WORLD TRADE ORGANIZATION

Dispute Settlement Reports

2002
Volume II

Pages 587-846

CAMBRIDGE
UNIVERSITY PRESS

PUBLISHED BY THE PRESS SYNDICATE OF THE UNIVERSITY OF CAMBRIDGE
The Pitt Building, Trumpington Street, Cambridge, United Kingdom

CAMBRIDGE UNIVERSITY PRESS
The Edinburgh Building, Cambridge CB2 2RU, UK
40 West 20th Street, New York, NY 10011–4211, USA
477 Williamstown Road, Port Melbourne, VIC 3207, Australia
Ruiz de Alarcón 13, 28014 Madrid, Spain
Dock House, The Waterfront, Cape Town 8001, South Africa

http://www.cambridge.org

First published 2004

Printed in the United Kingdom at the University Press, Cambridge

A catalogue record for this book is available from the British Library

Library of Congress Cataloguing in Publication data

ISBN 0 521 84839 3 hardback

THE WTO DISPUTE SETTLEMENT REPORTS

The *Dispute Settlement Reports* of the World Trade Organization (the "WTO") in-
include panel and Appellate Body reports, as well as arbitration awards, in disputes
concerning the rights and obligations of WTO Members under the provisions of the
Marrakesh Agreement Establishing the World Trade Organization. The *Dispute
Settlement Reports* are available in English, French and Spanish. Starting with 2002,
volume contains a cumulative index of published disputes.

This volume may be cited as DSR 2002:II

TABLE OF CONTENTS

Page

UNITED STATES – SECTION 211 OMNIBUS APPROPRIATIONS ACT OF 1998

Report of the Appellate Body
WT/DS176/AB/R

Adopted by the Dispute Settlement Body
on 1 February 2002

European Communities,
Appellant/Appellee

United States, *Appellant/Appellee*

Present:

Ehlermann, Presiding Member

Bacchus, Member

Lacarte-Muró, Member

TABLE OF CONTENTS

I. INTRODUCTION

1.   The European Communities and the United States appeal from certain issues of law and legal interpretations in the Panel Report, *United States – Section 211 Omnibus Appropriations Act of 1998* (the "Panel Report").[1] The Panel was established on 26 September 2000 to consider a complaint by the European Communities with respect to Section 211 of the United States Omnibus Appropriations Act of 1998 ("Section 211").[2] The European Communities alleged that Section 211 is inconsistent with certain obligations of the United States under the *Agreement on Trade-Related Aspects of Intellectual Property Rights* (the "*TRIPS*

---

[1]   WT/DS176/R, 6 August 2001.

[2]   Section 211 of the Department of Commerce Appropriations Act, 1999, as included in the Omnibus Consolidated and Emergency Supplemental Appropriations Act 1999, Public Law 105-277, 112 Stat. 2681, which became law in the United States on 21 October 1998, referred to in this dispute as "Section 211".

Agreement"), as read with the relevant provisions of the *Paris Convention for the Protection of Industrial Property*, as amended by the Stockholm Act of 1967 (the "Paris Convention (1967)"), which are incorporated by reference into the *TRIPS Agreement*.

2.   The background to this dispute and the measure at issue are described in detail in the Panel Report.[3] Here, we set out those aspects of the measure that are relevant to this appeal.

3.   The complaint by the European Communities relates to Section 211, which was signed into law on 21 October 1998. Section 211 states as follows:

>   (a)   (1)   Notwithstanding any other provision of law, no transaction or payment shall be authorized or approved pursuant to section 515.527 of title 31, Code of Federal Regulations, as in effect on September 9, 1998, with respect to a mark, trade name, or commercial name that is the same as or substantially similar to a mark, trade name, or commercial name that was used in connection with a business or assets that were confiscated unless the original owner of the mark, trade name, or commercial name, or the bona fide successor-in-interest has expressly consented.

>   [a]   (2)   No U.S. court shall recognize, enforce or otherwise validate any assertion of rights by a designated national based on common law rights or registration obtained under such section 515.527 of such a confiscated mark, trade name, or commercial name.

>   (b)   No U.S. court shall recognize, enforce or otherwise validate any assertion of treaty rights by a designated national or its successor-in-interest under sections 44 (b) or (e) of the Trademark Act of 1946 (15 U.S.C. 1126 (b) or (e)) for a mark, trade name, or commercial name that is the same as or substantially similar to a mark, trade name, or commercial name that was used in connection with a business or assets that were confiscated unless the original owner of such mark, trade name, or commercial name, or the bona fide successor-in-interest has expressly consented.

>   (c)   The Secretary of the Treasury shall promulgate such rules and regulations as are necessary to carry out the provisions of this section.

>   (d)   In this section:

>   (1)   The term "designated national" has the meaning given such term in section 515.305 of title 31, Code of Federal Regulations, as in effect on September 9, 1998, and includes a national of any foreign country who is a successor-in-interest to a designated national.

---

[3]   Panel Report, paras. 1.1-2.13.

> (2)   The term "confiscated" has the meaning given such term in section 515.336 of title 31, Code of Federal Regulations, as in effect on September 9, 1998.

4.   Section 211 applies to a defined category of trademarks, trade names and commercial names, specifically to those trademarks, trade names and commercial names that are "the same as or substantially similar to a mark, trade name, or commercial name that was used in connection with a business or assets that were confiscated" by the Cuban Government on or after 1 January 1959.[4]   Section 211(d) states that the term "designated national" as used in Section 211 has the meaning given to that term in Section 515.305 of Title 31, Code of Federal Regulations ("CFR"), and that it includes "a national of any foreign country who is a successor-in-interest to a designated national."   The term "confiscated" is defined as having the meaning given that term in Section 515.336 of Title 31 CFR. Part 515 of Title 31 CFR sets out the Cuban Assets Control Regulations (the "CACR"), which were enacted on 8 July 1963 under the Trading with the Enemy Act of 1917.[5]   Under these regulations, "designated national" is defined as Cuba, a national of Cuba or a specially designated national.[6] "Confiscated" is defined as nationalized or expropriated by the Cuban Government on or after 1 January 1959 without payment of adequate and effective compensation.[7]

---

[4]   Before the Panel, the United States submitted that "trade names" and "commercial names" are synonymous under its principal federal statute on trademark protection. As in the Panel Report, a reference in this Report to trade names should be read to include commercial names. See Panel Report, para. 8.21.

[5]   50 U.S.C. App. 1 ff.

[6]   See 31 CFR 515.305, which defines the term "designated national" as follows:
§515.305 Designated national.
For the purposes of this part, the term *designated national* shall mean Cuba and any national thereof including any person who is a specially designated national.
See also, 31 CFR 515.306, which defines the term "specially designated national" as follows:
(a)   The term *specially designated national* shall mean:
(1)   Any person who is determined by the Secretary of Treasury to be a specially designated national,
(2)   Any person who on or since the "effective date" has acted for or on behalf of the Government or authorities exercising control over a designated foreign country, or
(3)   Any partnership, association, corporation or other organization which on or since the "effective date" has been owned or controlled directly or indirectly by the Government or authorities exercising control over a designated foreign country or by any specially designated national.

[7]   See 31 CFR 515.336, which defines the term "confiscated" as follows:
§515.336 Confiscated.
As used in §515.208, the term *confiscated* refers to:
(a)   The nationalization, expropriation, or other seizure by the Cuban Government of ownership or control of property, on or after January 1, 1959:
(1)   Without the property having been returned or adequate and effective compensation provided; or
(2)   Without the claim to the property having been settled pursuant to an international claims settlement agreement or other mutually accepted settlement procedure; and

5.   Section 211(a)(1) relates to licensing regulations contained in the CACR. The CACR are administered by the Office of Foreign Assets Control ("OFAC"), an agency of the United States Department of the Treasury. Under United States law, all transactions involving property under United States jurisdiction, in which a Cuban national has an interest, require a licence from OFAC.[8] OFAC has the authority to grant either of two categories of licences, namely general licences and specific licences. A general licence is a general authorization for certain types of transactions set out in OFAC regulations.[9] Such a licence is, in effect, a standing authorization for the types of transactions that are specified in the CACR. A specific licence, by contrast, is one whose precise terms are not set out in the regulations, so that a person wishing to engage in a transaction for which a general licence is not available must apply to OFAC for a specific licence.[10]

6.   Section 211 refers to Section 515.527 of Title 31 CFR. Prior to the entry into force of Section 211, a general licence was available under Section 515.527 for the registration and renewal of trademarks previously owned by Cuban nationals irrespective of whether such trademarks had been confiscated by the Cu-

---

(b)   The repudiation by the Cuban Government of, the default by the Cuban Government on, or the failure of the Cuban Government to pay, on or after January 1, 1959:

(1)   A debt of any enterprise which has been nationalized, expropriated, or otherwise taken by the Cuban Government;

(2)   A debt which is a charge on property nationalized, expropriated, or otherwise taken by the Cuban Government; or

(3)   A debt which was incurred by the Cuban Government in satisfaction or settlement of a confiscated property claim.

[8]   See 31 CFR 515.201, which provides:

§515.201   Transactions involving designated foreign countries or their nationals; effective date.

(a)   All of the following transactions are prohibited, except as specifically authorized by the Secretary of the Treasury (or any person, agency, or instrumentality designated by him) by means of regulations, rulings, instructions, licenses, or otherwise, if either such transactions are by, or on behalf of, or pursuant to the direction of a foreign country designated under this part, or any national thereof, or such transactions involve property in which a foreign country designated under this part, or any national thereof, has at any time on or since the effective date of this section had any interest of any nature whatsoever, direct or indirect:

…

(b)   All of the following transactions are prohibited, except as specifically authorized by the Secretary of the Treasury (or any person, agency, or instrumentality designated by him) by means of regulations, rulings, instructions, licenses, or otherwise, if such transactions involve property in which any foreign country designated under this part, or any national thereof, has at any time on or since the effective date of this section had any interest of any nature whatsoever, direct or indirect:

…

(2)   All transfers outside the United States with regard to any property or property interest subject to the jurisdiction of the United States.

[9]   See 31 CFR 515.317, which provides:

A general license is any license or authorization the terms of which are set forth in this part.

[10]   31 CFR 515.318.

ban Government. Before the enactment of Section 211, Section 515.527 read as follows:

> Section 515.527   Certain transactions with respect to United States intellectual property.
>
> (a)   Transactions related to the registration and renewal in the United States Patent and Trademark Office or the United States Copyright Office of patents, trademarks, and copyrights in which the Government of Cuba or a Cuban national has an interest are authorized.

7.   On 10 May 1999, some six months after the entry into force of Section 211, the CACR were amended by adding a new subparagraph (a)(2) to Section 515.527, which effectively prohibits registration and renewal of trademarks and trade names used in connection with a business or assets that were confiscated without the consent of the original owner or *bona fide* successor-in-interest. This provision reads:

> (a)   (2)   No transaction or payment is authorized or approved pursuant to paragraph (a)(1) of this section with respect to a mark, trade name, or commercial name that is the same as or substantially similar to a mark, trade name, or commercial name that was used in connection with a business or assets that were confiscated, as that term is defined in section 515.336, unless the original owner of the mark, trade name, or commercial name, or the bona fide successor-in-interest has expressly consented.

8.   The effect of Section 211, as read with the relevant provisions of the CACR, is to make inapplicable to a defined category of trademarks and trade names certain aspects of trademark and trade name protection that are otherwise guaranteed in the trademark and trade name law of the United States. In the United States, trademark and trade name protection is effected through the common law as well as through statutes. The common law provides for trademark and trade name creation through use. The Trademark Act of 1946 (the "Lanham Act")[11] stipulates substantive and procedural rights in trademarks as well as trade names and governs unfair competition. Section 211(b) refers to Sections 44(b) and (e) of the Lanham Act.[12]

---

[11]   15 U.S.C. §1051 ff. The Lanham Act also defines the scope of a trademark, the process by which a federal registration for a trademark can be obtained from the United States Patent and Trademark Office (the "USPTO"), and prescribes penalties for trademark infringement. Under the law of the United States, trade names do not need to be registered.

[12]   Section 44 of the Lanham Act (15 U.S.C. §1126) states, in relevant part:

> (b)   Any person whose country of origin is a party to any convention or treaty relating to trademarks, trade or commercial names, or the repression of unfair competition, to which the United States is also a party, or extends reciprocal rights to nationals of the United States by law, shall be entitled to the benefits of this section under the conditions expressed herein to the extent necessary to give effect to any provision of such convention, treaty or reciprocal law, in addition to the rights to which any owner of a mark is otherwise entitled by this chapter.
>
> . . .

9.   Before the Panel, the European Communities argued that: Section 211(a)(1) is inconsistent with Article 2.1 of the *TRIPS Agreement* in conjunction with Article 6*quinquies* A(1) of the Paris Convention (1967) and Article 15.1 of the *TRIPS Agreement*; Section 211(a)(2) is inconsistent with Article 2.1 of the *TRIPS Agreement* in conjunction with Articles 2(1), 6*bis* (1) and 8 of the Paris Convention (1967), and Articles 3.1, 4, 16.1 and 42 of the *TRIPS Agreement*; and Section 211(b) is inconsistent with Article 2.1 of the *TRIPS Agreement* in conjunction with Articles 2(1), 6*bis* (1) and 8 of the Paris Convention (1967), and Articles 3.1, 4, 16.1 and 42 of the *TRIPS Agreement*.

10.   In the Panel Report circulated on 6 August 2001, the Panel found that:

(a)   Section 211(a)(1) is not inconsistent with Article 15.1 of the TRIPS Agreement;

(b)   Section 211(a)(1) is not inconsistent with Article 2.1 of the TRIPS Agreement in conjunction with Article 6*quinquies*A(1) of the Paris Convention (1967);

(c)   it has not been proved that Section 211(a)(2) is inconsistent with Article 16.1 of the TRIPS Agreement;

(d)   Section 211(a)(2) is inconsistent with Article 42 of the TRIPS Agreement;

(e)   Section 211(a)(2) is not inconsistent with Article 2.1 of the TRIPS Agreement in conjunction with Article 6*bis* of the Paris Convention (1967);

(f)   Section 211(a)(2) is not inconsistent with Article 2.1 of the TRIPS Agreement in conjunction with Article 8 of the Paris Convention (1967);

(g)   Section 211(a)(2) is not inconsistent with Article 3.1 of the TRIPS Agreement and Article 2.1 of the TRIPS Agreement in conjunction with Article 2(1) of the Paris Convention (1967);

(h)   Section 211(a)(2) is not inconsistent with Article 4 of the TRIPS Agreement;

(i)   it has not been proved that Section 211(b) is inconsistent with Article 16.1 of the TRIPS Agreement;

(j)   it has not been proved that Section 211(b) is inconsistent with Article 42 of the TRIPS Agreement;

(e)   A mark duly registered in the country of origin of the foreign applicant may be registered on the principal register if eligible, otherwise on the supplemental register in this chapter provided. Such applicant shall submit, within such time period as may be prescribed by the Director, a certification or a certified copy of the registration in the country of origin of the applicant. The application must state the applicant's bona fide intention to use the mark in commerce, but use in commerce shall not be required prior to registration.

(k)   it has not been proved that Section 211(b) is inconsistent with Article 2.1 of the TRIPS Agreement in conjunction with Article 6*bis* of the Paris Convention (1967);

(l)   Section 211(b) is not inconsistent with Article 2.1 of the TRIPS Agreement in conjunction with Article 8 of the Paris Convention (1967);

(m)   Section 211(b) is not inconsistent with Article 3.1 of the TRIPS Agreement and Article 2.1 of the TRIPS Agreement in conjunction with Article 2(1) of the Paris Convention (1967); and

(n)   Section 211(b) is not inconsistent with Article 4 of the TRIPS Agreement. [13]

11.   The Panel ruled that trade names are not a category of intellectual property covered by the *TRIPS Agreement*. Consequently, the Panel limited its review to an examination of Section 211 as it relates to trademarks. [14] The Panel recommended that the Dispute Settlement Body (the "DSB") request the United States to bring its measures into conformity with its obligations under the *TRIPS Agreement*. [15]

12.   On 4 October 2001, the European Communities notified the DSB of its intention to appeal certain issues of law covered in the Panel Report and certain legal interpretations developed by the Panel, pursuant to paragraph 4 of Article 16 of the *Understanding on Rules and Procedures Governing the Settlement of Disputes* (the "DSU"), and filed a Notice of Appeal pursuant to Rule 20 of the *Working Procedures for Appellate Review* (the "*Working Procedures*"). On 15 October 2001, the European Communities filed its appellant's submission. [16] On 19 October 2001, the United States filed an other appellant's submission. [17] On 26 October 2001, the European Communities and the United States each filed an appellee's submission. [18]

13.   On 2 November 2001, pursuant to Rule 28(1) of the *Working Procedures*, the Division hearing the appeal requested that the participants submit additional written memoranda on the interpretation by domestic courts of Article 6*quinquies* of the Paris Convention (1967), or the interpretation by domestic courts of legislation incorporating Article 6*quinquies*. Both participants filed the additional written memoranda on 6 November 2001, and served these memoranda on each other. Pursuant to Rule 28(2) of the *Working Procedures*, the Division gave the participants an opportunity to respond to these memoranda at the oral hearing in this appeal.

---

[13] Panel Report, para. 9.1.
[14] *Ibid.*, para. 8.41.
[15] *Ibid.*, para. 9.3.
[16] Pursuant to Rule 21 of the *Working Procedures*.
[17] Pursuant to Rule 23(1) of the *Working Procedures*.
[18] Pursuant to Rules 22 and 23(3) of the *Working Procedures*.

14.   The oral hearing in this appeal was held on 7, 8 and 9 November 2001. The participants presented oral arguments and responded to questions put to them by the Members of the Division.

II.   ARGUMENTS OF THE PARTICIPANTS

A.   Claims of Error by the European Communities – Appellant

1.   Article 6quinquies of the Paris Convention (1967)

15.   The European Communities argues that the Panel erred in finding that Section 211(a)(1) is not inconsistent with Article 2.1 of the *TRIPS Agreement* in conjunction with Article 6*quinquies* A(1) of the Paris Convention (1967). Contrary to the Panel's conclusion, Article 6*quinquies* A(1) does not address solely the form of the trademark. According to the European Communities, Article 6*quinquies* A(1) addresses all features of a trademark.

16.   The European Communities submits that the Panel correctly found that the term "as is" (or "*telle quelle*" in the French version of Article 6*quinquies* A(1)) refers to the trademark. This term encompasses all the features of a trademark, and under no circumstances can the term be understood as being limited to the form of a trademark. This is confirmed by the context of Article 6*quinquies* A(1).

17.   The European Communities argues that Article 6*quinquies* of the Paris Convention (1967) facilitates the obtaining of trademark protection in a Paris Union country when a trademark is already registered in the country of origin. [19] This facilitation is limited to the registration stage of the trademark. Trademarks created by registration in different countries will afterwards be "fully independent". [20]   Therefore, Article 6*quinquies* limits the discretion of WTO Members with respect to the imposition of conditions for trademark registration. There is thus no apparent conflict between Articles 6 and 6*quinquies*, contrary to what the Panel suggests in paragraph 8.79, second sentence.

18.   The European Communities submits that Article 6*quinquies* B provides important contextual guidance. This provision enumerates an exclusive list of exceptions to Article 6*quinquies* A that refer to elements going well beyond form. Article 6*quinquies* B(3) provides, for example, an exception when trademarks are "contrary to morality and public order", requiring an assessment of all the elements of the trademark including, but not limited to, its form.

19.   In the view of the European Communities, the Panel's recourse to preparatory work is an erroneous invocation of the supplementary means of interpretation in Article 32 of the *Vienna Convention on the Law of Treaties* ("*Vienna Convention*"). [21]   According to the European Communities, none of the condi-

---

[19]   The term "Paris Union" refers to the countries to which the Paris Convention (1967) applies. See Article 1(1) of the Paris Convention (1967).

[20]   European Communities' appellant's submission, para. 53.

[21]   Done at Vienna, 23 May 1969, 1155 U.N.T.S. 331; 8 International Legal Materials 679.

tions which justify recourse to supplementary means of interpretation is present in this dispute. Moreover, the documents related to the history of the Paris Convention (1967) used by the Panel in its analysis, fail to provide a clear indication of the intentions of the negotiators.

20.   The European Communities infers, given that Article 6*quinquies* A(1) of the Paris Convention (1967) is not limited to form, the consent of a third party required for registration of a trademark by Section 211(a)(1) must be analyzed with respect to the exceptions provided in Article 6*quinquies* B. As Section 211(a)(1) is not covered by any of the exceptions in Article 6*quinquies* B, it is inconsistent with Article 2.1 the *TRIPS Agreement* together with Article 6*quinquies* A(1) of the Paris Convention (1967).

2.   Article 15 of the TRIPS Agreement

21.   The European Communities claims that the Panel erred in finding that Section 211(a)(1) is not inconsistent with Article 15.1 of the *TRIPS Agreement*. The Panel was incorrect in considering that Section 211(a)(1) is domestic legislation within the meaning of Article 6(1) of the Paris Convention (1967), and that it is covered under "other grounds" as set out in Article 15.2 of the *TRIPS Agreement*.

22.   In the view of the European Communities, Section 211(a)(1) is not a measure related to ownership but a measure that establishes a particular condition, or an additional procedural step, for the registration or renewal of registration of certain trademarks. It is unrelated to the transfer or cessation of an asset. Furthermore, when the provision is applied in the context of a renewal, the registered trademark ceases to exist in the hands of any owner and the signs or combinations of signs that constitute the trademark fall into the public domain. The European Communities notes that Article 18 of the *TRIPS Agreement* provides that trademarks are renewable indefinitely. In sum, the consent for the registration or renewal of trademarks required under Section 211(a)(1) creates a curtailment on the continued enjoyment of an existing trademark and prevents new registrations from being granted.

23.   According to the European Communities, the Panel began its assessment by looking at paragraph 1 of Article 15 and then concluded that it had to be considered "in tandem" with paragraph 2. While not precisely clear on the basis for this approach, the European Communities understands that the Panel found Section 211(a)(1) to be inconsistent with Article 15.1 of the *TRIPS Agreement*, but nevertheless not WTO-inconsistent because it is covered by Article 15.2.

24.   The European Communities argues that, contrary to the Panel's position, Article 15.2 should be interpreted as allowing only those exceptions that are expressly foreseen in the Paris Convention (1967). This is consistent with the general recognition that exceptions must be interpreted narrowly. There is a relatively small number of express exceptions to Article 15.1 of the *TRIPS Agreement* that are contained in the Paris Convention (1967) or the *TRIPS Agree-*

ment.[22] These would make little sense if Article 15.2 of the *TRIPS Agreement* were to allow any exception not expressly prohibited. The broader interpretation given by the Panel to Article 15.2 would also render obsolete the disciplines established by Article 15.1. The Panel recognized this danger but, instead of revisiting its conclusions, it referred to the doctrine of "*abus de droit*", without drawing any conclusions from it for the interpretation of Article 15.

25.   The European Communities maintains that no provision exists, either in the *TRIPS Agreement* or in the Paris Convention (1967), that allows WTO Members to require the consent of third parties for the registration or renewal of registration of a trademark. Section 211(a)(1) is therefore incompatible with Article 15 of the *TRIPS Agreement*.

26.   The European Communities adds that, even under the Panel's interpretation of Article 15.2, Section 211(a)(1) would still be inconsistent with Article 15 of the *TRIPS Agreement* with respect to trademarks registered under Article 6*quinquies* of the Paris Convention (1967), because it is not covered by any of the exceptions enumerated in subparagraph B's exclusive list.

3.   Article 16 of the TRIPS Agreement

Section 211(a)(2)

27.   The European Communities argues that the Panel erred in finding that it had not proved that Section 211(a)(2) is inconsistent with Article 16.1 of the *TRIPS Agreement*. The Panel incorrectly applied the rules on burden of proof established by the Appellate Body.

28.   The European Communities submits that it provided ample evidence on how to interpret Section 211(a)(2), and demonstrated how this provision conflicts with the obligations of the United States under Article 16.1 of the *TRIPS Agreement*. That there has not yet been litigation in the United States giving rise to final judgments interpreting Section 211(a)(2), and that there is no legislative history with respect to this measure, cannot be used against the European Communities.

29.   The European Communities submits that the Panel erroneously distinguished between the owner of the registered trademark and the trademark itself, when both are intricately intertwined. Although disputes may arise with respect to who is the lawful owner of a registered trademark, the existence of a registered trademark necessarily implies that there is an owner.

30.   According to the European Communities, the Panel did not provide support for its conclusion that "[u]nder the exceptional circumstances dealt with under Section 211(a)(2), there may be a successful challenge concerning the

---

[22]   The European Communities cites the following provisions as express exceptions to Article 15.1 of the *TRIPS Agreement* contained in the Paris Convention (1967) or the *TRIPS Agreement*: Articles 22.3, 23.2, 24.5, and 62.1 of the *TRIPS Agreement* and Articles 6(2), 6*ter*, 6*quinquies* (B), C(2) and D of the Paris Convention (1967). (European Communities' appellant's submission, para. 73; European Communities' responses to questioning at the oral hearing.)

prima facie ownership rights in relation to the registration".[23] Section 211(a)(2) does not address the fate of the registered trademark in terms of its status in the register. Nor does the Panel explain the relevance of Section 211(a)(2) for purposes of determining who is the owner of a registered trademark under the relevant provisions of the Lanham Act.

31.   The European Communities asserts that Section 211(a)(2) does not address the ownership issue. This is particularly the case when it is invoked by an infringer other than the original owner, when the trademark has been abandoned by the original owner, or when no original owner exists because no United States trademark existed at the time of confiscation or the original owner is no longer alive.

32.   The European Communities concludes, therefore, that the owner of a registered trademark under Article 16.1 of the *TRIPS Agreement* is the holder of the registration until such time as it ceases to hold the registration. Further, it makes no sense to consider an original owner who is not in the register as the lawful owner. This conclusion is supported by the fact that under Section 211(a)(2), this original owner has no exclusive rights to prevent others from using the registered trademark.

Section 211(b)

33.   The European Communities argues that the Panel erred in finding that it has not been proven that Section 211(b) is inconsistent with Article 16.1 of the *TRIPS Agreement*. The Panel completely disregarded the partial agreement between the parties as to the proper reading of Section 211(b). The burden of proof is relevant only for the elements on which the parties disagree.

34.   According to the European Communities, the United States argued that Section 211(b) is limited to situations covered by Section 44(e) of the Lanham Act, namely, situations where a registered United States trademark is obtained on the basis of a trademark registered in a foreign country or where registration is applied for in a foreign country. The European Communities agrees with the United States that Section 211(b) covers such situations and that it prohibits United States courts from recognizing, enforcing or otherwise validating any rights asserted by a designated national flowing from a United States trademark obtained under Section 44(e) of the Lanham Act, provided that such a trademark was used in connection with a business or assets confiscated in Cuba.

35.   However, the European Communities submits that Section 211(b) covers other situations as well. According to the European Communities, Section 211(b) covers all cases in which foreigners, who are nationals of a WTO Member, hold registered trademarks or trade names in the United States. This is because Section 211(b) refers also to Section 44(b) of the Lanham Act, in which no mention is made of a registration or application for a trademark in the country of origin. It refers to benefits to persons whose country of origin is a party to any "convention or treaty relating to trademarks, trade or commercial names", which obvi-

---

[23]   Panel Report, para. 8.111; European Communities' appellant's submission, para. 107.

ously includes the *TRIPS Agreement*. In addition, the reading suggested by the United States would render the reference to trade names in Section 44(b) redundant because registration is not necessary for such rights.

36.   To further support its view, the European Communities cites a decision issued by a United States court in *Havana Club Holding, S.A. v. Galleon S.A.* (*"Havana Club Holding"*).[24] The European Communities emphasizes that the court decision stems from a final judgment in a case that went through the entire United States court system, up to the United States Supreme Court that denied *certiorari*.

37.   Given these elements, the European Communities considers that it has met its burden of proof with respect to that part of Section 211(b) for which the parties have a divergent reading. The evidence presented clearly demonstrates that Section 211(b) applies to all United States trademarks and trade names held by foreigners who are nationals of a WTO Member.

38.   Finally, as the denial and curtailment of trademark and trade name rights under Section 211(b) is the same as under Section 211(a)(2), the European Communities submits that its arguments about the inconsistency between the latter provision and Article 16.1 of the *TRIPS Agreement* apply also to Section 211(b). This refers both to the proper reading and to the scope of Section 211(b), that is, the narrower reading on which the parties agree as a minimum, as well as the wider reading as to its scope put forward by the European Communities.

4.   *Article 42 of the TRIPS Agreement*

39.   The European Communities argues that the Panel erred in finding that it has not been proven that Section 211(b) is inconsistent with Article 42 of the *TRIPS Agreement*. The Panel did not carry out an objective assessment of the evidence before it.

40.   The European Communities submits that throughout the proceedings, both parties suggested that Section 211(a)(2), which was found to be inconsistent with Article 42, and Section 211(b) have to be read together. Moreover, there was partial agreement between the parties as to the scope of Section 211(b). Furthermore, the Panel did not consider the final ruling in the *Havana Club Holding* decision, a case that made its course through the entire United States federal court system up to the Supreme Court, and which provides unequivocal proof of the denial of judicial enforceability of trade names effected by Section 211(b). That Section 211(b) is inconsistent with Article 42 of the *TRIPS Agreement* is evident irrespective of whether a broader or narrower reading is given to its scope.

---

[24]   *Havana Club Holding, S.A. v. Galleon S.A.*, 62 F.Supp.2d 1085 (S.D.N.Y. 1999); See also *Havana Club Holding, S.A. v. Galleon S.A.*, 203 F.3d 116 (2d Cir. 2000).

5. Article 2 of the Paris Convention (1967) and Article 3 of the TRIPS Agreement

41.   The European Communities submits that the Panel erred in finding that Section 211(a)(2) is not inconsistent with Article 3.1 of the *TRIPS Agreement* and Article 2.1 of the *TRIPS Agreement* together with Article 2(1) of the Paris Convention (1967).

42.   The European Communities argues that Section 211(a)(2) is discriminatory on its face because it applies exclusively to "designated nationals", which is defined in Section 515.305 of the CACR as Cuba or Cuban nationals, and was extended by Section 211(d)(1) to include foreign (that is, non-United States) successors-in-interest. According to the European Communities, under no circumstances can a United States national be considered a "designated" national. Furthermore, it is logically inconsistent, according to the European Communities, to argue that the CACR regulations as administered by OFAC could counterbalance this discrimination.

43.   The European Communities argues that the Panel considered only the discriminatory treatment between United States nationals and foreign nationals at the level of successors-in-interest. It did not consider the discriminatory treatment at the level of original registrants. According to the European Communities, Section 211(a)(2) discriminates at the level of original registrants between Cuban nationals on the one hand, and United States and non-Cuban foreign nationals on the other.

44.   The European Communities notes that Section 211(a)(2) applies to registered United States trademarks for which registration has been obtained under Section 515.527 of the CACR. Section 515.527 is relevant only if the rightholder is a Cuban national. It does not apply if the original registrant is a United States national or non-Cuban foreign national. According to the European Communities, this means that a United States trademark in the hands of a United States national or non-Cuban foreign national, even if it is the same as or substantially similar to a trademark used in connection with a business or assets that were confiscated in Cuba, is not covered by Section 211(a)(2).

45.   The European Communities notes that the CACR as administered by OFAC have no role in such cases because they apply only to United States assets owned by Cuba or Cuban nationals. Therefore, it is logically inconsistent to argue that the CACR and OFAC could, even theoretically, do anything to counterbalance the discrimination on the face of Section 211(a)(2) between Cuba and Cuban nationals on the one hand, and other nationals on the other.

46.   The European Communities argues that the Panel was also incorrect with respect to its conclusions regarding discrimination at the level of successors-in-interest. The European Communities acknowledges that if a United States trademark or trade name is acquired from a Cuban seller, the transaction would have to be authorized by OFAC and such authorization would be necessary regardless of the nationality of the buyer (the buyer may be a Cuban, United States or other foreign national) or the origin of the trademark or trade name (that is, whether it has any relationship with a confiscated asset). However, the European Commu-

nities argues that the burden was on the United States to demonstrate that the operation of Section 515.201 of the CACR would, in each and every factual situation, necessarily and fully compensate the discrimination created by Section 211(a)(2) between United States successors-in-interest and Cuban or other foreign successors-in-interest.

47.   The European Communities argues further that even if the United States were to meet that burden, there would nevertheless continue to be discriminatory treatment between United States nationals and foreigners because the United States nationals would have only to clear one hurdle (the OFAC process), while a foreign successor-in-interest would have to clear that hurdle as well as the constraints imposed by Section 211(a)(2).

48.   The European Communities is of the view that the situation in that case would be similar to that found to be discriminatory treatment prohibited under Article III of GATT 1947 in *United States – Section 337 of the Tariff Act of 1930* (*"US – Section 337"*), where foreign goods were subject to two cumulative enforcement measures for alleged infringements of intellectual property rights, while United States goods were subject to only one such measure.[25]

49.   The European Communities alleges that the Panel also erred in finding that Section 211(b) is not inconsistent with Article 3.1 of the *TRIPS Agreement*, and Article 2.1 of the *TRIPS Agreement* together with Article 2(1) of the Paris Convention (1967). It argues that this finding is erroneous in the light of its arguments presented earlier as to the scope of Section 211(b) and the burden of proof. Given that both provisions operate in exactly the same manner, the arguments submitted with respect to the different levels of discrimination that result from Section 211(a)(2) also apply to Section 211(b).

6.   Article 4 of the TRIPS Agreement

50.   The European Communities argues that the Panel erred in finding that Section 211(a)(2) is not inconsistent with Article 4 of the *TRIPS Agreement*.

51.   The European Communities is of the view that, as regards original owners of trademarks and trade names, the discrimination is obvious as Section 211(a)(2) "targets" only Cuba and Cuban nationals. Therefore, United States and foreign nationals, other than Cubans, who are original owners, are unaffected by Section 211(a)(2). The European Communities argues further that the CACR and OFAC could not offset this discrimination because they do not play a role in relation to non-Cuban original owners.

52.   The European Communities also submits that the Panel erred in finding that Section 211(b) is not inconsistent with Article 4 of the *TRIPS Agreement*. Given that Section 211(a)(2) has identical coverage to that of Section 211(b), the European Communities alleges that its arguments with respect to the former provision apply equally to the latter. This result is independent of the scope given to

---

[25]   Panel Report, adopted 7 November 1989, BISD 36S/345.

Section 211(b), whether it be the broader scope advanced by the European Communities or the narrower one on which the parties at a minimum agree.

7.   Article 8 of the Paris Convention (1967) – Trade Names

53.   The European Communities argues that the Panel erred in finding that trade names are not covered in the *TRIPS Agreement*. The Panel's finding comes "as a surprise"[26] because both the European Communities and the United States had agreed that trade names were included in the scope of the *TRIPS Agreement*. The issue of coverage of trade names was not raised specifically before the Panel until the interim review stage, when the participants commented on the Panel's finding that trade names were not covered.

54.   The European Communities maintains that the Panel erred in its analysis by considering that Article 1.2 of the *TRIPS Agreement* contains an exhaustive definition of intellectual property. The European Communities considers that Article 1.2 is illustrative and is no more than a very general definition of intellectual property rights covered by the *TRIPS Agreement*. Article 1.2 does not define the details of such intellectual property rights with conclusive precision.

55.   In the view of the European Communities, a proper analysis should begin with Article 2.1 of the *TRIPS Agreement*. The Panel's interpretation reduces the express inclusion in Article 2.1 of Article 8 of the Paris Convention (1967) to inutility. The Panel's interpretation also suggests that the negotiators of the *TRIPS Agreement* committed a blatant error. The European Communities supports its argument by referring to several matters that are included within the disciplines of the *TRIPS Agreement*, but that are not specifically referenced in Article 1.2. Finally, the European Communities disagrees with the Panel that the negotiating history of the *TRIPS Agreement* supports the Panel's finding that trade names are not covered.

56.   The European Communities argues that the Panel did not undertake any analysis in relation to Article 8 of the Paris Convention (1967), and simply concluded that Sections 211(a)(2) and (b) are not inconsistent with Article 2(1) of the *TRIPS Agreement* together with Article 8 of the Paris Convention (1967). Thus, the European Communities maintains that the Appellate Body should complete the analysis with respect to other provisions of the *TRIPS Agreement* that it claims are violated by Section 211.

57.   The European Communities argues that Sections 211(a)(2) and (b) deny court enforcement for trade names. This denial of court enforcement is tantamount to denying protection altogether, because trade names can only be effectively enforced with the help of the court system. The European Communities submits, therefore, that Sections 211(a)(2) and (b) are inconsistent with Article 8 of the Paris Convention (1967).

58.   The European Communities submits that, given that trade names are covered by the *TRIPS Agreement*, Article 42 applies equally to trade names. As Sec-

---

[26]   European Communities' appellant's submission, para. 22.

tions 211(a)(2) and (b) deny judicial enforceability to registered trademarks and also to trade names, the Panel's finding of inconsistency of Section 211(a)(2) with Article 42 of the *TRIPS Agreement* applies equally to trade names in respect of Sections 211(a)(2) and (b).

59.   Finally, the European Communities submits that, as Sections 211(a)(2) and (b) address trade names in the same manner as trademarks, its arguments · with respect to the inconsistency of Sections 211(a)(2) and (b) with Articles 2.1, 3.1 and 4 of the *TRIPS Agreement* apply in respect of both trademarks and trade names.

B.   Arguments of the United States – Appellee

1.   Article 6quinquies of the Paris Convention (1967)

60.   The United States argues that the Panel correctly found that Article 6*quinquies* A(1) does not require Members to accept for filing and protect without question *all* trademarks duly registered in their country of origin. Rather, Article 6*quinquies* A(1) prevents Members from denying such registration on the basis of the *form* of the trademark. As Section 211(a)(1) does not deal with the form of the trademark, it is not inconsistent with Article 2.1 of the *TRIPS Agreement*, in conjunction with Article 6*quinquies* of the Paris Convention (1967).

61.   The United States submits that the European Communities' arguments with respect to the Panel's sound interpretation of Article 6*quinquies* A(1) are incorrect. The European Communities makes no serious attempt at a textual analysis to support its position, inaccurately criticizes part of the Panel's analysis of the context of the provision, improperly tries to interpret the exceptions to Article 6*quinquies* A(1) as overriding the ordinary meaning of Article 6*quinquies* A(1), and incorrectly argues that the need to resort to supportive historical documents somehow undercuts the Panel's analysis.

62.   According to the United States, even if Article 6 *quinquies* A(1) were read to require WTO Members to accept for filing and protect any trademarks duly registered abroad in the country of origin, regardless of whether the registrant is the proper owner under domestic law, Article 6*quinquies* B would provide exceptions to these obligations. Contrary to the European Communities' arguments, two of these exceptions would cover the situations represented by Section 211.

63.   The United States notes that, according to Article 6*quinquies* B(1), registration of trademarks may be denied or invalidated when the trademarks are of such a nature as to infringe rights acquired by third parties in the country where protection is claimed. To the extent that the original owner of a confiscated asset, who used a trademark in connection with that asset, has rights that would be impaired if the entity which confiscated the asset could acquire ownership of the mark in the United States, it is consistent with Article 6*quinquies* B of the Paris Convention (1967) to deny registration by the confiscating entity, unless the original owner consents.

64.   The United States also notes that, according to Article 6*quinquies* B(3), registration may be denied if the trademarks are contrary to *ordre public*. Courts have found that giving domestic effect to foreign confiscation with respect to domestic assets is contrary to *ordre public*. Therefore, even if Article 6*quinquies* A(1) could be read to extend beyond matters of trademark form, then, in the case of foreign confiscation, the United States is justified in denying registration in the situations covered by Section 211 for reasons of *ordre public*.

2.   Article 15 of the TRIPS Agreement

65.   The United States argues that the questions raised by the European Communities with respect to Section 211(a)(1) are questions of fact, not law, and are therefore outside the scope of appellate review. Further, neither in its notice of appeal nor in its appellant's submission does the European Communities claim that the Panel did not fulfill its obligation under Article 11 of the DSU.

66.   Even assuming that the European Communities had properly raised this issue on appeal, the United States is of the view that such an appeal should fail. Section 211(a)(1) is no less about "ownership" of the trademark simply because it identifies who is *not* the owner, without legally assigning another. Further, the European Communities is effectively asking the Appellate Body to reweigh the evidence as to the ownership elements in Section 211. This, however, is properly within the scope of the Panel's discretion, and may not be reversed unless the Panel exceeded the bounds of its discretion under Article 11 of the DSU.

67.   The United States submits that the Appellate Body should also uphold the Panel's legal conclusion that Article 15 of the *TRIPS Agreement* does not prevent Members from denying registration to those who do not own the trademark. The European Communities appears to concede that the Panel's textual analysis is sound, but argues that the provision's context and object and purpose lead to the conclusion that Article 15 permits Members to deny trademark registrations only if specifically authorized by a particular provision of the *TRIPS Agreement* or the Paris Convention (1967). In the view of the United States, the European Communities' interpretation, however, is at odds with the ordinary meaning of Article 15, and creates conflicts with other provisions of the *TRIPS Agreement*.

68.   The United States further submits that the European Communities' reading of the context of this provision is inaccurate because paragraph 2 of Article 15 providing for denial on "other grounds" is not an exception, as alleged by the European Communities, and, if it were, there would still be no justification for interpreting it narrowly. The United States also argues that the object and purpose of the *TRIPS Agreement* is not frustrated by reserving registration to those that own the trademarks. In addition, the European Communities failed to acknowledge the Panel's finding that there are *TRIPS Agreement* disciplines in place to prevent such frustration.

69.   The United States maintains that the Appellate Body should reject the European Communities' contention that, even if Article 15 does not prohibit Members from denying registration on ownership grounds, Article 6*quinquies* A(1) does. First, the Panel was correct to find that Arti-

cle 6*quinquies* A(1) is limited to matters of the *form* of the trademark. Second, even assuming that it were not, the exceptions in Article 6*quinquies* B would cover the situations represented by Section 211.

3. Article 16 of the TRIPS Agreement

Section 211(a)(2)

70.   According to the United States, the European Communities' only substantive argument depends on the false assumption that a trademark registrant is necessarily the owner of the trademark, either under United States law or under the *TRIPS Agreement*. The Panel correctly noted that under a system in which trademark registration is not the same as trademark ownership, but only gives rise to a presumption of trademark ownership, the status of the trademark registration itself is not dispositive of the issue of ownership. Under such a system, if a defendant successfully overcomes the registrant's presumption of ownership, it may or may not decide to seek cancellation of the registration. Declining to seek cancellation does not make the defendant any less an owner of the trademark, or the registrant any more of one.

71.   The United States contends that, based on the Panel's analysis, it is clear that, whether or not the European Communities failed to present specific evidence, there is no basis for finding that Section 211(a)(2) denies Article 16.1 rights to persons who are "owners of registered trademarks". Even if there were, however, the United States submits, as it did before the Panel, that Section 211(a)(2) would be covered by the exceptions from Article 16 in Article 17 of the *TRIPS Agreement*.

Section 211(b)

72.   The United States argues that Section 211(b) is not inconsistent with Article 16.1 of the *TRIPS Agreement*. In support of its appeal with respect to Section 211(b) and Article 16.1, the European Communities simply cross-references its argument made in relation to Section 211(a)(2). With respect to Section 211(b), the Panel correctly found that the European Communities had not submitted sufficient evidence of a breach of Article 16.1 of the *TRIPS Agreement*.

73.   The United States maintains that, even if the European Communities had sustained its burden of proof with respect to the meaning of Section 211(b), the Appellate Body should nevertheless find that the European Communities did not sustain its evidentiary burden with respect to the alleged breach of Article 16.1. Further, if the Appellate Body finds that the European Communities did sustain its burden in both instances, it should nevertheless find that Section 211(b) is not inconsistent with Article 16.1, for the reasons stated above in connection with Section 211(a)(2).

4. Article 42 of the TRIPS Agreement

74. The United States submits that Section 211(b) is not inconsistent with Article 42 of the *TRIPS Agreement*. Although the European Communities argues that the Panel undertook a selective consideration of the evidence, the European Communities does not refer to or make any allegations concerning Article 11 of the DSU. To support its claim, the European Communities incorrectly suggests that the Panel seemed doubtful about its own finding by suggesting that Section 211(b) might raise concerns similar to those arising in respect of Section 211(a)(2). However, the Panel was merely reiterating that the European Communities had failed to present evidence that Section 211(b) was inconsistent with obligations of the *TRIPS Agreement*.

75. The United States notes the submission of the European Communities that both the European Communities and the United States agree on the scope of Section 211(b). In response to this submission, the United States argues that in its submissions on this issue, it was only responding "in kind" to the European Communities' vague arguments. The United States submits further that the European Communities incorrectly suggests that the Panel ignored a court decision interpreting Section 211(b), when, in fact, the Panel specifically found that the language from the court decision did not explain what the Panel needed to know for the purposes of this dispute.

76. Even assuming that Section 211(a)(2) and Section 211(b) are sufficiently "parallel" such that there are sufficient uncontested facts for the Appellate Body to complete the analysis not undertaken by the Panel, the United States argues that the Appellate Body should conclude that Section 211(b) is consistent with Article 42 of the *TRIPS Agreement*. Even if there were an inconsistency with respect to trademarks, there is no factual basis for finding an inconsistency with respect to trade names.

5. Article 2 of the Paris Convention (1967) and Article 3 of the TRIPS Agreement

77. The United States argues that the Panel correctly found that Section 211(a)(2) does not provide more favourable treatment to United States nationals than it does to non-United States nationals, and, therefore, is not inconsistent with the national treatment provisions of the *TRIPS Agreement* and the Paris Convention (1967). The European Communities claims that the Panel erred in its assessment of the facts. As the European Communities has not alleged any violations of Article 11 of the DSU, in the view of the United States this claim is outside the scope of appellate review.

78. According to the United States, the European Communities' claim is based on its assumption that OFAC regulations impose a licensing requirement only with respect to United States assets owned by Cuban nationals, such that United States or other nationals are unaffected. This is incorrect. OFAC regulations are very broad, and generally prohibit any transactions involving property in which a designated national has had any interest of any nature whatsoever, direct or indirect. This includes transactions by persons of any nationality with

respect to trademarks that are identical or similar to trademarks in which a designated national has had an interest. Moreover, in claiming that there is discrimination with respect to original registrants, the European Communities disregards the fact that, as to original owners, there is no distinction made according to nationality.

79.   The United States notes the European Communities' argument that, as the Panel's finding was based on OFAC's discretionary licensing authority, the United States has the burden of demonstrating that this authority would be exercised in an even-handed fashion. In the view of the United States, this is incorrect. It is the European Communities' burden to demonstrate that Section 211(a)(2), on its face, mandates WTO-inconsistent action.

80.   The United States argues that Section 211(b) is not inconsistent with the national treatment obligation in the *TRIPS Agreement* and the Paris Convention (1967). The European Communities' sole argument with respect to Section 211(b) and the national treatment obligation is to refer to its arguments under Section 211(a)(2), because the two sections operate in the same manner. However, the European Communities' argument with respect to Section 211(a)(2) is based in significant part on its observation that Section 211(a)(2) does not specifically mention United States nationals as successors-in-interest. Section 211(b), by contrast, specifically includes United States nationals as successors-in-interest. This difference alone undermines the European Communities' assertion that its arguments by cross-reference are supportable and meaningful. In the view of the United States, the European Communities' Section 211(a)(2) argument is largely irrelevant to Section 211(b).

81.   If the Appellate Body concludes that the European Communities' arguments regarding Section 211(a)(2) are germane to the analysis of Section 211(b), the United States submits that its own arguments with regard to Section 211(a)(2) demonstrate that Section 211(b) is not inconsistent with the national treatment obligation in the *TRIPS Agreement* and the Paris Convention (1967).

6.   Article 4 of the TRIPS Agreement

82.   In the view of the United States, the Panel correctly found that Section 211(a)(2) is not inconsistent with the most-favoured-nation obligation of the *TRIPS Agreement*. The European Communities' sole argument is that there is discrimination at the level of original owners. This is incorrect. The original owner, of whatever nationality, consents to his own registration, so Section 211(a)(2) creates no differential treatment according to the nationality of the original owner. Further, there is no discrimination with respect to the nationality of the entity confiscating assets in Cuba. Entities of other nationalities were not in a position to confiscate the original properties in Cuba; they become relevant only if they become successors-in-interest to the confiscating entity. As the Panel correctly found, Section 211(a)(2) treats all foreign successors-in-interest in the same manner.

83.   The United States also argues that Section 211(b) is not inconsistent with the most-favoured-nation obligation of the *TRIPS Agreement*. The European

Communities has failed to make specific arguments with respect to the most-favoured-nation obligation under Section 211(b). However, if the Appellate Body concludes that the European Communities' arguments with respect to Section 211(a)(2) are germane to its analysis of Section 211(b), the United States refers the Appellate Body to its own arguments in respect of Section 211(a)(2).

7. Article 8 of the Paris Convention (1967) – Trade Names

84.　The United States agrees with the European Communities that the Panel erred in finding that the *TRIPS Agreement* contains no obligations with respect to trade names. Article 2.1 of the *TRIPS Agreement* identifies trade names, which are protected under Article 8 of the Paris Convention (1967), as a category of intellectual property covered "in respect of Parts II, III and IV" of the *TRIPS Agreement*. The United States is of the view that if upheld, the Panel's finding would render this specific identification of trade names in Article 8 of the Paris Convention (1967) a nullity.

85.　However, the United States does not agree with the European Communities that the Appellate Body should complete the Panel's analysis with respect to whether Section 211 is inconsistent with the obligations under the *TRIPS Agreement* and the Paris Convention (1967) regarding the protection of trade names. According to the United States, there are insufficient factual findings with respect to trade name protection in the United States so that the Appellate Body should decline to complete the analysis not undertaken by the Panel. In particular, the United States submits that the Panel examined thoroughly United States law with respect to trademarks and trademark registrations, but made no findings on how trade name ownership is established, or whether the issue of registration or non-registration of trade names affects the rights of the person asserting ownership of a trade name.

86.　However, if the Appellate Body decides nevertheless to complete the analysis, the United States submits that the Appellate Body should find that Section 211(a)(2) is not inconsistent with any trade name obligations of the *TRIPS Agreement* and the Paris Convention (1967).

C. Claims of Error by the United States – Appellant

1. Article 42 of the TRIPS Agreement

87.　The United States argues that the Panel erred in finding that Section 211(a)(2) breaches the requirements for fair and equitable procedures detailed in Article 42 of the *TRIPS Agreement*.

88.　The Panel found that, inconsistently with this Article, "Section 211(a)(2) limits, under certain circumstances, right holders' effective access to and, hence, the availability of civil judicial procedures".[27] However, the United States submits that the Panel erred by overlooking the fact that under Section 211, the "certain circumstances" under which a court will not recognize, enforce, or otherwise

---

[27]　Panel Report, para. 8.102.

validate the assertion of ownership rights are no more than the very "circumstances" in which the claimant is not the legitimate owner (or right holder) according to United States law.

89.   The United States contends further that the Panel erroneously concluded that Section 211(a)(2) prevents persons who claim ownership of a trademark on the basis of registration from having the ability to substantiate their claims in a trademark infringement action. According to the United States, the Panel found nothing in Section 211(a)(2) that prevents parties, including trademark registrants, from initiating a judicial proceeding, from presenting all relevant evidence in support of their claims, and, if they are trademark registrants, from enjoying the presumption of validity that registration confers.

D.   Arguments of the European Communities – Appellee

1.   Article 42 of the TRIPS Agreement

90.   The European Communities argues that the Panel did not err in finding that Section 211(a)(2) is inconsistent with Article 42 of the *TRIPS Agreement*. According to the European Communities, Article 42 requires that, in a civil judicial procedure, a plaintiff must be able to pursue all issues relevant for the enforcement of an intellectual property right covered by the *TRIPS Agreement* and not just the plaintiff's entitlement to enforce the right conferred by the intellectual property right.

91.   The European Communities contends further that the United States argument is based on a mis-characterization of Section 211(a)(2) as an ownership rule. Accordingly, the European Communities argues that the United States' circular reasoning that if somebody is not the rightful owner of a registered trademark, there is nothing this person can enforce in civil judicial procedures, has to be rejected. Even assuming that Section 211(a)(2) contains an element that can be of relevance to the issue of ownership, the European Communities contends that the owner of record of a registered United States trademark must benefit fully from the protection offered by Article 42 until such moment that the trademark is definitively removed from the register.

92.   The European Communities argues that Section 211(a)(2) limits the issues subject to litigation and thus excludes issues that are typically relevant in trademark-related litigation, such as use of the trademark, identity or similarity of signs, class of products or services covered by the trademark, existence and scope of a licence, among others.

III.   ISSUES RAISED IN THIS APPEAL

93.   The measure at issue in this dispute is Section 211 of the United States Omnibus Appropriations Act, 1999, ("Section 211")[28], which became law in the United States on 21 October 1998. Section 211 consists of four subsections. In

---

[28]   See *supra*, footnote 2.

its request for the establishment of a panel, the European Communities indicated that it was challenging only subsections (a)(1), (a)(2) and (b).[29] At the oral hearing in this appeal, the European Communities confirmed this by stating that the measure "includes 211(a)(1), 211(a)(2), and 211(b)" and that "[t]he other provisions are definitions and are auxiliary".[30] The United States agreed.[31]

94.   With this in mind, we confine our rulings in this appeal to subsections (a)(1), (a)(2) and (b) of Section 211. We address subsections (c) and (d) only to the extent that the definitions they contain are relevant to our examination of the consistency of subsections (a) and (b) with the provisions of the *TRIPS Agreement* and of the Paris Convention (1967) that have been invoked by the European Communities.

95.   Section 211 makes reference to Section 515.527 of the Cuban Assets Control Regulations (the "CACR").[32] The CACR were enacted on 8 July 1963 pursuant to the Trading with the Enemy Act, a statute enacted by the United States Congress on 6 October 1917.[33] After the entry into force of Section 211, the CACR were amended by adding a new subparagraph (a)(2) to Section 515.527 of Title 31 CFR.[34] Both parties to this dispute agree that neither the CACR nor the Trading with the Enemy Act is part of the measure at issue in this appeal. Thus, we refer to the CACR and to the Trading with the Enemy Act only to the extent that they are relevant for the interpretation of Section 211 and have been addressed by the participants in their arguments in this dispute.

96.   This dispute focuses on the protection of trademarks.[35] In the legal regimes of most WTO Members, the ownership of a trademark is established exclusively through registration. The Panel established that this is not so under United States law.[36] Before the Panel, the United States submitted that, under United States law, "'use' in connection with a business or assets may create ownership rights in the trademark".[37] The Panel established, further, that, in the

---

[29]   WT/DS176/2.
[30]   European Communities' responses to questioning at the oral hearing.
[31]   United States' responses to questioning at the oral hearing.
[32]   31 CFR §§515.101 – 515.901 (1999).
[33]   See *supra*, footnote 5.
[34]   After this, paragraph (a) of Section 515.527 became subparagraph (a)(1). The amendment entered into force on 10 May 1999. The text of Sections 515.527(a)(1) and (a)(2) are set out in paragraphs 6 and 7 of this Report.
[35]   Before the Panel, the European Communities also made claims in relation to trade names, and, on appeal, the European Communities challenges the Panel's finding that trade names are not covered in the *TRIPS Agreement*. In Sections V-X of this Report, we address the European Communities' appeal as it relates to trademarks. We address the issue of trade names, and the Panel's findings with respect to this issue, in Section XI below.
[36]   See Panel Report, paras. 8.62-8.64, where the Panel stated that:

> [W]e are obliged to examine first how the United States determines trademark ownership under its laws.
>
> . . .
>
> According to the United States, trademark ownership is generally established through use and thus the owner of a trademark is generally the party who controls the nature and quality of the goods sold or services rendered under the trademark.
> We note that trademark ownership is generally determined by use under US law.

[37]   *Ibid*., para. 4.215.

United States, "the registration of a trademark confers a *prima facie* presumption of the registrant's ownership of the registered trademark."[38] The European Communities agreed with the submission of the United States that "if the person registering a trademark in the United States is not the true owner of the trademark under [United States] law, the registration may be cancelled."[39]

97.   Both the European Communities and the United States agree that, in the United States, the principal federal statute on trademark and trade name protection is the Trademark Act of 1946 (which is commonly referred to as the "Lanham Act").[40] Both parties to this dispute have also agreed that the Lanham Act also is not part of the measure at issue in this appeal. Thus, we refer to the Lanham Act only to the extent that it is relevant for the interpretation of Section 211.

98.   On appeal, the United States submits that the European Communities has not challenged the *application* of Section 211.[41] At the oral hearing in this appeal, the European Communities confirmed that it has not challenged the application of the statute, and clarified that, instead, it is challenging the statute on its face.[42] The European Communities confirmed as well that, in this dispute, the European Communities is not challenging the WTO-consistency of the decisions in *Havana Club Holding, S.A. v. Galleon S.A.* (the "*Havana Club Holding* decisions").[43] Like the Panel, the only applications of Section 211 we are aware of are the two United States court decisions relating to Section 211(b) in 1999 and in 2000 in *Havana Club Holding, S.A. v. Galleon S.A.* The request by the European Communities for the establishment of a panel does not contain any reference to the *Havana Club Holding* decisions. Thus, in this appeal, we examine the WTO-consistency of Section 211 on its face. The question of the WTO-consistency of the *Havana Club Holding* decisions is not before us. However, as the European Communities has argued and as the United States has agreed, the *Havana Club Holding* decisions are relevant as evidence of how Section 211(b), as the European Communities has put it, "operates in practice".[44] We agree.

99.   Therefore, the measure at issue in this dispute consists of subsections (a)(1), (a)(2) and (b) of Section 211. With respect to this measure, the following issues are raised in this appeal:

---

[38]   Panel Report, para. 8.99.

[39]   Panel Report, para. 4.240. United States' other appellant's submission, para. 24. European Communities' responses to questioning at the oral hearing. See also McCarthy, J. Thomas, *McCarthy on Trademarks and Unfair Competition* (West Publishing Group, 2000), Vol. I, p. 19-13.

[40]   See *supra*, footnote 11.

[41]   United States' other appellant's submission, para. 19.

[42]   European Communities' responses to questioning at the oral hearing.

[43]   *Havana Club Holding, S.A. v. Galleon S.A.*, 203 F.3d 116 (2d Cir. 2000); *Havana Club Holding, S.A. v. Galleon S.A.*, 62 F.Supp.2d 1085 (S.D.N.Y. 1999). These two decisions followed three decisions issued earlier in the same dispute, before Section 211 was enacted: *Havana Club Holding, S.A. v. Galleon, S.A.*, 961 F.Supp. 498 (S.D.N.Y. 1997); *Havana Club Holding, S.A. v. Galleon S.A.*, 974 F.Supp. 302 (S.D.N.Y. 1997); *Havana Club Holding, S.A. v. Galleon S.A.*, 1998 WL 150983 (S.D.N.Y.). Because they were issued before Section 211 was enacted, these three earlier decisions are not relevant.

[44]   European Communities' appellant's submission, para. 145.

(a)   whether the Panel erred in finding that Section 211(a)(1) is not inconsistent with Article 2.1 of the *TRIPS Agreement* in conjunction with Article 6*quinquies* A(1) of the Paris Convention (1967);

(b)   whether the Panel erred in finding that Section 211(a)(1) is not inconsistent with Article 15.1 of the *TRIPS Agreement*;

(c)   whether the Panel erred in finding that the European Communities has not proved that Sections 211(a)(2) and (b) are inconsistent with Article 16.1 of the *TRIPS Agreement*;

(d)   whether the Panel erred in finding that:

    (i)   Section 211(a)(2) is inconsistent with Article 42 of the *TRIPS Agreement* with respect to the protection of trademarks; and

    (ii)   the European Communities has not proved that Section 211(b) is inconsistent with Article 42 of the *TRIPS Agreement* with respect to the protection of trademarks;

(e)   whether the Panel erred in finding that Sections 211(a)(2) and (b) are not inconsistent with Article 2.1 of the *TRIPS Agreement* in conjunction with Article 2(1) of the Paris Convention (1967) and Article 3.1 of the *TRIPS Agreement* in respect of the protection of trademarks;

(f)   whether the Panel erred in finding that Sections 211(a)(2) and (b) are not inconsistent with Article 4 of the *TRIPS Agreement* in respect of the protection of trademarks; and

(g)   whether the Panel erred in finding that trade names are not covered by the *TRIPS Agreement* and, consequently:

    (i)   erred in not finding that Sections 211(a)(2) and (b) are inconsistent with Article 2.1 of the *TRIPS Agreement* in conjunction with Article 2(1) of the Paris Convention (1967) and Article 3.1 of the *TRIPS Agreement* in respect of the protection of trade names;

    (ii)   erred in not finding that Sections 211(a)(2) and (b) are inconsistent with Article 4 of the *TRIPS Agreement* in respect of the protection of trade names;

    (iii)   erred in not finding that Sections 211(a)(2) and (b) are inconsistent with Article 42 of the *TRIPS Agreement* in respect of the protection of trade names; and

    (iv)   erred in finding that Sections 211(a)(2) and (b) are not inconsistent with Article 2.1 of the *TRIPS Agreement* in conjunction with Article 8 of the Paris Convention (1967).

IV.   PRELIMINARY MATTERS

A.   *The Scope of Appellate Review*

100.   We begin by addressing a preliminary question that is central to our disposition of the specific issues raised in this appeal. This question is the scope of appellate review in this appeal.

101.   With respect to the scope of appellate review, the United States argues that we are bound on appeal by the Panel's conclusions about the meaning of the measure at issue. The United States submits that a panel's review of a Member's domestic law is, in any dispute, a question of fact[45], and that, therefore, the European Communities' allegations, in this dispute, about the Panel's appreciation of the meaning of the terms of Section 211 are questions of fact. The United States points to our mandate under Article 17.6 of the DSU, which limits appeals to "issues of law covered in the panel report and legal interpretations developed by the panel." The United States reminds us of our observation in our Report in *EC Measures Concerning Meat and Meat Products (Hormones)* ("*EC – Hormones*") that "[f]indings of fact, as distinguished from legal interpretations or legal conclusions, by a panel are, in principle, not subject to review by the Appellate Body."[46] The United States reminds us as well of Article 11 of the DSU, which obliges a panel to "make an objective assessment of the matter before it, including an objective assessment of the facts of the case". Although the United States acknowledges that the question whether a panel has made such an objective assessment of the facts is indeed a legal question, the United States insists that, for such a question to fall within the scope of appellate review, it must be properly raised on appeal. The United States emphasizes that the European Communities has not made a claim under Article 11 of the DSU in this appeal. From this, the United States concludes that the findings of the Panel on the meaning of Section 211 are not within the scope of this appeal.

102.   The European Communities argues that we are in no way bound on appeal by the Panel's characterization of the meaning of Section 211. The European Communities sees this as a "question of law"[47] that is fully within the scope of appellate review under the DSU. The European Communities contends that the findings of the Panel in relation to Section 211 are based, *inter alia*, on an erroneous reading of Section 211 itself. The European Communities argues further that these erroneous findings are based on erroneous interpretations of the relevant provisions of the *TRIPS Agreement* and of the relevant provisions of the Paris Convention (1967) that have been incorporated by reference into the *TRIPS Agreement.*[48] The European Communities insists that the Appellate Body is empowered to review the result of a panel's examination of a WTO Member's domestic law for the purpose of ascertaining its consistency with the *Marrakesh*

---

[45]   United States' appellee's submission, paras. 19 and 20.
[46]   Appellate Body Report, WT/DS26/AB/R, WT/DS48/AB/R, adopted 13 February 1998, DSR 1998:1, 135, para. 132.
[47]   European Communities' responses to questioning at the oral hearing.
[48]   European Communities' appellant's submission, paras. 80-81.

Agreement Establishing the World Trade Organization (the "*WTO Agreement*"). At the oral hearing, the European Communities explained that understanding what is the measure that is the subject of the dispute is a question of law and, if the subject of a dispute is simply a provision of a domestic law which is being attacked as such, then understanding that measure correctly is a question of law.

103.　In addressing the scope of appellate review in this case, we begin by recalling our ruling in *EC – Hormones* that:

> The consistency or inconsistency of a given fact or set of facts with the requirements of a given treaty provision is ... a legal characterization issue. It is a legal question.[49]

104.　We believe that our ruling in *India – Patent Protection for Pharmaceutical and Agricultural Chemical Products* ("*India – Patents (US)*") is of even greater relevance. We stated there, in relevant part, that:

> In public international law, an international tribunal may treat municipal law in several ways. Municipal law may serve as evidence of facts and may provide evidence of state practice. However, municipal law may also constitute evidence of compliance or non-compliance with international obligations. ... (footnote omitted)

> It is clear that an examination of the relevant aspects of Indian municipal law and, in particular, the relevant provisions of the Patents Act as they relate to the "administrative instructions", is essential to determining whether India has complied with its obligations under Article 70.8(a). There was simply no way for the Panel to make this determination without engaging in an examination of Indian law. But, as in the case cited above before the Permanent Court of International Justice, in this case, the Panel was not interpreting Indian law "as such"; rather, the Panel was examining Indian law solely for the purpose of determining whether India had met its obligations under the *TRIPS Agreement*. ...

> And, just as it was necessary for the Panel in this case to seek a detailed understanding of the operation of the Patents Act as it relates to the "administrative instructions" in order to assess whether India had complied with Article 70.8(a), *so, too, is it necessary for us in this appeal to review the Panel's examination of the same Indian domestic law.*[50] (emphasis added)

105.　Our rulings in these previous appeals are clear: the municipal law of WTO Members may serve not only as evidence of facts, but also as evidence of compliance or non-compliance with international obligations. Under the DSU, a panel may examine the municipal law of a WTO Member for the purpose of determining whether that Member has complied with its obligations under the *WTO Agreement*. Such an assessment is a legal characterization by a panel. And, there-

---

[49]　Appellate Body Report, *EC – Hormones, supra*, footnote 46, para. 132.

[50]　Appellate Body Report, WT/DS50/AB/R, adopted 16 January 1998, DSR 1998:I, 9, paras. 65-66 and 68.

fore, a panel's assessment of municipal law as to its consistency with WTO obligations is subject to appellate review under Article 17.6 of the DSU.

106.   To address the legal issues raised in this appeal, we must, therefore, necessarily examine the Panel's interpretation of the meaning of Section 211 under United States law. An assessment of the consistency of Section 211 with the Articles of the *TRIPS Agreement* and of the Paris Convention (1967) that have been invoked by the European Communities necessarily requires a review of the Panel's examination of the meaning of Section 211. Likewise, that assessment necessarily requires a review also of the Panel's examination of the meaning of both the CACR and the Lanham Act, to the extent that they are relevant for assessing the meaning of Section 211. This is an interpretation of the meaning of Section 211 solely for the purpose of determining whether the United States has fulfilled its obligations under the *TRIPS Agreement*. The meaning given by the Panel to Section 211 is, thus, clearly within the scope of our review as set out in Article 17.6 of the DSU.

B.   The Nature of the Measure

107.   Having determined that it is appropriate for us to review the Panel's conclusions about the meaning of the measure at issue in this appeal, we turn now to that task. A number of the legal issues raised in this appeal turn on the meaning or nature of Section 211. We begin our consideration of this pivotal issue by noting that Section 211(a)(1) provides:

> Notwithstanding any other provision of law, no transaction or payment shall be authorized or approved pursuant to section 515.527 of title 31, Code of Federal Regulations, as in effect on September 9, 1998, with respect to a mark, trade name, or commercial name that is the same as or substantially similar to a mark, trade name, or commercial name that was used in connection with a business or assets that were confiscated *unless the original owner of the mark, trade name, or commercial name, or the bona fide successor-in-interest has expressly consented.* (emphasis added)

108.   Before the Panel, the United States submitted that Section 211 concerns ownership. The European Communities argued that it does not. The Panel concluded that "the language of Section 211(a)(1) indicates that it is a measure that *deals* with ownership of trademarks used in connection with confiscated assets." [51] (emphasis added) The Panel concluded also that Section 211(a)(1) "regulates ownership". [52] The Panel explained these conclusions as follows:

> The language of Section 211(a)(1) *addresses* the rights of a person registering a trademark to assert an *ownership interest* in the trademark concerned. Section 211(a)(1), together with OFAC regulations, creates an additional procedural step that relates to the

---

[51]   Panel Report, para. 8.59.
[52]   *Ibid.*, para. 8.83.

registration of a trademark or the renewal of a trademark registration in the United States, namely the requirement that an applicant obtain a licence—a general or a specific licence—in order to be able to pay the registration or renewal fee. In the absence of such a licence, the applicant is not able to pay the required fee and this, in turn, results in the rejection of the application. As a part of this procedure, the US authorities examine, in the case where the trademark in question is one that was used in connection with confiscated assets, whether the applicant is the *proper owner* of that trademark in accordance with US law or has the consent of the original owner or the latter's successor-in-interest. If a trademark was used in connection with confiscated assets, the failure to obtain the required consent or to meet the condition of being the *proper owner* as defined under US law has the practical effect of denying trademark registration. However, if the applicant is the *original owner* under US law or has the consent of such *original owner* or its bona fide successor-in-interest, the licence will be granted and, hence, the trademark will be registered or the registration will be renewed.[53] (emphasis added).

109. Relying on this view of Section 211(a)(1), the Panel found:

We find that Section 211(a)(1) is not inconsistent with Article 15.1 of the TRIPS Agreement because the term "other grounds" as used in Article 15.2 of the TRIPS Agreement may include a measure that denies trademark registration on the basis that the applicant is *not the owner* under national, in this case, US law and Section 211(a)(1) is a measure that deals with the ownership of trademarks used in connection with confiscated assets.[54] (emphasis added)

110. On appeal, the participants continue to disagree about the nature of Section 211. Unlike the Panel, the European Communities does not see Section 211 as a measure that "deals with" or "regulates" ownership. Rather, the European Communities maintains that the purpose of Section 211 "consists in curtailing the enjoyment and existence of certain trademarks and trade names in the hands of certain categories of rightholders."[55] The European Communities explains that the Panel assumed erroneously that Section 211(a)(1) "has as its function to *allocate* ownership to a litigious trademark"[56] (emphasis added) because, as the Panel itself observed, Section 211(a)(1), together with the OFAC regulations, merely "creates an additional procedural step that *relates* to the registration of a trademark or the renewal of a trademark registration in the United States".[57] (emphasis added) On this basis, the European Communities argues that Sec-

---

[53] Panel Report, para. 8.60.
[54] *Ibid.*, para. 8.70.
[55] European Communities' appellant's submission, para. 2.
[56] *Ibid.*, para. 83.
[57] Panel Report, para. 8.60.

tion 211 does not in any way establish ownership of trademarks and that, therefore, Section 211 is not, by nature, an ownership measure.[58]

111.   The United States sees Section 211 differently. The United States, like the Panel, sees Section 211 as a measure that "deals with" and "regulates" ownership. The United States explains that Section 211 "deals with" and "regulates" ownership in a limited and specific set of circumstances – those that are described in the measure relating to confiscation.[59] The United States contends that Section 211 is an expression of the longstanding doctrine[60] of the United States that those whose claim to ownership of a trademark is based on an uncompensated confiscation of assets cannot claim rights of ownership in the United States, absent the consent of the owners whose assets were confiscated.[61] The United States asserts that whether Section 211 affirmatively attributes ownership of the trademark to someone else is irrelevant.[62] As the United States sees it, the measure is no less an ownership measure because it identifies only who is *not* the owner and does not establish who *is* the owner of a particular trademark in the circumstances in which Section 211 applies.[63]

112.   With these arguments of the parties in mind, we examine the measure at issue in this appeal. In doing so, we observe, like the European Communities, that Section 211(a)(1) does not positively "allocate" – that is, it does not attribute or establish – trademark ownership for one person or another. Yet, we disagree with the European Communities that the "consent requirement introduced by Section 211(a)(1) has nothing to do with an ownership related measure such as a transfer or cessation of an asset."[64]

113.   In our view, a measure such as the one before us that conditions rights on obtaining the express consent of the original owner *is*, unquestionably, a measure that deals with ownership. We do not agree with the European Communities that a measure must *establish* ownership in order to be one that is, in its nature, an ownership measure. A measure need not deal exhaustively with a particular subject in order to be considered as a measure dealing with that subject.

114.   Therefore, we agree instead with the United States that the mere fact that Section 211(a)(1) does *not* affirmatively establish ownership[65] does not, in and of itself, render that measure one that does not deal with ownership. Further, we agree with the United States that, although Section 211(a)(1) does not determine who *does* own a trademark, it can, in the particular circumstances in which it applies, determine who *does not*. To us, this alone is sufficient to make Sec-

---

[58]   European Communities' responses to questioning at the oral hearing. At the oral hearing, in response to one question, the European Communities confirmed that, by "allocate", in this context, the European Communities means "attribute".

[59]   We refer here and throughout this Report to the term "confiscated" as it is defined in Section 515.336 of Title 31 CFR. See *supra*, footnote 7.

[60]   United States' appellee's submission, para. 1.

[61]   *Ibid.*, para. 16; Panel Report, para. 4.14.

[62]   United States' appellee's submission, para. 23.

[63]   *Ibid.*

[64]   European Communities' appellant's submission, para. 64.

[65]   United States' appellee's submission, para. 23.

tion 211(a)(1) a measure that, in its nature, relates to the *ownership* of trademarks and trade names.

115.   The text of the measure supports this interpretation. As we have observed, the text of Section 211(a)(1) contains a phrase that specifically refers to ownership, namely: "a mark, trade name, or commercial name that was used in connection with a business or assets that were confiscated unless the original owner of the mark, trade name or commercial name, or the *bona fide* successor-in-interest has expressly consented." [66]   Section 211(a)(2) does not contain this phrase. Rather, Section 211(a)(2) reads:

> No U.S. court shall recognize, enforce or otherwise validate any assertion of rights by a designated national based on common law rights or registration obtained under such section 515.527 of *such* a confiscated mark, trade name, or commercial name. (emphasis added)

116.   This raises the issue of the import of the word "such" in the phrase "such a confiscated mark, trade name, or commercial name." Although it is clear that the "such" in Section 211(a)(2) refers back to Section 211(a)(1), the question is: to what part of paragraph (a)(1) does paragraph (a)(2) refer? On the one hand, "such a confiscated mark, trade name, or commercial name" could conceivably refer *only* to the phrase "mark, trade name, or commercial name that is the same as or substantially similar to a mark, trade name, or commercial name that was used in connection with a business or assets that were confiscated". On the other hand, it could refer – *in addition* – to the phrase immediately following, that is, to "unless the original owner of the mark, trade name, or commercial name, or the bona fide successor-in-interest has expressly consented."

117.   The Panel interpreted Section 211(a)(2) to refer back to both phrases; that is, the Panel determined that Section 211(a)(2) includes the consent requirement found in Section 211(a)(1), when it stated that:

> Under the exceptional circumstances dealt with under Section 211(a)(2), there may be a successful challenge concerning the *prima facie* ownership rights in relation to the registration, obtained by a designated national pursuant to a general OFAC licence without the consent of the original owner, of a trademark used in connection with confiscated assets. [67]

118.   We agree with the Panel on the import of the second "such" in Section 211(a)(2). Moreover, in response to questions posed at the oral hearing, both the

---

[66]   Section 211(a)(1) reads:
> Notwithstanding any other provision of law, no transaction or payment shall be authorized or approved pursuant to section 515.527 of title 31, Code of Federal Regulations, as in effect on September 9, 1998, *with respect to a mark, trade name, or commercial name that is the same as or substantially similar to a mark, trade name, or commercial name that was used in connection with a business or assets* that were confiscated <u>unless the original owner of the mark, trade name, or commercial name, or the bona fide successor-in-interest has expressly consented.</u> (emphasis and underlining added)

[67]   Panel Report, para. 8.111.

European Communities and the United States responded that, likewise, in their view, the second "such" in Section 211(a)(2) refers to both parts of the phrase in Section 211(a)(1) that is omitted from Section 211(a)(2), including the requirement to obtain express consent.[68]

119. We turn next to the text of Section 211(b), which reads:

> No U.S. court shall recognize, enforce or otherwise validate any assertion of treaty rights by a designated national or its successor-in-interest under sections 44 (b) or (e) of the Trademark Act of 1946 (15 U.S.C. 1126 (b) or (e)) for a mark, trade name, or commercial name that is the same as or substantially similar to a mark, trade name, or commercial name that was used in connection with a business or assets that were confiscated *unless the original owner of such mark, trade name, or commercial name, or the bona fide successor-in-interest has expressly consented.* (emphasis added)

Here we note that the wording of Section 211(b) specifically includes the express consent requirement.

120. Thus, the consent requirement is present alike in each of Sections 211(a)(1), 211(a)(2) and 211(b), and, as a consequence, so too is the element of the measure that "deals with" and "regulates" ownership.

121. Accordingly, we will address each of the legal issues raised in this appeal with the understanding that the measure before us, in the particular circumstances in which it applies, is, in its nature, one that relates to the ownership of a defined category of trademarks and trade names.

V. ARTICLE 6*QUINQUIES* OF THE PARIS CONVENTION (1967)

122. We turn now to the claims of the European Communities as they relate to Article 6*quinquie*s of the Paris Convention (1967). Article 6*quinquies* A(1) reads:

> Every trademark duly registered in the country of origin shall be accepted for filing and protected *as is* in the other countries of the Union, subject to the reservations indicated in this Article. Such countries may, before proceeding to final registration, require the production of a certificate of registration in the country of origin, issued by the competent authority. No authentication shall be required for this certificate. (emphasis added)

123. Article 6*quinquies* forms part of the Stockholm Act of the Paris Convention, dated 14 July 1967. The Stockholm Act is a revision of the original *Paris Convention for the Protection of Industrial Property*, which entered into force on

---

[68] European Communities' responses to questioning at the oral hearing; United States' responses to questioning at the oral hearing. The United States suggested that this omission may merely be an instance of legislative "shorthand" as there is no reason to think that the framers of the measure would have wanted to omit from Section 211(a)(2) what is required in Section 211(a)(1).

7 July 1884.[69] The parties to the Paris Convention, who are commonly described as the "countries of the Paris Union", are obliged to implement the provisions of that Convention.

124. Article 2.1 of the *TRIPS Agreement* provides that: "[i]n respect of Parts II, III and IV of this Agreement, Members shall comply with Articles 1 through 12, and Article 19, of the Paris Convention (1967)." Thus, Article 6*quinquies* of the Paris Convention (1967), as well as certain other specified provisions of the Paris Convention (1967), have been incorporated by reference into the *TRIPS Agreement* and, thus, the *WTO Agreement*.

125. Consequently, WTO Members, whether they are countries of the Paris Union or not, are obliged, under the *WTO Agreement*, to implement those provisions of the Paris Convention (1967) that are incorporated into the *TRIPS Agreement*. As we have already stated, Article 6*quinquies* of the Paris Convention (1967) is one such provision.

126. Before the Panel, the European Communities claimed that Section 211(a)(1) is inconsistent with Article 2.1 of the *TRIPS Agreement* in conjunction with Article 6*quinquies* A(1) of the Paris Convention (1967), an allegation contested by the United States.[70]

127. The Panel found:

> The ordinary meaning of the term "as is" and read in its context and as confirmed by the negotiating history indicates that Article 6*quinquies* A(1) addresses the form of the trademark; that is, those trademarks duly registered in one country, even when they do not comply with the provisions of domestic law of a Member concerning the permissible form of trademarks, have nevertheless to be accepted for filing and protection in another country. Therefore, we do not agree with the EC's assertion that the Member in which registration is sought does not have any right to question the existence of a trademark in the hands of an owner as defined by the laws of the country of origin. However, as we noted above in our examination of Section 211(a)(1) in relation to Article 15.1 of the TRIPS Agreement, Section 211(a)(1) is a measure that regulates ownership and does not deal with the form of the signs of which the trademark is composed. For these reasons, Section 211(a)(1) is not inconsistent with Article 6*quinquies* A(1) of the Paris Convention (1967). (footnote omitted)
>
> ...
>
> We conclude that Article 6*quinquies* A(1) addresses the form of the trademark and therefore find that Section 211(a)(1) is not inconsistent with Article 6*quinquies* A(1) of the Paris Convention

---

[69] The original Paris Convention was concluded in 1883.
[70] Panel Report, paras. 8.71-8.73.

(1967) as incorporated into the TRIPS Agreement by means of a reference in its Article 2.1.[71]

128.   The European Communities appeals this finding and argues on appeal, as before the Panel, that Article 6*quinquies* A(1) requires that a trademark duly registered in a country of origin that is a country of the Paris Union must be accepted for registration and protected "as is" in every respect in other countries of the Paris Union, subject only to the specific exceptions set forth in that Article. Thus, the European Communities sees Article 6*quinquies* A(1) as applying to more than merely the *form* of a trademark. According to the European Communities, Section 211(a)(1) violates Article 6*quinquies* A(1) because it does not permit the filing and protection of the trademark "as is". Rather, it prevents the owner of a trademark registered in another country from acquiring or maintaining a trademark registration in the United States by preventing the payment of the required fees necessary for registration and renewal in the United States, unless the original owner or the *bona fide* successor-in-interest has expressly consented.

129.   The United States views Article 6*quinquies* A(1) differently and, thus, the United States views its obligation under Article 6*quinquies* A(1) as it relates to Section 211(a)(1) differently as well. The United States agrees with the Panel that the obligation in Article 6*quinquies* A(1) to register a foreign trademark "as is" concerns only the form of the trademark. Given this, the United States concludes that Section 211(a)(1) is not inconsistent with Article 6*quinquies* A(1) because Section 211(a)(1) does not address the form of the trademark. As the United States sees it, nothing in Article 6*quinquies* obliges the United States to accept the registration or renewal of a trademark if the person registering or renewing it is not the true owner of the trademark under United States law. The United States portrays Section 211(a)(1) as dealing with ownership of trademarks. The United States does not see anything in Article 6*quinquies* or in any other provision of the Paris Convention (1967) that specifies how trademark ownership is to be determined. Instead, the United States interprets the Paris Convention (1967) and, now, the *TRIPS Agreement*, as leaving the determination of trademark ownership to the national laws of each WTO Member, subject only to the requirements against discrimination that are found in that Convention and in that Agreement.

130.   Before examining the text of Article 6*quinquies*, we note that the Paris Convention (1967) provides two ways in which a national of a country of the Paris Union may obtain registration of a trademark in a country of that Union other than the country of the applicant's origin: one way is by registration under Article 6 of the Paris Convention (1967); the other is by registration under Article 6*quinquies* of that same Convention.

131.   Article 6(1) of the Paris Convention (1967) provides:

---

[71]   Panel Report, paras. 8.83 and 8.89.

> The conditions for the filing and registration of trademarks shall be determined in each country of the Union by its domestic legislation.

132.   Article 6(1) states the general rule, namely, that each country of the Paris Union has the right to determine the *conditions* for filing and registration of trademarks in its domestic legislation. This is a reservation of considerable discretion to the countries of the Paris Union – and now, by incorporation, the Members of the WTO – to continue, in principle, to determine for themselves the conditions for filing and registration of trademarks. Thus, in our view, the general rule under the Paris Convention (1967) is that national laws apply with respect to trademark registrations within the *territory* of each country of the Paris Union, subject to the requirements of other provisions of that Convention.[72] And, likewise, through incorporation, this is also now the general rule for all WTO Members under the *TRIPS Agreement*.

133.   Therefore, an applicant who chooses to seek registration of a trademark in a particular foreign country under Article 6 must comply with the conditions for filing and registration specified in that country's legislation. Such an applicant is *not* obliged to register a trademark first in its country of origin in order to register that trademark in another country of the Paris Union.[73] However, that applicant must comply with the conditions of that other country where registration is sought.[74]

134.   As we have stated, Article 6 is not the only way to register a trademark in another country. If an applicant *has* duly registered a trademark in its country of origin, Article 6*quinquies* A(1) provides an alternative way of obtaining protection of that trademark in other countries of the Paris Union.

135.   This alternative way of seeking acceptance in another country of the Paris Union of a trademark registered in the applicant's country of origin, afforded by Article 6*quinquies* A(1), is subject to two prerequisites. First, that trademark must be *duly registered* according to the domestic legislation of the country of origin, and, second, it must be registered in the applicant's *country of origin*, as defined in Article 6*quinquies* A(2).[75] Article 6*quinquies* D confirms that the

---

[72]   The discretion of countries of the Paris Union to legislate conditions for filing and registration is not unlimited. It is subject to the international minimum standard of trademark disciplines provided for in other Articles of the Paris Convention (1967). These include, for example, national treatment, as well as internationally agreed reasons for denying trademark registration, such as those provided for in Article 6*ter*. The Paris Convention (1967) limits also the legislative discretion of countries of the Union under Article 6(1) by setting out reasons that countries cannot invoke to deny trademark registration, for example in Article 6(2).

[73]   Article 6(2) of the Paris Convention (1967) provides:

> However, an application for the registration of a mark filed by a national of a country of the Union in any country of the Union may not be refused, nor may a registration be invalidated, on the ground that filing, registration, or renewal, has not been effected in the [national's] country of origin.

[74]   Article 6(3) of the Paris Convention (1967) further states:

> A mark duly registered in a country of the Union shall be regarded as *independent* of marks registered in the other countries of the Union, including the country of origin. (emphasis added)

[75]   Article 6*quinquies* A(2) of the Paris Convention (1967) reads:

recognition of a trademark in another country of the Paris Union under Article 6*quinquies* is dependent on registration in the country of origin.[76] These two prerequisites though are not at issue in this appeal. The issue in this appeal relates to the extent of the obligations established by Article 6*quinquies* A(1), assuming that these two prerequisites have been met.

136.   By virtue of Article 6*quinquies* A(1), WTO Members are obliged to confer an exceptional right on an applicant in a Paris Union country other than its country of origin, one that is over and above whatever rights the other country grants to its own nationals in its domestic law. A national who files for registration of a trademark in his own country must comply *fully* with the conditions for filing and registration as determined by the national legislation of that country. But, if that country is a Member of the Paris Union – and, now, of the WTO – then an applicant from another WTO Member who seeks registration in that country of a trademark duly registered in its country of origin has the *additional rights* that WTO Members are obliged to confer on that applicant under Article 6*quinquies* A(1).

137.   The participants to this dispute disagree on the scope of the requirement imposed by Article 6*quinquies* A(1) to accept for filing and protect trademarks duly registered in the country of origin "as is". Looking first to the text of Article 6*quinquies* A(1), we see that the words "as is" (or, in French, "telle quelle"[77]) relate to the trademark to be "accepted for filing and protected" in another country based on registration in the applicant's country of origin. The ordinary meaning of the words "as is" is "in the existing state".[78]   The French term "telle quelle" can be defined as "sans arrangement, sans modification."[79]   This suggests to us that the requirement of Article 6*quinquies* A(1) to accept for filing and protect a trademark duly registered in the applicant's country of origin relates at least to the *form* of the trademark as registered in the applicant's country of origin.[80]   The question before us is whether the scope of this requirement also encompasses other features and aspects of that trademark as registered in the country of origin.

138.   According to one expert:

> Shall be considered the country of origin the country of the Union where the applicant has a real and effective industrial or commercial establishment, or, if he has no such establishment within the Union, the country of the Union where he has his domicile, or, if he has no domicile within the Union but is a national of a country of the Union, the country of which he is a national.

[76]   Article 6*quinquies* D of the Paris Convention (1967) states:
> No person may benefit from the provisions of this Article if the mark for which he claims protection is not registered in the country of origin.

[77]   Article 29(1)(c) of the Paris Convention (1967) provides: "In case of differences of opinion on the interpretation of the various texts, the French text shall prevail."

[78]   *The New Shorter Oxford English Dictionary*, L. Brown (ed.), (Clarendon Press, 1993), Vol. I, p. 123.

[79]   *Le Petit Robert Dictionnaire de la Langue Française* (1995), p. 2220. Or in English, as it stands; without adjustments; without modification.

[80]   The participants agree that the requirement of Article 6*quinquies* A(1) *at the very least* relates to the form of the trademark, but they disagree on what else beyond form, if anything at all, that requirement includes.

... whenever a trademark is duly registered in the country of origin, the other countries of the Union are obliged to accept and protect it, even if, as regards its form, that is, with regard to the signs of which it is composed, such trademark does not comply with the requirements of the domestic legislation, subject to the additional rules, particularly the grounds for refusal or invalidation of any mark, considered on its individual merits, established in the Article. This rule will therefore apply to trademarks consisting of numbers, letters, surnames, geographical names, words written or not written in a certain language or script, and other signs of which the trademark is composed.[81] (italics and footnotes omitted)

139.   However, this view is not determinative of the question before us. To resolve this question, we look to the context of Article 6*quinquies* A(1). We find that there is considerable contextual support for the view that the requirement to register a trademark "as is" under Article 6*quinquies* A(1) does *not* encompass all the features and aspects of that trademark. As we have stressed, Article 6(1) of the Paris Convention (1967) reserves to the countries of the Paris Union the right to determine the *conditions* for filing and registration of trademarks by their domestic legislation.[82] Article 6(1) confirms that the countries of the Paris Union did not relinquish their right to determine the conditions for filing and registration of trademarks by entering into the Paris Convention (1967) – subject, of course, to the other obligations of Paris Union countries under the Paris Convention (1967).[83]   Clearly, if Article 6*quinquies* A(1) were interpreted too broadly, the legislative discretion reserved for Members under Article 6(1) would be significantly undermined.

140.   To illustrate this point, we will assume for the moment, and solely for the sake of argument, that, as the European Communities argues, Article 6*quinquies* A(1) does require other countries to accept for filing and to protect duly registered trademarks in respect of *all their aspects*, including those other than the form of a trademark. If this were so, an applicant who is a national of a country of the Paris Union would have two choices: that applicant could request trademark registration under Article 6 in another country of the Paris Union – in which case, that registration would be subject to the trademark law of that other country. Or, that applicant could register the trademark in its country of origin and then invoke the right, pursuant to Article 6*quinquies* A(1), to request acceptance of that trademark for filing and protection in another country. In the latter case, that registration would be governed by the trademark law, not

---

[81]   See, Bodenhausen, G.H.C, *Guide to the Application of the Paris Convention for the Protection of Industrial Property as revised at Stockholm in 1967*, (hereinafter "*Guide to the Paris Convention*"), United International Bureaux for the Protection of Intellectual Property, (1968, reprinted 1991), pp. 110-111.

[82]   We note that prior to the Revision Conference of Lisbon (1958), the requirements now found in Articles 6 and 6*quinquies* were contained in a single (original) Article 6. At the Revision Conference, it was decided to split the original Article in order to make clear the difference between the two alternative ways to obtain trademark registration explained above.

[83]   See *supra*, footnote 72.

of the country in which the applicant sought registration under Article 6*quinquies* A(1), but of the applicant's country of origin. The "conditions" for registration imposed in the law of the other country of the Paris Union where registration was sought under Article 6*quinquies* A(1) would be irrelevant. If this were so, any such applicant would be able to choose between trademark registration under Article 6 and trademark registration under Article 6*quinquies*, depending on which *conditions* for filing and registration were viewed by the applicant as more favourable to the applicant's interests.[84] Consequently, within the territory of any country of the Paris Union other than the applicant's country of origin, a national of a country of that Union could ensure that it would be subject to *either* the domestic trademark registration requirements of the country of origin (through recourse to Article 6*quinquies*) *or* the domestic trademark registration requirements of the other country where trademark registration is sought (through recourse to Article 6) – *whichever it preferred*. In other words, a national of a Paris Union country could circumvent the "use" requirements of a particular regime by registering in the jurisdiction that does not impose "use" requirements.

141.   We are persuaded that the drafters of the Paris Convention did not intend such a result. If, even today, WTO Members have – as the European Communities concedes – reserved the right under the *TRIPS Agreement* to maintain domestic regimes of trademark ownership based on use, then it does not seem credible to us to contend – as the European Communities does – that many of those very same countries intended more than a century ago, in concluding the Paris Convention, or on the occasion of one of the subsequent Revision Conferences of the Paris Convention, to establish a global system for determining trademark ownership that could circumvent, and thereby undermine, a domestic regime of trademark ownership based on use.

142.   We note that Article 6*quinquies* B provides that registration of a trademark covered by this Article may be neither denied nor invalidated, except for the reasons listed in subparagraphs B(1) through (3).[85] These exceptions refer,

---

[84]   As far as trademark protection within the territory of the Paris Union national's country of origin is concerned, such national could not avoid being subject to national trademark law.

[85]   Article 6*quinquies* B provides:

Trademarks covered by this Article may be neither denied registration nor invalidated except in the following cases:

1.   when they are of such a nature as to infringe rights acquired by third parties in the country where protection is claimed;

2.   when they are devoid of any distinctive character, or consist exclusively of signs or indications which may serve, in trade, to designate the kind, quality, quantity, intended purpose, value, place of origin, of the goods, or the time of production, or have become customary in the current language or in the bona fide and established practices of the trade of the country where protection is claimed;

3.   when they are contrary to morality or public order and, in particular, of such a nature as to deceive the public. It is understood that a mark may not be considered contrary to public order for the sole reason that it does not conform to a provision of the legislation on marks, except if such provision itself relates to public order.

inter alia, to acquired rights of third parties; to distinctiveness of character; and to morality, public order ("*ordre public*") and deceptiveness.

143.   The European Communities maintains that these exceptions contemplated by Article 6*quinquies* B(1) through (3) refer to various elements going well beyond the form of a trademark. The European Communities argues that this gives contextual support to the European Communities' notion that the obligation of a Paris Union country, under Article 6*quinquies* A(1), to accept a trademark duly registered in the applicant's country of origin "as is" includes matters going beyond form.[86]   In contrast, the United States contends that these exceptions relate only to the form of the trademark.[87]

144.   We note that the *form* of a trademark may be of such a nature as to infringe rights acquired by third parties within the meaning of paragraph 1 of Article 6*quinquies* B. The *form* of a trademark may be devoid of distinctive character within the meaning of paragraph 2 of that Article. Equally, the *form* of a trademark may be contrary to morality or public order, or of such a nature as to deceive the public, within the meaning of paragraph 3 of Article 6*quinquies* B. Therefore, in our view, if the requirements of Article 6*quinquies* A(1) are interpreted as covering *only* the *form* of a trademark, all the exceptions in Article 6*quinquies* B(1) through (3) can be given full meaning and effect.

145.   Finally, we look to an agreed interpretation adopted at the conclusion of the original Paris Convention in 1883. The Final Protocol of the Paris Convention (1883) was considered to form an integral part of that Convention.[88]   Paragraph 4 of that Final Protocol in 1883 explained that the provision, which later became Article 6*quinquies* A(1)[89]:

> ... should be understood in the sense that no trademark may be excluded from protection in one of the States of the Union for the sole reason that it does not comply, with regard to the signs of which it is composed, with the conditions of the laws of that State, provided it complies on this point with the laws of the country of origin and that it has been properly filed there. Subject to this exception, *which only concerns the form of the mark*, and subject to the provision of the other Articles of the Convention, *each State shall apply its domestic law.*[90] (emphasis added)

146.   As the European Communities has observed, this agreed interpretation was omitted at the Washington Revision Conference of 1911. Yet, like the Panel, we note that no delegation to that conference expressed the view at that time that this omission should change the meaning of the provision.[91]   Indeed, as one

---

This provision is subject, however, to the application of Article 10*bis*.
[86]   European Communities' appellant's submission, para. 54.
[87]   United States' appellee's submission, para. 9.
[88]   Final Protocol of the Paris Convention (1883), para. 7.
[89]   See *supra*, footnote 82.
[90]   Final Protocol of the Paris Convention (1883), para. 4.
[91]   "[I]t is not possible to conclude from this decision [at the Washington Conference of 1911] that agreement was reached regarding a different scope of application of the provision." Bodenhausen, *Guide to the Paris Convention, supra*, footnote 81, p. 110. Panel Report, para. 8.82.

WIPO publication states, "it is generally believed that such omission did not alter the intended sense of 'telle quelle' as it was made explicit in 1883."[92] On this, we simply observe that our interpretation of Article 6*quinquies* A(1) is not inconsistent with this interpretation.

147.   We have already stated that we agree with the Panel that Section 211(a)(1) is a measure dealing, in the particular circumstances in which it applies, with the ownership of a defined category of trademarks.[93] We also agree that the obligation of countries of the Paris Union under Article 6*quinquies* A(1) to accept for filing and protect a trademark duly registered in the country of origin "as is" does not encompass matters related to ownership.[94]

148.   For these reasons, we uphold the finding of the Panel in paragraph 8.89 of the Panel Report that Section 211(a)(1) is not inconsistent with Article 2.1 of the *TRIPS Agreement* in conjunction with Article 6*quinquies* A(1) of the Paris Convention (1967).

VI.   ARTICLE 15 OF THE *TRIPS AGREEMENT*

149.   Article 15.1 of the *TRIPS Agreement* defines "protectable subject matter" eligible for registration as trademarks. Before the Panel, the European Communities claimed that Section 211(a)(1) is inconsistent with Article 15.1 because Section 211(a)(1) prohibits registration of trademarks that are "protectable". In contrast, the United States contended that Section 211(a)(1) does not concern "protectable subject matter" and thus does not violate Article 15.1. In the alternative, the United States submitted that, even if Section 211(a)(1) did concern "protectable subject matter", there is no violation of Article 15.1 because Section 211(a)(1) falls within the exception in Article 15.2, which permits denial of registration on "other grounds" provided they do not derogate from the provisions of the Paris Convention (1967). The European Communities argued in turn that Article 15.2 would apply only if Section 211(a)(1) fell within an exception "expressly foreseen" under the Paris Convention (1967).[95] In the view of the European Communities, Section 211(a)(1) does not do so and, therefore, violates Article 15.1.

150.   The Panel found that :

> ... Section 211(a)(1) is not inconsistent with Article 15.1 of the TRIPS Agreement because the term "other grounds" as used in Article 15.2 of the TRIPS Agreement may include a measure that denies trademark registration on the basis that the applicant is not the owner under national, in this case, US law and Section 211(a)(1) is

---

[92]   Paris Centenary, 1983, WIPO Publication No. 875. Panel Report, footnote 124 to para. 8.82.
[93]   See *supra*, para. 121.
[94]   Panel Report, para. 8.83.
[95]   European Communities' appellant's submission, para. 72.

a measure that deals with the ownership of trademarks used in connection with confiscated assets. [96]

151.   The European Communities appeals this finding. According to the European Communities, WTO Members must register trademarks that meet the requirements of Article 15.1. The European Communities argues that Section 211(a)(1) violates Article 15.1 by creating, in the form of a consent requirement, a "curtailment" that prevents both the continued enjoyment of existing trademarks and the registration of new trademarks. [97]

152.   In reply, the United States submits that Article 15.1 is a more limited provision than envisioned by the European Communities. The United States sees Article 15.1 as simply describing what "subject matter" is "protectable" as a trademark. As the United States sees it, Article 15.1 does not establish an affirmative obligation to register *every* trademark that is "eligible for registration". Accordingly, the United States concludes that Section 211(a)(1) is not inconsistent with Article 15.1 because Section 211(a)(1) has nothing to do with whether certain signs are capable of constituting a trademark. [98]

153.   Article 15.1 of the *TRIPS Agreement* provides:

Protectable Subject Matter

> Any sign, or any combination of signs, capable of distinguishing the goods or services of one undertaking from those of other undertakings, *shall be capable of constituting a trademark*. Such signs, in particular words including personal names, letters, numerals, figurative elements and combinations of colours as well as any combination of such signs, *shall be eligible for registration as trademarks*. Where signs are not inherently capable of distinguishing the relevant goods or services, Members may make registrability depend on distinctiveness acquired through use. Members may require, as a condition of registration, that signs be visually perceptible. (emphasis added)

154.   Article 15.1 defines which signs or combinations of signs are *capable of* constituting a trademark. These signs include words such as personal names, letters, numerals, figurative elements and combinations of colours, as well as any combination of such signs. This definition is based on the distinctiveness of signs as such, or on their distinctiveness as acquired through use. If such signs are capable of distinguishing the goods or services of one undertaking from those of other undertakings, then they become *eligible for* registration as trademarks. [99] To us, the title of Article 15.1 – "Protectable Subject Matter" – indicates that

---

[96]   Panel Report, para. 8.70.
[97]   European Communities' appellant's submission, para. 67.
[98]   United States' opening statement at the oral hearing.
[99]   According to Article 15.1, in respect of signs not inherently capable of distinguishing goods or services, registrability may be made dependent on distinctiveness acquired through use. In addition, Members may require, as a condition for registration, that signs be visually perceptible.

Article 15.1 embodies a *definition* of what can constitute a trademark. WTO Members are obliged under Article 15.1 to ensure that those signs or combinations of signs that meet the distinctiveness criteria set forth in Article 15.1 – and are, thus, *capable of constituting a trademark* – are *eligible for registration* as trademarks within their domestic legislation.

155.   Thus, in our view, the European Communities sees an obligation in Article 15.1 that is not there. Identifying certain signs that are *capable of* registration and imposing on WTO Members an obligation to make those signs *eligible for* registration in their domestic legislation is not the same as imposing on those Members an obligation to register *automatically* each and every sign or combination of signs that are *capable of* and *eligible for* registration under Article 15.1. This Article describes which trademarks are "capable of" registration. It does not say that all trademarks that are capable of registration "shall be registered". This Article states that such signs or combinations of signs "shall be *eligible* for registration" as trademarks. It does not say that they "shall be registered". To us, these are distinctions with a difference. And, as we have said, supporting these distinctions is the fact that the title of this Article speaks of subject matter as "protectable", and not of subject matter "to be protected". In this way, the title of Article 15 expresses the notion that the subject matter covered by the provision is subject matter that *qualifies* for, but is not necessarily *entitled to*, protection.

156.   It follows that the wording of Article 15.1 allows WTO Members to set forth in their domestic legislation conditions for the registration of trademarks that do *not* address the definition of either "protectable subject matter" or of what constitutes a trademark.

157.   This interpretation is supported by the context of Article 15.1. We look first to Article 15.2 of the *TRIPS Agreement*, which provides:

> Paragraph 1 shall not be understood to prevent a Member from denying registration of a trademark on *other grounds*, provided that they *do not derogate from* the provisions of the Paris Convention (1967). (emphasis added)

158.   To us, the reference in Article 15.2 to Article 15.1 makes it clear that "other grounds" for denial of trademark registration are grounds *different from* those already mentioned in Article 15.1, such as lack of inherent distinctiveness of signs, lack of distinctiveness acquired through use, or lack of visual perceptibility. We agree with the Panel that:

> Such interpretation is borne out contextually by Article 15.2 of the TRIPS Agreement which provides that "paragraph 1 shall not be understood to prevent a Member from denying registration on other grounds". [100]

159.   The right of Members under Article 15.2 to deny registration of trademarks on grounds other than the failure to meet the distinctiveness requirements

---

[100]   Panel Report, para. 8.49. We address the meaning of the latter part of Article 15.2 below, when we discuss the relevant provisions of the Paris Convention (1967).

set forth in Article 15.1 implies that Members are not obliged to register any and every sign or combination of signs that meet those distinctiveness requirements.

160.   Additionally, Article 15.4 of the *TRIPS Agreement* states:

> The nature of the goods or services to which a trademark is to be applied shall in no case form an obstacle to registration of the trademark.

161.   If Article 15.1 were to be interpreted to *require* registration of all signs or combinations of signs meeting the distinctiveness criteria set forth in that Article, it would not have been necessary to establish *positively* in the *TRIPS Agreement* that "[t]he nature of the goods or services to which a trademark is to be applied shall in no case form an obstacle to registration of the trademark".[101] Such an interpretation of Article 15.1 would reduce Article 15.4 to redundancy and inutility.[102]

162.   Furthermore, we note that Article 15.3 of the *TRIPS Agreement* provides:

> Members may make registrability depend on use. However, actual use of a trademark shall not be a condition for filing an application for registration. An application shall not be refused solely on the ground that intended use has not taken place before the expiry of a period of three years from the date of application.

163.   In establishing explicitly that Members may make registrability depend on use, Article 15.3, first sentence, addresses an element of registration other than "protectable subject matter". In other words, Article 15.1 refers to "use" as a basis for signs which are not inherently distinctive to acquire distinctiveness and thus qualifying as "protectable subject matter". Article 15.3 relates to "use" as a basis for registrability of a trademark by a particular applicant. At first sight, Article 15.3, first sentence, might seem to suggest that, implicitly, Article 15.1 goes beyond the definition of what constitutes a trademark. However, we do not believe that the presence of Article 15.3, first sentence, obliges us to interpret Article 15.1 as having a meaning inconsistent with its actual wording.

164.   Article 15.3, first sentence, makes explicit one of the "other grounds" mentioned generally in Article 15.2, and the two sentences that follow limit this one ground. In other words, we see the significance of Article 15.3 less in its first sentence than in the two sentences that follow that circumscribe, in other respects, the condition of use for registrability.

---

[101]   Article 7 of the Paris Convention (1967) provides for a similar obligation, which is limited, however, to the nature of *goods*. Article 7 states:

> The nature of the goods to which a trademark is to be applied shall in no case form an obstacle to the registration of the mark.

Our considerations with respect to Article 15.4 of the *TRIPS Agreement* apply *mutatis mutandis* to Article 7 of the Paris Convention (1967).

[102]   Appellate Body Report, *United States – Standards for Reformulated and Conventional Gasoline* ("*US – Gasoline*"), WT/DS2/AB/R, adopted 20 May 1996, DSR 1996:I, 3, at 21. See also, Appellate Body Report, *Japan – Taxes on Alcoholic Beverages* ("*Japan – Alcoholic Beverages II*"), WT/DS8/AB/R, WT/DS10/AB/R, WT/DS11/AB/R, adopted 1 November 1996, DSR 1996:I, 97, at 106.

165.   As with our interpretation of Article *6quinquies*, here, too, we recall that Article 6(1) of the Paris Convention (1967), which has become a WTO provision by incorporation through Article 2.1 of the *TRIPS Agreement*, reserves to each country of the Paris Union the right to determine the "conditions" for filing and registration of trademarks in its domestic legislation.[103] If Article 15.1 required the registration of any and every sign or combination of signs that meets the distinctiveness criteria specified in that Article, then WTO Members would be deprived of the legislative discretion they enjoy under Article 6(1) of the Paris Convention (1967). In our view, Article 15.1 of the *TRIPS Agreement* limits the right of Members to determine the "conditions" for filing and registration of trademarks under their domestic legislation pursuant to Article 6(1) *only* as it relates to the distinctiveness requirements enunciated in Article 15.1.

166.   With all this in mind, we consider the consistency of Section 211(a)(1) with the requirements of Article 15.1. Section 211(a)(1) prohibits any transaction or payment with respect to a defined category of marks, trade names or commercial names unless the original owner of the mark, trade name or commercial name (or the *bona fide* successor-in-interest) has expressly consented. We have concluded already that Section 211(a)(1) is a measure that relates to ownership in that, in certain circumstances, it determines who is *not* the owner of a defined category of trademarks and trade names under United States trademark law.[104] Therefore, Section 211(a)(1) does not in any way concern those issues that are addressed by Article 15.1, such as the inherent distinctiveness of signs, distinctiveness acquired through use and visual perceptibility. Section 211(a)(1) does not in any way prevent or preclude the registration of signs or combinations of signs that meet the requirements of Article 15.1, so long as the application for registration as a trademark is not made by a person who is not the legitimate owner of the sign or combination of signs according to United States law. Therefore, Section 211(a)(1) is not inconsistent with the requirements of Article 15.1 concerning "protectable subject matter".

167.   As far as we are concerned, this conclusion is dispositive of the European Communities' challenge to Section 211(a)(1) under Article 15. However, the European Communities also appeals a legal interpretation, within the meaning of Article 17.6 of the DSU, developed by the Panel in respect of Article 15.2. So we look next at Article 15.2.

168.   The Panel found:

> Article 15.2 states that Members are not prevented from denying registration of trademarks on "other grounds" so long as such grounds do not "derogate" from the provisions of the Paris Convention (1967). Thus, if a measure comes within the scope of

---

[103]   The reservation of legislative discretion to Paris Union countries that are also WTO Members is limited by commonly agreed grounds for denying trademark registration (for example, Article 6*ter*), commonly agreed grounds for *not* denying trademark registration (for example Article 6(2)) and subject to, *inter alia*, the national treatment obligation under the Paris Convention (1967), as well as other relevant provisions of the *TRIPS Agreement*. See *supra*, footnote 72.

[104]   See *supra*, para. 121.

"other grounds", a Member may deny trademark registration to signs that meet the requirements of Article 15.1. It is in this context that we assess the consistency of Section 211(a)(1) with Article 15.1 of the TRIPS Agreement.[105]

169. In addition to arguing that Section 211(a)(1) violates Article 15.1, the European Communities submits that Section 211(a)(1) could not in any event be justified on the "other grounds" contemplated by the exception found in Article 15.2 because, as the European Communities sees it, under Article 15.2, "only those *exceptions which are expressly foreseen* in the Paris Convention are permissible."[106] The European Communities argues that none of the exceptions contained in the *TRIPS Agreement*, nor any of the exceptions provided for in the Paris Convention (1967), expressly permit the requirement in Section 211(a)(1) that consent must be obtained from the original owner or its *bona fide* successor-in-interest before registration will be allowed under United States law.

170. The United States argues, in reply, that, even if Section 211(a)(1) were in violation of Article 15.1, the denial of registration on the ground that the applicant is not the true owner would nevertheless be justified under Article 15.2. The United States sees nothing in Article 15.2 that requires that such "other grounds" be "expressly provided" in the Paris Convention (1967). Instead, the United States contends that it is sufficient that the Paris Convention (1967) not forbid such "other grounds".

171. The specific reference to Article 15.1 in Article 15.2 makes it clear that the "other grounds" for denial of registration to which Article 15.2 refers are different from those mentioned in Article 15.1. Given this, the key phrase relating to the issue before us is the limitation found in the final phrase of Article 15.2, which requires that those grounds "do not derogate from the provisions of the Paris Convention (1967)."

172. As always, we consider first the ordinary meaning of the treaty text. The ordinary meaning of "derogate" is "to detract from" or "to take away [] so as to lessen or impair".[107] With this meaning in mind, we consider the circumstances

---

[105] Panel Report, para. 8.51.

[106] European Communities' appellant's submission, para. 72. In this respect, the European Communities refers to, *inter alia*, Article 6(2), Article 6*ter*, Article 6*quinquies* B(1) through (3), C, D and E, and Article 10*bis*.

Article 6(2) of the Paris Convention prohibits a Paris Union country from refusing an application for registration or invalidating registration of a mark filed by a Paris Union national in any Paris Union country other than its country of origin on the ground that filing, registration, or renewal, has not been effected in the country of origin.

Article 6*ter* prohibits, *inter alia*, trademarks concerning state emblems, official hallmarks and emblems of intergovernmental organizations without authorization of competent authorities.

For the text of Article 6*quinquies* B(1) through (3), see *supra*, footnote 85.

Article 10*bis*(1): "Unfair Competition" provides: "The countries of the Union are bound to assure to nationals of such countries effective protection against unfair competition. ...".

See, *inter alia*, European Communities' appellant's submission, para. 72, and European Communities' responses to questioning at the oral hearing.

[107] *The New Shorter Oxford English Dictionary*, *supra*, footnote 78, Vol. I, p. 642.

in which grounds for the denial of trademark registration determined by a Member in its domestic legislation may "derogate from" the Paris Convention (1967).

173.   The participants do not dispute that "other grounds" that are *expressly* provided for in the exceptions contained in the Paris Convention (1967) do *not* derogate from that Convention, within the meaning of Article 15.2 of the *TRIPS Agreement*.[108] The participants agree, for example, that the exceptions stated in Article 6*quinquies* B(1) through (3) of the Paris Convention (1967) qualify as such "other grounds", within the meaning of Article 15.2. What is more, we note that the European Communities does not question that exceptions explicitly mentioned in the *TRIPS Agreement* may be "other grounds" for the denial of trademark registration which "do not derogate from" the Paris Convention (1967).[109]

174.   Rather, the question before us with respect to Article 15.2 is the extent to which, if at all, Members are permitted to deny trademark registration on grounds *other than those expressly provided for* in the *TRIPS Agreement* and the Paris Convention (1967).

175.   In this respect, we recall, once again, that Article 6(1) of the Paris Convention (1967) reserves to each country of the Paris Union the right to determine *conditions for the filing and registration* of trademarks by its domestic legislation. The authority to determine such conditions by domestic legislation must, however, be exercised consistently with the obligations that countries of the Paris Union have under the Paris Convention (1967). These obligations include internationally agreed grounds for *refusing* registration, as stipulated in the Paris Convention (1967).[110]

176.   The right of each country of the Paris Union to determine conditions for filing and registration of trademarks by its domestic legislation is also constrained by internationally agreed grounds for *not* denying trademark registration.[111] This means, by implication, that the right reserved to each country of the Paris Union to determine, under Article 6(1), conditions for the filing and registration of trademarks includes the right to determine by domestic legislation con-

---

[108]   European Communities' and United States' responses to questioning at the oral hearing.

[109]   The European Communities refers, *inter alia*, to Articles 22.3 and 23.2 of the *TRIPS Agreement*, which ensure that the protection of geographical indications is not undermined through the use of trademarks that contain or consist of geographical indications. The European Communities also mentions Article 24.5 of the *TRIPS Agreement* (concerning rights to trademarks – acquired through registration or use in good faith – which are identical or similar to geographical indications) and Article 62.1 of the *TRIPS Agreement* (concerning compliance with reasonable procedures and formalities as a condition for acquisition and maintenance of intellectual property rights and related *inter partes* procedures). European Communities' appellant's submission, para. 73.

[110]   For example, Article 6*bis* (denial of registration of well-known marks) and Article 6*ter* (prohibition of trademarks including state emblems) contain express exceptions from the regulatory discretion conferred on Members by virtue of Article 6(1).

[111]   For example, Article 6(2) limits the legislative discretion of countries of the Paris Union by providing that an application for registration by a national of a country of the Paris Union may not be refused on the ground that the national has not filed for registration or renewal in its country of origin. This exception does not concern a particular ground for *refusing* trademark registration. Rather, it stipulates when – despite the legislative discretion granted to countries of the Union by Article 6(1) – trademark registration must *not* be refused.

ditions to *refuse* acceptance of filing and registration on grounds other than those explicitly prohibited by the Paris Convention (1967).[112]

177.   Therefore, a condition need not be expressly mentioned in the Paris Convention (1967) in order not to "derogate" from it. Denial of registration on "other grounds" would derogate from the Paris Convention (1967) only if the denial were on grounds that are inconsistent with the provisions of that Convention.

178.   For all these reasons, we conclude that Section 211(a)(1) is not inconsistent with the definition of "protectable subject matter" in Article 15.1 of the *TRIPS Agreement*, and conclude also that "other grounds" for the denial of registration within the meaning of Article 15.2 of the *TRIPS Agreement* are not limited to grounds expressly provided for in the exceptions contained in the Paris Convention (1967) or the *TRIPS Agreement*. Hence, we uphold the Panel's finding in paragraph 8.70 of the Panel Report.

VII.   ARTICLE 16 OF THE *TRIPS AGREEMENT*

179.   Before the Panel, the European Communities claimed that the denial of access to United States courts for designated nationals (or their successors-in-interest) under Sections 211(a)(2) and (b) deprives certain trademark owners of the exclusive rights conferred by Article 16.1 of the *TRIPS Agreement*. The United States contended that Sections 211(a)(2) and (b) do not violate Article 16.1 because only those persons who are not owners of a trademark under United States law are denied rights under Sections 211(a)(2) and (b).

180.   With respect to the alleged inconsistency of Section 211(a)(2) with Article 16.1, the Panel found that:

> [t]he European Communities has not provided any evidence to us that would enable us to conclude that US courts would interpret Section 211(a)(2) in a manner that would deprive a person, who has been determined by the court to be the owner of a registered trademark, of its exclusive rights.[113]

> ... the European Communities has not proved that Section 211(a)(2) is inconsistent with Article 16.1 of the TRIPS Agreement.[114]

181.   Similarly, with respect to the alleged inconsistency of Section 211(b) with Article 16.1, the Panel found that:

> ... the European Communities, as the complaining party, has not presented evidence and legal arguments sufficient to demonstrate the violation it alleges. Therefore, it has not been proved that Sec-

---

[112]   See *supra*, footnote 72.
[113]   Panel Report, para. 8.111.
[114]   *Ibid.*, para. 8.112.

tion 211(b) is inconsistent with Article 16.1 of the TRIPS Agreement.[115]

182.   According to the Panel, "[n]either Article 16.1 nor other provisions contained in the TRIPS Agreement define how the owner of a trademark is determined."[116] The Panel reasoned, instead, that "[t]o determine who the owner of a registered trademark is, it is necessary to have recourse to the national law of the Members. ... the TRIPS Agreement does not contain a regime of ownership of trademarks that is valid for and applicable to all Members."[117]

183.   The European Communities appeals these findings and alleges that the Panel erroneously distinguished between the owner of a registered trademark and the trademark itself, which are in reality "intertwined".[118] The European Communities maintains that, although disputes may arise with respect to who is the lawful owner of a registered trademark, the very existence of a registered trademark implies that there must be an owner. And, in the view of the European Communities, the holder of a registration must, under Article 16.1, be considered the owner of the trademark until such time as it ceases to hold the registration.[119]

184.   The United States asks us to uphold the findings of the Panel and argues that the Panel correctly concluded that, under a system such as that of the United States in which trademark registration does not confer trademark ownership, the status of the trademark registration itself is not dispositive of the issue of ownership.[120] The United States submits that Article 16.1 specifically anticipates that the owner of a trademark – the person in a position to assert exclusive rights under domestic law – may be someone other than the person who has registered the trademark. The United States emphasizes that, under the federal trademark law of the United States, if a person other than the registrant can show a superior claim to the trademark based, for example, on previous use, then that person can be adjudged the true "owner" of the trademark.[121] The United States stresses that such a system of making trademark rights available "on the basis of use" is specifically permitted under the last sentence of Article 16.1.

185.   Article 16 of the *TRIPS Agreement* is entitled "Rights Conferred". Article 16.1 provides:

> The owner of a registered trademark shall have the exclusive right
> to prevent all third parties not having the owner's consent from us-
> ing in the course of trade identical or similar signs for goods or
> services which are identical or similar to those in respect of which
> the trademark is registered where such use would result in a likeli-
> hood of confusion. In case of the use of an identical sign for iden-
> tical goods or services, a likelihood of confusion shall be pre-

---

[115]   Panel Report, para. 8.159.
[116]   *Ibid.*, para. 8.108.
[117]   *Ibid.*
[118]   European Communities' appellant's submission, para. 106.
[119]   *Ibid.*, para. 109.
[120]   Panel Report, footnote 116 to para. 8.64 and para. 8.109.
[121]   *Ibid.*, para. 8.104; United States' appellee's submission, para. 60.

sumed. The rights described above shall not prejudice any existing prior rights, nor shall they affect the possibility of Members making rights available on the basis of use.

186.   As we read it, Article 16 confers on the *owner* of a registered trademark an internationally agreed minimum level of "exclusive rights" that all WTO Members must guarantee in their domestic legislation. These exclusive rights protect the owner against infringement of the registered trademark by unauthorized third parties. [122]

187.   We underscore that Article 16.1 confers these exclusive rights on the "owner" of a registered trademark. As used in this treaty provision, the ordinary meaning of "owner" can be defined as the proprietor or the person who holds the title or dominion of the property constituted by the trademark. [123] We agree with the Panel that this ordinary meaning does not clarify how the ownership of a trademark is to be determined. [124] Also, we agree with the Panel that Article 16.1 does not, in express terms, define how ownership of a registered trademark is to be determined. Article 16.1 confers exclusive rights on the "owner", but Article 16.1 does not tell us who the "owner" *is*.

188.   As the United States reminds us, and as the European Communities concedes, the last sentence of Article 16.1 acknowledges that WTO Members may make the rights available "on the basis of use" of the trademark. We read this to permit WTO Members to make the "exclusive rights" contemplated by Article 16.1 available within their respective jurisdictions on the basis of registration or use. The Panel concluded that Article 16.1 contemplates that different forms of entitlement may exist under the laws of different Members, and we agree. [125] However, the *TRIPS Agreement* does not establish or prescribe a regime of ownership of trademarks.

189.   In the absence of any *explicit* provisions defining ownership in the *TRIPS Agreement*, it is useful to look also at whether the *TRIPS Agreement* – including the Articles of the Paris Convention (1967) incorporated into it – contains an *implicit* definition of ownership. Turning first to the Paris Convention (1967), we see that, in response to a request for information by the Panel [126], the Director-General of the International Bureau of the World Intellectual Property Organization ("WIPO") stated that "no provision [of the Paris Convention (1967)] addresses the question how the owner of a trademark has to be determined under the domestic law of States party to the Paris Convention." [127] The Panel did not

---

[122]   We note that, prior to the entry into force of the *TRIPS Agreement*, only Article 10*bis*(3) of the Paris Convention (1967) provided for a prohibition of "all acts of such a nature as to create confusion by any means whatever with the establishment, the goods, or the industrial or commercial activities of a competitor." See, Gervais, D., *The TRIPS Agreement – Drafting History and Analysis*, Sweet & Maxwell, London (1998), pp. 109-110.

[123]   *The New Shorter Oxford English Dictionary*, *supra*, footnote 78, Vol. II, p. 2059; *Black's Law Dictionary*, 7th ed., B.A. Garner (ed.), (West Group, 1999), p. 1130.

[124]   Panel Report, para. 8.108.

[125]   Panel Report, para. 8.108.

[126]   Pursuant to Article 13 of the DSU.

[127]   The letter from the Director-General of the International Bureau of WIPO, dated 2 March 2001, states:

discuss this. However, the Panel seems to have taken the view that the definition of the conditions of ownership has been left to the legislative discretion of individual countries of the Paris Union by Article 6(1) of the Paris Convention (1967). We agree.

190.   The European Communities suggests that there are several direct or indirect references to ownership in the *TRIPS Agreement* that give guidance to WTO Members on how to determine ownership. [128] Specifically, the European Communities points to Articles 15.1, 16.1 and 19.1 as giving such guidance.

191.   The European Communities argues that Article 15.1 of the *TRIPS Agreement* creates a link between the trademark, on the one hand, and the goods or services emanating from an "undertaking", on the other. This implies, in the view of the European Communities, that only an "undertaking" can be the owner of a trademark. We express no view on the validity of this assertion. In any event, assuming *arguendo* that this argument is correct, the fact remains that Article 15.1 nevertheless does not define *which* "undertaking" would be the owner. Thus, this argument does not make the European Communities' case.

192.   The European Communities likewise submits that there is an equation in Article 16.1 of the *TRIPS Agreement* between the owner of the trademark and the "undertakings" whose goods or services are distinguished by the trademark. On this, we note only that Article 16.1 of the *TRIPS Agreement* refers to the "owner of a registered trademark" and to the "goods or services" in respect of which trademarks are used. Unlike Article 15.1, Article 16.1 does not include the word "undertakings". Nor does it mention the owner of the goods or services for which the trademark is used. So, unlike the European Communities, we fail to see any basis in Article 16.1 for the assertion that this provision equates the owner of a trademark with the undertaking whose goods or services are distinguished by the trademark.

193.   Lastly, the European Communities argues that Article 19.1 of the *TRIPS Agreement* seems also to equate the owner of the trademark with the undertaking using the trademark for its goods or services. Here, we note that Article 19.1 addresses the situation where a Member's domestic legislation requires use of the trademark for the purposes of maintaining its registration and those circumstances when use by a person other than the owner of the trademark is recognized as use for the purposes of maintaining a registration. Here, as well, there is no mention of the "undertaking" that uses the trademark for its goods or services. Thus, here, too, unlike the European Communities, we find no basis for viewing this provision as relevant to the argument the European Communities is making.

Even though some provisions of the Paris Convention refer to the concept of trademark ownership (Article 5C(2) and (3), and Article 6*septies*: "proprietor", Article 6*ter*(1)(c): "owner", Article 6*bis*(1) "being already the mark of a person entitled to the benefits of this Convention"), *no provision addresses the question how the owner of a trademark has to be determined under the domestic law of States party to the Paris Convention.* (emphasis added)

Reproduced in relevant part in para. 6.41 of the Panel Report.

[128]   European Communities' response to question 50 from the Panel. The European Communities also repeated this argument before us at the oral hearing.

194.   Accordingly, we do not agree with the argument of the European Communities that, under the *TRIPS Agreement*, the "undertaking" that uses the trademark to distinguish its goods or services must be regarded as the owner of the trademark.

195.   For all these reasons, we conclude that neither Article 16.1 of the *TRIPS Agreement*, nor any other provision of either the *TRIPS Agreement* and the Paris Convention (1967), determines who owns or who does not own a trademark.

196.   With this conclusion in mind, we consider next whether Sections 211(a)(2) and (b) are inconsistent with Article 16.1.

197.   The Panel stated that:

> [u]nder the exceptional circumstances dealt with under Section 211(a)(2), there may be a successful challenge concerning the *prima facie* ownership rights in relation to the registration, obtained by a designated national pursuant to a general OFAC licence without the consent of the original owner, of a trademark used in connection with confiscated assets. In circumstances where the presumptive ownership would be successfully challenged within effective civil judicial procedures, the provisions of Section 211(a)(2) would not stand in the way of the person whom the court would deem to be the proper owner of the trademark under US law from asserting its rights. In this way, Section 211(a)(2) allows for the person whom the court considers to be the proper owner of the registered trademark under US law to be granted exclusive rights. [129]

198.   Based on this view of Section 211(a)(2), the Panel concluded that the European Communities had not provided "any evidence" for concluding that United States courts would interpret Section 211(a)(2) in a manner that would deprive a person who had been determined by the court to be the owner of a registered trademark of that person's exclusive rights. [130]

199.   We recall that the European Communities contends that the Panel created an artificial distinction between the owner of a registered trademark and the trademark itself. [131] We disagree with the apparent equation by the European Communities of trademark registration with trademark ownership. [132] Here, again, the European Communities appears to us to overlook the necessary legal distinction between a trademark system in which ownership is based on registration and a trademark system in which ownership is based on use. As we have

---

[129]   Panel Report, para. 8.111.
[130]   *Ibid.*
[131]   European Communities' appellant's submission, para. 106.
[132]   "Common sense would suggest that a registered trademark can only exist if there is a registration. In turn a registration must be for the benefit of an owner. Therefore the owner of the registered trademark under Article 16(1) is the holder of the registration until such time as when he ceases to hold the registration. It would make no sense to consider an ill-defined 'original owner' who is not in the register to be the lawful owner of the registered trademark in the sense of Article 16(1) [of the] TRIPS [Agreement]." European Communities' appellant's submission, para. 109.

noted more than once, United States law confers exclusive trademark rights, not on the basis of registration, but on the basis of use. There is nothing in Article 16.1 that compels the United States to base the protection of exclusive rights on registration. Indeed, as we have also observed more than once, the last sentence of Article 16.1 confirms that WTO Members may make such rights available on the basis of use. The United States has done so. Therefore, it necessarily follows that, under United States law, registration is *not* conclusive of ownership of a trademark. Granted, under United States law, the registration of a trademark does confer a *prima facie* presumption of the registrant's ownership of the registered trademark and of the registrant's exclusive right to use that trademark in commerce.[133] But, while we agree with the Panel that the presumptive owner of the *registered* trademark must be entitled, under United States law, to the exclusive rights flowing from Article 16.1 unless and until the presumption arising from registration is successfully challenged through court or administrative proceedings, we do not agree with the European Communities' evident equation of registration with ownership.[134]

200.   As we have concluded earlier, Section 211(a)(2) is related to ownership of a defined category of trademarks.[135] As such, Section 211(a)(2) can be invoked against the presumptive ownership of a registered trademark. If successfully invoked, Section 211(a)(2) will eviscerate the presumption of ownership flowing under United States' law from registration of a trademark. But Section 211(a)(2) is not inconsistent with Article 16.1. For neither Article 16 nor any other Article of the *TRIPS Agreement* determines who owns or does not own a trademark.

201.   Turning to the alleged inconsistency of Section 211(b) with Article 16.1, we recall that we concluded earlier that, like Section 211(a)(2), Section 211(b) is related to ownership of a defined category of trademarks.[136] Like Section 211(a)(2), Section 211(b) can be invoked against the presumptive ownership of a registered trademark. Like Section 211(a)(2), Section 211(b), if successfully invoked, will eviscerate the presumption of ownership flowing under United States' law from registration of a trademark. Therefore, we conclude that, like Section 211(a)(2), Section 211(b) is not inconsistent with Article 16, as neither this Article nor any other Article of the *TRIPS Agreement* determines who owns or does not own a trademark. Therefore, in our view, it has not only "not been proved that Section 211(b) is inconsistent with Article 16.1"[137], but, we conclude also that Section 211(b) is not inconsistent with that Article.

202.   For all these reasons, we find that Sections 211(a)(2) and (b) are not inconsistent with Article 16.1 of the *TRIPS Agreement*.

---

[133]   Panel Report, para. 8.109.
[134]   Panel Report, para. 8.110.
[135]   See *supra*, paras. 118 and 121.
[136]   See *supra*, paras. 119 and 121.
[137]   Panel Report, para. 8.159.

VIII. ARTICLE 42 OF THE *TRIPS AGREEMENT*

203.   Both the United States and the European Communities appeal the Panel's findings on Article 42 of the *TRIPS Agreement*. The United States appeals the conclusion of the Panel that Section 211(a)(2) violates Article 42 of the *TRIPS Agreement*.[138] The European Communities appeals the Panel's finding that "it has not been proved that Section 211(b) is inconsistent with Article 42 of the TRIPS Agreement".[139]

204.   We begin our analysis with the text of Article 42 of the *TRIPS Agreement*, which provides:

Fair and Equitable Procedures

Members shall make available to the right holders [footnote 11] civil judicial procedures concerning the enforcement of any intellectual property right covered by this Agreement. Defendants shall have the right to written notice which is timely and contains sufficient detail, including the basis of the claims. Parties shall be allowed to be represented by independent legal counsel, and procedures shall not impose overly burdensome requirements concerning mandatory personal appearances. *All parties to such procedures shall be duly entitled to substantiate their claims and to present all relevant evidence.* The procedure shall provide a means to identify and protect confidential information, unless this would be contrary to existing constitutional requirements. (emphasis added)

Footnote 11: For the purpose of this Part, the term "right holder" includes federations and associations having legal standing to assert such rights.

205.   Article 42 forms part of Part III on "Enforcement of Intellectual Property Rights". Part III has broad coverage. It applies to all intellectual property rights covered by the *TRIPS Agreement*. According to Article 1.2 of the *TRIPS Agreement*, the term "intellectual property" refers to "all categories of intellectual property that are the subject of Sections 1 through 7 of Part II" of that Agreement.

206.   Section 1 of Part III lays out "General Obligations" of Members. According to Article 41.1 of Section 1, Members are required to ensure that enforcement procedures as specified in Part III are available under their domestic law "so as to permit effective action against any act of infringement of intellectual property rights covered by [the TRIPS] Agreement". These enforcement procedures must include expeditious remedies to prevent infringements and remedies which constitute a deterrent to further infringements. At the same time, these

---

[138]   Panel Report , para. 8.102.
[139]   Panel Report, para. 8.162.

procedures must be applied in such a manner as to avoid the creation of barriers to legitimate trade and to provide safeguards against their abuse. These procedures provide for an internationally-agreed minimum standard which Members are bound to implement in their domestic legislation.

207.   Section 2 of Part III is entitled "Civil and Administrative Procedures and Remedies". Article 42 deals with enforcement action in judicial proceedings, and contains detailed requirements which ensure that "civil judicial procedures" are "fair and equitable". Like Section 1 of Part III, Section 2 introduces an international minimum standard which Members are bound to implement in their domestic legislation.

208.   Before the Panel, the European Communities claimed that Sections 211(a)(2) and (b) are inconsistent with Article 42 of the *TRIPS Agreement* because they "expressly deny[] the availability of [United States] courts to enforce the rights targeted" by Section 211.[140]

209.   The United States contended before the Panel that Sections 211(a)(2) and (b) do not violate Article 42 because nothing in the measure precludes a person asserting ownership rights in the trademark from having access to civil judicial procedures and a full opportunity "to substantiate [its] claim" to ownership and "to present all relevant evidence."[141]

210.   On Section 211(a)(2), the Panel found:

> We note the US argument that Section 211(a)(2) does not affect the availability of judicial procedures to any party to assert a right to a trademark. However, given the clear wording of Section 211(a)(2) which provides that "[n]o U.S. court shall recognize, enforce or otherwise validate any assertion of rights" in certain circumstances, we fail to see how a right holder would be able effectively to assert its rights under these circumstances. While Section 211(a)(2) would not appear to prevent a right holder from initiating civil judicial procedures, its wording indicates that the right holder is not entitled to effective procedures as the court is *ab initio* not permitted to recognize its assertion of rights if the conditions of Section 211(a)(2) are met. In other words, the right holder is effectively prevented from having a chance to substantiate its claim, a chance to which a right holder is clearly entitled under Article 42, because effective civil judicial procedures mean procedures with the possibility of an outcome which is not pre-empted *a priori* by legislation.[142] (footnote omitted)
>
> ...
>
> [G]iven that Section 211(a)(2) limits, under certain circumstances, right holders' effective access to and, hence, the availability of

---

[140]   Panel Report, paras. 4.91 and 4.147.
[141]   *Ibid.*, paras. 8.93 and 8.161.
[142]   *Ibid.*, para. 8.100.

civil judicial procedures, we find that Section 211(a)(2) is inconsistent with Article 42 of the TRIPS Agreement.[143]

211.   On Section 211(b), the Panel concluded:

We note that it is plausible that similar concerns mentioned in respect of Section 211(a)(2) might arise in connection with Section 211(b). However, as we noted above, the European Communities did not explain the meaning of various terms contained in Sections 44(b) and (e) even though Article 211(b) explicitly refers to "treaty rights...under sections 44(b) or (e)". Therefore, for the reasons set out in paragraphs 8.157 and 8.158, it has not been proved that Section 211(b) is inconsistent with Article 42 of the TRIPS Agreement.[144]

212.   On appeal, the United States submits that a court would refuse to recognize, enforce or otherwise validate a designated national's assertion of rights under Sections 211(a)(2) or (b) only *after* making a number of findings.[145] According to the United States, these provisions do not constitute legislation that *a priori* pre-empts a positive outcome of an assertion of rights by a designated national. Rather, the United States maintains that it is only *after* effective civil judicial procedures have been made available that a court would refuse to recognize, enforce or validate an assertion of rights by a designated national. The United States emphasizes that, in any event, Article 42 does not create obligations with respect to a person who is not the holder of an intellectual property right covered by the *TRIPS Agreement*. On this basis, the United States argues that Article 42 does not require judicial authorities to provide enforcement procedures once a finding is made that the claimant does not hold any intellectual property right to enforce. Accordingly, the United States concludes that Sections 211(a)(2) and (b) cannot possibly deny enforcement rights guaranteed under Article 42 to a person who is not the legitimate owner of a trademark under United States law.[146]

213.   In contrast, the European Communities emphasizes on appeal that Article 42 entitles parties to more than mere access to civil judicial procedures, which it concedes the United States courts would provide when applying Sections 211(a)(2) and (b). For the European Communities, Article 42 is violated unless domestic civil judicial procedures enable a plaintiff to pursue *all* issues or claims that arise and to present *all* relevant evidence in the context of the enforcement of an intellectual property right covered by the *TRIPS Agreement*. In the view of the European Communities, Sections 211(a)(2) and (b) each limit the

---

[143]   Panel Report, para. 8.102.
[144]   Panel Report, para. 8.162.
[145]   The United States mentions, for example, the following: whether the trademark at issue was used in connection with a certain business or assets; whether the business or assets were confiscated; whether adequate and effective compensation was paid to the original owner; whether the person claiming ownership is a designated national or a successor-in-interest; whether the original owner expressly consents to the use of that trademark by the claimant. See United States' other appellant's submission, para. 18.
[146]   United States' other appellant's submission, para. 13.

issues of possible litigation to the elements referred to in those Sections[147], while excluding from judicial inquiry other issues that are typically relevant in trademark-related litigation and regulated by, *inter alia*, the Lanham Act.[148] On this reasoning, the European Communities alleges that both Sections 211(a)(2) and (b) are inconsistent with Article 42.

214.   In making their respective arguments about the consistency or inconsistency of Sections 211(a)(2) and (b) with Article 42, the participants referred mainly to the first and fourth sentences of that provision. The first sentence of Article 42 requires "Members [to] make available to right holders civil judicial procedures concerning the enforcement of any intellectual property right covered by [the TRIPS] Agreement." The fourth sentence of Article 42 provides that "[a]ll parties to such procedures shall be duly entitled to substantiate their claims and to present all relevant evidence."

215.   The first sentence of Article 42 requires Members to make certain civil judicial procedures "available" to right holders. Making something *available* means making it "obtainable", putting it "within one's reach" and "at one's disposal" in a way that has sufficient force or efficacy.[149] We agree with the Panel that the ordinary meaning of the term "make available" suggests that "right holders" are entitled under Article 42 to have *access* to civil judicial procedures that are effective in bringing about the enforcement of their rights covered by the Agreement.[150]

216.   Article 42, first sentence, does not define what the term "civil judicial procedures" in that sentence encompasses. The *TRIPS Agreement* thus reserves, subject to the procedural minimum standards set out in that Agreement, a degree of discretion to Members on this, taking into account "differences in national legal systems".[151] Indeed, no Member's national system of civil judicial procedures will be identical to that of another Member.

217.   Pursuant to the first sentence of Article 42, civil judicial procedures must be made available to "right holders" of intellectual property rights covered by the *TRIPS Agreement* so as to enable them to protect those rights against infringement. The United States seems to suggest that access to those rights may be limited to the *owner* of a trademark under United States law.[152] The Panel defined the term "right holders" as persons who have the legal capacity to assert

---

[147]   These issues include: whether the original owner or *bona fide* successor-in-interest has expressly consented; whether a trademark which is composed of the same or substantially similar signs as a trademark which was used in connection with a business or assets that were confiscated; whether an uncompensated confiscation of a business or asset took place in Cuba. United States' other appellant's submission, para. 18.

[148]   These are issues such as use of the trademark; alleged deficiency of a registration; identity or similarity of signs in general; class of goods or services covered by the trademark; existence and scope of a licence. European Communities' appellee's submission, para. 22.

[149]   *The New Shorter Oxford English Dictionary, supra*, footnote 78, Vol. I, p. 154.

[150]   Panel Report, para. 8.95.

[151]   Recital 2(c) of the Preamble to the *TRIPS Agreement*.

[152]   United States' other appellant's submission, para. 4.

rights. [153] We agree with the Panel that the term "right holders" as used in Article 42 is not limited to persons who have been established as owners of trademarks. Where the *TRIPS Agreement* confers rights exclusively on "owners" of a right, it does so in express terms, such as in Article 16.1, which refers to the "owner of a registered trademark". By contrast, the term "right holders" within the meaning of Article 42 also includes persons who claim to have legal standing to assert rights. This interpretation is also borne out by the fourth sentence of Article 42, which refers to "parties". Civil judicial procedures would not be fair and equitable if access to courts were not given to both complainants and defendants who purport to be owners of an intellectual property right.

218.   In this respect, the Panel stated:

> As we have already noted, in the United States, the registration of a trademark confers a *prima facie* presumption of the registrant's ownership of the registered trademark. This means that, in the United States, the holder of a registration is deemed to be the owner unless otherwise proven. A person who enjoys the presumption of being the owner of a trademark under US law must be entitled to a level of protection of its rights that meets the US obligations under the TRIPS Agreement, including Article 42. Consequently, in our interpretation, this presumptive owner must have access to civil judicial procedures that are effective in terms of bringing about the enforcement of its rights *until the moment that there is a determination by the court that it is, in fact, not the owner of the trademark that it has registered* or that there is some other disqualifying ground which is compatible with international obligations. [154] (emphasis added)

For the reasons we have stated, we agree with the Panel that the "right holders" to whom Members must make the procedural rights of Article 42 available include trademark registrants who are presumptive owners under United States law. In our view, these procedural rights extend as well to all other "right holders".

219.   WTO Members must also guarantee to all "parties" the right to "substantiate their claims", as required by the fourth sentence of Article 42. The use of the words "their claims" suggests that, under Article 42, the choice of which claims or how many issues to raise in civil judicial procedures is left to each party. The use of the word "substantiate" implies that litigants have the right to do more than simply initiate claims; Members must duly entitle all litigants to

---

[153]   Panel Report, para. 8.98. In its reasoning, the Panel relied on footnote 11 to Article 42. The footnote states that "the term 'right holder' includes federations and associations having legal standing to assert such rights." At the oral hearing, both participants submitted that footnote 11 does not resolve the issue on which they disagree in respect of Article 42, and submitted further that, in their view, that footnote was irrelevant to this dispute.

[154]   Panel Report, para. 8.99.

"give substance" to, or "give good grounds" for, their claims in order to prove the truth of a charge, and to demonstrate or verify it by evidence.[155]

220.   Litigants are also entitled under the fourth sentence of Article 42 to "present all relevant evidence" in such procedures. These words indicate that parties have the right to file "all relevant evidence" in support of their claims with the courts.

221.   From all this, we understand that the rights which Article 42 obliges Members to make available to right holders are *procedural* in nature. These *procedural* rights guarantee an international minimum standard for nationals of other Members within the meaning of Article 1.3 of the *TRIPS Agreement*.

222.   With this understanding, we turn now to the measure before us and examine whether Sections 211(a)(2) and (b) are consistent with the procedural requirements set out in the first and fourth sentences of Article 42. In doing so, we first recall our conclusion that, in the circumstances in which they apply, Sections 211(a)(2) and (b) deal with the *substantive* requirements of ownership in a defined category of trademarks.[156]   Thus, while not affirmatively establishing ownership, Sections 211(a)(2) and (b) determine who does *not* own those trademarks. We also recall our conclusion that neither the *TRIPS Agreement*, nor the provisions of the Paris Convention (1967) that are incorporated into the *TRIPS Agreement*, determines who owns or does not own a trademark.[157]   Accordingly, the regulation of such ownership is, in principle, reserved to the legislative discretion of Members pursuant to Article 6(1) of the Paris Convention (1967).

223.   The United States submitted at the oral hearing that the procedural provisions of the Lanham Act and of the United States Federal Rules of Civil Procedure[158] apply and guarantee "fair and equitable ... civil judicial procedures" in respect of Section 211. The European Communities agreed. Accordingly, the participants agree that designated nationals and successors-in-interest have access to civil judicial procedures. At the oral hearing, the European Communities also agreed that the Federal Rules of Evidence are applicable in such proceedings.[159]   It is, therefore, our understanding that both participants agree that designated nationals and successors-in-interest have – to the same extent, and in the same way, as any claimant and defendant – the rights provided under the Federal Rules of Civil Procedure and the Federal Rules of Evidence. These rights are the rights to "substantiate their claims" and "present all relevant evidence" with respect to all elements mentioned in Sections 211(a)(2) and (b). We also understand both participants to agree that Sections 211(a)(2) and (b) do not require or authorize a United States court to reject a claim by a designated national or successor-in-interest as inadmissible or unfounded without having applied fully the Federal Rules of Civil Procedure and the Federal Rules of Evidence. The Euro-

---

[155]   *The New Shorter Oxford English Dictionary, supra,* footnote 78, Vol. II, p. 3124.
[156]   See *supra,* para. 121.
[157]   See *supra,* para. 195.
[158]   FED. R. CIV.
[159]   FED. R. EVID.

pean Communities has not claimed that either the Federal Rules of Civil Procedure or the Federal Rules of Evidence do not comply with the obligation in Article 42.

224.   We further understand the European Communities to acknowledge that, in a situation where the recognition of an intellectual property right depends on the fulfilment of cumulative substantive conditions, the failure to meet a single one of those substantive conditions (such as ownership of a disputed trademark) would prevent a court from recognizing that right. At the oral hearing, the European Communities also conceded that a court may, in such a situation, abstain from ruling on all the other substantive conditions that may be relevant (for example, on the distinctiveness of the trademark, or on the existence of an infringement).

225.   However, unlike the United States, the European Communities believes that, under Article 42, the decision whether or not to abstain from ruling on substantive conditions or requirements other than those mentioned in Sections 211(a)(2) and (b) must be left to the discretion of the courts. According to the European Communities, a statute must not limit the discretion of the courts by directing the courts to examine certain substantive requirements before, and to the exclusion of, other substantive requirements. [160]   As we understand it, the European Communities argues that, in requiring the courts to examine the circumstances they address as a matter of priority, and to the exclusion of other issues typically arising in trademark-related litigation, Sections 211(a)(2) and (b) interfere with the discretion of the courts.

226.   In our view, a conclusion by a court on the basis of Section 211, after applying the Federal Rules of Civil Procedure and the Federal Rules of Evidence, that an enforcement proceeding has failed to establish ownership – a requirement of substantive law – with the result that it is impossible for the court to rule in favour of that claimant's or that defendant's claim to a trademark right, does not constitute a violation of Article 42. There is nothing in the *procedural* obligations of Article 42 that prevents a Member, in such a situation, from legislating whether or not its courts must examine *each and every* requirement of substantive law at issue before making a ruling.

227.   With this in mind, we turn to the alleged inconsistency of Section 211(a)(2) with Article 42. Section 211(a)(2) does not prohibit courts from giving right holders access to fair and equitable civil judicial procedures and the opportunity to substantiate their claims and to present all relevant evidence. Rather, Section 211(a)(2) only requires the United States courts not recognize, enforce or otherwise validate any assertion of rights by designated nationals or successors-in-interest who have been determined, after applying United States Federal Rules of Civil Procedure and Federal Rules of Evidence, not to own the trademarks referred to in Section 211(a)(2). As we have said, Section 211(a)(2) deals with the substance of ownership. Therefore, we do not believe that Section 211(a)(2) denies the *procedural* rights that are guaranteed by Article 42.

---

[160]   European Communities' responses to questioning at the oral hearing.

228. For this reason, we conclude that Section 211(a)(2) *on its face* is not inconsistent with the requirements of Article 42 of the *TRIPS Agreement.*

229. Turning next to Section 211(b), we recall that the Panel concluded that "it has not been proved that Section 211(b) is inconsistent with Article 42."[161] We further recall our conclusion that, like Section 211(a)(2), Section 211(b) is related to ownership of a defined category of trademarks.[162] Like Section 211(a)(2), Section 211(b) can be invoked against the presumptive ownership of a registered trademark. Like Section 211(a)(2), Section 211(b), if successfully invoked, will eviscerate the presumption of ownership flowing under United States' law from registration of a trademark. Like Section 211(a)(2), Section 211(b) does not prohibit courts from giving right holders access to civil judicial procedures and the opportunity to substantiate their claims and to present all relevant evidence. Like Section 211(a)(2), Section 211(b) only requires the United States courts not recognize, enforce or otherwise validate any assertion of rights by designated nationals or successors-in-interest who have been determined, after applying United States Federal Rules of Civil Procedure and Federal Rules of Evidence, not to own the trademarks referred to in Section 211. As we have said, Section 211(b) deals with the substance of ownership. Therefore, we do not believe that Section 211(b) denies the *procedural* rights that are guaranteed by Article 42.

230. For this reason, we conclude that Section 211(b) *on its face* is not inconsistent with the requirements of Article 42 of the *TRIPS Agreement.*

231. And, for all these reasons, we find that Sections 211(a)(2) and (b) *on their face* are not inconsistent with the requirements of Article 42 of the *TRIPS Agreement.* Therefore, we reverse the Panel's finding on Section 211(a)(2) in paragraph 8.102 of the Panel Report and uphold its finding on Section 211(b) in paragraph 8.162 of the Panel Report.

232. Finally, we emphasize that the European Communities has challenged Sections 211(a)(2) and (b) *on their face.* The European Communities has not challenged the application of Sections 211(a)(2) and (b) in particular instances by United States courts. Accordingly, our conclusions that Sections 211(a)(2) and (b) are not inconsistent with Article 42 relate to that measure *on its face.* We do not rule on whether a particular United States court has, or has not, violated the requirements of Article 42 in applying Sections 211(a)(2) and (b) in any particular case.

IX. ARTICLE 2(1) OF THE PARIS CONVENTION (1967) AND ARTICLE 3.1 OF THE *TRIPS AGREEMENT*

233. We turn now to the issue of national treatment. In this appeal we have been asked to address, for the first time, this fundamental principle of the world trading system as it relates to intellectual property. There are two separate na-

---

[161] Panel Report, para. 8.162.
[162] See *supra*, para. 121.

tional treatment provisions that cover trademarks as well as other intellectual property rights covered by the *TRIPS Agreement.* The European Communities claims, on appeal, that Sections 211(a)(2) and (b) violate both.

234.   One national treatment provision at issue in this appeal is Article 2(1) of the Paris Convention (1967), which states:

> Nationals of any country of the Union shall, as regards the protection of industrial property, enjoy in all the other countries of the Union the advantages that their respective laws now grant, or may hereafter grant, to nationals; all without prejudice to the rights specially provided for by this Convention. Consequently, they shall have the same protection as the latter, and the same legal remedy against any infringement of their rights, provided that the conditions and formalities imposed upon nationals are complied with.

235.   As we have already explained, the Stockholm Act of the Paris Convention, dated 14 July 1967, is but the most recent version of that important international intellectual property convention.[163]   Article 2(1) was part of the Paris Convention in 1883. Since that time, it has remained a treaty obligation of all the countries that have been party to the Paris Convention.

236.   The parties to this dispute are not unacquainted with the national treatment obligation and other protections for trademarks and other forms of industrial property provided by the Paris Convention. Every one of the fifteen Member States of the European Union has long been a country of the Paris Union. Most of the current Member States of the European Union became party to the Paris Convention in the 1880's.[164]   The most recent did so in 1925 – seventy-seven years ago. Likewise, the United States has, from almost the very beginning, been a country of the Paris Union. The United States became a country of the Paris Union on 30 May 1887 – one hundred and fifteen years ago.

237.   Thus, the national treatment obligation is a longstanding obligation under international law for all the countries directly involved in this dispute, as well as for many more countries of the Paris Union that, like the parties to this dispute, are also Members of the WTO. If there were no *TRIPS Agreement,* if there were no WTO, the parties to this dispute would be bound, nevertheless, under Article 2(1) of the Paris Convention (1967), to accord national treatment to other countries of the Paris Union.

238.   As we have explained, what *is* new is that, as a consequence of the Uruguay Round, Article 2(1) of the Paris Convention (1967) was made part of the *WTO Agreement.*[165]   And, as we have previously explained, by virtue of Article

---

[163]   See *supra,* para. 123.

[164]   The dates on which adhesion of the current Member States of the European Union to the Paris Union took effect, are as follows: Austria, 1 January 1909; Belgium, 7 July 1884; Denmark, 1 October 1894; Finland, 20 September 1921; France, 7 July 1884; Germany, 1 May 1903; Greece, 2 October 1924; Ireland, 4 December 1925; Italy, 7 July 1884; Luxembourg, 30 June 1922; the Netherlands, 7 July 1884; Portugal, 7 July 1884; Spain, 7 July 1884; Sweden, 1 July 1885; and, the United Kingdom, 7 July 1884.

[165]   See *supra,* para. 124.

2.1 of the *TRIPS Agreement*, Article 2(1) of the Paris Convention (1967), as well as certain other specified provisions of the Paris Convention (1967), have been incorporated into the *TRIPS Agreement* and, thus, the *WTO Agreement*.[166] Consequently, these obligations of countries of the Paris Union under the Paris Convention (1967) are also now obligations of all WTO Members, whether they are countries of the Paris Union or not, under the *WTO Agreement*, and, thus, are enforceable under the DSU.[167]

239.   In addition to Article 2(1) of the Paris Convention (1967), there is also another national treatment provision in the *TRIPS Agreement*. The other national treatment provision at issue in this appeal is Article 3.1 of the *TRIPS Agreement*, which states in relevant part:

> Each Member shall accord to the nationals of other Members treatment no less favourable than that it accords to its own nationals with regard to the protection [footnote 3] of intellectual property, subject to the exceptions already provided in, respectively, the Paris Convention (1967), the Berne Convention (1971), the Rome Convention or the Treaty on Intellectual Property in Respect of Integrated Circuits.

> _____

> Footnote 3: For the purposes of Articles 3 and 4, "protection" shall include matters affecting the availability, acquisition, scope, maintenance and enforcement of intellectual property rights as well as those matters affecting the use of intellectual property rights specifically addressed in this Agreement.

240.   Thus, in drafting the *TRIPS Agreement*, the framers of the *WTO Agreement* saw fit to include an additional provision on national treatment. Clearly, this emphasizes the fundamental significance of the obligation of national treatment to their purposes in the *TRIPS Agreement*.

241.   Indeed, the significance of the national treatment obligation can hardly be overstated. Not only has the national treatment obligation long been a cornerstone of the Paris Convention and other international intellectual property conventions.[168]   So, too, has the national treatment obligation long been a cornerstone of the world trading system that is served by the WTO.

242.   As we see it, the national treatment obligation is a fundamental principle underlying the *TRIPS Agreement*, just as it has been in what is now the GATT 1994. The Panel was correct in concluding that, as the language of Article 3.1 of the *TRIPS Agreement*, in particular, is similar to that of Article III:4 of the GATT 1994, the jurisprudence on Article III:4 of the GATT 1994 may be useful in interpreting the national treatment obligation in the *TRIPS Agreement*.

[166]   See *supra*, para. 124.
[167]   See *supra*, para. 125.
[168]   For example, see Article 2 of the International Convention for the Protection of Performers, Producers of Phonograms and Broadcasting Organizations ("Rome Convention (1961)"), adopted at Rome on 26 October 1961; and also Article 5 of the Treaty on Intellectual Property in Respect of Integrated Circuits ("IPIC Treaty"), adopted at Washington on 26 May 1989.

243.   As articulated in Article 3.1 of the *TRIPS Agreement*, the national treatment principle calls on WTO Members to accord no less favourable treatment to non-nationals than to nationals in the "protection" of trade-related intellectual property rights. The footnote to Article 3.1 clarifies that this "protection" extends to "matters affecting the availability, acquisition, scope, maintenance and enforcement of intellectual property rights as well as those matters affecting the use of intellectual property rights specifically addressed" in the *TRIPS Agreement*. As we have previously concluded, neither the *TRIPS Agreement* nor the Paris Convention (1967) requires WTO Members to adopt any particular "ownership regime".[169]

244.   The European Communities claims that Sections 211(a)(2) and (b) violate the national treatment obligation in both Article 2(1) of the Paris Convention (1967) and Article 3.1 of the *TRIPS Agreement* by treating non-United States nationals less favourably than United States nationals in two different situations to which the measure applies: first, that of successors-in-interest or *bona fide* successors-in-interest to original owners; and, second, that of original owners. The European Communities contends that this discrimination occurs in different ways in these two different situations, but, in each situation, they see a violation of the fundamental obligation of national treatment.

245.   We examine first the European Communities' claims relating to the alleged discrimination among successors-in-interest under Sections 211(a)(2) and (b).

246.   Before the Panel, the European Communities argued that Section 211(a)(2) applies only to Cuban nationals and to other foreign (that is, non-United States) successors-in-interest. The European Communities argued that this violates the national treatment obligation in Article 2(1) of the Paris Convention (1967) and Article 3.1 of the *TRIPS Agreement* because it imposes restrictions on Cubans and other foreign nationals that it does not impose on United States nationals.

247.   In response to the claim by the European Communities that Section 211(a)(2) violates the national treatment obligation of the United States with respect to successors-in-interest, the Panel reasoned as follows:

> Section 211(a)(2) provides that no US courts are to recognize, enforce or validate any rights by a "designated national" based on registration of trademarks obtained through a licence from OFAC. We note that the term "designated national" is defined in Section 211(d)(1) to include (1) Cuba, (2) any Cuban national, (3) "a specially designated national" or (4) "a national of any foreign country who is a successor-in-interest to a designated national." We consider that the term "designated national" must be read as a whole and cannot be segregated into two tiers. We note that "designated national" is defined to include "[a] national of *any foreign country* who is a successor-in-interest to a designated national" and

---

[169] See *supra*, para. 195.

does not include US nationals. *Thus, it is plausible that while a foreign national who is a successor-in-interest to a designated national may not have its rights to the underlying mark recognized, enforced or validated, a US national who is a successor-in-interest to a designated national can have US courts recognize, enforce or validate rights in respect of the underlying mark that was registered pursuant to a specific licence granted by OFAC. Such differential treatment in respect of intellectual property right protection could be considered to provide a less favourable treatment to nationals of other Members as it denies effective equality of opportunities to non-US nationals in the United States.*[170] (emphasis added)

248.   Thus, with respect to successors-in-interest, the Panel stated that Section 211(a)(2), *in and of itself*, "could be considered" to provide less favourable treatment to non-United States nationals than to United States nationals. Yet, the Panel refrained from making, at that stage, findings with respect to Article 2(1) of the Paris Convention (1967) and Article 3.1 of the *TRIPS Agreement.* Instead, the Panel went on to examine the argument of the United States that any more favourable treatment that might arise under Section 211(a)(2) for United States nationals was offset[171] by OFAC's practice under Section 515.201 of the CACR of not issuing specific licences to United States nationals to become successors-in-interest to "designated nationals". As the Panel summarized it, the United States argued that:

> ... Section 211(a)(2) is not inconsistent with Article 3.1 on the basis that US nationals, although not specifically set out in the measure, cannot become successors-in-interest to designated nationals because Section 515.201 of 31 CFR prohibits US nationals from becoming successors-in-interest without obtaining a specific licence from OFAC. The United States submitted that OFAC has never issued a specific licence to a US national for the purpose of becoming a successor-in-interest to trademarks that were used in connection with confiscated assets. The United States asserted that a law is only WTO-inconsistent on its face if it mandates WTO-inconsistent actions and that if the law allows the national authority to act in [*sic*] manner consistent with the WTO Agreement,

---

[170]   Panel Report, para. 8.133. Like the Panel, we note that Section 211(d)(1) broadened the definition of "designated national" to include, in addition to Cuba and any Cuban national, nationals of any foreign country (that is, non-United States nationals) who are successors-in-interest to a designated national. Section 211(d)(1) provides:

> The term "designated national" has the meaning given such term in section 515.305 of title 31, Code of Federal Regulations, as in effect on September 9, 1998, and includes a national of any foreign country who is a successor-in-interest to a designated national.

[171]   For purposes of this appeal, we use the term "offset" to describe a situation in which an action counterbalances, counteracts or neutralizes the effect of a contrary action. See *infra*, paras. 259-269 .

panels should not assume that a Member will use its discretion in a manner contrary to its international obligations. [172]

249.   Thus, before the Panel, the United States argued that Section 211(a)(2) does not apply to United States nationals because, under the CACR, United States nationals are prohibited from owning or having an interest in property that was confiscated by the Cuban Government and, therefore, cannot become successors-in-interest. The United States acknowledged that OFAC has the discretion administratively to authorize specific licences with respect to certain transactions that would enable United States nationals to deal with such property. The United States asserted, however, that this discretion has little practical effect because OFAC has never issued such a licence to a United States national for purposes of becoming a successor-in-interest to a confiscating entity. [173]   The United States submitted further to the Panel that there is no reason to believe that OFAC would ever issue such a licence, and that, therefore, as a matter of law, the Panel should not assume that OFAC, an agency of the executive branch, would take an action that might put the United States in violation of its international obligations. [174] For these reasons, the United States maintained that it does not provide more favourable treatment to United States nationals than to Cubans and other non-nationals.

250.   The Panel accepted this argument by the United States with respect to successors-in-interest and went on to state that:

> Although the term "designated national" is defined to include a national of any foreign country who is a successor-in-interest, we note that Section 515.201 of 31 CFR imposes a general prohibition on US nationals from becoming successors-in-interest unless OFAC grants a specific licence. The question that needs to be addressed in determining the consistency of Section 211(a)(2) with the national treatment principle is whether OFAC accords a more favourable treatment to US nationals in considering whether to grant licences to US nationals to become successors-in-interest. [175]

251.   As regards the treatment of successors-in-interest, the Panel focused on the discretionary authority enjoyed by OFAC. In so doing, the Panel relied on the report of the panel in *United States Measures Affecting the Importation, Internal Sale and Use of Tobacco* ("*US – Tobacco*") [176], and on our Report in *United States – Anti-Dumping Act of 1916* ("*US – 1916 Act*") [177] concerning the issue of discretionary authority. Based on those previous Reports, the Panel concluded that, where discretionary authority is vested in the executive branch of a WTO Member, it cannot be assumed that that Member will exercise that authority in violation of its obligations under any of the covered agreements.

---

[172]   Panel Report, para. 8.134.
[173]   *Ibid.*
[174]   *Ibid.*, para. 4.126.
[175]   Panel Report, para. 8.135.
[176]   Panel Report, adopted 4 October 1994, BISD 41S/I/131, para. 118.
[177]   Appellate Body Report, WT/DS136/AB/R, WT/DS162/AB/R, adopted 26 September 2000, DSR 2000:X, 4793, para. 88.

252.   The Panel found, as a matter of fact, that OFAC has never granted a specific licence to allow any United States national to become a successor-in-interest to a "designated national". [178] Further, the Panel found that the European Communities had not demonstrated that, in exercising its discretionary authority, OFAC had acted in a manner that was inconsistent with the national treatment obligation in Article 2(1) of the Paris Convention (1967) and Article 3.1 of the *TRIPS Agreement*. [179]

253.   In view of this, the Panel concluded that:

> Because US nationals are unable to obtain licences so as to become a successor-in-interest and OFAC has not granted any such licence for such purpose and in light of our conclusion that Section 211(a)(2) does not accord a treatment less favourable to foreign original owners than it accords to original owners who are US nationals, we find that Section 211(a)(2) is not inconsistent with Article 3.1 of the TRIPS Agreement and Article 2.1 of the TRIPS Agreement in conjunction with Article 2(1) of the Paris Convention (1967). [180]

254.   The European Communities appeals these findings. The European Communities does not dispute that OFAC can deny United States nationals the specific licences required under the CACR to become successors-in-interest to "designated nationals". Nor does the European Communities dispute that, to date, OFAC has never granted such a specific licence to United States nationals. Rather, the European Communities argues that the offsetting effect of this admittedly longstanding OFAC practice does not cure the discrimination in Section 211(a)(2) with respect to successors-in-interest who are *not* United States nationals.

255.   According to the European Communities, the discriminatory treatment in favour of successors-in-interest who are United States nationals and against successors-in-interest who are *not* United States nationals continues to exist because of what the European Communities sees as an "extra hurdle" that non-United States nationals face procedurally under United States law.

256.   That "extra hurdle" is this. United States nationals who are successors-in-interest must go successfully only through the OFAC procedure. In the circumstances addressed by Section 211, they are not subject to the constraints imposed by Section 211(a)(2). [181] In contrast, non-United States successors-in-interest not only must go successfully through the OFAC procedure, but also find themselves *additionally* exposed to the "extra hurdle" of an additional proceeding under Section 211(a)(2). [182] In sum, United States nationals face only *one* proceeding, while non-United States nationals face *two*. It is on this basis that the European Communities claims on appeal that Section 211(a)(2), as it relates to successors-

---

[178]   Panel Report, para. 8.140.
[179]   *Ibid.*, para. 8.138.
[180]   Panel Report, para. 8.140.
[181]   European Communities' appellant's submission, para. 124.
[182]   *Ibid.*

in-interest, violates the national treatment obligation in the *TRIPS Agreement* and the Paris Convention (1967).

257.   At the oral hearing in this appeal, the United States reiterated that it is very unlikely that a United States national would ever be licensed to become a successor-in-interest to a "designated national"; therefore, the United States argues that it does not matter "what happens to such a successor-in-interest when he gets to the enforcement level".[183] In any event, the United States continues, if a United States national were ever granted a specific licence, the United States courts would apply the "longstanding principle against the recognition of foreign confiscations."[184]

258.   In considering the European Communities' appeal, we look first at the reasoning and the conclusions of the Panel. As we have noted, initially, the Panel concluded, on a plain reading of the statute, that Section 211(a)(2) affords "differential treatment" between United States and non-United States nationals, and that such treatment "could be considered to provide a less favourable treatment to nationals of other Members as it denies effective equality of opportunities" to non-United States nationals in the United States.[185] We agree.

259.   Next, the Panel considered the supposed offsetting effect of the consistent practice of OFAC. Here, as we have also noted, the Panel relied on previous rulings addressing the issue of legislation that gives discretionary authority to the executive branch of a Member's government. As the Panel rightly noted, in *US – 1916 Act*, we stated that a distinction should be made between legislation that mandates WTO-inconsistent behaviour, and legislation that gives rise to executive authority that can be exercised with discretion. We quoted with approval there the following statement of the panel in *US – Tobacco*:

> ... panels had consistently ruled that legislation which mandated action inconsistent with the General Agreement could be challenged as such, whereas legislation which merely gave the discretion to the *executive authority* of a contracting party to act inconsistently with the General Agreement could not be challenged as such; only the actual application of such legislation inconsistent with the General Agreement could be subject to challenge.[186]

Thus, where discretionary authority is vested in the executive branch of a WTO Member, it cannot be assumed that the WTO Member will fail to implement its obligations under the *WTO Agreement* in good faith.[187] Relying on these rul-

---

[183]   United States' responses to questioning at the oral hearing.
[184]   United States' responses to questioning at the oral hearing.
[185]   Panel Report, para. 8.133.
[186]   Appellate Body Report, *US – 1916 Act*, *supra*, footnote 177, para. 88, quoting from Panel Report, *US – Tobacco*, *supra*, footnote 176, para. 118.
[187]   We made a similar observation in a somewhat different context in *Chile – Taxes on Alcoholic Beverages*, where we stated:

> [M]embers of the WTO should not be assumed, in any way, to have *continued* previous protection or discrimination through the adoption of a new measure. This would come close to a presumption of bad faith. Accordingly, we hold that the

ings, and interpreting them correctly, the Panel concluded that it could not assume that OFAC would exercise its discretionary executive authority inconsistently with the obligations of the United States under the *WTO Agreement*. Here, too, we agree.

260.   But here, the Panel stopped. We are of the view that, having reached the conclusion it did with respect to the offsetting effect of OFAC practice, the Panel should not have stopped but should have gone on and considered the argument made by the European Communities about the "extra hurdle" faced by non-United States successors-in-interest. For this reason, we do so now.

261.   We note, as did the Panel, the report of the panel in *US – Section 337*.[188] That panel reasoned that "the mere fact that imported products are subject under Section 337 to legal provisions that are different from those applying to products of national origin is in itself not conclusive in establishing inconsistency with Article III:4."[189]

262.   That panel stated further that:

> [I]t would follow ... that any unfavourable elements of treatment of imported products could be offset by more favourable elements of treatment, provided that the results, as shown in past cases, have not been less favourable. *[E]lements of less and more favourable treatment could thus only be offset against each other to the extent that they always would arise in the same cases and necessarily would have an offsetting influence on the other.*[190] (emphasis added)

263.   And that panel, importantly for our purposes, concluded that:

> ... *while the likelihood of having to defend imported products in two fora is small, the existence of the possibility is inherently less favourable than being faced with having to conduct a defence in only one of those fora.*[191] (emphasis added)

264.   We agree with this approach and consider it to be particularly relevant to this appeal. It is not disputed that Section 515.201 of the CACR imposes a limitation – a "hurdle" – on both successors-in-interest who are United States nationals and successors-in-interest who are not. It is also not disputed that Section 211(a)(2) applies only to successors-in-interest who are *not* United States nationals. It is likewise not disputed that, under Section 211(a)(2), in *every individual situation* where a non-United States successor-in-interest seeks to assert

---

Panel committed legal error in taking this factor into account in examining the issue of "so as to afford protection". (footnote omitted)

     See, Appellate Body Report, WT/DS87/AB/R, WT/DS110/AB/R, adopted 12 January 2000, DSR 2000:I, 281, para. 74.

[188]   Panel Report, *US – Section 337*, *supra*, footnote 25. Central to that dispute was a situation where the proceedings that were applicable to imported products alleged to infringe United States patents were different in a number of respects from those applicable before a federal district court when a product of foreign origin was challenged on the grounds of patent infringement.

[189]   Panel Report, *US – Section 337*, *supra*, footnote 25, para. 5.11.

[190]   *Ibid.*, para. 5.12.

[191]   *Ibid.*, para. 5.19.

its rights without the express consent of the original owner or its *bona fide* successor-in-interest, the United States courts are required not to recognize, enforce or otherwise validate any assertion of rights. We emphasize that this situation exists under the statute *on its face*, and that, therefore, unlike the situation with respect to the granting of a special licence to United States successors-in-interest by OFAC, this situation assumes no action by OFAC or by any other agency of the United States Government.

265.   The United States may be right that the likelihood of having to overcome the hurdles of both Section 515.201 of Title 31 CFR and Section 211(a)(2) may, echoing the panel in *US – Section 337*, be *small*. But, again echoing that panel, even the *possibility* that non-United States successors-in-interest face two hurdles is *inherently less favourable* than the undisputed fact that United States successors-in-interest face only one.

266.   Both before the Panel and before us, the United States has submitted that Section 211 is a statutory articulation of the longstanding doctrine of non-recognition of foreign confiscation[192] that is recognized in "virtually every jurisdiction".[193] Thus, the United States argues that, in the unlikely[194] event that a United States national did somehow succeed in getting a specific licence from OFAC, this longstanding doctrine would be applied by United States courts to prevent such a national from enforcing its rights as a successor-in-interest. The United States argues, therefore, that the prohibition imposed by Section 211(a)(2) with respect to non-United States successors-in-interest would also be applied to United States successors-in-interest. We are not persuaded by this argument.

267.   The United States has not shown, as required under the national treatment obligation, that, in every individual case, the courts of the United States would not validate the assertion of rights by a United States successor-in-interest. Moreover, even if there is, as the United States argues, a *likelihood* that United States courts would not enforce rights asserted by a United States successor-in-interest, the fact remains, nevertheless, that non-United States successors-in-interest are placed by the measure, *on its face*, in an inherently less favourable situation than that faced by United States successors-in-interest. And, even if we were to accept the United States argument about the doctrine of non-recognition of foreign confiscation, presumably that doctrine would apply to those who are not nationals of the United States as well as to those who are. Any application of this doctrine would therefore not offset the discrimination in Section 211(a)(2), because it would constitute yet another, separate obstacle faced by nationals and non-nationals alike. Hence, it would not offset the effect of Section 211(a)(2), which applies only to successors-in-interest who are not United States nationals.

268.   Accordingly, we conclude that Section 211(a)(2) imposes an additional obstacle on successors-in-interest who are not nationals of the United States that is not faced by United States successors-in-interest. And, therefore, we conclude

---

[192]   We recall that the term "confiscated" is defined in the CACR. See *supra*, footnote 7.
[193]   United States' appellee's submission, para. 16.
[194]   United States' responses to questioning at the oral hearing.

that, by applying the "extra hurdle" imposed by Section 211(a)(2) only to non-United States successors-in-interest, the United States violates the national treatment obligation in Article 2(1) of the Paris Convention (1967) and Article 3.1 of the *TRIPS Agreement* .

269.   For this reason, we reverse the Panel's conclusion in paragraph 8.140 of the Panel Report that "[b]ecause US nationals are unable to obtain licences so as to become a successor-in-interest and OFAC has not granted any such licence for such purpose … Section 211(a)(2) is not inconsistent with Article 3.1 of the TRIPS Agreement and Article 2.1 of the TRIPS Agreement in conjunction with Article 2(1) of the Paris Convention (1967)."

270.   The European Communities also raised claims at the level of successors-in-interest against Section 211(b).[195] With respect to these claims, the Panel concluded that:

> Section 211(b) states that US courts shall not recognize, enforce or validate any assertion of treaty rights by a "designated national or *its successor-in-interest*". The difference between Section 211(a)(2) and Section 211(b) is that the latter contains the additional term "its successor-in-interest" whereas the former just refers to "a designated national". Moreover, the term "its successor-in-interest" as set out in Section 211(b) is not limited to foreign nationals which means that it includes US nationals. This would mean that any transfer of trademarks used in connection with confiscated assets to any national, including US nationals, would be subject to Section 211(b). For these reasons, Section 211(b) does not accord a treatment less favourable to nationals of other Members than it accords to US nationals.[196] (emphasis in original)

271.   We agree with the Panel that Section 211(b) applies to successors-in-interest of *any origin*, including United States nationals and that, consequently, Section 211(b) does not accord less favourable treatment to non-United States nationals than to United States nationals.

272.   Therefore, we uphold the Panel's conclusion in paragraph 8.173 of the Panel Report that – at the level of successors-in-interest – Section 211(b) is not inconsistent with Article 2.1 of the *TRIPS Agreement* in conjunction with Article 2(1) of the Paris Convention (1967) and Article 3.1 of the *TRIPS Agreement*.

273.   We turn now to the European Communities' claims relating to Sections 211(a)(2) and (b) with respect to the other form of discrimination alleged by the European Communities – that of discrimination among *original owners*.

274.   On this, the Panel found with respect to Sections 211(a)(2) and (b):

> In respect of original owners, Section 211(a)(2) does not accord a treatment less favourable to foreign original owners than it accords

---

[195]   European Communities' appellant's submission, para. 157.
[196]   Panel Report, para. 8.171.

> to original owners who are US nationals with respect to protection of intellectual property rights. [197]
>
> ...
>
> Similarly, in respect of original owners, Section 211(b) does not accord a treatment less favourable to foreign original owners than it accords to original owners who are US nationals. [198]

In contrast to its reasoned explanation on alleged discrimination relating to successors-in-interest, the Panel gave no further explanation for its conclusion on alleged discrimination among original owners.

275.   On appeal, the European Communities argues that the Panel erred in its conclusion about discrimination among original owners. The European Communities maintains that, on their face, both Sections 211(a)(2) and 211(b) violate the national treatment obligation under the *TRIPS Agreement* and the Paris Convention (1967) because they provide less favourable treatment to Cuban nationals who are original owners than to United States nationals who are original owners. The European Communities supports this position by relying on a particular set of circumstances that exists under the statute that, according to the European Communities, illustrates how Sections 211(a)(2) and (b), on their face, discriminate in favour of United States nationals who are original owners and against Cuban nationals who are original owners. The European Communities believes this situation demonstrates the discriminatory treatment implicit in Sections 211(a)(2) and (b). [199]

276.   Specifically, the European Communities asks us to consider the following particular set of circumstances that exists under the statute. There are two separate owners who acquired rights, either at common law or based on registration, in two separate United States trademarks, before the Cuban confiscation occurred. Each of these two United States trademarks is the same, or substantially similar to, the signs or combination of signs of which a trademark registered in Cuba is composed. That same or similar Cuban trademark was used in connection with a business or assets that were confiscated in Cuba. Neither of the two original owners of the two United States trademarks was the owner of that same or similar trademark that was registered in Cuba. Those two original owners each seek to assert rights in the United States in their two respective United States trademarks. The situation of these two original owners of these two United States trademarks is identical in every relevant respect, but one. That one difference is this: one original owner is a national of Cuba, and the other original owner is a national of the United States.

277.   The European Communities asks us to consider this specific situation involving these two original owners, one from Cuba and one from the United States. The European Communities argues that, on the face of the statute, in this

---

[197]   Panel Report, para. 8.139.
[198]   *Ibid.*, para. 8.172.
[199]   European Communities' appellant's submission, paras. 115 and 157; European Communities' opening statement at the oral hearing; European Communities' responses to questioning at the oral hearing.

situation, the original owner who is a Cuban national is subject to Sections 211(a)(2) and (b), and the original owner who is a United States national is not. This alone, as the European Communities sees it, is sufficient for us to find that Sections 211(a)(2) and (b) violate the national treatment obligation of the United States.

278.   Like the European Communities, we see this situation as critical to our determination of whether the treatment of original owners under Section 211 is consistent with the national treatment obligation of the United States under Article 2(1) of the Paris Convention (1967) and Article 3.1 of the *TRIPS Agreement*.

279.   The situation highlighted by the European Communities on appeal exists because Sections 211(a)(2) and (b) apply to "designated nationals". A "designated national" is defined in Section 515.305 of Title 31 CFR as "Cuba and any national thereof including any person who is a specially designated national."[200] Thus, Sections 211(a)(2) and (b) apply to original owners that are Cuban nationals. Original owners that are United States nationals are not covered by the definition of "designated national" and, thus, are not subject to the limitations of Sections 211(a)(2) and (b).

280.   Thus, in our view, the European Communities is correct on this issue. Sections 211(a)(2) and (b) are discriminatory *on their face*.

281.   We conclude, therefore, that the European Communities has established a *prima facie* case that Sections 211(a)(2) and (b) discriminate between Cuban nationals and United States nationals, both of whom are original owners of trademarks registered in the United States which are composed of the same or substantially similar signs as a Cuban trademark used in connection with a business or assets that were confiscated in Cuba.

282.   The United States attempts to rebut this argument by the European Communities by maintaining that Sections 211(a)(2) and (b) are not applicable to original owners, regardless of their nationality, because original owners are always in a position to consent expressly to their own assertion of rights under Sections 211(a)(2) and (b).[201] Section 211(a)(2), when read together with Section 211(a)(1), and Section 211(b) do indeed provide an exception for designated nationals who have the express consent of "the original owner of the mark, trade name, or commercial name, or the bona fide successor-in-interest".[202] However, the United States erroneously assumes in its argument on this issue that the Cuban original owner of the United States trademark is necessarily the same person as the original owner of the same or substantially similar Cuban trademark used in connection with a business or assets that were confiscated. This is by no means necessarily the case, as is demonstrated in the specific situation posed by the European Communities. In that situation, the Cuban national who holds the

---

[200]   The definition also includes successors-in-interest, but the situation discussed here does not involve successors-in-interest. Nor does it involve "specially designated nationals", given that there is no claim that a person is acting for or on behalf of the Cuban government. The term "specially designated national" is defined in Section 515.306 of 31 CFR, see *supra*, footnote 6.
[201]   United States' appellee's submission, para. 71.
[202]   See *supra*, para. 120.

trademark rights in the United States would be unable to use its own consent to avoid the court's denial of any assertion of rights under Sections 211(a)(2) and (b) because it was not the original owner of the same or similar Cuban trademark.

283.   The United States also argues in rebuttal that Section 211(a)(2) does not apply to Cuban nationals in the situation posed by the European Communities because Section 515.527 of the CACR was not in effect when the original owners in this situation obtained their trademark rights in the United States.[203] We note that Section 211(a)(2) refers to the assertion of rights "based on common law rights or registration obtained under such section 515.527". Thus, it is clear from the text of Section 211(a)(2) that the reference to Section 515.527 relates to rights based on registration, and not to common law rights. Indeed, the United States conceded as much in response to our questions at the oral hearing. Thus, this argument may address the discrimination against Cuban nationals who are original owners of trademark rights in the United States *based on registration*. But it does not address the discrimination against Cuban nationals who are original owners of trademark rights in the United States *based on common law*.

284.   For trademark rights based on registration, it is true that, in the situation posed by the European Communities, Section 515.527 of the CACR would not have been in effect when the Cuban original owner obtained its trademark rights in the United States, namely before the Cuban confiscation. However, we recall that Section 515.527 of the CACR applies not only to the registration, but also to the *renewal* of registered trademarks.[204] Although the Cuban national's initial registration, carried out before the Cuban confiscation, would not have been obtained pursuant to Section 515.527, a renewal of such registration would come within the purview of that provision. Hence, Section 211(a)(2) could apply to a Cuban national who registered a United States trademark before confiscation *and renewed it after that date*.

285.   For trademark rights based on common law, the United States contends that the Cuban original owner could not have maintained its rights in the United States trademark because it would not have been able to import the trademarked goods from Cuba and, thus, would not have been able to continue using the trademark "in commerce".[205] Yet, this argument assumes that the Cuban national who owns the trademark in the United States could have imported the trademarked goods *only from Cuba*. We understand that from the European Communities' responses to questioning at the oral hearing, the Cuban holder of common law trademark rights in the United States could import the trademarked

---

[203]   United States' responses to questioning at the oral hearing.

[204]   Section 515.527(a)(1) of 31 CFR provides:

> Transactions related to the registration and *renewal* in the United States Patent and Trademark Office or the United States Copyright Office of patents, trademarks, and copyrights in which the Government of Cuba or a Cuban national has an interest are authorized. (emphasis added)

[205]   Section 1 of the Lanham Act, 15 U.S.C. §1051. United States' responses to questioning at the oral hearing.

goods from a country other than Cuba. The United States did not deny this at the oral hearing. [206] We are, therefore, not persuaded by this argument.

286. On this point, the United States replied as well that the Cuban original owner could be "unblocked" under the OFAC regulations, an argument that the United States did not make before the Panel or in its written submissions in this appeal. The relevant regulation is Section 515.505 of the CACR, which lists those persons that are "licensed as unblocked nationals" or who may apply to be "unblocked". [207] According to the United States, as an "unblocked national" [208], such a Cuban original owner would have the same status as a United States national. [209] Yet, to fulfill the national treatment obligation, less favourable treatment must be offset, and thereby eliminated, in *every* individual situation that exists under a measure. Therefore, for this argument by the United States to succeed, it must hold true for *all* Cuban original owners of United States trademarks, and not merely for *some* of them.

287. Accordingly, we examine three possible situations to determine whether the discrimination is eliminated in every individual instance that might arise under Section 515.505. The first example involves a Cuban original owner residing in the United States. The second involves a Cuban original owner residing in a

---

[206] European Communities' responses to questioning at the oral hearing. We note also the following excerpt from a judgment by the United States District Court, Southern District New York:

> In 1995, Bacardi-Martini began to distribute rum in the United States which was produced in the Bahamas under the authority of Galleon, Bacardi & Co.'s predecessor-in-interest, bearing the trademark Havana Club.

Havana Club Holding, S.A. v. Galleon S.A., 62 F.Supp.2d 1085, 1090.
United States' responses to questioning at the oral hearing.

[207] Section 515.505 of 31 CFR provides:

> (a)   The following persons are hereby licensed as unblocked nationals.
> (1)   Any person resident in, or organized under the laws of a jurisdiction in, the United States or the authorized trade territory who or which has never been a designated national;
> (2)   Any individual resident in the United States who is not a specially designated national; and
> (3)   Any corporation, partnership or association that would be a designated national solely because of the interest therein of an individual licensed in paragraph (a) or (b) of this section as an unblocked national.
> (b)   Individual nationals of a designated country who have taken up residence in the authorized trade territory may apply to the Office of Foreign Assets Control to be specifically licensed as unblocked nationals.
> (c)   The licensing of any person as an unblocked national shall not suspend the requirements of any section of this chapter relating to the maintenance or production of records.

[208] An "unblocked national" is defined in Section 515.307 of 31 CFR as:

> Any person licensed pursuant to §515.505 licensed as an *unblocked national* shall, while so licensed, be regarded as a person within the United States who is not a national of any designated foreign country: *Provided, however,* That the licensing of any person as an *unblocked national* shall not be deemed to suspend in any way the requirements of any section of this chapter relating to reports, or the production of books, documents, and records specified therein.

[209] United States' responses to questioning at the oral hearing.

country other than the United States or Cuba.[210] The third involves a Cuban original owner residing in Cuba.

288. According to the United States, a Cuban original owner residing in the United States is, in fact, "unblocked" by Section 515.505(a)(2) of the CACR.[211] We agree with this reading of Section 515.505(a)(2). This eliminates the less favourable treatment of this Cuban original owner. The other examples, however, yield a different result.

289. A Cuban original owner residing in a country other than the United States or Cuba, for example, in the European Communities, could apply to OFAC to be "specifically licensed as [an] unblocked national[]." This is pursuant to Section 515.505(b) of the CACR, because the United States does not impose sanctions on the European Communities and, therefore, the European Communities would be considered part of the "authorized trade territory" described in Section 515.322 of the CACR.[212] This could eliminate less favourable treatment *in practice*. Yet, the very existence of the additional "hurdle" that is imposed by requiring application to OFAC is, in itself, inherently less favourable. Sections 211(a)(2) and (b) do not apply to United States original owners; no application to OFAC is required. But Cuban original owners residing in the "authorized trade territory" must apply to OFAC. Thus, such Cuban original owners must comply with an administrative requirement that does not apply to United States original owners.[213] By virtue alone of having to apply to OFAC, even Cuban original owners that reside in the "authorized trade territory" described in Section 515.332 are treated less favourably than United States original owners. So, in this second situation, the discrimination remains.

290. A Cuban original owner residing in Cuba is discriminated against as well. Cuba is not part of the "authorized trade territory" because it is subject to sanctions administered by OFAC under the CACR. From our reading of the regulations, it seems to us that a Cuban national who resides in Cuba could not, under any circumstances, be "unblocked" under Sections 515.505(a) or (b) of Title 31 CFR. Nor has the United States suggested otherwise. Thus, in this third situation, the discrimination remains as well.

291. We turn now to the United States' argument that Section 515.201 of the CACR offsets *any* discrimination implicit in Sections 211(a)(2) and (b). Section 515.201 of the CACR sets out a list of transactions that are prohibited, except as specifically authorized by the Secretary of the Treasury:

---

[210] We are referring here to a country which is within the "authorized trade territory", as defined in Section 515.322 of 31 CFR. See *infra*, footnote 212.

[211] United States' responses to questioning at the oral hearing.

[212] Section 515.322 of 31 CFR provides:

§515.322 Authorized trade territory; member of the authorized trade territory.

(a) The term *authorized trade territory* includes all countries, including any colony, territory, possession, or protectorate, except those countries subject to sanctions pursuant to this chapter. The term does not include the United States.

(b) The term member of the *authorized trade territory* shall mean any of the foreign countries or political subdivisions comprising the authorized trade territory.

[213] See Panel Report, *US – Section 337, supra*, footnote 25, paras. 5.11-5.14.

§515.201 Transactions involving designated foreign countries or their nationals; effective date.

(a) All of the following transactions are prohibited, except as specifically authorized by the Secretary of the Treasury (or any person, agency, or instrumentality designated by him) by means of regulations, rulings, instructions, licenses, or otherwise, if either such transactions are by, or on behalf of, or pursuant to the direction of a foreign country designated under this part, or any national thereof, or such transactions involve property in which a foreign country designated under this part, or any national thereof, has at any time on or since the effective date of this section had any interest of any nature whatsoever, direct or indirect ...

(b) All of the following transactions are prohibited, except as specifically authorized by the Secretary of the Treasury (or any person, agency, or instrumentality designated by him) by means of regulations, rulings, instructions, licenses, or otherwise, if such transactions involve property in which any foreign country designated under this part, or any national thereof, has at any time on or since the effective date of this section had any interest of any nature whatsoever, direct or indirect ...

292.   The United States argues that Section 515.201 of the CACR could apply to a United States original owner in the situation described above, thereby offsetting the less favourable treatment of the Cuban national that otherwise occurs under Sections 211(a)(2) and (b). [214] The United States asserts that, in this way, the United States original owner would be barred from asserting rights in the trademark pursuant to Section 515.201 of the CACR, just as a Cuban original owner would be barred from doing so under Sections 211(a)(2) and (b).

293.   In making this argument, the United States maintains that Section 515.201 of the CACR has a very broad reach – so far that it reaches United States nationals who are pre-confiscation original owners of a United States trademark that is the same or substantially similar to a Cuban trademark used in connection with a Cuban business or assets that were confiscated. We understand the United States to argue that, because the United States trademark is the same or similar to a trademark used in connection with a business or assets confiscated in Cuba, it would be considered as "involv[ing] property in which a foreign country designated under this part, or any national thereof, has at any time on or since the effective date of this section had any interest of any nature whatsoever, direct or indirect", and hence a transaction that is prohibited under Section 515.201 of the CACR. [215]

294.   We disagree. We do not believe that Section 515.201 of the CACR would *in every case* offset the discriminatory treatment imposed by Sections 211(a)(2) and (b). For this argument by the United States to hold true in each and every

---

[214] United States' responses to questioning at the oral hearing.
[215] United States' appellee's submission, para. 72.

situation, the scope of the phrase "having an interest in" in Section 515.201 would necessarily have to overlap in coverage with the scope of the phrase "used in connection with" in Sections 211(a)(2) and (b). However, the United States was unable to point to evidence substantiating that the different standards used in Section 515.201 and in Sections 211(a)(2) and (b) overlap completely.[216] We are, therefore, not satisfied that Section 515.201 would offset the inherently less favourable treatment present in Sections 211(a)(2) and (b) in each and every case. And, because it has not been shown by the United States that it would do so in each and every case, the less favourable treatment that exists under the measure cannot be said to have been offset and, thus, eliminated.

295.   Finally, the United States referred to its longstanding doctrine of non-recognition of foreign confiscations.[217] However, this policy could not possibly apply to trademarks that existed *in the United States* when a business or assets connected with a trademark composed of the same or substantially similar signs were confiscated *in Cuba*.

296.   Thus, we conclude that Sections 211(a)(2) and (b) are inconsistent with the national treatment obligation of the United States under the Paris Convention (1967) and the *TRIPS Agreement* at the level of original owners. And, therefore, we reverse the Panel's findings in paragraphs 8.140 and 8.173 of the Panel Report that Section 211(a)(2) and Section 211(b) are "not inconsistent with Article 3.1 of the TRIPS Agreement and Article 2.1 of the TRIPS Agreement in conjunction with Article 2(1) of the Paris Convention (1967)" to the extent that they concern the treatment of original owners.

X.   ARTICLE 4 OF THE *TRIPS AGREEMENT*

297.   Like the national treatment obligation, the obligation to provide most-favoured-nation treatment has long been one of the cornerstones of the world trading system. For more than fifty years, the obligation to provide most-favoured-nation treatment in Article I of the GATT 1994 has been both central and essential to assuring the success of a global rules-based system for trade in goods. Unlike the national treatment principle, there is no provision in the Paris Convention (1967) that establishes a most-favoured-nation obligation with respect to rights in trademarks or other industrial property. However, the framers of the *TRIPS Agreement* decided to extend the most-favoured-nation obligation to the protection of intellectual property rights covered by that Agreement. As a cornerstone of the world trading system, the most-favoured-nation obligation must be accorded the same significance with respect to intellectual property rights under the *TRIPS Agreement* that it has long been accorded with respect to trade in goods under the GATT. It is, in a word, fundamental.

298.   Article 4 of the *TRIPS Agreement* provides, in relevant part:

---

[216] United States' responses to questioning at the oral hearing.

[217] United States' appellee's submission, paras. 16 and 76; United States' responses to questioning at the oral hearing.

With regard to the protection of intellectual property, any advantage, favour, privilege or immunity granted by a Member to the nationals of any other country shall be accorded immediately and unconditionally to the nationals of all other Members. [footnote 3]

Footnote 3: For the purposes of Articles 3 and 4, 'protection' shall include matters affecting the availability, acquisition, scope, maintenance and enforcement of intellectual property rights as well as those matters affecting the use of intellectual property rights specifically addressed in this Agreement."

299.   The European Communities claimed before the Panel that Sections 211(a)(2) and (b) are inconsistent with Article 4 of the *TRIPS Agreement*.

300.   The Panel found that:

Section 211(a)(2) does not deny Cuban nationals any advantage, favour, privilege or immunity that it accords to other foreign nationals. We therefore find that Section 211(a)(2) is not inconsistent with Article 4 of the TRIPS Agreement. [218]

301.   With respect to Section 211(b), the Panel stated that the issue was the same as that examined in connection with Section 211(a)(2), and concluded:

As we are faced with the same issue that was examined in connection with Section 211(a)(2), we refer to our reasons set out in paragraphs 8.145 to 8.147 and find that Section 211(b) is not inconsistent with Article 4 of the TRIPS Agreement. [219]

302.   The European Communities appeals these findings of the Panel on both Section 211(a)(2) and Section 211(b).

303.   Before proceeding with our analysis, we find it necessary to address the scope of our examination of this issue. In the light of the claim raised by the European Communities, the Panel limited its examination and findings to the particular situation of Cuban confiscations. [220] Neither the European Communities nor the United States has disputed this point on appeal. Therefore, we also restrict our analysis to that particular situation.

---

[218] Panel Report, para. 8.148.

[219] *Ibid.*, para. 8.176.

[220] In para. 8.143, the Panel explained the parties' position on this issue as follows:

In response to the question as to whether Article 4 of the TRIPS Agreement allows a Member to have a certain policy applicable to confiscations of trademarks in one Member on the condition that all WTO Member nationals are treated similarly or whether Article 4 requires that a similar policy be applied to confiscations of trademarks in all other Members, the European Communities states that the most-favoured-nation treatment flowing from Article 4 attaches to persons and not to situations. The European Communities argues, therefore, that Article 4 requires that all nationals of other Members be treated similarly in respect of a certain event. In response to the same question, the United States submitted that because the European Communities is alleging a violation of the most-favoured-nation principle based on the first situation described by the Panel, there is no need to examine the question of whether Article 4 applies to the second situation.

304.   We note also that, with respect to the most-favoured-nation obligation, the European Communities has not presented arguments on appeal addressing the Panel's findings with respect to the level of successors-in-interest. Thus, we do not consider this to be before us on appeal, and, therefore, we will limit our discussion to the Panel's findings with respect to the alleged discrimination involving *original owners*.

305.   The allegations submitted by the European Communities on most-favoured-nation treatment of original owners are similar to those described in the previous section on national treatment. As it did with respect to national treatment, the European Communities supports its claim under Article 4 of the *TRIPS Agreement* by focusing on a particular set of circumstances that exists under the statute, *on its face*, involving original owners. [221]

306.   Like the situation posed by the European Communities earlier, the one set forth in the most-favoured-nation treatment involves two separate owners who acquired rights, either at common law or based on registration, in two separate United States trademarks, before the Cuban confiscation occurred. Each of these two United States trademarks is the same, or substantially similar to, signs or a combination of signs of which a trademark registered in Cuba is composed. That same or similar Cuban trademark was used in connection with a business or assets that were confiscated in Cuba. Neither of the two original owners of the two United States trademarks was the owner of that same or similar trademark that was registered in Cuba. Those two original owners each now seek to assert rights in the United States in their two respective United States trademarks. The situation of these two original owners of these two United States trademarks is identical in every relevant respect, but one. That one difference is this: one original owner is a national of Cuba, and the other original owner is a national of a country other than Cuba or the United States. We will refer, for the sake of convenience, to this other original owner as "a non-Cuban foreign national".

307.   Pointing to this particular situation, the European Communities argues that, on the face of the statute, the original owner who is a Cuban national is subject to Sections 211(a)(2) and (b), and the original owner who is a non-Cuban foreign national is not. This alone, as the European Communities sees it, is sufficient for us to find that Sections 211(a)(2) and (b) violate the most-favoured-nation obligation of the United States.

308.   We agree with the European Communities that the situation it describes on appeal is within the scope of the statute *on its face*. As we explained earlier, the term "designated national" as defined in Section 515.305 of 31 CFR and Section 211(d)(1) includes non-Cuban foreign nationals only when they are successors-in-interest to Cuba or a Cuban national. [222] Non-Cuban foreign nationals

---

[221]   See *supra*, para. 276. We also note that the European Communities confirmed this in its responses to questioning at the oral hearing.
[222]   The situation discussed here does not involve successors-in-interest. See *supra*, para. 279.

who are original owners are not covered by the definition of "designated national"[223] and are thereby not subject to Sections 211(a)(2) and (b).

309.   Therefore, here too, as with national treatment, the European Communities has established a *prima facie* case that Sections 211(a)(2) and (b) are discriminatory on their face, as between a Cuban national and a non-Cuban foreign national both of whom are original owners of United States trademarks composed of the same or substantially similar signs as a trademark used in connection with a business or assets that were confiscated in Cuba.

310.   As it did in respect of the national treatment claim, the United States attempts to rebut the European Communities' most-favoured-nation claim with arguments intended to demonstrate that Sections 211(a)(2) and (b) do not apply to a Cuban national who is an original owner of a United States trademark. The United States arguments on this claim are the same as their arguments on national treatment. We have already addressed these arguments. And, as these United States arguments have not changed, our conclusions have not changed either. We will, nevertheless, recall, briefly, the arguments submitted by the United States and will also restate our conclusions with respect to each.

311.   The United States submits that Sections 211(a)(2) and (b) do not apply to Cuban nationals that are original owners because they have their own consent. We explained earlier that this is not necessarily the case where a Cuban original owner of a trademark in the United States is not the same person as the original owner of the same or substantially similar Cuban trademark.[224]

312.   The United States also argues that Section 211(a)(2) does not apply to the Cuban nationals in the situation posed by the European Communities because Section 515.527 of Title 31 CFR was not in effect when the original owners in this situation obtained their trademark rights in the United States. Previously, we explained that this argument does not apply to common law rights and that registered trademarks eventually would become subject to the application of Section 515.527 of Title 31 CFR upon renewal of the registration after entry into force of that Section.[225]

313.   In addition, the United States alleges that the Cuban original owner could not have maintained its common law rights in the United States trademark because it would have been unable to import the trademarked goods from Cuba. Previously, we stated that this argument is not persuasive because the Cuban holder of common law trademark rights in the United States could import the trademarked goods from a country other than Cuba.[226]

314.   The United States further asserts that the Cuban original owner could be "unblocked" by OFAC under Section 515.505. As we explained in our analysis of the national treatment claim, using three distinct situations as examples, only

---

[223]   The term "designated national" also includes persons that are "specially designated nationals". However, as we noted earlier, the situation posed by the European Communities does not involve a "specially designated national". See *supra*, footnote 200.

[224]   See *supra*, para. 282.

[225]   See *supra*, paras. 283 and 284.

[226]   See *supra*, para. 285 and footnote 206.

Cuban nationals that reside in the United States are automatically licensed as "unblocked".[227] Cuban nationals that reside in a country that is part of the "authorized trade territory"[228], such as the Members States of the European Communities, can apply to OFAC to be "unblocked". This implies that Cuban nationals that reside in the "authorized trade territory" face an additional administrative procedure that does not apply to non-Cuban foreign nationals who are original owners, because the latter are not "designated nationals".[229] Therefore, as we stated earlier, treatment that is inherently less favourable persists. Those Cuban nationals that reside in countries not part of the "authorized trade territory", such as Cuba, are not licensed as "unblocked" nor can they apply to be "unblocked". Thus, discrimination remains in this third situation as well.[230]

315.   The United States also argues that any discrimination found in Sections 211(a)(2) and (b) would be offset by Section 515.201 of Title 31 CFR. In the context of the national treatment claim, we analyzed this argument in relation to United States nationals. In the context of the claim under Article 4 at issue here, we must examine whether Section 515.201 of Title 31 CFR also applies to non-Cuban foreign nationals.

316.   Section 515.201 of Title 31 CFR essentially applies to transactions carried out by persons in the United States or subject to United States jurisdiction. In this regard, Section 515.201 of Title 31 CFR does not apply exclusively to United States nationals. It could apply to a non-Cuban foreign national as well.

317.   The fact that Section 515.201 of Title 31 CFR *could* also apply to a non-Cuban foreign national does not mean, however, that it would offset *in each and every case* the discriminatory treatment imposed by Sections 211(a)(2) and (b) on Cuban original owners. As we explained before, for the United States argument to hold true in each and every situation, the scope of "having an interest in" that is found in Section 515.201 would necessarily have to overlap in coverage with the scope of the "used in connection with" criterion found in Sections 211(a)(2) and (b). The United States was unable to point to evidence substantiating that these two standards overlap completely.[231] We are, therefore, not satisfied that Section 515.201 would offset the inherently less favourable treatment present in Sections 211(a)(2) and (b) in each and every case.[232]

318.   Finally, the United States referred to its longstanding doctrine of non-recognition of foreign confiscations.[233] Earlier, we concluded that this policy could not possibly apply to trademarks that existed *in the United States* at the time when a business or assets were confiscated *in Cuba* in connection with

---

[227]   See *supra*, para. 288.
[228]   The term "authorized trade territory" essentially includes countries that are not subject to OFAC sanctions. See *supra*, footnote 212.
[229]   See *supra*, para. 289.
[230]   See *supra*, para. 290.
[231]   United States' responses to questioning at the oral hearing.
[232]   See *supra*, para. 294.
[233]   United States' appellee's submission, para. 16.

which a trademark composed of the same or substantially similar signs was used.[234]

319.   We, therefore, reverse the Panel's findings in paragraphs 8.148 and 8.176 of the Panel Report, to the extent that they concern the treatment of original owners, and find, in this respect, that Section 211(a)(2) and Section 211(b) are inconsistent with Article 4 of the *TRIPS Agreement*.

XI.   ARTICLE 8 OF THE PARIS CONVENTION (1967) – TRADE NAMES

320.   We turn, lastly, to the issue of whether trade names are covered by the *TRIPS Agreement*.

321.   Article 8 of the Paris Convention (1967) provides:

> A trade name shall be protected in all the countries of the Union without the obligation of filing or registration, whether or not it forms part of a trademark.

322.   There is no question that trade names are covered by the Paris Convention (1967). The question before us is whether trade names are also covered by the *TRIPS Agreement*. On this, the Panel found:

> *[W]e conclude that the categories of intellectual property covered by the TRIPS Agreement are those referred to in Article 1.2.* Article 8 of the Paris Convention (1967) is relevant as part of the TRIPS Agreement to the extent that it may affect the protection of the categories of intellectual property covered by the Agreement. As *trade names are not a category of intellectual property covered by the TRIPS Agreement*, Members do not have obligations under the TRIPS Agreement to provide protection to trade names.[235] (emphasis added)

323.   As a consequence of this conclusion, the Panel limited its finding on the inconsistency of Section 211(a)(2) with Article 42 of the *TRIPS Agreement* to trademarks.[236] Also as a consequence of this conclusion, the Panel found that Sections 211(a)(2) and (b) are not inconsistent with Article 2.1 of the *TRIPS Agreement* in conjunction with Article 8 of the Paris Convention (1967).[237] However, we do not find a similarly clear limitation in the Panel's findings with respect to Articles 3.1 and 4 of the *TRIPS Agreement*.

324.   The European Communities asks us to reverse the Panel's finding that trade names are not covered in the *TRIPS Agreement*. In addition, the European Communities asks us to:

---

[234]   See *supra*, para. 295.
[235]   Panel Report, para. 8.41.
[236]   *Ibid.*, paras. 8.102 and 9.1(d).
[237]   *Ibid.*, paras. 8.122 and 9.1(f) and paras. 8.165 and 9.1(l).

(a)   reverse the Panel's findings that Sections 211(a)(2) and (b) are not inconsistent with Article 2.1 of the *TRIPS Agreement* in conjunction with Article 8 of the Paris Convention (1967);

(b)   find that Sections 211(a)(2) and (b) are inconsistent with Article 42 of the *TRIPS Agreement* with respect of trade names;

(c)   find that Sections 211(a)(2) and (b) are inconsistent with Article 2.1 of the *TRIPS Agreement* in conjunction with Article 2(1) of the Paris Convention (1967) and with Article 3.1 of the *TRIPS Agreement* with regard to trade names; and

(d)   find that Sections 211(a)(2) and (b) are inconsistent with Article 4 of the *TRIPS Agreement* with regard to trade names.

325.   The United States agrees with the European Communities that the Panel erred in finding that the *TRIPS Agreement* contains no obligations with respect to trade names.

326.   On this issue, we begin with a review of the Panel's analysis of whether trade names are covered by the *TRIPS Agreement*. The Panel looked first to Article 1.2 of the *TRIPS Agreement*, which provides:

> For the purposes of this Agreement, the term "intellectual property" refers to all categories of intellectual property that are the subject of Sections 1 through 7 of Part II.

327.   The Panel reasoned that:

> Sections 1 through 7 of Part II of the TRIPS Agreement deal with *the following categories of intellectual property*: copyright and related rights; trademarks; geographical indications; industrial designs; patents; layout-designs (topographies) of integrated circuits; and protection of undisclosed information. The categories of related rights covered by Article 14 are protection of performers, producers of phonograms and broadcasting organizations.[238] (emphasis added)

328.   The Panel assumed that "[c]ategories of protectable subject matters not dealt within Sections 1 to 7 of Part II of the TRIPS Agreement are not included in the definition of 'intellectual property' in Article 1.2" and observed that "Sections 1 to 7 of Part II do not contain any reference to trade names".[239] The Panel referred to the interpretive principles found in Article 31 of the *Vienna Convention*, and drew the following conclusion:

> We interpret the terms "intellectual property" and "intellectual property rights" with reference to the definition of "intellectual property" in Article 1.2 of the TRIPS Agreement. The textual reading of Article 1.2 is that it establishes an inclusive definition and

---

[238]   Panel Report, para. 8.24.
[239]   *Ibid.*, para. 8.25.

this is confirmed by the words "all categories"; the word "all" indicates that this is an exhaustive list.[240]

329.   Having thus determined provisionally that trade names are not covered in the *TRIPS Agreement*, the Panel then addressed the meaning to be given to Article 2.1 of the *TRIPS Agreement*, which provides as follows:

> In respect of Parts II, III and IV of this Agreement, Members shall comply with Articles 1 through 12, and Article 19, of the Paris Convention (1967).

330.   As we pointed out earlier, Article 8 of the Paris Convention (1967) specifically requires trade name protection.

331.   However, the Panel interpreted the words "in respect of" in Article 2.1 as limiting the incorporation of the provisions of the Paris Convention (1967), including Article 8, to Parts II, III and IV of the *TRIPS Agreement*. The Panel reasoned as follows:

> The second subclause of Article 2.1 obliges Members to comply with the provisions of the Paris Convention (1967) which are identified in that provision. However, the second subclause is conditioned by the first subclause: Members shall comply with the obligations "*[i]n respect of* Parts II, III and IV of this Agreement". As the ordinary meaning of the term "in respect of" is in "relation [to], connection [with], reference [to]" and it refers to Parts II, III and IV explicitly, *we consider that Members have to comply with Articles 1 through 12 and 19 of the Paris Convention (1967) "in respect" of what is covered by those parts of the TRIPS Agreement identified therein*, namely copyright and related rights; trademarks; geographical indications; industrial designs; patents; layout-designs (topographies) of integrated circuits; and protection of undisclosed information.[241] (underlining added, footnotes omitted)

332.   Relying on Article 32 of the *Vienna Convention*, the Panel also reviewed the negotiating history of Articles 1.2 and 2.1 of the *TRIPS Agreement* and concluded that this history confirmed its interpretation of the scope of the *TRIPS Agreement*.[242]

333.   We disagree with the Panel's reasoning and with the Panel's conclusion on the scope of the *TRIPS Agreement* as it relates to trade names.

334.   To explain, we turn first to the Panel's interpretation of Article 1.2 of the *TRIPS Agreement*, which, we recall, provides:

> For the purposes of this Agreement, the term "intellectual property" refers to all categories of intellectual property that are the subject of Sections 1 through 7 of Part II.

---

[240]   Panel Report, para. 8.26.
[241]   Panel Report, para. 8.30.
[242]   *Ibid.*, paras. 8.31-8.40.

335. The Panel interpreted the phrase "'intellectual property' refers to all categories of intellectual property that are the *subject* of Sections 1 through 7 of Part II" (emphasis added) as if that phrase read "intellectual property means those categories of intellectual property appearing in the *titles* of Sections 1 through 7 of Part II." To our mind, the Panel's interpretation ignores the plain words of Article 1.2, for it fails to take into account that the phrase "the subject of Sections 1 through 7 of Part II" deals not only with the categories of intellectual property indicated in each section *title*, but with other *subjects* as well. For example, in Section 5 of Part II, entitled "Patents", Article 27(3)(b) provides that Members have the option of protecting inventions of plant varieties by *sui generis* rights (such as breeder's rights) instead of through patents.[243] Under the Panel's theory, such *sui generis* rights would not be covered by the *TRIPS Agreement*. The option provided by Article 27(3)(b) would be read out of the *TRIPS Agreement*.

336. Moreover, we do not believe that the Panel's interpretation of Article 1.2 can be reconciled with the plain words of Article 2.1. Article 2.1 explicitly incorporates Article 8 of the Paris Convention (1967) into the *TRIPS Agreement*.

337. The Panel was of the view that the words "in respect of" in Article 2.1 have the effect of "conditioning" Members' obligations under the Articles of the Paris Convention (1967) incorporated into the *TRIPS Agreement*, with the result that trade names are not covered. We disagree.

338. Article 8 of the Paris Convention (1967) covers only the protection of trade names; Article 8 has no other subject. If the intention of the negotiators had been to exclude trade names from protection, there would have been no purpose whatsoever in including Article 8 in the list of Paris Convention (1967) provisions that were specifically incorporated into the *TRIPS Agreement*. To adopt the Panel's approach would be to deprive Article 8 of the Paris Convention (1967), as incorporated into the *TRIPS Agreement* by virtue of Article 2.1 of that Agreement, of any and all meaning and effect. As we have stated previously:

> One of the corollaries of the "general rule of interpretation" in the *Vienna Convention* is that interpretation must give meaning and effect to all the terms of a treaty. An interpreter is not free to adopt a reading that would result in reducing whole clauses or paragraphs of a treaty to redundancy or inutility.[244]

---

[243] Article 27.3(b) of the *TRIPS Agreement* provides:
  Members may also exclude from patentability:

  …

  (b)   plants and animals other than micro-organisms, and essentially biological processes for the production of plants or animals other than non-biological and microbiological processes. However, Members shall provide for the protection of plant varieties either by patents or by an effective *sui generis* system or by any combination thereof. The provisions of this subparagraph shall be reviewed four years after the date of entry into force of the WTO Agreement.

[244] Appellate Body Report, *US – Gasoline, supra*, footnote 102, DSR 1996:I, 3, at 21. See also, Appellate Body Report, *Japan – Alcoholic Beverages II*, *supra*, footnote 102, DSR 1996:I, 97, at 106.

339.   As for the import of the negotiating history, we do not see it as in any way decisive to the issue before us. The documents on which the Panel relied are not conclusive of whether the *TRIPS Agreement* covers trade names. The passages quoted by the Panel from the negotiating history of Article 1.2 do not even refer to trade names. There is nothing at all in those passages to suggest that Members were either for or against their inclusion. Indeed, the only reference to a debate about the categories for coverage in the *TRIPS Agreement* relates, not to trade names, but to trade secrets. [245] The Panel itself acknowledged that "[t]he records do not contain information on the purpose of the addition" [246] of the words "in respect of" at the beginning of Article 2.1. Therefore, we do not consider that any conclusions may be drawn from these records about the interpretation of the words "in respect of" in Article 2.1 as regards trade names.

340.   Thus, in our view, the Panel's interpretation of Articles 1.2 and 2.1 of the *TRIPS Agreement* is contrary to the ordinary meaning of the terms of those provisions and is, therefore, not in accordance with the customary rules of interpretation prescribed in Article 31 of the *Vienna Convention*. [247] Moreover, we do not believe that the negotiating history confirms, within the meaning of Article 32 of the *Vienna Convention*, the Panel's interpretation of Articles 1.2 and 2.1.

341.   For all these reasons, we reverse the Panel's finding in paragraph 8.41 of the Panel Report that trade names are not covered under the *TRIPS Agreement* and find that WTO Members do have an obligation under the *TRIPS Agreement* to provide protection to trade names.

342.   Having reversed the Panel's finding, we consider next whether we should complete the legal analysis with respect to the application of Section 211 to trade names and to the consistency of Section 211 with Article 2.1 of the *TRIPS Agreement* in conjunction with Article 8 of the Paris Convention (1967), with Article 2.1 of the *TRIPS Agreement* in conjunction with Article 2(1) of the Paris Convention (1967) and Article 3.1 of the *TRIPS Agreement*, with Article 4 of the *TRIPS Agreement*, and with Article 42 of the *TRIPS Agreement*.

343.   In the past, we have completed the analysis where there were sufficient factual findings in the panel report or undisputed facts in the panel record to enable us to do so [248], and we have not completed the analysis where there were

---

[245]   Panel Report, para. 8.34.

[246]   *Ibid.*, para. 8.39.

[247]   See Article 3.2 of the DSU.

[248]   See Appellate Body Report, *US – Gasoline, supra*, footnote 102, DSR 1996:I, 3, at 18 ff; Appellate Body Report, *Canada – Certain Measures Concerning Periodicals*, WT/DS31/AB/R, adopted 30 July 1997, DSR 1997:I, 449, at 469 ff; Appellate Body Report, *EC – Hormones, supra*, footnote 46, paras. 222 ff; Appellate Body Report, *European Communities – Measures Affecting the Importation of Certain Poultry Products*, WT/DS69/AB/R, adopted 23 July 1998, DSR 1998:V, 2031, paras. 156 ff; Appellate Body Report, *Australia – Measures Affecting Importation of Salmon* ("*Australia – Salmon*"), WT/DS18/AB/R, adopted 6 November 1998, DSR 1998:VIII, 3327, paras. 117 ff, 193 ff and 227 ff; Appellate Body Report, *United States – Import Prohibition of Certain Shrimp and Shrimp Products*, WT/DS58/AB/R, adopted 6 November 1998, DSR 1998:VII, 2755, paras. 123 ff; Appellate Body Report, *Japan – Measures Affecting Agricultural Products*, WT/DS76/AB/R ("*Japan – Agricultural Products II*"), *supra*, footnote 102, paras. 112 ff; Appellate Body Report, *United States – Tax Treatment for "Foreign Sales Corporations"*, WT/DS108/AB/R, adopted 20 March 2000, DSR

---

not.[249] In one instance, we declined to complete the analysis with respect to a "novel" issue that had not been argued in sufficient detail before the panel.[250]

344. In this appeal, the European Communities argues that we should complete the analysis, while the United States contends that we should not do so because, in its view, there are insufficient factual findings by the Panel about trade name protection under United States law for us to do so. The United States argues further that should we decide to complete the analysis, we should find that Sections 211(a)(2) and (b) are not inconsistent with any trade name obligations under either the *TRIPS Agreement* or the Paris Convention (1967).

345. We believe that there are sufficient undisputed facts in the Panel record regarding trade name protection to enable us to complete the analysis dealing with the alleged inconsistency of Sections 211(a)(2) and (b) with Articles 3.1, 4, and 42 of the *TRIPS Agreement*, and with Article 2.1 of that Agreement in conjunction with Articles 2(1) and 8 of the Paris Convention (1967).

346. In this respect, we note that Sections 211(a)(2) and (b) do not distinguish on their face between trademarks and trade names. Both types of intellectual property are subject to Sections 211(a)(2) and (b). We note also that both participants agree that the Panel's finding with respect to coverage of trade names under the *TRIPS Agreement* was in error. Both participants referred to protection of trade names as well as trademarks throughout their submissions before the Panel, often interchangeably, both "accepting as a given that trade names are within the scope of [the] TRIPS [Agreement]".[251] The result is that there is sufficient information about trade names in the Panel record.

347. The Panel inquired specifically into the protection of trade names under United States law. The United States gave the following response regarding trade

---

2000:III, 1619, paras. 133 ff; Appellate Body Report, *Canada – Measures Affecting the Export of Civilian Aircraft, Recourse by Brazil to Article 21.5 of the DSU*, WT/DS70/AB/RW, adopted 4 August 2000, DSR 2000:IX, 4299, paras. 43 ff; Appellate Body Report, *United States – Definitive Safeguard Measures on Imports of Wheat Gluten from the European Communities*, WT/DS166/AB/R, adopted 19 January 2001, DSR 2001:II, 717, paras. 80 ff and 127 ff, Appellate Body Report, *European Communities – Measures Affecting Asbestos and Asbestos-Containing Products* ("*EC – Asbestos*"), WT/DS135/AB/R, adopted 5 April 2001, DSR 2001:VII, 3243, paras. 133 ff, Appellate Body Report, *United States – Safeguard Measures on Imports of Fresh, Chilled or Frozen Lamb Meat from New Zealand and Australia*, WT/DS177/AB/R, WT/DS178/AB/R, adopted 16 May 2001, DSR 2001:IX, 4051, paras. 150 ff and 172 ff.

[249] See Appellate Body Report, *Australia – Salmon, supra*, footnote 248, paras. 209 ff, 241 ff and 255; Appellate Body Report, *Korea – Definitive Safeguard Measure on Imports of Certain Dairy Products*, WT/DS98/AB/R, adopted 12 January 2000, DSR 2000:I, 3, paras. 91 ff and 102 ff; Appellate Body Report, *Canada – Certain Measures Affecting the Automotive Industry*, WT/DS139/AB/R, WT/DS142/AB/R, adopted 19 June 2000, DSR 2000:VI, 2985, paras. 133 ff and 144 ff; Appellate Body Report, *Korea – Measures Affecting Imports of Fresh, Chilled and Frozen Beef*, WT/DS161/AB/R, WT/DS169/AB/R, adopted 10 January 2001, DSR 2001:I, 5, paras. 128 ff; Appellate Body Report, *EC – Asbestos, supra*, footnote 248, paras. 78 ff; Appellate Body Report, *Canada – Measures Affecting the Importation of Milk and the Exportation of Dairy Products, Recourse to Article 21.5 of the DSU by New Zealand and the United States*, WT/DS103/AB/RW, WT/DS113/AB/RW, adopted 18 December 2001, DSR 2001:XIII, 6829, paras. 98 ff.

[250] Appellate Body Report, *EC – Asbestos, supra*, footnote 248, para. 84.

[251] European Communities' appellant's submission, footnote 7 to para. 21, quoting the United States' request to the Panel to review precise aspects of the interim report.

---

name protection to a question posed by the Panel, suggesting that trade name protection is identical to that afforded common law trademarks:[252]

> Section 43 of the Trademark Act, 15 U.S.C. 1125, provides the legal basis for pursuing unfair competition claims with respect to trademarks, trade names and commercial names. The owner of any of these types of property may assert rights as a plaintiff.
>
> ...
>
> A "trade name" and a "commercial name" (hereinafter collectively: "trade name") are synonymous under the Lanham Act and are defined as "any name used by a person to identify his or her business or vocation". *See* Sec. 45 of the Lanham Act (Definitions), 15 U.S.C. §1127 (Exhibit US-28). Trade names are not entitled to federal registration under the Lanham Act. Trade names are protectable under the common law, upon a showing of secondary meaning. *A party claiming a trade name infringement may bring a suit in state court or initiate a federal suit under §43(a) of the Lanham Act, 13 U.S.C. §1125(a), in the same manner as a party claiming common-law-rights in an unregistered trademark. No presumptions of validity or ownership are accorded to a trade-name or common law trademark owner.* (emphasis added)

348.   Regarding the protection afforded trade names under Article 2.1 of the *TRIPS Agreement* in conjunction with Article 8 of the Paris Convention (1967), the position of the United States before the Panel was as follows:

> The obligations of Article 8 are straightforward. A Member has to offer some protection to trade names, without the requirement of filing or registration and regardless of whether it forms part of a trademark
>
> ...
>
> Article 8 does not impose any requirements on the scope of protection, other than, through Article 2 [of the Paris Convention], the requirement of national treatment.[253]

349.   The European Communities also submitted that the scope of protection under Article 8 was not precise. It said:

> The European Communities argues that Article 8 of the Paris Convention (1967) requires that WTO Members extend protection to trade names independently from whether they form part of a trademark. While Article 8 does not precisely stipulate the way in which this protection for trade/commercial names has to be granted, one of the leading commentators writes that "[t]he protection will generally be given against unlawful acts of third parties

---

[252]   Question 9 from the Panel to the United States reads: "Please explain how common law rights in relation to trademarks, trade names and commercial names are protected under US law."
[253]   United States' first submission to the Panel, para. 94. See also Panel Report, para. 4.105.

> consisting, for example, of use of the same or a confusingly similar trade name [...], if such use is liable to cause confusion among the public".[254] (footnote and underlining omitted)

350.   Moreover, in their submissions before the Panel on the consistency of Sections 211(a)(2) and (b) with Article 2.1 of the *TRIPS Agreement* in conjunction with Article 2(1) of the Paris Convention (1967), Articles 3.1, 4 and 42 of the *TRIPS Agreement*, both participants put forward the same arguments on trade names that they did with respect to trademarks. The United States also argued before the Panel that:

> ... it cannot be asserted that the protections given trade names must be more stringent than those given trademarks. Therefore, for reasons asserted throughout this submission with respect to trademarks, sections 211(a)(2) and 211(b) are not inconsistent with Article 8 of the Paris Convention.[255]

351.   We note further that, in its request pursuant to Article 15 of the DSU for interim review of certain aspects of the Panel Report, the United States argued that "the analysis of the [European Communities'] claims with request [*sic*] to trade names would not differ from that relating to trademarks."[256] This argument by the United States was quoted in this appeal by the European Communities without objection by the United States.

352.   On the basis of:

— the fact that Sections 211(a)(2) and (b) do not distinguish on their face between trade marks and trade names;

— the participants' approach in submitting the same arguments and using the same analyses regarding trade name and trademark protection, suggesting that the obligations regarding protection of one are no different from those regarding protection of the other;

— the information in the Panel record about the participants' interpretation of Article 8 of the Paris Convention (1967); and

— the information in the Panel record about trade name protection under United States law;

we conclude that the Panel record contains sufficient factual findings and facts undisputed between the participants to permit us to complete the analysis regarding the consistency of Sections 211(a)(2) and (b) – in respect of trade names – with Article 2.1 of the *TRIPS Agreement* in conjunction with Article 2(1) of the Paris Convention (1967) and Article 3.1 of the *TRIPS Agreement*, with Article 4 of the *TRIPS Agreement*, with Article 42 of the *TRIPS Agreement*, and with Article 2.1 of that Agreement in conjunction with Article 8 of the Paris Convention (1967).

---

[254]   Panel Report, para. 4.102.

[255]   United States' first submission to the Panel, para. 95. See also Panel Report, para. 4.106.

[256]   European Communities' appellant's submission, footnote 7 to para. 21, quoting the United States' request to the Panel to review precise aspects of the interim report.

353.   In respect of the alleged inconsistency of Sections 211(a)(2) and (b) with Article 2.1 of the *TRIPS Agreement* in conjunction with Article 2(1) of the Paris Convention (1967) and Article 3.1 of the *TRIPS Agreement*, and with Article 4 of the *TRIPS Agreement*, we recall our conclusions above that these Sections impose on designated nationals and their successors-in-interest the requirement to obtain the express consent of the original owners or their *bona fide* successors-in-interest.[257] We note that the requirement to obtain express consent applies not only to the defined category of *trademarks* referred to in those Sections. It applies also to the defined category of *trade names* referred to in those Sections.[258]   We also recall that Section 211(a)(2), read in conjunction with Section 211(d), applies only to successors-in-interest of non-United States origin, whereas Section 211(b) applies to successors-in-interest of any origin.[259]

354.   Therefore, we find that our conclusion in paragraph 268 above that, by applying the "extra hurdle" imposed by Section 211(a)(2) only to non-United States successors-in-interest to trademark rights referred to in that Section, the United States violates the national treatment obligation in Article 2.1 of the *TRIPS Agreement* in conjunction with Article 2(1) of the Paris Convention (1967) and Article 3.1 of the *TRIPS Agreement*, applies also to successors-in-interest in trade names referred to in that Section.

355.   We find further that our conclusion in paragraph 272 above that, at the level of successors-in-interest to trademark rights referred to in that Section, Section 211(b) is not inconsistent with Article 2.1 of the *TRIPS Agreement* in conjunction with Article 2(1) of the Paris Convention (1967) and Article 3.1 of the *TRIPS Agreement*, applies also to successors-in-interest to trade names referred to in that Section.

356.   We find also that our conclusion in paragraph 296 above that Sections 211(a)(2) and (b) are inconsistent with Article 2.1 of the *TRIPS Agreement* in conjunction with Article 2(1) of the Paris Convention (1967) and Article 3.1 of the *TRIPS Agreement*, to the extent that they concern the treatment of original owners of trademarks referred to in those Sections, applies also to original owners of trade names referred to in Sections 211(a)(2) and (b).

357.   We find as well that our conclusion in paragraph 319 above that Sections 211(a)(2) and (b) are inconsistent with Article 4 of the *TRIPS Agreement*, to the extent that they concern the treatment of original owners of trademarks referred to in those Sections, applies also to original owners of trade names referred to in Sections 211(a)(2) and (b).

358.   We recall our conclusion in paragraph 231 above that Sections 211(a)(2) and (b) are *not* inconsistent with Article 42 of the *TRIPS Agreement* as far as holders of rights in trademarks referred to in those Sections are concerned. We note that, as with right holders in trademarks, those Sections only require the United States courts not to recognize, enforce or otherwise validate any assertion

---

[257]   See *supra*, paras. 120 and 121.
[258]   See *supra*, para. 2.
[259]   See *supra*, paras. 268 and 271.

of rights by designated nationals or successors-in-interest who have been determined, after applying United States Federal Rules of Civil Procedure and Federal Rules of Evidence, not to own the trade names referred to in Sections 211(a)(2) and (b). Therefore, we find that Sections 211(a)(2) and (b) are not inconsistent with Article 42 of the *TRIPS Agreement* as regards holders of rights in trade names referred to in those Sections.

359.   We recall further our conclusion in paragraph 195 above of the section addressing Article 16.1 of the *TRIPS Agreement* that neither the Paris Convention (1967) nor the *TRIPS Agreement* determines who owns or who does not own a trademark. We believe that the Paris Convention (1967) and the *TRIPS Agreement* also do not determine who owns or does not own a trade name. Given our view that Sections 211(a)(2) and (b) relate to ownership[260], we conclude that these Sections are not inconsistent with Article 2.1 of the *TRIPS Agreement* in conjunction with Article 8 of the Paris Convention (1967).

XII.   FINDINGS AND CONCLUSIONS

360.   For the reasons set out in this Report, the Appellate Body:

   (a)   upholds the Panel's finding in paragraph 8.89 of the Panel Report that Section 211(a)(1) is not inconsistent with Article 2.1 of the *TRIPS Agreement* in conjunction with Article 6*quinquies* A(1) of the Paris Convention (1967);

   (b)   upholds the Panel's finding in paragraph 8.70 of the Panel Report that Section 211(a)(1) is not inconsistent with Article 15.1 of the *TRIPS Agreement*;

   (c)   upholds the Panel's findings in paragraphs 8.112 and 8.159 of the Panel Report and finds that Sections 211(a)(2) and (b) are not inconsistent with Article 16.1 of the *TRIPS Agreement*;

   (d)   with respect to Article 42 of the *TRIPS Agreement*, and in relation to trademarks:

      (i)   reverses the Panel's finding in paragraph 8.102 of the Panel Report and finds that Section 211(a)(2) is not inconsistent with this Article; and

      (ii)   upholds the Panel's finding in paragraph 8.162 of the Panel Report and finds that Section 211(b) is not inconsistent with this Article;

   (e)   with respect to Article 2.1 of the *TRIPS Agreement* in conjunction with Article 2(1) of the Paris Convention (1967) and Article 3.1 of the *TRIPS Agreement*, and in relation to trademarks:

      (i)   regarding successors-in-interest:

---

[260]   See *supra*, para. 121.

> (a) reverses the Panel's finding in paragraph 8.140 of the Panel Report and finds that Section 211(a)(2) is inconsistent with these Articles;
>
> (b) upholds the Panel's finding in paragraph 8.173 of the Panel Report and finds that Section 211(b) is not inconsistent with these Articles;

> (ii) regarding original owners, reverses the Panel's findings in paragraphs 8.140 and 8.173 of the Panel Report and finds that Section 211(a)(2) and Section 211(b) are inconsistent with these Articles;

(f) reverses the Panel's findings in paragraphs 8.148 and 8.176 of the Panel Report regarding original owners and finds that, in this respect, and in relation to trademarks, Sections 211(a)(2) and (b) are inconsistent with Article 4 of the *TRIPS Agreement.*

(g) reverses the Panel's finding in paragraph 8.41 of the Panel Report that trade names are not covered under the *TRIPS Agreement*, and finds that WTO Members do have an obligation under the *TRIPS Agreement* to provide protection to trade names, and accordingly:

> (i) with respect to Article 2.1 of the *TRIPS Agreement* in conjunction with Article 2(1) of the Paris Convention (1967) and Article 3.1 of the *TRIPS Agreement,* and in relation to trade names:
>
> > (a) regarding successors-in-interest, finds that Section 211(a)(2) is inconsistent with these Articles;
> >
> > (b) regarding successors-in-interest, finds that Section 211(b) is not inconsistent with these Articles;
> >
> > (c) regarding original owners, finds that Section 211(a)(2) and Section 211(b) are inconsistent with these Articles;
>
> (ii) finds that, in relation to trade names, Sections 211(a)(2) and (b) are inconsistent with Article 4 of the *TRIPS Agreement*;
>
> (iii) finds that, in relation to trade names, Sections 211(a)(2) and (b) are not inconsistent with Article 42 of the *TRIPS Agreement*; and
>
> (iv) finds that Sections 211(a)(2) and (b) are not inconsistent with Article 2.1 of the *TRIPS Agreement* in conjunction with Article 8 of the Paris Convention (1967).

361. The Appellate Body *recommends* that the DSB request the United States to bring its measure, found in this Report and in the Panel Report as modified by this Report to be inconsistent with the *TRIPS Agreement*, into conformity with its obligations under that Agreement.

XIII. CONCLUDING REMARKS

362.   We wish to emphasize that this ruling is not a judgment on confiscation as that term is defined in Section 211.[261] The validity of the expropriation of intellectual or any other property rights without compensation by a WTO Member within its own territory is not before us. Nor do we express any view, nor are we required to express any view in this appeal, on whether a Member of the WTO should, or should not, recognize in its own territory trademarks, trade names, or any other rights relating to any intellectual or other property rights that may have been expropriated or otherwise confiscated in other territories.

363.   However, where a WTO Member chooses not to recognize intellectual property rights in its own territory relating to a confiscation of rights in another territory, a measure resulting from and implementing that choice must, if it affects other WTO Members, comply with the *TRIPS Agreement*, by which all WTO Members are voluntarily bound. In such a measure, that WTO Member must accord "no less favourable treatment" to the nationals of all other WTO Members than it accords to its own nationals, and must grant to the nationals of all other WTO Members "any advantage, favour, privilege or immunity" granted to any other WTO Member. In such a measure, a WTO Member may not discriminate in a way that does not respect the obligations of national treatment and most-favoured-nation treatment that are fundamental to the *TRIPS Agreement*.

---

[261]   See *supra*, footnote 7.

UNITED STATES – SECTION 211 OMNIBUS APPROPRIATIONS ACT OF 1998

Report of the Panel
WT/DS176/R

*Adopted by the Dispute Settlement Body on 1 February 2002
as Modified by the Appellate Body Report*

TABLE OF CONTENTS

Page

I.   INTRODUCTION

1.1   On 7 July 1999, the European Communities and their member States (hereafter referred to as the "European Communities") requested consultations with the United States under Article 4 of the Understanding on Rules and Procedures Governing the Settlement of Disputes (the "DSU") and, to the extent it incorporates by reference Article XXIII of the General Agreement on Tariffs and Trade 1994, Article 64.1 of the Agreement on Trade-Related Aspects of Intellectual Property Rights (the "TRIPS Agreement") regarding Section 211 of the Omnibus Appropriations Act of 1998 (the "OAA").[1,2]

1.2   The European Communities and the United States held consultations on 13 September and 13 December 1999, but failed to reach a mutually satisfactory solution. On 30 June 2000, the European Communities requested the establishment of a panel under Article 6 of the DSU and Article 64.1 of the TRIPS Agreement.[3]

1.3   At its meeting on 26 September 2000, the Dispute Settlement Body (the "DSB") established a panel in accordance with Article 6 of the DSU with the following standard terms of reference:

> "To examine, in the light of the relevant provisions of the covered agreements cited by the European Communities and their member States in document WT/DS176/2, the matter referred to the DSB by the European Communities and their member States in that document and to make such findings as will assist the DSB in making the recommendations or in giving the rulings provided for in those agreements."[4]

1.4   Canada, Japan and Nicaragua reserved their rights to participate in the panel proceedings as third parties.

1.5   On 17 October 2000, the European Communities made a request, with reference to paragraph 7 of Article 8 of the DSU, to the Director-General to determine the composition of the Panel. This paragraph states:

> If there is no agreement on the panelists within 20 days after the date of the establishment of a panel, at the request of either party, the Director-General, in consultation with the Chairman of the DSB and the Chairman of the relevant Council or Committee, shall determine the composition of the panel by appointing the panelists whom the Director-General considers most appropriate in accordance with any relevant special or additional rules or procedures of the covered agreement or covered agreements which are at issue in the dispute, after consulting with the parties to the dispute. The

---

[1]   Section 211 of the Department of Commerce Appropriations Act, 1999, as included in Public Law 105-277, Section 101(b), 112 Stat. 2681, referred to in this dispute as "Section 211 Omnibus Appropriations Act of 1998".

[2]   See document WT/DS176/1; IP/D/20 (15 July 1999).

[3]   See document WT/DS176/2 (7 July 2000), reproduced in Annex 1 to this report.

[4]   See document WT/DS176/3 (27 October 2000), reproduced in Annex 2 to this report.

Chairman of the DSB shall inform the Members of the composition of the panel thus formed no later than 10 days after the date the Chairman receives such a request.

1.6   On 26 October 2000, the Director-General composed the Panel as follows:

Chairperson: Mr. Wade Armstrong

Members: Mr. François Dessemontet

                    Mr. Armand de Mestral

1.7   The Panel met with the parties on 24-25 January and 7 March 2001. It met with the third parties on 25 January 2001.

1.8   On 1 February 2001, the Panel sent a letter to the International Bureau of the World Intellectual Property Organization ("WIPO"), which is responsible for the administration of the Paris Convention for the Protection of Industrial Property. In that letter, the Panel requested factual information, consistent with Article 13 of the DSU, on the provisions of the Stockholm Act of 1967 of that Convention (the "Paris Convention (1967)"), incorporated into the TRIPS Agreement by its Article 2.1, that are relevant to the matter. It also expressed its interest in obtaining factual information on the way the determination of the owner of a trademark may have been addressed in the negotiating history of the Convention or in subsequent developments. The International Bureau of WIPO provided such information in a letter dated 2 March 2001.

1.9   The Panel submitted its interim report to the parties on 11 June 2001. The Panel submitted its final report to the parties on 3 July 2001.

II.   FACTUAL ASPECTS

2.1   The dispute concerns Section 211 of the OAA, signed into law on 21 October 1998. Section 211 deals with trademarks, trade names, and commercial names that are the same as or substantially similar to trademarks, trade names, or commercial names that were used in connection with businesses or assets that were confiscated by the Cuban Government on or after 1 January 1959. Section 211 reads as follows:

SEC. 211.   (a)(1) Notwithstanding any other provision of law, no transaction or payment shall be authorized or approved pursuant to section 515.527 of title 31, Code of Federal Regulations, as in effect on September 9, 1998, with respect to a mark, trade name, or commercial name that is the same as or substantially similar to a mark, trade name, or commercial name that was used in connection with a business or assets that were confiscated unless the original owner of the mark, trade name, or commercial name, or the bona fide successor-in-interest has expressly consented.

(2)   No U.S. court shall recognize, enforce or otherwise validate any assertion of rights by a designated national based on common

law rights or registration obtained under such section 515.527 of such a confiscated mark, trade name, or commercial name.

(b)   No U.S. court shall recognize, enforce or otherwise validate any assertion of treaty rights by a designated national or its successor-in-interest under sections 44 (b) or (e) of the Trademark Act of 1946 (15 U.S.C. 1126 (b) or (e)) for a mark, trade name, or commercial name that is the same as or substantially similar to a mark, trade name, or commercial name that was used in connection with a business or assets that were confiscated unless the original owner of such mark, trade name, or commercial name, or the bona fide successor-in-interest has expressly consented.

(c)   The Secretary of the Treasury shall promulgate such rules and regulations as are necessary to carry out the provisions of this section.

(d)   In this section:

>   (1)   The term "designated national" has the meaning given such term in section 515.305 of title 31, Code of Federal Regulations, as in effect on September 9, 1998, and includes a national of any foreign country who is a successor-in-interest to a designated national.

>   (2)   The term "confiscated" has the meaning given such term in section 515.336 of title 31, Code of Federal Regulations, as in effect on September 9, 1998.

2.2   Part 515 of title 31 of the Code of Federal Regulations (the "CFR") contains the Cuban Assets Control Regulations (the "CACR"). Section 515.305 of that Part (hereafter cited as 31 CFR 515.305) contains the definition of the term "designated national" referred to in Section 211(d)(1). It reads:

>   Section 515.305   Designated national.

>   For the purposes of this part, the term *designated national* shall mean Cuba and any national thereof including any person who is a specially designated national.[5]

2.3   Section 515.336 of title 31 of the CFR contains the definition of the term "confiscated" referred to in Section 211(d)(2). It reads:

>   Section 515.336   Confiscated.

>   As used in Section 515.208, the term *confiscated* refers to:

---

[5]   The term "specially designated national" is defined in Section 515.306 of 31 CFR, which reads:
(a) The term specially designated national shall mean:
(1) Any person who is determined by the Secretary of Treasury to be a specially designated national,
(2) Any person who on or since the "effective date" has acted for or on behalf of the Government or authorities exercising control over a designated foreign country, or
(3) Any partnership, association, corporation or other organization which on or since the "effective date" has been owned or controlled directly or indirectly by the Government or authorities exercising control over a designated foreign country or by any specially designated national.

(a) The nationalization, expropriation, or other seizure by the Cuban Government of ownership or control of property, on or after January 1, 1959:

(1) Without the property having been returned or adequate and effective compensation provided; or

(2) Without the claim to the property having been settled pursuant to an international claims settlement agreement or other mutually accepted settlement procedure; and

(b) The repudiation by the Cuban Government of, the default by the Cuban Government on, or the failure of the Cuban Government to pay, on or after January 1, 1959:

(1) A debt of any enterprise which has been nationalized, expropriated, or otherwise taken by the Cuban Government;

(2) A debt which is a charge on property nationalized, expropriated, or otherwise taken by the Cuban Government; or

(3) A debt which was incurred by the Cuban Government in satisfaction or settlement of a confiscated property claim.

2.4   Section 211(a) refers to Section 515.527 of 31 CFR, which read at the time, 21 October 1998, when Section 211 was signed into law:

Section 515.527 Certain transactions with respect to United States intellectual property.

(a) Transactions related to the registration and renewal in the United States Patent and Trademark Office or the United States Copyright Office of patents, trademarks, and copyrights in which the Government of Cuba or a Cuban national has an interest are authorized.

(b) This section authorizes the payment from blocked accounts or otherwise of fees currently due to the United States Government in connection with any transaction authorized in paragraph (a) of this section.

(c) This section further authorizes the payment from blocked accounts or otherwise of the reasonable and customary fees and charges currently due to attorneys or representatives within the United States in connection with the transactions authorized in paragraph (a) of this section.

2.5   After the entry into force of Section 211, the CACR were amended by adding a new subparagraph (a)(2) to Section 515.527 of 31 CFR. After this, its paragraph (a) became subparagraph (a)(1). The amendment entered into force on 10 May 1999. The new subparagraph (a)(2) reads:

(a)(2) No transaction or payment is authorized or approved pursuant to paragraph (a)(1) of this section with respect to a mark, trade name, or commercial name that is the same as or substantially similar to a mark, trade name, or commercial name that was used in connection with a business or assets that were confiscated, as that term is defined in section 515.336, unless the original owner of the mark, trade name, or commercial name, or the bona fide successor-in-interest has expressly consented.

2.6   Section 211(b) refers to Sections 44(b) and (e) of the Trademark Act of 1946, also referred to as the Lanham Act (15 U.S.C. § 1126 (b) and (e)), which read:

> Section 44 (15 U.S.C. §1126). International conventions; register of marks
>
> (...)
>
> (b)   Any person whose country of origin is a party to any convention or treaty relating to trademarks, trade or commercial names, or the repression of unfair competition, to which the United States is also a party, or extends reciprocal rights to nationals of the United States by law, shall be entitled to the benefits of this section under the conditions expressed herein to the extent necessary to give effect to any provision of such convention, treaty or reciprocal law, in addition to the rights to which any owner of a mark is otherwise entitled by this Act.
>
> (...)
>
> (e)   A mark duly registered in the country of origin of the foreign applicant may be registered on the principal register if eligible, otherwise on the supplemental register herein provided. Such applicant shall submit, within such time period as may be prescribed by the Director, a certification or a certified copy of the registration in the country of origin of the applicant. The application must state the applicant's bona fide intention to use the mark in commerce, but use in commerce shall not be required prior to registration.
>
> (...)

2.7   Section 211(a)(1) relates to licensing regulations contained in the CACR. Under US law, all transactions involving property under US jurisdiction in which a Cuban national has an interest require a licence from the Office of Foreign Assets Control of the US Treasury Department ("OFAC").[6] OFAC's regulations recognize two categories of licences for this purpose: specific licences and general licences. A general licence is an authorization for certain types of transactions that is set forth specifically in OFAC's regulations.[7] In effect, these are standing authorizations for the types of transactions specified in the regulations, and a person wishing to engage in such transactions does not have to apply to OFAC. A specific licence, by contrast, is one whose precise terms are not set

---

[6]   31 CFR 515.201.
[7]   31 CFR 515.317.

forth in OFAC's regulations.[8] Generally, a person wanting to engage in a transaction for which a general licence is not available applies to OFAC for a specific licence.

2.8   One of the general licences available under OFAC regulations is contained in 31 CFR 515.527 cited above. It is for transactions related to the registration and renewal in the United States Patent and Trademark Office (the "USPTO") and United States Copyright Office of patents, trademark registrations, and copyright registrations in which the Government of Cuba or a Cuban national has an interest. Section 211(a)(1) changed this OFAC general licence provision by stating that the coverage of this general licence would not include transactions or payments with respect to certain marks, trade names and commercial names – i.e., those that are the same as or similar to marks, trade names or commercial names used in connection with a business or assets confiscated by the Government of Cuba (unless the original owner or his successor-in-interest consents).

2.9   The practical effect of Section 211(a)(1) is that a general licence is not available. Section 211(a)(1) does not address OFAC specific licences, which is another means by which payments of application fees may be authorized. A decision by OFAC not to approve any transaction or payment related to the registration or renewal of a trademark would, if not set aside on judicial review, prevent such registration or renewal because the statutory fees for the filings would not be deemed to have accompanied the filing.[9]

2.10   Section 211(a)(2) directs that "[n]o U.S. court shall recognize, enforce or otherwise validate any assertion of rights by a designated national based on common law rights or registration obtained under such section 515.527 of such a confiscated mark, trade name, or commercial name". As regards registered trademarks, if a "designated national" (1) has obtained such a trademark registration under a general OFAC licence, and (2) the trademark is identical or similar to a trademark used in connection with a business confiscated without compensation by the Cuban Government, US courts will not recognize, enforce or otherwise validate any assertion of trademark rights by that person. The same is true of common law rights, including trademarks, trade names and commercial names, except that there is no federal requirement for registration.

2.11   A "designated national", in the first instance, is "Cuba and any national thereof". This is under the first part of the definition in Section 211(d)(1), which incorporates the definition of "designated national" in 31 CFR 515.305. Section 211(d)(1) provides that "designated national" includes a national of any for-

---

[8]   31 CFR 515.318.

[9]   Sub-paragraph (a)(1) of 15 U.S.C. § 1051 on "Registration of trademarks" provides that "[t]he owner of a trademark used in commerce may request registration of its trademark on the principal register hereby established by paying the prescribed fee and filing in the Patent and Trademark Office an application [...]". See also sub-paragraph (b)(1) of the same Section dealing with trademarks intended for use in commerce. Paragraph (a) of 15 U.S.C. § 1059 on "Renewal of registration" provides that "[...] each registration may be renewed for periods of 10 years at the end of each successive 10-year period following the date of registration upon payment of the prescribed fee and the filing of a written application [...]".

eign country who is a successor-in-interest to a designated national. Any transaction by which a US person could become a successor-in-interest to a Cuban confiscating entity is prohibited under 31 CFR 515.201. US nationals would need to obtain a specific licence from OFAC for that purpose. OFAC has never issued a specific licence for such a purpose.

2.12   Section 211(a)(2) provides that no US court shall recognize, enforce or otherwise validate any assertion of treaty rights by a designated national or its successor-in-interest under Sections 44 (b) or (e) of the Trademark Act of 1946 (15 U.S.C. 1126 (b) or (e)) for such a confiscated trademark, trade name, or commercial name.

2.13   The Panel notes that the only application of Section 211 by US courts to date of which the parties are aware was the application of Section 211(b) to a trade name issue in *Havana Club Holdings, S.A. v. Galleon S.A.*[10]

III.   FINDINGS AND RECOMMENDATIONS REQUESTED BY THE PARTIES

3.1   The European Communities alleges that:

(a)   Section 211(a)(1) of the OAA is inconsistent with Article 2.1 of the TRIPS Agreement in conjunction with Article 6*quinquies* A(1) of the Paris Convention (1967) and Article 15.1 of the TRIPS Agreement;

(b)   Section 211(a)(2) of the OAA is inconsistent with Article 2.1 of the TRIPS Agreement in conjunction with Articles 2(1), 6*bis* (1) and 8 of the Paris Convention (1967), and Articles 3.1, 4, 16.1 and 42 of the TRIPS Agreement; and

(c)   Section 211(b) of the OAA is inconsistent with Article 2.1 of the TRIPS Agreement in conjunction with Articles 2(1), 6*bis* (1) and 8 of the Paris Convention (1967), and Articles 3.1, 4, 16.1 and 42 of the TRIPS Agreement.

3.2   In the view of the European Communities, these measures cause prejudice to the legitimate rights of trademark owners and owners of trade/commercial names, thus nullifying and impairing the rights of the European Communities.

3.3   The European Communities requests the Panel to find that the United States has violated its obligations under Articles 3.1, 4, 15.1, 16.1 and 42 of the TRIPS Agreement as well as Article 2.1 of the TRIPS Agreement in conjunction with Articles 2(1), 6*bis* (1), 6*quinquies* A(1) and 8 of the Paris Convention (1967) and recommend that the United States bring its domestic legislation into conformity with its obligations under the TRIPS Agreement.

3.4   The United States requests the Panel to find that Section 211 of the OAA is not inconsistent with Articles 3.1, 4, 15.1, 16.1 or 42 of the TRIPS Agreement, or with Article 2.1 of the TRIPS Agreement in conjunction with Articles 2(1),

---

[10]   *Havana Club Holdings, S.A. v. Galleon S.A.*, 203 F.2d 116 (2d Cir. 2000).

6bis (1), *6quinquies* A(1) and 8 of the Paris Convention (1967) and reject the claims of the European Communities in their entirety.

IV.   ARGUMENTS OF THE PARTIES

A.   Introduction

4.1   This part of the report contains a summary of the claims and arguments contained in the parties' written submissions to the Panel and the written versions of the oral presentations they made at the Panel's meetings with the parties. Section B of this part summarizes the introductions to the parties' first written submissions. Section C summarizes the parties' claims and arguments that are specific to the inconsistencies between Section 211 and the TRIPS Agreement alleged by the European Communities. The claims and arguments are set out sequentially, starting with the arguments contained in the parties' first written submissions and followed by a summary of the arguments contained in subsequent submissions and statements. In its defence, the United States raised two horizontal issues that are relevant to all alleged inconsistencies between Section 211 and the TRIPS Agreement, namely the principle of non-recognition of foreign confiscations and the determination of the owner of a trademark. Section D summarizes the parties' arguments on these thematic issues. It also contains the arguments concerning burden of proof contained in the first US written submission. The parties' responses to the questions posed by the Panel are referenced where they add relevant information to the arguments contained in the parties' submissions. In general, the language used in the parties' submissions has been maintained close to its original form, subject to abridging and consolidating. Unless indicated otherwise, emphasis is used as in the parties' submissions.

4.2   Part V contains a summary of the arguments made by the third parties and part VI a summary of the letter from the Chair of the Panel to the Director General of WIPO and his response thereto.

4.3   The Panel's findings can be found in part VIII and its conclusions and recommendations in part IX of this report.

B.   Introductions by the Parties

4.4   In the introduction to its first written submission, the *European Communities* summarizes the reasons why it considers that certain aspects of the US legislation relating to the protection of trademarks and trade/commercial names are incompatible with the United States' obligations stemming from the TRIPS Agreement. The European Communities alleges that the objective of Section 211 of the OAA consists in curtailing the enjoyment and existence of certain trademarks and trade names in the hands of certain categories of right holders.

4.5   The European Communities submits that US trademarks (including trade names and commercial names) can be owned and enjoyed by Cuban legal or natural persons. Until the enactment of Section 211, this included the possibility to pay registration and prolongation fees to the US Patent and Trademark Office (the "USPTO"). This also meant that such trademarks could be licensed or assigned and the right holder could request the US judicial system to take the measures available under US law to enforce his trademarks rights vis-à-vis infringers. Until the enactment of Section 211 it was irrelevant if such a US trademark had any relation to or resemblance with a trademark used or held by a Cuban entity which was confiscated during the Cuban revolution. Through the introduction of Section 211 the enjoyment of such rights in which the Government of Cuba, a Cuban national or any foreign successor-in-title to the latter have an interest, have been fundamentally curtailed.

4.6   The European Communities argues that Section 211(a)(1) disallows any transaction related to the registration and renewal in the USPTO of trademarks in which Cuba or a Cuban national has an interest. Such transactions are only permissible if the historic owner of a confiscated Cuban entity, which held the same or a similar mark, expressly consents to them. The practical result of this provision is to take away – over time – existing US trademarks from their lawful owners, because they will no longer be able to renew the trademark registration. Furthermore, this provision prevents somebody from registering such a trademark if it has previously not yet been registered in the USPTO.

4.7   The European Communities claims that Section 211(a)(2) prohibits US courts from enforcing any such US trademark in the United States on the request of a Cuban national or any foreign successor-in-interest. In other words, it makes the trademark devoid of any practical value because the exclusive rights flowing from a trademark cannot be enforced by the owner in any other meaningful way than by having recourse to courts.

4.8   The European Communities submits that Section 211(b) prohibits US courts from enforcing any treaty rights concerning a trademark under the same conditions as pointed out in Section 211(a)(2), except that the prohibition applies here to all successors-in-interest.

4.9   The European Communities adds that all three operative elements contained in Section 211, while not immediately doing away with the US trademark or trade/commercial name concerned, make it devoid of any practical effect and terminate its existence over time, where renewal is necessary.

4.10   The European Communities argues that a US trademark or trade name that is subject to Section 211 is legally distinct from the property affected by the actions of the Cuban authorities in 1960. US assets, which include US trademarks or trade names, were completely unaffected by the Cuban confiscation measures, because the United States did not recognize – and subsequently has never recognized – any effects on the ownership of assets located in the United States as a consequence of the Cuban actions. In other words, tangible (e.g., real property, vehicles, machines) or intangible (e.g., receivables, bank deposits and intellectual property rights) assets located in the United States continue to belong to their original owners, despite the confiscation operated by the Cuban authorities in Cuba. The curtailment intended by Section 211 is targeted at situations where the original US trademark or trade name had ceased to exist, e.g., for lack of renewal by its owner, or where such a right has never existed in the US.

4.11   In the view of the European Communities, these measures are in violation of the United States' obligations under the TRIPS Agreement as specified in paragraph 3.1 of Part III of this report.

4.12   The European Communities also brings to the attention of the Panel a statement made by US government officials concluding that a draft that was the basis of the provision that later became Section 211 would have violated US TRIPS obligations.[11]

4.13   The European Communities concludes its summary by stating that its economic interests in this matter are significant. Section 211 has already directly affected at least one well-known, commercially valuable trademark (Havana Club for spirit drinks). The rights to this mark and trade name are owned by a Cuban entity and have been licensed to a joint venture between that entity and an EC company. Given the great number of trademarks and trade/commercial names used in connection with Cuban enterprises before 1960, however, the effects of Section 211 are likely to prejudice a great number of commercial relationships by EC enterprises not only with Cuban entities but other partners that fall within the scope of Section 211.[12]

4.14   In an introduction to its first written submission, the *United States* contends that the core issue presented by the dispute is whether the TRIPS Agreement requires the United States to recognize and enforce trademarks used in connection with assets that have been confiscated – i.e., expropriated without compensation[13] – from their rightful owners. The United States submits that it does not. Under US law – both Section 211 and long-standing case law - those whose claim to a trademark is based on an uncompensated confiscation of assets cannot claim rights of ownership in the United States, absent consent of the owners whose assets were confiscated. Indeed, in the United States' view, this is a principle that has been widely recognized throughout the world, and, in particular, by many WTO Members. According to the United States, the European Communities' view in this dispute, by contrast, is that a person's assets may be confiscated by a governmental authority which can then, invoking TRIPS and the Paris Convention, enforce those "rights" in the United States in a manner

---

[11]   The European Communities refers to a memorandum, dated 30 October 1998, to Ambassador Barshefsky on congressional trade actions prepared by United States Trade Representative officials. They wrote in relation to an earlier draft of Section 211 that "Senator Mack inserted language into the omnibus appropriations bill that prohibits US courts from enforcing trademarks held by a designated national or successor-in-interest that was used with a business that was confiscated. This provision addresses a longstanding dispute between the Cuban government and Bacardi rum. The language is problematic because it violates our obligations under the TRIPS agreement." (Inside US Trade, Issue: Vol. 16, No. 47, 27 November 1998, page 18). The Panel was not provided a copy of the draft that was the subject of the comments quoted above.

[12]   The European Communities recalls that Section 211 has also been discussed at the Council for Trade-Related Aspects of Intellectual Property Rights. *See* paragraph 16 of document IP/C/19 and paragraph 16 of document IP/C/22 (the Council's annual reports for the years 1999 and 2000).

[13]   The United States clarifies that, unless otherwise indicated, it uses the term "confiscation" to refer to an expropriation without payment of adequate and effective compensation. *See* Section 211(d)(2) of the OAA, referencing the definition in 31 CFR 515.336.

contrary to US law. TRIPS does not require such a result, and the negotiators of TRIPS could not have intended such a result.

4.15   The United States argues that, contrary to the assertions of the European Communities in its introduction, Section 211 is not targeted at situations where the US trademark has ceased to exist or never existed, and is not distinct from the well-recognized right of sovereign nations not to recognize foreign confiscations. Section 211 is targeted at the assertion of rights by a confiscating entity or its US or non-US successors vis-à-vis the rights of the original owners of the confiscated assets, the precise target of the principle against giving extraterritorial effect to uncompensated confiscations. According to the United States, the European Communities is arguing that TRIPS and the Paris Convention require Members to recognize and enforce trademark rights asserted by foreign confiscating entities, even if that right is based on a foreign confiscation. The United States contends that the European Communities is, indeed, challenging the sovereign right of a Member not to give effect to foreign uncompensated confiscations, a right reflected in numerous judicial decisions both in Europe and in the United States.

4.16   The United States submits consequently that the European Communities inaccurately "sets the stage" throughout its introduction by implying that, before Section 211 was enacted, confiscating entities could assert rights to US trademarks based on their uncompensated confiscation, and that Section 211 takes away these legitimate rights. It has never been the case, in the United States or elsewhere, that confiscating entities or their successors could establish ownership rights in assets not within their jurisdiction. Section 211 is a statutory reflection of the principle that they cannot do so.

4.17   The United States argues that the European Communities has a heavy burden in this dispute - to demonstrate that the well-established principle against giving extraterritorial effect to foreign confiscations has always been contrary to the Paris Convention, and is now contrary to TRIPS. The United States submits that the European Communities cannot meet this burden, and that its assertions of conflict between Section 211 and TRIPS are unfounded.

C.   Arguments Concerning the Alleged Inconsistencies with the TRIPS Agreement

1.   Section 211(a)(1) of the OAA

4.18   The *European Communities* alleges that, "in practical terms", Section 211(a)(1) prevents the registration or renewal of already registered trademarks as targeted by its provisions. Specifically, Section 211(a)(1) operates to prevent an act (i.e., payment of the required fees) that must be performed by the right holder in order to register a mark or to ensure the renewal of trademarks that were duly registered in the United States.

4.19   The *United States* contends that nothing in Article 15.1 of the TRIPS Agreement or Article 6*quinquies* of the Paris Convention (1967) as incorporated into the TRIPS Agreement requires the United States to accept the registration or renewal of trademarks, if the person registering or renewing the trademark registration is not the true owner of the trademark under US law. Indeed, neither the TRIPS Agreement nor the Paris Convention dictates who Members must recognize as the owner of a trademark. That decision is left to the domestic law of the Members. The United States also submits that the European Communities' claim of TRIPS inconsistency is based on two errors. First, the European Communities misunderstands the scope and effects of Article 15.1 of the TRIPS Agreement and Article 6*quinquies* (A)(1) of the Paris Convention (1967) as incorporated into the TRIPS Agreement, the two substantive provisions cited by the European Communities as the sources of the alleged obligations of the United States. Second, in formulating its argument, the European Communities ignores both Article 15.2 of the TRIPS Agreement, which limits the scope of Article 15.1, and Article 6*quinquies* (B) of the Paris Convention, which expressly provides for exceptions to the obligations established by Article 6*quinquies* (A)(1).

(a)   Section 211(a)(1) of the OAA in Relation to Article 15.1 of the TRIPS Agreement

4.20   The *European Communities* claims that Article 15.1 of the TRIPS Agreement constitutes one of the fundamental trademark provisions of the Agreement by creating an obligation on WTO Members to make "any sign, or any combination of signs" which meet the criteria defined in the final sentence of this provision "eligible for registration as trademarks".

4.21   The European Communities submits that the trademarks targeted by Section 211(a)(1), i.e., those which are "[...] the same as or substantially similar to a mark, trade name, or commercial name that was used in connection with a business or assets that were confiscated [...]" fully meet the criteria set out in Article 15.1 of the TRIPS Agreement to make a "sign, or combination of signs" eligible for trademark protection. This is further evidenced by the fact that Section 211(a)(1) also disallows the renewal of trademarks which have been duly registered by the USPTO, thus necessarily meeting all requirements which make a sign or a combination of signs a trademark.[14]

4.22   The European Communities further argues that there is no provision in the TRIPS Agreement or the Paris Convention (1967) which would allow a WTO Member to make the registration or renewal of a trademark dependent on the express consent of the former owner of such a mark or similar marks anywhere in the world.

4.23   Therefore, the European Communities claims that Section 211(a)(1) is at variance with the United States' obligations under Article 15.1 of the TRIPS Agreement.

4.24   Before considering the specific provisions of Article 15.1 of the TRIPS Agreement and Article 6*quinquies* of the Paris Convention (1967) as incorporated into the TRIPS Agreement in its first written submission, the *United States*

---

[14]   In a footnote, the European Communities notes that the second sentence of Article 18 of the TRIPS Agreement confirms that "[t]he registration of a trademark shall be renewable indefinitely".

submits that nothing in those two Articles requires the United States to accept the registration or renewal of trademarks, if the person registering or renewing the trademark registration is not the true owner of the trademark under US law. The United States claims that neither the TRIPS Agreement nor the Paris Convention dictates who Members must recognize as the owner of a trademark; that decision is left to the domestic law of the Members.

4.25   Given that the arguments presented by the United States, and subsequently by the European Communities, concerning the determination of the owner of a trademark are relevant to several inconsistencies between Section 211 and the TRIPS Agreement alleged by the European Communities, these arguments are presented below in a thematic manner in Section D.2 of this part of the report.

4.26   As regards Article 15.1 of the TRIPS Agreement, the United States contends that Section 211(a)(1) is not inconsistent with its provisions. Article 15.1 defines eligible subject matter of trademarks and limits the ability of Members to claim that a trademark is not capable of constituting a trademark, and is therefore not eligible for registration, because of the form of the trademark. It does not contain an affirmative obligation to register all eligible trademarks. For instance, under Article 15.1, a Member could not refuse trademark registration on the grounds that it is made up of personal names, or of letters, or on other grounds related to form, so long as the signs of which the trademark is composed are capable of distinguishing the goods or services or one undertaking from another. Article 15.2 emphasizes that this does *not* mean that a Member is prevented from denying registration of a trademark on *other* grounds, provided such other grounds do not derogate from the provisions of the Paris Convention.

4.27   The United States argues that the restrictions imposed by Section 211(a)(1) are not based on the *form* of the trademark. Section 211(a)(1) is concerned with trademarks, regardless of the form, that are similar or identical to trademarks used in connection with assets confiscated without compensation, and are being registered without the permission of the original owner. It relates solely to the rights of the person registering the trademark to assert an ownership interest in that trademark. For this reason, Section 211(a)(1) is not inconsistent with Article 15.1.

4.28   The United States further argues that if one would assume, for the sake of argument, that Article 15.1 of the TRIPS Agreement could be interpreted as imposing on Members an independent affirmative obligation to register those trademarks that it declares "eligible for registration", such an obligation would be limited by Article 15.2, which provides that Article 15.1 does not "prevent a Member from denying registration of a trademark on other grounds, provided that they do not derogate from the provisions of the Paris Convention (1967)". Therefore, Article 15.1 does not prevent a Member from denying registration of a trademark on other grounds, as long as doing so is not inconsistent with the Paris Convention. Because nothing in Section 211(a)(1) is inconsistent with the Paris Convention, Section 211(a)(1) is not inconsistent with TRIPS Article 15.1.

4.29   The *European Communities* disagrees with the United States' assertion that Article 15.1 of the TRIPS Agreement contains a simple definition of a trademark. The European Communities claims that such a reading of this provision would lead to, in its view, absurd result that a WTO Member does not have an obligation to allow trademarks to be registered and protected in the first place. When looking at the ordinary meaning of the words used in Article 15.1 and reading it together with Article 16 of the TRIPS Agreement there can be no reasonable doubt that Article 15.1 stipulates an obligation on WTO Members to register trademarks which meet the requirements set out in this provision. This is further confirmed by looking at Articles 6 and 6*quinquies* of the Paris Convention.

4.30   The European Communities claims that registration under Article 15.2 can only be refused in the exceptional cases expressly mentioned in TRIPS and the Paris Convention. Such provisions can be found in Articles 22.3, 23.2 and 24.5 of the TRIPS Agreement, and Articles 6(2), 6*ter* and 6*quinquies* B of the Paris Convention. In the absence of a specific optional or mandatory exception, a request for registration has to be granted under Article 15.1 of the TRIPS Agreement. It submits that the United States has not invoked any specific exception provided for under TRIPS or the Paris Convention to justify Section 211(a)(1). In its view, in the absence of a specific optional or mandatory exception, a request for registration has to be granted under Article 15.1 the TRIPS Agreement and registrations have to be indefinitely renewable; as regards the renewal of registrations, the European Communities refers to Article 18 of the TRIPS Agreement.

4.31   The Panel requested the European Communities to clarify its position as to whether Article 15.1 precludes a Member from (a) determining any requirements concerning the capacity or eligibility of a natural or legal person to file a trademark application; (b) requiring, in case a legal entity files an application, that such legal entity complies with the formalities and substantive requirements under its law concerning the existence of a legal person; or (c) requiring the registrant to be an undertaking having its own industrial or commercial assets. In response, the European Communities submits that Article 62 of the TRIPS Agreement allows WTO Members to require compliance with reasonable procedures and formalities as a condition for the acquisition or maintenance of intellectual property; and that sub-questions (a) and (b) appear to be covered by Article 62 of the Agreement. On sub-question (c), the European Communities submits that the conditions would appear to be more of a substantive nature and would thus not be covered by Article 62. The European Communities argues that as concerns the "undertaking" quality of the registrant, this would appear to be the normal requirement for a trademark owner; and that from a purely logical point of view any "undertaking" must necessarily have some minimal assets in order to pursue its activities (e.g., one staff and telephone); but that a requirement that the applicant has his own industrial or commercial assets would not appear to be permissible under Article 15.1, since it would appear that an applicant who produces or distributes his goods with the help of subcontractors with their material and staff assets is fully entitled to the benefits of Article 15.1.

4.32   The *United States* asserts that the European Communities is wrong to claim that TRIPS Article 15.1 contains an affirmative obligation to register all trademarks regardless of whether a Member considers the registrant to be the true owner of the trademark. That a sign is "capable of constituting a trademark", does not create an obligation to accept the registration of that trademark by whoever wants to register it. The *text* of Article 15.1 is clear, and it is the *text* that is the starting point in any interpretation of an agreement, under the customary rules of interpretation reflected in the Vienna Convention. Article 15.1 limits the ability of Members to refuse registration of trademarks based solely on the signs of which it is composed. It does not require a Member to register a trademark that does not, under the laws of the Member, belong to the person applying for registration. In other words, Article 15.1 might prevent a Member from declaring that particular signs are ineligible to be trademarks. There is nothing in Article 15.1 that prevents a Member from declaring that confiscating entities cannot claim an ownership interest in trademarks associated with a confiscated asset.

4.33   The United States argues that under Article 15.1, entitled "protect*able*" - not "protect*ed*" - subject matter", any sign or combination of signs capable of distinguishing goods is "capable" of constituting a trademark. In other words, a Member cannot reject a registration based on a contention that a qualifying sign or combination of signs is not "capable" of constituting a trademark. Nowhere does Article 15.1 require a Member to register and protect all signs or combinations of signs that are capable of constituting a trademark. And despite the European Communities' reference to "indirect guidance", Article 15.1 says absolutely nothing about who is the proper owner of the trademark. The United States claims that Article 15.1 stands for the proposition that the signs must be capable of distinguishing the goods of one undertaking from those of another in order to function as a trademark. But this says nothing about whether a particular undertaking must be considered to "own" the trademark. Signs that are capable of distinguishing the goods of one entity from those of another might be claimed by two different entities; Article 15.1 says nothing about which of the two (if either) owns the trademark; it only says that the trademark cannot be rejected on the grounds of its form.

4.34   The United States submits that Section 211(a)(1) has nothing to do with whether certain signs are capable of constituting trademarks; it has only to do with who may assert the rights in such a trademark. It is, therefore, not inconsistent with Article 15.1 of the TRIPS Agreement.

4.35   The United States argues that Article 15.1 simply does not answer the question of who is the owner of the trademark. The fact that there are, in all Members, opportunities to challenge the registration based on the true ownership of the trademark means that a Member is not obliged to register a trademark in the name of a particular person, just because the trademark is made up of signs making it "capable of constituting a trademark" under Article 15.1.

4.36   The United States further argues that Article 15.2 makes it clear that Article 15.1 does not prevent a Member from denying registration of a trademark on grounds *other than* its form, provided that those grounds do not derogate from the provisions of the Paris Convention. As the Paris Convention does not dictate national laws on the ownership of trademarks, any denial of a trademark registration on grounds of lack of ownership does not derogate from the provisions of the Paris Convention.

4.37   The United States claims that Paris Convention Article 6*quinquies* and TRIPS Article 15.1 are the only two Articles that the European Communities alleges are violated by Section 211(a)(1). The United States submits that both of these Articles limit the ability of Members to reject trademark registrations based on deficiencies in the *form* of the trademark. Neither imposes any limits on the ability of Members to reject registrations because the registrant is not the true owner of the trademark.

4.38   The United States argues that there is no support in the text of Article 15.1 for the EC assertion that Article 15.1 requires that any sign or combination of signs "capable" of being a trademark be registered. The text of Article 15.1 only defines the signs that must be considered eligible subject matter for protection as trademarks. The United States similarly argues that there is no support for the contention that registration can only be refused in the "exceptional cases expressly mentioned in TRIPS and the Paris Convention". In the view of the United States, that is not what Article 15.2 says. Article 15.2 clarifies that Article 15.1 - defining the form of a trademark - does *not* prevent Members from denying registration of a trademark on *other grounds* ("other", that is, than the form of the trademark). It adds that, of course, those grounds must not derogate from the Paris Convention. This is very different from saying that registration may *only* be denied on particular specified grounds set forth in particular named sub-Articles of the Paris Convention. The Paris Convention does not prescribe any rules that say that Members must give ownership rights to confiscating entities. Therefore, denying a trademark registration on the grounds that the registrant is not the true owner of the trademark is not inconsistent with Article 15.1, and does not derogate from any provision of the Paris Convention under Article 15.2.

4.39   The United States submits that the European Communities offers no "exception" to TRIPS Article 15.1 that would permit a Member to determine that it will not give effect in its territory to a foreign confiscation. It claims that, under the European Communities' interpretation, Article 15.1 does not permit a Member to decide that the confiscating entity is not the owner of the trademark used in connection with the confiscated assets.

4.40   The United States contends that Section 211(a)(1) does not require the United States to take any actions inconsistent with its TRIPS obligations. It submits that Section 211(a)(1) makes OFAC general licences unavailable for certain trademark registrations and renewals, i.e., those trademarks that are identical or substantially similar to trademarks used in connection with a business or assets that were confiscated *and* for which the consent of the original owner of the trademark has not been obtained. This provision does not randomly deny the registration of trademarks. It focuses on those trademarks that were used in connection with an asset confiscated by the Cuban Government, and on the original owners of those trademarks. It protects the original owners of those trademarks by saying that the confiscating entity or its successors must get the consent of those owners before it can take advantage of a general OFAC licence to register or renew the trademark. It does not say those trademarks cannot be registered or renewed: it simply says that the consent of the original owners must be obtained to take advantage of a general licence.[15]

> (b)   Section 211(a)(1) of the OAA in Relation to Article *6quinquies* (A)(1) of the Paris Convention (1967) as Incorporated into the TRIPS Agreement

4.41   The *European Communities* argues that Article *6quinquies* (A)(1) of the Paris Convention (1967) as incorporated into the TRIPS Agreement means, "in practical terms", that "whenever a trademark is duly registered in the country of origin, the other countries of the Union are obliged to accept and protect it". In the view of the European Communities, all trademarks duly registered in their country of origin are covered, independently of issues of form of the trademark. It claims that Section 211(a)(1) prevents the owner of a mark registered in another WTO Member or a party to the Paris Union from obtaining and maintaining in force a trademark registration within the United States. Section 211(a)(1) forecloses the possibility of performing an act (i.e., payment of required fees) that is a prerequisite to obtaining a registration or a requirement for maintaining the registration in force. There exists no possibility for the holder of a mark "duly registered" in another country that is party to the Paris Convention or is a WTO Member and which is included in the scope of Section 211 to register the mark in the United States.[16]

---

[15]   In response to a question from the Panel, the United States clarifies that "Section 211(a)(1) addresses the availability of *general* OFAC licences to register certain trademarks. It does not address specific OFAC licences, which are another means of obtaining the authorization to make payments related to the registration or renewal of a trademark. The legal effect of the application of Section 211(a)(1) is, therefore, only that the OFAC general licence is not available to register such trademarks." In response to a question on whether the legal effect of Section 211(a)(1) could amount to a taking of an acquired right in a situation where the lack of an authorization of a payment of a renewal fee leads to the expiration of a trademark registration resulting from a failure to pay the renewal fee, the United States responds that "making general licenses unavailable for certain trademarks is not the taking of an acquired right, for several reasons. First, a general license is not itself an acquired right – it is one vehicle under which payments are authorized under OFAC's licensing authority. OFAC reserves the right to impose exclusions or restrictions from the scope of such general licenses. 31 C.F.R. 515.503. The other vehicle is a specific license. Second, if, in fact, a confiscating entity (or its successor in interest) is not the legitimate owner of the trademark, that entity never had rights in the trademark to begin with. Since there were no acquired rights in the trademark, denying the registration or renewal of the trademark is not a taking of an acquired right. Regardless of Section 211, a trademark registration or renewal is always subject to challenge on the grounds that the registrant is not the legitimate owner of the trademark. This was the situation before 1998, and remains the situation today."

[16]   The European Communities adds that an illustrative example is the "Havana Club" trademark which in its view played an important role in the legislative history of Section 211, which was and is duly registered in Cuba and more than 150 other countries and territories. The European Communities claims that, by the operation of Section 211(a)(1), this trademark, which is also registered in the United States, cannot be renewed once its present term of registration expires and thus will be taken away over time from its lawful owner.

4.42   Therefore, in the view of the European Communities, Section 211(a)(1) is at variance with the US obligations under Article 2.1 of the TRIPS Agreement together with Article 6*quinquies* A(1) of the Paris Convention (1967).

4.43   The *United States* argues that, contrary to the assertions of the European Communities, Article 6*quinquies* of the Paris Convention (1967) does not force the United States to register and protect all trademarks duly registered in a Member country of origin when the registrant traces its ownership "right" to the trademark to an uncompensated confiscation and when the United States does not recognize such a right under US law. In its view, it is simply incorrect that Article 6*quinquies* leaves no latitude to US domestic law to determine whether the original owner – the one whose business or assets were taken from him without compensation – is the true owner of the trademark right in the United States.

4.44   The United States argues that, in fact, Article 6*quinquies* provides a limited exception to the rule that it is the Member's national laws that determine the conditions for filing and registration of trademarks. It in no way interferes with the United States' ability to determine whether the applicant is the proper owner of the trademark. Article 6(1) of the Paris Convention sets forth the general rule that "[t]he conditions for the filing and registration of trademarks shall be determined in each country of the Union by its domestic legislation". Articles 2 and 3 of the Paris Convention guarantee to all nationals of other Members the same rights that a Member grants to its own nationals (national treatment).

4.45   The United States adds that Article 6*quinquies*, by contrast, is aimed at the *exceptional* circumstance in which a national of a Member, who has a registered trademark in his country of origin, claims *better* than national treatment with respect to a registration of his trademark in its original form in another Member. This provision was necessary because of differences in domestic legislation with regard to the form of the trademark. Where, for instance, domestic legislation prohibited foreign words or simple numbers or letters from being registered as a trademark, a national of one Member might be precluded from registering his trademark even under national treatment principles. This was contrary to the interests of owners of trademarks and the public in having the same trademark apply to the same goods in various countries.

4.46   The United States argues that, to address this situation, in which a trademark registered in one Member might not otherwise be registerable in another member *because of its form* (e.g., because it is in a foreign language or contains numbers), Article 6*quinquies* provides an exceptional "national treatment 'plus'" avenue:

> "Every trademark duly registered in the country of origin shall be accepted for filing and protected as is [in the authentic French text, *telle quelle*] in the other countries of the Union, subject to the reservations indicated in this Article."

4.47   In the US view, the phrase "as is", or "*telle quelle*" in the authentic French text of the Convention, is important in defining the scope of Article 6*quinquies*. According to one commentator, Professor Bodenhausen, "*telle quelle*" in the original Convention of 1883 meant "in its original form", and the Final Protocol to that Convention made clear that the scope of what was later to become Article 6*quinquies* was limited to situations in which domestic law would refuse to protect a trademark solely because of the signs of which it is composed:

> "Paragraph 1 of Article 6 should be understood in the sense that no trademark may be excluded from protection in one of the States of the Union for the sole reason that it does not comply, *with regard to the signs of which it is composed*, with the conditions of the laws of that State, provided it complies on this point with the laws of the country of origin and that it has been properly filed there. Subject to this exception, *which only concerns the form of the mark*, and subject to the provision of the other Articles of the Convention, each State shall apply its domestic law."[17]

4.48   The United States submits that, under the exceptional circumstances in which Article 6*quinquies* is invoked, therefore, Members are obliged to accept trademarks duly registered in the country of origin for filing and registration, if the only objection to the trademark is that it does not comply with the provisions of domestic law concerning the permissible form of a trademark. Nothing in Article 6*quinquies* prevents Members from applying other provisions of their domestic law to trademark applications under Article 6(1) of the Paris Convention.

4.49   The United States argues that nothing in Article 6*quinquies* requires the United States to accept for filing and protection trademarks that, although duly registered in the country of origin, are not duly registered by the persons that the United States considers under its domestic laws to be the proper owners of the trademark. The exceptional circumstance represented by Article 6*quinquies* – where the United States might be required to accept a trademark that is inconsistent with US law *as to the form of the trademark* – cannot reasonably be read to require the United States to accept and protect a trademark filed by the person who, under US law, is not the legitimate owner.

4.50   The United States adds that even assuming, for the sake of argument, that the scope of paragraph (A)(1) of Article 6*quinquies* of the Paris Convention could be interpreted as not being limited to the form of a trademark, Section 211(a)(1) would still not be contrary to this Article, because of the exceptions or reservations set forth in paragraph (B) of the same Article.

4.51   The United States submits that, under Article 6*quinquies* (B), the Members of the Paris Union have reserved the right to deny registration to, or to invalidate, a foreign-origin trademark when such a registration would be "contrary to [...] public order". It is plain that any exception based on *ordre public* would include the principle of non-recognition of foreign confiscations.[18] In the US

---

[17]   The United States refers to Bodenhausen, Professor G.H.C., *Guide to the Application of the Paris Convention for the Protection of Industrial Property*, United International Bureaux for the Protection of Intellectual Property (BIRPI) (1969) (reprinted 1991) ("Bodenhausen"), page 110, quoting the Final Protocol. Emphasis by the author.

[18]   The United States emphasizes that it does not believe that Article 6*quinquies* (A) imposes an obligation to accept for filing and protect all trademarks filed in Member countries, if, under US law, the filing entity is not the true owner of the trademark. Therefore, the United States does not believe

view, the customary international law on expropriation is clear: a State may not expropriate private assets of nationals of other States in its territory unless the expropriation is (1) for a public purpose, (2) on a non-discriminatory basis and in accordance with due process of law, and (3) subject to prompt, adequate and effective compensation. It is on the basis of *ordre public* that courts in Europe, the United States, and elsewhere around the world have refused to give effect in the forum to claims of title based on a foreign confiscation. In particular, courts in many countries of the world - and in particular those in Europe and in the United States - have declined to recognize claims to title to trademarks that were expropriated without compensation. While courts justify their decisions in accordance with the technical peculiarities of each system, the conclusions they reach are consistent: the forum will refuse to give extraterritorial effects to a claim of title derived from a foreign confiscation because such confiscation is contrary to the *ordre public* of the forum.

4.52   The United States submits that Section 211 reflects the principle that no extraterritorial effect will be given to a claim of title based on a foreign confiscation. If Section 211(a)(1) restricts the recognition of a claim of title based on a foreign confiscation, in so doing, it properly prevents the application in the United States of a foreign confiscatory decree. Indeed, giving *telle quelle* protection to a foreign-origin trademark that has been confiscated by a foreign government would amount to giving extraterritorial effect in the United States to the foreign confiscation. Neither TRIPS nor the Paris Convention requires the United States to do this. Accordingly, even if the Panel came to the view that Article 6*quinquies* (A)(1) contains an obligation to register and protect a trademark on behalf of a person that the United States does not consider the owner of the trademark - a view that the United States believes is incorrect - the *ordre public* exception in Article 6*quinquies* (B) would excuse the United States from such an obligation where the result would be to give extraterritorial application to foreign confiscations. Therefore, Section 211(a)(1) cannot be inconsistent with the obligations of the United States under Article 6*quinquies* of the Paris Convention.

4.53   In response, the *European Communities* argues that it is true that questions of form played a certain role in the Diplomatic Conference that adopted Article 6*quinquies* A(1) of the Paris Convention. However, in WTO dispute settlement procedures, the interpretation of the norms at stake is based on the international customary rules of treaty interpretation codified by the Vienna Convention. On this basis, the words of Article 6*quinquies* A(1) are to be given their ordinary meaning, in their context and in the light of the treaty's object and purpose. The text of Article 6*quinquies* A(1) unequivocally states that "every trademark duly registered in the country of origin shall be accepted for filing and protected as such in the other countries". The European Communities argues further that Article 6*quinquies* B, in particular its sub-paragraph B(3), is not limited to

---

that the exceptions under Article 6*quinquies* (B) are relevant. However, it argues that were Article 6*quinquies* (A) considered to impose such an obligation, the *ordre public* exception under Article 6*quinquies* (B) would encompass the principle against the recognition of foreign confiscations.

the form of a trademark. An issue of form would for example concern the use of a certain language or script for visual signs. For the European Communities it would appear difficult to imagine situations in which the use of a certain language or script in itself would be contrary to morality or public order. In the EC view, it is rather the deceptive impression which all aspects of the signs or combination of signs have on the public, which determine whether or not trademarks are contrary to morality or public order.

4.54   According to the European Communities, a respected commentator to the Paris Convention, which is also cited by the United States, supports the interpretation[19] that pleads for a comprehensive duty for registration and protection.

4.55   The European Communities adds that even if the US interpretation were acceptable, Section 211(a)(1) would continue to be at variance with Article 6*quinquies* A(1), because it denies registration also for such trademarks which would meet the particular circumstances as to form claimed by the United States.

4.56   The Panel requested the European Communities to clarify its position as to whether Article 6*quinquies* precludes a Member from (a) determining any requirements concerning the capacity or eligibility of a natural or legal person to file a trademark application; (b) requiring, in case a legal entity files an application, that such legal entity complies with the formalities and substantive requirements under its law concerning the existence of a legal person; or (c) requiring the registrant to be an undertaking having its own industrial or commercial assets. The European Communities responded that the answers it gave to a similar question concerning Article 15.1 of the TRIPS Agreement would appear to also apply to applications made on the basis of Article 6*quinquies* of the Paris Convention.[20]

4.57   The European Communities argues that Article 6*quinquies* B of the Paris Convention allows in well-defined circumstances the refusal of the registration of trademarks. The denial is in particular permissible if the trademark is contrary to morality or public order and of a nature to deceive the public. The European Communities emphasizes that it is the trademark for which registration or protection is sought which must be contrary to morality or public order. This defect must directly attach to the trademark and its perception by the public and does not attach to its owner.[21] The fact that a trademark is the same or similar to one that has been confiscated cannot by itself have a deceptive effect vis-à-vis the public. In its view, the Havana Club case is a good illustration that foreign confiscations do not affect the good morality or public order of a trademark or trade name, because this trademark has been duly registered by the USPTO. If this trademark had been considered as immoral, deceptive or scandalous, the USPTO would have had to refuse the registration *ex officio* under Section 2 of the Trademark Act. The European Communities claims that it is difficult to see for what reasons but for the introduction of Section 211 it had now become all of a

---

[19]   The European Communities refers to Bodenhausen, page 110.
[20]   *See* paragraph 4.31 above.
[21]   The European Communities refers to Bodenhausen, page 116-117.

sudden contrary to morality or public order after having existed for several decades unchallenged.

4.58   The European Communities reiterates that Section 211 applies to trademarks which have never been the object of a confiscation by a foreign country. It would appear obvious that in this respect Article 6*quinquies* B(3) cannot be invoked to excuse Section 211, even if one were to accept the US argument.

4.59   In the view of the European Communities, Article 6*quinquies* represents a limited exception to the territoriality principle, because it requires a country to accord rights as a consequence of the existence of rights in another country. In other words, a trademark has to be registered and protected, because a trademark exists in another country. In the view of the European Communities, the country where registration is sought has under this provision no right to question the existence of a trademark in the hands of an owner as defined by the laws of the country of origin. The European Communities adds that, once granted, the new trademark will become fully subject to the principle of territoriality and independence from the trademark in the country of origin.

4.60   The *United States* notes that the European Communities cited with approval the treatise by a respected commentator on the Paris Convention, Professor Bodenhausen, at page 110, which the European Communities termed a plea "for a comprehensive duty for registration and protection". The European Communities reads this as an interpretation that Article 6*quinquies* applies broadly to matters other than form. In the US view, what the European Communities neglected to say, however, is that Professor Bodenhausen is very clear on pages 110 and 111 that Article 6*quinquies* goes to the *form* of the trademark. Recalling that it has quoted an extensive passage to that effect in its written submission,[22] the United States adds that Professor Bodenhausen further elaborates as follows on pages 110 and 111, which follows an initial discussion of Article 6*quinquies*:

> "This leads to the following conclusions:
>
> Whenever a trademark is duly registered in the country of origin, the other countries of the Union are *obliged to accept and protect it,* even if, as regards *its form,* that is, *with regard to the signs of which it is composed,* such trademark does not comply with the requirements of the domestic legislation, *subject* to the additional rules, *particularly the grounds for refusal or invalidation of any mark, considered on its individual merits,* established in the Article. This rule will therefore apply to trademarks consisting of numbers, letters, surnames, geographical names, words written or not written in a certain language or script, and other signs of which the trademark is composed."

4.61   And further down on page 111:

> "Member States are equally free, regardless of Article 6*quinquies*, to apply to trademark applications other provision of their domestic law not concerning the signs of which a trademark is com-

---

[22]   *See* paragraph 4.47 above.

posed, such as a requirement of previous use of the mark, or the condition that the applicant must possess an industrial or commercial enterprise."[23]

4.62   The United States sums up by asserting that Article 6*quinquies* of the Paris Convention does not prevent a Member from denying registration of a trademark duly registered abroad, where the registrant is not the true owner of the trademark.

4.63   The United States reiterates that Article 6*quinquies* A of the Paris Convention limits the ability of Members to deny protection to trademarks on the grounds that the *form* of the trademark is inconsistent with national rules. Under Article 6*quinquies*, a Member cannot refuse to register or protect a trademark duly registered in its country of origin on the grounds that the trademark does not conform to national rules *as to the form of the trademark*. In the words of Article 6*quinquies*, such a trademark shall be accepted for filing and protected "*telle quelle*", which means "as is" or "in its original form": the trademark, in other words, does not have to be changed to conform to national laws on trademark form. In the US view, any interpretation of this obligation extending it to matters beyond the form of the trademark would impermissibly read the key words "*telle quelle*" out of this Article. Such an interpretation would also ignore the object and purpose of the Article — to prevent denials based on the *form* of the trademark. In sum, an examination of the ordinary meaning of the terms of Article 6*quinquies* A, read in their context, and in light of their object and purpose, establishes that the European Communities' interpretation is incorrect. The United States further argues that the material provided by WIPO on this provision's negotiating history confirms this. Under the customary rules of interpretation of international law, as reflected in Article 32 of the Vienna Convention, the WIPO materials may serve this confirmatory role.

4.64   The United States adds that Section 211 has nothing to do with the form of the trademark, and everything to do with the ownership of the trademark.

4.65   According to the United States, the European Communities claims that Article 6*quinquies* A requires the United States to "accept for filing and protect" a trademark that has been confiscated in the country of origin, so long as it is duly registered there. The United States interprets this to mean that if the government of a Member confiscates the business assets of a company, including its duly registered trademarks in that Member (the country of origin), Article 6*quinquies* would, according to the European Communities, require all other Members to accept for filing and protect that trademark in their territories. The United States argues that this is tantamount to requiring Members to give effect in their own territory to foreign confiscations of trademarks. For example, if Member A confiscates a company in its territory, including its trademarks, and asks Member B to protect an existing trademark in the name of the confiscated company, the European Communities' interpretation of Article 6*quinquies* A is that Member A would be required to do so, and thereby to give effect, in its terri-

---

[23]   Emphasis in original; footnotes omitted with respect to both quoted passages.

tory, to the confiscation. The United States adds that, yet, the European Communities concedes that Members are *not* obligated to give such effect under the TRIPS Agreement or the Paris Convention. In short, the European Communities' extraordinarily broad reading of Article 6*quinquies* leads to a result that both parties agree is wrong.

4.66   According to the United States, the European Communities has suggested that this – in the US view undeniably incorrect - result can be avoided by invoking the "exceptions" provision in paragraph B(1) of Article 6*quinquies*, which permits a Member to invalidate or avoid registering trademarks "when they are of such a nature as to infringe rights acquired by third parties in the country where protection is claimed".

4.67   The United States recalls its view that Article 6*quinquies* A does not undercut the principle that Members do not have to give effect in their territories to foreign confiscations. It argues that this provision deals only with issues of "form" and there is no need, absent the European Communities' misreading of this provision, to resort to "exceptions" to preserve this important principle. The WIPO materials show that, in negotiating the original version of Article 6*quinquies*, the delegates specifically rejected the use of the word "property" in this Article, because they agreed that the provision did *not* address the question of trademark ownership.[24] The United States further argues that, even if the Panel were to resort to the Article 6*quinquies* exceptions to preserve this important principle, it is not at all clear why it should resort to the exception for "rights acquired by third parties" under Article 6*quinquies* B(1), rather than the exception for "*ordre public*" under Article 6*quinquies* B(3). The United States submits that the European Communities has not cited a single situation in which "rights acquired by third parties" have been used to justify the non-recognition of foreign confiscations, whereas the United States has cited scores of decisions in which "*ordre public*" has been cited as the reason for not giving effect to foreign confiscations. It seems apparent that *if* the Panel *has* to resort to an exception to Article 6*quinquies* A to preserve this important principle – which the United States believes not to be necessary - the exception for "*ordre public*" is the appropriate exception. Furthermore, the United States argues that there is no support for the European Communities' suggestion that the "*ordre public*" exception is limited to situations in which the trademark deceives the public. It is clear from the text of Article 6*quinquies* that trademarks that deceive the public are just one of the kinds of trademarks included within the morals and "*ordre public*" exception. Moreover, numerous courts throughout the world have found that giving domestic effect to foreign confiscations, including with respect to trademarks, is against "*ordre public*".[25]

---

[24]   The United States refers to *Actes de Paris*, 1880, pp. 70-79. Annex I of the letter from WIPO.

[25]   The United States adds that, nevertheless, the European Communities has offered the Article 6*quinquies* B(1) exception for "rights acquired by third parties" as the sole foundation on which, under Article 6*quinquies*, the entire principle of non-recognition relies for survival. The United States examines how this exception might be invoked to preserve the principle of non-recognition. A Member confiscates the assets of ABC Company, including its trademarks registered in that Member and in the United States. The original owners of ABC Company come to the United States and claim that

4.68   The United States adds that, perhaps more significantly, the exception under Article 6*quinquies* B(1) says nothing about *how* a Member makes the determination that the "third parties" have acquired rights that would be infringed by the foreign trademark. Even if the Panel were to adopt the European Communities' strained reading of Article 6*quinquies* B(1), that Article says nothing about how a Member is to determine who the true owners of the US trademark are whose "acquired" rights would be infringed. Article 6*quinquies* B(1) leaves this decision to the national laws of the Members. The United States argues that, therefore, even if the European Communities' construction of Article 6*quinquies* were correct, the Panel is still left with the conclusion that, under Article 6*quinquies* B(1), it is up to the national laws of the Members to determine who the proper owner of the trademark is, a determination that is not dictated by either the Paris Convention or TRIPS. Thus, the European Communities ends up where the United States began.

4.69   The United States does not share the European Communities' view that if TRIPS does not dictate trademark ownership rules, the disciplines of TRIPS are worthless. In the United States' view, the TRIPS Agreement contains numerous disciplines that prevent arbitrary allocations of trademark ownership, including national treatment, most-favoured-nation treatment, and many procedural protections. Members' national rules on ownership issues may differ in the context of other intellectual property rights covered by TRIPS, and these acknowledged differences have not undermined the TRIPS disciplines. Nevertheless, even if the lack of ownership rules were a flaw in the Agreement, the European Communi-

---

they, and not the confiscated ABC Company, have the rights to the US trademark. According to the European Communities, Article 6*quinquies* A requires the United States to protect the ownership interests of the confiscated company in the US trademark. Article 6*quinquies* B(1), however, again according to the European Communities, permits the United States to decide that the original owners of ABC Company are "third parties" that have acquired rights in the United States that are infringed by confiscated ABC Company's US trademark. Only by invoking this exception, in the European Communities' view, can the United States avoid the requirement under Article 6*quinquies* A that it recognize the confiscated ABC Company as the rightful owner of the US trademark.

The United States argues that this approach strains the ordinary meaning of the Article 6*quinquies* B(1) exception beyond recognition. And it does so without really addressing the ultimate issue of "ownership" in a way different from that presented by the United States. The approach requires the Panel to find that the original owners of ABC Company who have fled to the United States are now "third parties" that "acquired" rights in the United States. But the original owners of the company are not really "third parties": they are the rightful owners of the ABC mark in the United States. And they did not "acquire" rights in the United States that pre-date and would be infringed by trademarks of the confiscated ABC Company if those trademarks were registered and protected. Rather, the trademarks claimed by the original owners are the same as the trademarks claimed by the confiscated ABC Company. Judging from the text of the Paris Convention, and from Professor Bodenhausen's explanation of the text, the exception in Article 6*quinquies* B.1 is aimed at the situation in which true third parties - parties not related to those claiming ownership in the foreign trademark – have pre-existing rights in the United States that would be infringed if a foreign trademark were registered and protected. It is only by virtue of a tortured construction that the European Communities can conclude that protection of "third party" rights acquired in the United States means recognizing the continued ownership of the original owners.

The United States adds that, yet, according to the European Communities' view, the very survival of the principle of non-recognition of foreign confiscations under the Paris Convention and TRIPS depends on this tortured construction.

ties' interpretation of Article 6*quinquies* B(1) would not address any such flaw in the slightest, because it does not determine how a Member decides that third parties have acquired rights. In other words, it does not result in the application of any additional disciplines on ownership. The United States claims that the European Communities arrives at the same conclusion as the United States: that Members are entitled to determine who is the proper owner of a trademark in their territory and have the right to prevent confiscating entities from asserting such ownership rights.

2.   Section 211(a)(2) of the OAA[26]

4.70   The *European Communities* claims that Section 211(a)(2) prevents the owner of a registered US trademark or the owner of a trade name from using a US court to enforce its rights. As such, the measure denies standing to certain owners of US rights to initiate or maintain proceedings in a US court to enforce the rights conferred on these parties through the Lanham Act. Since such rights, whether in the form of Federal trademark registrations or rights in trade names, may only be enforced through actions in a Federal court, this measure operates to foreclose any judicial recourse for actions that would infringe such rights.

4.71   The *United States* submits that Section 211(a)(2) provides that "[n]o court shall recognize, enforce, or otherwise validate any assertion of rights by a designated national based on common law rights or registration obtained under [the OFAC general licensing provision discussed above] of such a confiscated mark, trade name or commercial name". In plain terms, anyone who traces "rights" in a US trademark to a confiscation in Cuba may not have those purported rights recognized or enforced by US courts. Section 211(b) contains a similar provision with respect to persons who claim trademark, trade name or commercial name rights in the United States by virtue of a trademark registration in a Member country. In other words, under Section 211(b), a confiscating entity, or its successors in interest, cannot – by virtue of having confiscated a business and duly registering its trademark in Cuba – claim ownership rights to that trademark in the United States. The European Communities claims, incorrectly, that these provisions are inconsistent with a number of TRIPS provisions.

---

[26]   The first written submission of the European Communities contained separate sections of arguments relating to Section 211(a)(2) and Section 211(b). The European Communities' arguments relating to Section 211(a)(2) are summarized in this Section of the report; its arguments relating to Section 211(b) contained in its first written and subsequent submissions are summarized in paragraphs 4.143-4.148 below. When addressing Section 211(b), the European Communities refers, in its first written submission, to its arguments concerning Section 211(a)(2) and argue that they apply *mutatis mutandis* to Section 211(b). However, the United States provided its arguments concerning both Section 211(a)(2) and Section 211(b) simultaneously. Therefore, the United States' arguments concerning both provisions are summarized in this Section of the report.

(a) Section 211(a)(2) of the OAA in Relation to Article 16.1 of the TRIPS Agreement

4.72   The *European Communities* argues that, given that trademarks as all other intellectual property rights are primarily enforced in the United States, like in most WTO Members, in the civil judicial system, the denial of access to the US Court system for certain trademark owners is tantamount to depriving the right holders of their exclusive rights altogether. There exists no other legal or practical way to prevent third parties not having the owner's consent from using in the course of trade identical or similar signs in the United States than the possibility to have recourse to the US judicial system.

4.73   The *United States* responds that Article 16.1 of the TRIPS Agreement confers certain rights on the "owner" of a "registered trademark", notably the exclusive right to prevent third parties not having the owner's consent from using the trademark under certain circumstances. Sections 211(a)(2) and (b) can only violate Article 16.1, therefore, if they prevent the owner of a registered trademark from asserting his exclusive rights vis-à-vis third parties. Sections 211(a)(2) and (b) do not do this, for two reasons. First, under Section 211, a person who traces his "rights" to an uncompensated confiscation is not an owner of the trademark under US law, and is in no position to assert any rights under TRIPS. Nothing in TRIPS requires the United States to confer ownership status on a person who traces his purported ownership status to an uncompensated confiscation. Second, with respect to the assertion of "common law rights" under Section 211(a)(2) – i.e., those rights based not on registration, but on use - these are not rights sought by "the owner of a registered trademark", which are the rights guaranteed by Article 16.1, but are rights sought by the owner of a common law trademark.

4.74   The United States argues that, with respect to the first point, TRIPS Article 16.1 clearly distinguishes between the registered trademark, on the one hand, and the owner of the trademark, who may assert his rights, on the other. Where a person is the owner of a trademark, and that trademark is registered by that owner, TRIPS guarantees that person exclusive rights to prevent third-party use. However, it may be, under Article 16.1, that the "owner" of the trademark is not the same as the person who has registered the trademark. While a US federal trademark registration carries with it the legal presumptions of ownership, validity, and priority, all of these presumptions are subject to challenge. If a person other than the registrant can show a superior claim to the trademark based, for example, on prior use, that person can be adjudged the true "owner" of the trademark. Article 16.1 specifically anticipates that the owner of the trademark - the person in a position to assert exclusive rights under domestic law - may be someone other than the registrant.

4.75   The United States submits that this is clear from the last sentence of Article 16.1, which states that the rights guaranteed by Article 16.1 do not "affect the possibility of Members making rights available on the basis of use". That sentence also provides more generally that the Article 16.1 rights "shall not prejudice any existing prior rights".[27] Aside from the specific mention of rights acquired by use, Article 16.1 does not specify what are the other "existing prior rights" that are not prejudiced by the Article 16.1 rights. The determination of existing prior rights, like the determination that trademark rights are acquired through use, is a question of national law not dealt with in the TRIPS Agreement.

4.76   The United States asserts that, in light of this interpretation, it is plain that Sections 211(a)(2) and (b) are not inconsistent with TRIPS Article 16.1.

4.77   The United States submits that Section 211(a)(2) provides that if a "designated national" – essentially the Cuban government, Cuban nationals, and their successors in interest – (1) has obtained a trademark registration under a general OFAC licence, *and* (2) the trademark is identical or similar to a trademark used in connection with a business confiscated without compensation by the Cuban Government, US courts will not recognize, enforce or otherwise validate any assertion of trademark rights by that person. Under Section 211(b), if a designated national has obtained a registration in his country of origin for such a trademark (that is, a trademark used in connection with a confiscated business), and asserts ownership rights to that trademark in the United States by virtue of the foreign registration, US courts will not recognize, enforce, or otherwise validate that assertion of rights.

4.78   The United States argues that this is not inconsistent with Article 16.1. Although the United States is not enforcing the trademark for the benefit of the trademark registrant, it is not denying exclusive rights to the "owner" of the registered trademark, which is the obligation set forth in Article 16.1. This is because, under US law, the successor to the confiscating entity is not the "owner" of the trademark in the United States. Whether to confer ownership status on a claimant to a trademark right is a matter that is reserved to the domestic law of the Member. TRIPS simply has nothing to say about the substantive issue of trademark ownership.[28] If the United States decides that confiscating entities that have provided no compensation for the property confiscated or their successors in interest cannot exercise the rights of ownership to the trademark associated with the confiscated business in the United States, it is fully within the authority of the United States to do so. There is no TRIPS provision that limits that right. Once a Member recognizes that the registrant is the owner of the trademark, TRIPS requires the Member to grant certain rights to that owner. Until that happens, it does not.[29]

---

[27]   The United States illustrates this by noting that, in the United States, if one person registers a trademark, but another person has "existing prior rights" based on use, it is the latter person, and not the registrant, who, consistent with domestic law implementing Article 16.1, can assert his rights.

[28]   The United States adds that there are certain important procedural protections and principles, such as national treatment and most-favoured-nation treatment, that would affect ownership rules from a procedural point of view. This is to be contrasted with the substantive requirements for ownership that Members are entitled to establish under their domestic laws.

[29]   The United States gives an illustration aimed at clarifying why, in its view, this result makes sense in light of the principle against the extraterritorial application of foreign confiscatory decrees. Under this principle, for example, if there were an uncompensated confiscation of a Cuban business

4.79   The United States submits that the plain language of Article 16.1 clearly envisions that, under domestic law, the rights of ownership may be given to someone other than the registrant. Further, it is inconceivable that the TRIPS negotiators intended, by means of Article 16.1, to reverse the established principle of US law against giving domestic effect to foreign uncompensated confiscations. According to the United States, this principle has been in effect in the much of the world, including the United States and Europe, for nearly one hundred years, and has been much in force and in evidence throughout the post-World War II period. There is no indication in the TRIPS text, or in its object and purpose, of any intention to overturn this long-standing principle.

4.80   The United States argues that Article 16.1 has as its object and purpose to define and protect the rights of the owner of a trademark, not to limit the ability of Members to determine who the owner is. In other words, the contribution of TRIPS Article 16.1 was enhanced enforcement of intellectual property rights, not curtailment of a sovereign nation's authority to determine who may assert those rights. Article 16.1 especially did not curtail such rights with respect to the basic decision whether to recognize uncompensated foreign confiscations.

4.81   The United States notes that the European Communities appears to argue that the extraterritorial effect of uncompensated confiscations is *not* the issue.[30] In the US view, the European Communities appears to concede that sovereign nations are entitled to refuse recognition foreign uncompensated confiscations at the time the confiscation takes place; for the European Communities, the issue presented by Section 211 is whether, *after* a foreign confiscation takes place, and after the original owner has abandoned his trademark, the United States can *still* prevent the confiscating entity from owning US trademark rights.

4.82   In the view of the United States, this argument draws a false distinction. Whether TRIPS has, despite its silence, overturned the principle against giving domestic effect to foreign confiscations is, indeed, the issue. The United States argues that either Article 16.1 takes away the ability of sovereign nations not to recognize the ownership of confiscating entities, or it does not. Nothing in Article 16.1 supports a distinction between the rights of confiscating entities at the time of the confiscation and those rights 20 years later. If, as the European Communities asserts, Article 16.1 says that Members are no longer free to determine who is and who is not the owner of a trademark right, a Member is no freer to make that determination at the time of the confiscation than it is after the

---

that had trademarks both in the United States and in Cuba, the confiscation would not affect the ownership of the trademark rights in the United States: those rights would still belong to the true owners of the business, not the confiscating entity. On this point, both EC and US judicial precedent seem to agree. Yet, if the US trademark were a common law trademark – that is, one established through use and not through registration – the confiscating entity might be able to register the trademark in its name. The United States claims that, under the EC reading of TRIPS Article 16.1, if the confiscating entity succeeded in registering the mark, it would be entitled under Article 16.1 to have its trademark enforced in the United States, to the detriment of the true owners. In the US view, this is a result that would be entirely contrary to the principle of not giving extraterritorial effect to foreign confiscations.

[30]   The United States refers to a paragraph in the introduction to the EC first submission referenced in paragraph 4.10 above.

trademark has allegedly fallen into the public domain. Article 16.1 does not change the rule that Members get to determine who may claim ownership of a trademark.

4.83   The United States reiterates that the ordinary meaning of Article 16.1 is that it confers certain exclusive rights to prevent third party use on the *owner* of a trademark that is registered. If a person is not the *owner* of the trademark – and ownership is determined under a Member's national laws – Article 16.1 does not confer rights on that person. In the context of Section 211, if a confiscating entity or its successor is not the owner of a trademark, Article 16.1 does not guarantee that entity any rights.

4.84   According to the United States, the European Communities' interpretation is that Article 16.1 confers exclusive rights on whoever registers the trademark. Article 16.1 might have been drafted to confer exclusive rights on the trademark registrant, but it was not. Instead, it specifically states that its presumptions and entitlements accrue to "[t]he owner of a registered trademark [...]". In fact, Article 16.1 could not be clearer that there is a distinction between the owner of the trademark and the trademark registrant: it specifically says that nothing in that Article prevents Members from making rights available based on use. In other words, a Member does not breach Article 16.1 by determining that the true owner of a trademark is the person who first used the mark, and *not* the person who registered the mark. If the European Communities' interpretation were accurate, Article 16.1 would require Members to give exclusive rights to the registrant, even if the rights based on use were conferred under national law on someone else. This position is directly contradicted by Article 16.1 itself. It therefore simply cannot be accurate that Article 16.1 imposes an obligation to confer rights on whoever registers the trademark.

4.85   The United States argues that the European Communities' assertion that there is one class of federal trademarks which are "owned" by whoever registers them and another class of trademarks whose ownership is based on use is not credible.[31] The very fact that a person can establish his ownership of a trademark based on prior use, and can disprove the ownership of the federal trademark registrant, demonstrates that there are not two distinct "classes" of trademarks. This is a situation specifically anticipated by Article 16.1. The United States argues that the EC interpretation of Article 16.1 - as requiring Members to confer exclusive rights on whoever registers the trademark - is unsupported by the text of that Article. It claims that this interpretation is particularly extreme and troublesome, given that the European Communities also believes that Article 15.1 requires Members to register without question any trademark that consists of qualifying signs, regardless of whether the registrant qualifies as an owner or not under national law, and regardless of whether the registrant claims to own the trademark in the United States on the basis of its ownership of confiscated assets abroad.

4.86   The United States argues that, given that the obligation imposed by TRIPS Article 16.1 is to confer rights on the "owner" of a trademark that is regis-

---

[31]   The United States refers to the European Communities' arguments cited in paragraph 4.178 below.

tered, the Panel must therefore determine whether Sections 211(a)(2) and (b) require actions that are inconsistent with this obligation. In its view, they do not. Sections 211(a)(2) and 211(b) do not deny exclusive rights to the true owners of registered trademarks. Rather, they reflect that courts are not obligated to find the trademark registrant to be the "owner" of the trademark where the registrant claims ownership by virtue of a confiscation and the original owner does not consent. Sections 211(a)(2) and 211(b) do not curtail recognized ownership rights in the United States. To the contrary, they exercise the recognized sovereign right of the United States to determine the criteria for trademark ownership in the United States, and to deny ownership, where appropriate, to those who derive their claim from an uncompensated confiscation.

4.87   In sum, the United States contends that Sections 211(a)(2) and (b) are not inconsistent with TRIPS Article 16.1, because Article 16.1 confers rights on the *owner* of a registered trademark, and Section 211 does not limit the rights of the true owners of registered trademarks.

4.88   The United States adds that, even if the Panel were to find an inconsistency between the rights referred to in Article 16.1 and Sections 211(a)(2) and 211(b), however, these Sections would still be consistent with TRIPS. This is because Article 17 allows WTO Members to make limited exceptions to the rights conferred by a trademark, provided that such limited exceptions take account of the legitimate interests of the owner of the trademark and of third parties. Sections 211(a)(2) and 211(b) would meet these requirements, because each of these provisions applies only to a very narrow and specified class of potential right holders and are therefore "limited". They are also limited in the sense that they merely impose one condition to the enforcement of asserted trademark rights: the consent of the original owner. This consent requirement is directly related to the purpose of the exception, which is to deny extraterritorial effects to a Cuban confiscation. Further, Sections 211(a)(2) and 211(b) take into account the legitimate interests of the owner of the trademark and of third parties. A designated national who claims to own the trademark rights has *no* legitimate interest in the mark because his claim is based, directly or indirectly, on the confiscation of the business associated with the mark. By contrast, the interest of the dispossessed owner has considerable legitimacy. The original owner created the trademark, first used it on his products, and built its distinctive reputation. The fact that he was deprived of his property, without compensation, by governmental fiat, in no way diminishes the policy justification for protecting his interest in the mark. A consent requirement sufficiently "takes account" of this history and allows the current claimant and the original owner to work out an accommodation of their respective interests. In other words, Section 211 is precisely targeted at the wrong it seeks to address.

4.89   Commenting on the US arguments relating to Article 17 of the TRIPS Agreement, the *European Communities* recalls that the panel in *Canada – Patent Protection of Pharmaceutical Products* had to interpret the term "limited exceptions" as used in Article 30 of the TRIPS Agreement in relation to patents. The panel said that "[t]he term 'limited exception' must therefore be read to connote a narrow exception – one which makes only a small diminution of the rights in question".[32] In the EC view, there can be no doubt that the outright denial of judicial enforceability goes well beyond "a small diminution of the rights in question", thus excluding the limited nature of the exception. The findings of the Panel in *United States -Section 110(5) of the US Copyright Act* in relation to "certain special cases" in Article 13 of the TRIPS Agreement[33] concerning copyright confirm this result.

4.90   The European Communities reiterates its view that Section 211 has nothing to do with the denial of effects of foreign confiscations in the United States. Therefore, the US argument concerning legitimate interests of third parties is not on the point. The European Communities argues that it would also appear that by denying any judicial enforceability to the trademark owner, his interests have not been taken account of at all. Finally it would appear to be excluded, also in light of the "fair use" example contained in Article 17 that the interests of a historic owner of an enterprise which has used such a or a similar trademark would qualify as a relevant interest under Article 17 of the TRIPS Agreement. The third parties who would qualify under Article 17 are those who intend to use the trademark, not those who want to prevent its use.

(b)   Section 211(a)(2) of the OAA in relation to Article 42 of the TRIPS Agreement

4.91   The *European Communities* claims that by expressly denying the availability of US courts to enforce the rights targeted by its provisions, Section 211(a)(2) constitutes a violation of the United States' obligations under the first sentence of Article 42 of the TRIPS Agreement. Article 42 together with Articles 44-46 and 50 of the Agreement require WTO Members to provide remedies expressly stipulated therein. These remedies include injunctions, damages and provisional measures.

4.92   The *United States* contends that Sections 211(a)(2) and (b) are consistent with Article 42 of the TRIPS Agreement, which requires WTO Members to make civil judicial procedures available for the enforcement of intellectual property rights covered by the Agreement. The plain text of Article 42 makes clear that it applies only with respect to intellectual property rights "covered by [the] Agreement", i.e., rights that a Member is required to enforce under the Agreement. Article 42 does not require WTO Members to provide right holders with procedures to enforce rights that do not exist. If a purported intellectual property right is not "covered by this Agreement", a Member is under no obligation to enforce it through its civil judicial system. Neither Article 16, nor any other provision of the TRIPS Agreement, addresses the question of who is the legitimate owner of a trademark under a Member's domestic law. Sections 211(a)(2) and (b) merely state that a person that holds no rights in a mark cannot enforce that mark. These Sections, therefore, do not violate Article 42.

---

[32]   *See Canada – Patent Protection of Pharmaceutical Products*, WT/DS114/R, DSR 2000:V, 2289, paragraph 7.30.
[33]   *See United States – Section 110(5) of the US Copyright Act*, WT/DS160/R, DSR 2000:VIII, 3769, paragraphs 6.102-6.113.

4.93   The United States argues that the same reasoning applies if the Panel finds that Section 211 falls within the TRIPS Article 17 exceptions provision. By definition, where a valid exception to trademark rights applies, such rights cannot be successfully asserted.

4.94   Consequently, the United States submits that Sections 211(a)(2) and (b) cannot violate Article 42. As the text of Article 42 makes clear, where TRIPS prescribes no right, it certainly does not require a remedy.

4.95   The United States adds that there can be no serious question that the United States makes available civil judicial procedures concerning the enforcement of intellectual property rights. The US civil judicial system is one of the most developed systems in the world and trademark holders regularly enforce their rights in US domestic courts. Notwithstanding the European Communities' – in the US view - erroneous assertions to the contrary, persons potentially affected by Section 211 do have access to US courts, and have standing to present their case.

4.96   The United States argues that Sections 211(a)(2) and (b) constitute substantive rules governing the ownership of trademark rights, not jurisdictional or standing rules regarding access to the court system. They do not affect the availability of judicial procedures to any party asserting a right to a trademark. Indeed, in order for a court to find that Section 211 applies, it must make a number of legal determinations - for instance, that the trademark is the same as, or similar to, a trademark used in connection with a confiscated business, that no adequate and effective compensation was paid, and that the person asserting the right is a designated national or a successor in interest. Nothing in Sections 211(a)(2) or (b) precludes the person asserting ownership rights in the trademark from having a full opportunity to substantiate his claim to ownership and to present all relevant evidence.

(c)   Section 211(a)(2) of the OAA in Relation to Article 6*bis* of the Paris Convention (1967) as Incorporated into the TRIPS Agreement

4.97   The *European Communities* argues that Article 6*bis* (1) of the Paris Convention (1967) mandates the enhanced protection to be granted for so-called well-known trademarks. The European Communities claims that Section 211(a)(2) denies protection to certain trademarks indiscriminately whether or not they are well-known and that it is, therefore, at variance with Article 6*bis* (1) of the Paris Convention (1967) as incorporated into the TRIPS Agreement by its Article 2.1.

4.98   The *United States* contends that Sections 211(a)(2) and (b) are not inconsistent with Article 6*bis* (1) of the Paris Convention (1967), because it only provides that Members shall undertake to refuse or cancel a registration, or prohibit the use of a trademark, when the competent authorities of that Member consider that the trademark is well-known in that Member's territory "as being already the mark of" another person claiming protection under that Article. Sections 211(a)(2) and (b) only come into play when US courts determine that the US trademark is not, in fact, "the mark of" the confiscating entity or its successors in interest. If, under US law, the confiscating entity does not have any rights of ownership in the trademark, the trademark cannot, as a matter of law, be "well-known as being already the mark of" the confiscating entity.

4.99   The *European Communities* claims that there can be no reasonable doubt that Sections 211(a)(2) and (b) deny Cuba, a Cuban national or a foreign successor-in-interest the benefit of Article 6*bis* of the Paris Convention. These persons will not be able to claim refusal or cancellation of a requested registration nor will they be in a position to prohibit the use of such a trademark.

4.100   The Panel requested the European Communities to give examples of situations under which Section 211(a)(2) could violate the United States' obligations under Article 6*bis* (1) of the Paris Convention as incorporated into the TRIPS Agreement. In response, the European Communities says that if the "Havana Club" trademark were not registered in the United States, but the United States would recognize it as a well-known mark in the sense of Article 6*bis* (1) of the Paris Convention, the operation of Section 211(a)(2) would not allow the owner of this well-known trademark to prevent somebody else from using this trademark in the United States. Given its broad language, Section 211(a)(2) applies to all kinds of trademarks, registered trademarks, common-law trademarks and well-known trademarks.

4.101   The *United States* argues that the European Communities has presented no argument whatsoever that Article 6*bis* requires Members to recognize the trademark ownership of particular entities. In fact, those Articles say nothing about who owns the trademark or trade name. Article 6*bis* specifically reserves to "the competent authority" of the Member the determination of whether a trademark is well known as the mark of a particular person. The United States submits that the WIPO communication acknowledges that this decision by the competent authorities relates to ownership, but specifies that "no provision [of the Paris Convention] addresses the question how the owner of a trademark has to be determined under the domestic law of [Members]".

    (d)   Section 211(a)(2) of the OAA in Relation to Article 8 of the Paris Convention (1967) as Incorporated into the TRIPS Agreement

4.102   The *European Communities* argues that Article 8 of the Paris Convention (1967) requires that WTO Members extend protection to trade names independently from whether they form part of a trademark. While Article 8 does not precisely stipulate the way in which this protection for trade/commercial names has to be granted, one of the leading commentators writes that "[t]he protection will generally be given against unlawful acts of third parties consisting, for example, of use of the same or a confusingly similar trade name [...], if such use is liable to cause confusion among the public".[34] Indeed, under US law, trade names are protected through a right of action under, among other things, Section 43(a) of

---

[34]   The European Communities refers to Bodenhausen at page 133.

the Lanham Act, which permits parties to prevent the use of a trade name in a manner likely to cause confusion or to deceive.

4.103 The European Communities claims that, in any event, the language of Section 211(a)(2) is of such a sweeping nature that there can be no doubt that the United States does not grant any protection to the trade/commercial names covered by this provision. Thus, the United States does not meet its obligations under Article 2.1 of the TRIPS Agreement together with Article 8 of the Paris Convention.

4.104 The European Communities underlines the importance it attaches to – in its view - the TRIPS deficient protection (in particular violation of Article 8 of the Paris Convention) in the United States of trade names and commercial names as a consequence of the operation of Sections 211(a)(2) and (b), because a great number of such – in its view often very valuable – US trade names are potentially affected by the curtailments introduced by Sections 211(a)(2) and (b). This economic importance is further highlighted by the fact that the Federal Circuit Court has indeed applied Section 211(b) to the Havana Club trade name and denied protection.

4.105 The *United States* contends that Sections 211(a)(2) and (b) are not inconsistent with Article 8 of the Paris Convention because Article 8 merely requires a Member to offer some protection to trade names, without the requirement of filing or registration and regardless of whether it forms part of a trademark. Article 8 does not impose any requirements on the scope of protection, other than, through Article 2 of the Paris Convention, the requirement of national treatment. For this reason alone, Sections 211(a)(2) and (b) do not violate Article 8 of the Paris Convention.

4.106 In any case, however, it cannot be asserted that the protections given trade names must be more stringent than those given trademarks. Because Sections 211(a)(2) and (b) are not inconsistent with TRIPS or the Paris Convention with respect to trademarks, therefore, they are not inconsistent with TRIPS or the Paris Convention with respect to trade names.

4.107 The United States adds that the European Communities has presented no argument whatsoever that Article 8 requires Members to recognize the trade name ownership of particular entities. In the US view, Article 8 is silent on the subject.

(e)   Section 211(a)(2) of the OAA in relation to Article 3.1 of the TRIPS Agreement and Article 2(1) of the Paris Convention (1967) as incorporated into the TRIPS Agreement

4.108 The *European Communities* submits that the language of Article 3.1 of the TRIPS Agreement on "National treatment" is based on Article III(4) of the General Agreement on Tariffs and Trade ("GATT"). However, while national treatment in GATT attaches to goods – not to the respective owners of the goods – it attaches under TRIPS to the person of the right holder. This modified "attachment" is systematically linked to the territorial character of intellectual property rights. In the EC view, the vast jurisprudence on Article III(4) of GATT, under the GATT dispute settlement system as well as under the WTO dispute settlement system, may give valuable insight for the interpretation of Article 3.1 of the TRIPS Agreement. In any event, the basic feature contained in Article 3.1 of the TRIPS Agreement would appear to be straight forward. A WTO Member cannot treat a national of another WTO Member in relation to an intellectual property right which its IPR system offers less favourably than it treats its own nationals in relation to such an intellectual property right.

4.109   The European Communities argues that Section 211(a)(2) denies the protection of US intellectual property rights to owners who are "designated nationals". A reference in Section 211(d)(1) of the OAA is made to 31 CFR 515.305 which provides that "[f]or the purposes of this part, the term 'designated national' shall mean Cuba and any national thereof including any person who is a specially designated national". Furthermore, Section 211(d)(1) extends the definition of a designated national beyond 31 CFR 515.305 to "[...] a national of any *foreign* country who is a successor-in-interest to a designated national".

4.110   The European Communities claims that the language of these provisions makes it utterly clear that Cuba, Cuban nationals and specially designated nationals are denied protection of their US intellectual property rights, while US nationals are enjoying such protection. Furthermore, protection is also denied to a foreign national which is a successor-in-interest to a designated national, while such a successor-in-interest of US nationality benefits from protection. This constitutes a *de jure* violation of Article 3.1 of the TRIPS Agreement.

4.111   The European Communities notes that the principle of national treatment is considered to be one of the basic rules of also the Paris Convention (1967), as provided in its Article 2(1). The European Communities submits that the texts of Article 3.1 of the TRIPS Agreement and Article 2(1) of the Paris Convention are not identical. In its view, the former stipulates negatively what a WTO Member may not do, while the latter stipulates positively what a country of the Paris Union has to do, namely, to confer on non-nationals of the country the same advantages conferred by the industrial property laws of that country on its own citizens. The Paris Convention thus imposes a specific obligation for identical treatment for foreign and domestic right holders. The underlying objective of both provisions remains however the same, i.e., to prohibit treatment that differs as a consequence of the nationality of the right holders.

4.112   The European Communities claims that the *de jure* discrimination created by Section 211(a)(2) between Cuban right holders, on the one hand, and US right holders, on the other, constitutes as much a violation of Article 2(1) of the Paris Convention (1967) as incorporated into the TRIPS Agreement by a reference in its Article 2.1 as it does in relation to Article 3.1 of the TRIPS Agreement.

4.113   The European Communities develops its arguments by claiming that Section 211(a)(2) operates a violation of the national treatment principles at two levels:

-       By expressly curtailing the protection of trademarks and trade or commercial names held by "designated nationals" which means basically Cuba and Cuban nationals, while granting US nationals the full enjoyment of their rights, Section 211(a)(2) creates a first level of discrimination, which constitutes the most obvious violation of the national treatment obligations contained both in TRIPS and the Paris Convention.

- At the second level the operation of Section 211(d)(1), which defines the term "designated national", creates a discrimination at the level of successors-in-interest. This provision does expressly deny protection to any foreign successor-in-interest to a Cuban national or Cuba, while allowing US successors-in-interest to Cuban nationals or Cuba the full enjoyment of their trademarks or trade names.

4.114 The European Communities adds that Articles 3 and 4 also apply to common-law trademarks. Therefore, the curtailments operated by Sections 211(a)(2) and (b) to US common law trademarks are also relevant for the case.

4.115 In this situation there can, in the view of the European Communities, be no reasonable doubt that Sections 211(a)(2) and (b) are at variance with the US obligations under Article 3 of the TRIPS Agreement and Article 2(1) of the TRIPS Agreement together with Article 2(1) the Paris Convention as well as Article 4 of the TRIPS Agreement.

4.116 The European Communities argues that this conclusion would be valid even if one were to qualify Section 211 as a measure to address the issue of foreign expropriations. Given that such a measure would undoubtedly affect the "acquisition, maintenance, enforcement and use" of intellectual property rights covered by TRIPS, such measures have to comply with Articles 3 and 4 of the TRIPS Agreement even if one were to argue that they are exempt from the specific obligations under Part II thereof.

4.117 The European Communities notes that the United States has repeatedly asserted that a US national can never become the owner of a trademark or trade name covered by Sections 211(a)(2) and (b). The European Communities argues that this assertion is false. For purposes of illustration, the European Communities mentions three trademarks/trade names which are owned by US entities and which are the same or substantially the same as trademarks/trade names used in conjunction with expropriated Cuban business. The European Communities submits that Punch and Partàgas trademarks, which were used in conjunction with expropriated Cuban cigar enterprises, are held by US companies and the Cohiba trademark, which has also been used in conjunction with a Cuban cigar enterprise and which was expropriated, is also registered for a US company.

4.118 The Panel requested to European Communities to indicate what were the particular facts that led the United States to determine the ownership of these three trademarks and, in particular, whether their owners could be the same as the original owners of the confiscated trademarks or their successors-in-title or US nationals that have compensated the original owners. The European Communities responds that it has no information over and above what is contained in the publicly available documents from the USPTO register that it had submitted.

4.119 The *United States* contends that Sections 211(a)(2) and (b) are not inconsistent with the national treatment provisions of TRIPS and the Paris Convention. Contrary to the European Communities' assertions, it is simply incorrect to claim that Cuba, Cuban nationals, and specially designated nationals are denied "protection of their intellectual property rights, while US nationals are enjoying such protection", or that foreign nationals who are successors in interest are denied such protection, while US nationals are not. First and foremost, those nationals that base their alleged trademark rights on a foreign confiscation are not the true owners under US law, and so have no ownership rights to assert under TRIPS.

4.120 The United States argues that neither Section 211(a)(2) nor Section 211(b) accords less favorable treatment to non-US nationals than it does to US nationals. Section 211(b) specifies that US courts shall not recognize, enforce, or otherwise validate any assertion of rights – by virtue of a foreign registration – in trademarks, trade names or commercial names used in connection with confiscated assets "by a designated national or its successor-in-interest". Section 211(b) applies, therefore, by its own terms, to designated nationals *and to any successor in interest*, whether Cuban or not. It applies to any person, *whether Cuban or not and whether US or not*, who claims a registration under US law by virtue of a foreign registration of a trademark used in connection with confiscated assets.[35]

4.121 The United States submits that Section 211(a)(2) provides that US courts may not recognize, enforce, or otherwise validate any assertion of alleged rights in a confiscated trademark "by a designated national" or a national *of any foreign country* who is a successor in interest to a designated national. US nationals who are successors in interest are not specifically mentioned in Section 211(a)(2),[36] but US nationals *cannot even become* successors in interest to a designated national - for instance, a Cuban entity that owns a confiscated business in Cuba - without getting a specific licence from OFAC. This is because any transaction by which a US person could become a successor-in-interest to a Cuban confiscating entity is prohibited under 31 CFR 515.201. OFAC has never issued a specific licence for such a purpose.

---

[35] The United States illustrates this by noting that:
- If the confiscating entity transfers its interest in the trademark to a Cuban national, that Cuban national will not be able to enforce the trademark in the United States.
- If the confiscating entity transfers its interest in the trademark to a French national, that French national will not be able to enforce that trademark in the United States.
- If the confiscating entity transfers its interest in the trademark to a US national, that US national will not be able to enforce that trademark in the United States.

[36] The United States notes that there are jurisdictional limits to OFAC's licensing authority. While it has the jurisdiction and authority to prevent US nationals from becoming successors in interest to a confiscating entity, it has no ability to prevent foreign nationals from becoming successors in interest to other foreign nationals in connection with property not subject to US jurisdiction.

4.122 The United States adds that, even assuming for the sake of argument that a US national were in a position to assert alleged rights in trademarks used in connection with assets confiscated abroad, that US person would, moreover, have to convince a US court that any such rights should be enforced in spite of the principle of non-recognition of foreign confiscatory measures. US judicial precedents have very specifically addressed situations involving a foreign confiscation without compensation that purports to affect trademarks or other property in the United States, and resulting disputes between the confiscating entity (or its successor) and the original owners. In those situations, which are equally addressed by Section 211, the precedent is clear and directly on point that it is the original owners of the asset in the United States (whose assets abroad were confiscated) that can assert ownership rights in the associated US trademark, *not* the confiscating entity or its successors.

4.123 In sum, the United States asserts that neither Section 211(a)(2) nor Section 211(b) gives non-US nationals less favorable treatment than US nationals.

4.124 Commenting on the European Communities' argument that Section (a)(1) operates a violation of the national treatment principle at two levels, the United States contends that Section 211 has to be read as a whole, and not split into small "national treatment/MFN" pieces. The United States submits that if Section 211 were limited to Cuba and Cuban nationals, this might be a different case, but it adds that Section 211 is not limited in such a way. Section 211 is directed at Cuba and Cuban nationals who trace their ownership claim to a confiscation *and* at any other nationals - Cuban or not, US or not - who trace their ownership claim to that confiscation. One cannot assess consistency with national and MFN treatment by focusing on only one part of the law. The law has to be considered as a whole.

4.125 In the view of the United States, in assessing whether Section 211 on its face, and not as applied, breaches the national treatment provisions of TRIPS, the Panel should examine whether Section 211 requires that US nationals be treated more favorably than non-US nationals. Although Section 211(a)(2) itself is directed at confiscating entities and "foreign" successors in interest, the omission of US successors-in-interest is without practical effect. Under OFAC regulations, US nationals are generally prohibited from becoming successors in interest to a confiscating entity. So the issue of whether, as a successor in interest, US nationals can assert ownership rights in confiscated trademarks under Section 211(a)(2) is academic. The issue would not even arise unless OFAC made an exception to the general prohibition and decided to grant a specific licence to allow a US national to become a successor in interest in the first place.

4.126 The United States submits that there is no reason to believe that OFAC would ever issue such a licence, and the Panel should not, as a matter of law, assume that OFAC, an executive branch office, would take an action that might put the United States in violation of its international obligations. A law is only WTO-inconsistent on its face if it *mandates* WTO-inconsistent actions. If the law permits the national authority to act in a manner consistent with the WTO

Agreement, panels should not assume that a Member will use its discretion to act in a manner contrary to its international obligations.

4.127 According to the United States, panels have, on numerous occasions, recognized this distinction between laws that mandate WTO-inconsistent action and those that do not. In *United States - Tobacco,*[37] the panel found that a law did not mandate GATT-inconsistent action, and was therefore not GATT-inconsistent, where the language of that law was susceptible of a range of meanings, including ones permitting GATT-consistent action. In *United States - Taxes on Petroleum and Certain Imported Substances,*[38] the US Superfund Act explicitly directed the US tax authorities to impose a penalty tax on imports that was inconsistent with national treatment, but permitted the US Treasury Department to avoid the imposition of the penalty by issuing a regulation. No regulation had been issued at the time of the panel report. Because the US authorities had the "possibility" of avoiding the GATT-inconsistent penalty in that dispute, the panel found that the law itself was not GATT-inconsistent. Indeed, a law that does not mandate WTO-inconsistent action is not, on its face, WTO-inconsistent, even if actions taken under that law are WTO-inconsistent. For example, the panel in *EEC - Regulation on Imports of Parts and Components.*[39] found that "the mere existence" of the anti-circumvention provision of the European Communities' anti-dumping legislation was not inconsistent with the European Communities' GATT obligations, even though the European Communities had taken GATT-inconsistent measures under that provision. The panel based its finding on its conclusion that the anti-circumvention provision "does not mandate the imposition of duties or other measures by the EEC Commission and Council; it merely authorizes the Commission and the Council to take certain actions".

4.128 The United States submits that, in this case, there is no indication that OFAC would license a US national to become a successor in interest to a confiscating entity. To the contrary, OFAC regulations generally prohibit such a transaction. Further, even if a US national were in the position of claiming trademark ownership rights derived from a foreign confiscation in a US court, the US principle against the extraterritorial application of foreign confiscations would be applied to such a claim. In short, there is nothing to suggest that, because of Section 211(a)(2), the United States is according more favorable treatment to US nationals than to other nationals. Section 211(a)(2), therefore, does not violate the TRIPS national treatment provisions.

4.129 According to the United States, the European Communities seems to believe it has proved something of relevance when it cites three US trademarks of apparent Cuban origin that are registered by US companies. The United States contends that there is no reason to believe that those registrants are successors in interest to any confiscating entity and, therefore, the European Communities'

---

[37] Panel Report on *United States - Measures Affecting the Importation, Internal Sale and Use of Tobacco,* adopted 4 October 1994, BISD 41S/131 ("*U.S. - Tobacco*").
[38] L/6175, adopted June 17, 1987, BISD 34S/136, 160, paras 5.2.1-5.2.2.
[39] Panel Report on *EEC - Regulation on Imports of Parts and Components,* adopted 16 May 1990, BISD 37S/132 ("*EEC - Parts*").

observation simply has no relevance to this dispute. Furthermore, the United States claims that it is not clear what point the European Communities seeks to prove by naming several so-called "Cuban origin" trademarks owned by US companies. If the point is that the ownership of US registrants cannot be challenged, and that the ownership of foreign registrants can be, then this point is wrong. The ownership of US nationals in trademarks can be challenged on the same basis as the ownership of any other nationals. If the European Communities' point was that Section 211 would have prevented such registrations by non-US nationals, but permits registrations by US nationals, this point is also incorrect. Section 211 focuses on the trademark ownership claims of those who, in the first instance, derive their ownership from a confiscation. Others are unaffected by Section 211. Section 211 does not prevent registration or ownership of "Cuban-origin" trademarks; it targets only assertions of ownership by confiscating entities or their successors, of whatever nationality, whether US or not, or whether Cuban or not.

4.130 The United States argues that the TRIPS and Paris Convention provisions cited by the European Communities - those related to national treatment and most-favoured-nation treatment – require that nationals of Members be treated no less favorably than one's own nationals, and that any advantage, favor, privilege or immunity granted to the nationals of any country be accorded to nationals of all Members. Sections 211(a)(2) and (b) are not inconsistent with either of these principles. Those Sections apply to *any person, regardless of nationality* that attempts to assert ownership rights in a trademark, trade name or commercial name that are derived from a confiscation in Cuba. The United States adds that courts would also apply the principle of non-recognition of foreign confiscations to any confiscations outside of Cuba.

4.131 The United States concludes that nothing in Section 211 requires that the United States take any action that is inconsistent with any TRIPS obligation.

(f)   Section 211(a)(2) of the OAA in Relation to Article 4 of the TRIPS Agreement

4.132 The *European Communities* argues that the dichotomy created by Section 211(a)(2) distinguishes between Cuba or Cuban nationals and others, the latter being US nationals or nationals of any other country. Therefore, this provision does not only discriminate between Cuban nationals and US nationals (violation of national treatment obligation) but also creates *de jure* discrimination between Cuba/Cuban nationals and other non-US nationals by denying protection of intellectual property rights held by Cuban nationals while granting such protection to nationals of other countries. It would appear obvious that none of the exceptions under sub-paragraphs (a) to (d) of Article 4 of the TRIPS Agreement on "Most-favoured-nation treatment" are relevant for the case at hand. Therefore, Section 211(a)(2) is at variance with the United States' obligations under Article 4 of the TRIPS Agreement.

4.133 The *United States* contends that it is simply incorrect to assert that Sections 211(a)(2) and (b) violate the TRIPS most-favoured-nation provision – Article 4 – because they "create[ ] *de jure* discrimination between Cuba/Cuban nationals and other non-US nationals by denying protection of intellectual property rights held by Cuban nationals while granting such protection to nationals of other countries". It is incorrect first because, under US law, persons basing their trademark claims on foreign confiscations are not the true owners of the trademarks and therefore have no rights to assert under TRIPS. It is also incorrect because Sections 211(a)(2) and (b) do not grant an "advantage, favour, privilege, or immunity" to non-Cuban nationals that they do not grant to Cuban nationals: neither one nor the other can enforce a trademark based on a foreign confiscation.

4.134 The United States submits that Sections 211(a)(2) and (b) apply in the first instance to those entities in Cuba that confiscated a business in Cuba without compensation and to any Cuban national, to whom the "rights" in connection with that business are transferred or made available.[40] These persons may not assert ownership rights in a US trademark, trade name, or commercial name used in connection with that confiscated business under Sections 211(a)(2) and (b). In other words, there must be a clean "chain of title" in order to assert ownership rights.[41] Sections 211(a)(2) and (b), therefore, are aimed at all those persons whose claim to a particular trademark, trade name or commercial name is based on an uncompensated confiscation of the business associated with that trademark, trade name or commercial name. That nationals of Cuba are specifically mentioned in Sections 211(a)(2) and (b) results from the territorial nature of trademarks: Cuban nationals who assert trademark rights used in connection with confiscated businesses in Cuba – unlike other nationals - are claiming a right by virtue of the confiscation. Further, the principle that the United States will not give extra-territorial effect to foreign confiscations is a principle that applies equally to all countries, and is not limited to confiscations in Cuba.

4.135 According to the United States, the TRIPS Agreement assures that, with respect to the protection of intellectual property, nationals of different Members are not granted different advantages, favours, privileges or immunities based purely on their nationality. It does not, however, prevent a Member from pursuing legitimate objectives - such as not recognizing rights in trademarks similar to those used in connection with a confiscated business in Cuba - as long as the advantages granted to the nationals of one Member are not withheld from the nationals of another Member. That Sections 211(a)(2) and (b) are focused on trademarks similar to those used in connection with confiscated businesses in

---

[40] The United States explains that a "designated national", in the first instance, is "Cuba [i.e., the Government of Cuba] and any national thereof". "Confiscated" means seized by the Cuban Government without compensation. In the first instance, therefore, Sections 211(a)(2) and (b) mean that the Cuban Government cannot enforce rights in the United States to a trademark, trade name or commercial name used in connection with a business that it seized without compensation. It can seize the physical assets of a business in Cuba, but it cannot assert trademark rights connected with that business in the United States.

[41] The United States analogizes Sections 211(a)(2) and (b) to a mandatory "title search" which operates to ensure that the entity asserting rights in the mark, trade name or commercial name is legally entitled to the benefits of ownership. This preserves not only the true owners' rights, but serves also to protect the public from misrepresentation.

Cuba - and not confiscated businesses elsewhere - does not amount to an MFN violation under the TRIPS Agreement, because it does not discriminate against Cuban nationals, as opposed to other nationals, who wish to assert such trademark rights.[42]

4.136 The United States adds that Sections 211(a)(2) and (b) do not limit their focus to Cuba and Cuban nationals: under those Sections, US courts will not enforce or recognize any asserted rights to such trademarks, trade names and commercial names by *any* successors-in-interest - *whether Cuban or not* - to any Cuban entities claiming rights based on confiscated assets. It does not matter if the "rights" associated with the confiscated assets are transferred by the confiscating entity to a Cuban, European, or US national: US courts will not recognize those assertions of rights as regards trademarks, trade names and commercial names in the United States. Sections 211(a)(2) and (b) do not, therefore, grant an "advantage, favour, privilege or immunity" to the nationals of, for instance, France that it does not grant to the nationals of Cuba with regard to the protection of intellectual property rights. Under Sections 211(a)(2) and (b), a Cuban national who is a successor-in-interest to a confiscated business will have all the advantages of a French national who is a successor-in-interest to a confiscated business, with regard to the protection of intellectual property rights. Neither one will be able to claim rights in the United States to a trademark, trade name, or commercial name of a confiscated business.

4.137 The United States submits that, consequently, Sections 211(a)(2) and 211(b) are not inconsistent with Article 4 of the TRIPS Agreement.

4.138 The *European Communities* argues that Articles 3 and 4 also apply to common-law trademarks. Therefore, the curtailments operated by Sections 211(a)(2) and (b) to US common law trademarks are also relevant for the case.

4.139 In this situation there can, in the view of the European Communities, be no reasonable doubt that Sections 211(a)(2) and (b) are at variance with the US obligations under Article 3 of the TRIPS Agreement and Article 2.1 of the TRIPS Agreement together with Article 2(1) of the Paris Convention as well as Article 4 of the TRIPS Agreement.

4.140 The European Communities argues that this conclusion would be valid even if one were to qualify Section 211 as a measure to address the issue of foreign expropriations. Given that such a measure would undoubtedly affect the "acquisition, maintenance, enforcement and use" of intellectual property rights covered by TRIPS, such measures have to comply with Articles 3 and 4 of the TRIPS Agreement, even if one were to argue that they are exempt from the specific obligations under Part II thereof.

---

[42] In response to a question from the Panel, the United States submits that it is not unusual in a common law system for the legislature to codify certain common law principles, and in so doing, to focus on one particular area of application of that principle. This does not imply that the principle no longer applies in the other areas; it only means that, for whatever reason, the legislature saw fit to clarify its application in the one particular area. With respect to Section 211, it is fair to conclude that the confiscations in Cuba presented a concrete situation which Congress saw fit to specifically address in legislation.

4.141 The Panel asked whether, in the view of the European Communities, Article 4 of the TRIPS Agreement allows a Member to have a certain policy applicable to confiscations of trademarks in one Member, on the condition that all WTO Member nationals are treated similarly in respect of such confiscations in that Member, or whether that Article requires that a similar policy has to be applied to confiscations of trademarks in all other Members. The European Communities responds that in its view the MFN obligations flowing from Article 4 of the TRIPS Agreement attach to persons, not to situations. It argues that Article 4 outlaws discrimination between nationals of other WTO Members (discrimination as between own nationals and nationals of other WTO Members are outlawed by Article 3 of the Agreement). Therefore, Article 4 requires that all nationals of other WTO Members are treated similarly in respect of a certain event. Article 4 does not require that similar events in all other WTO Members are dealt with in a similar way, as long as this does in reality not create a discrimination between persons. Thus, extending the scope of Section 211 to "all expropriations everywhere in the world at all times" would not do away with the violation of Article 4 of the TRIPS Agreement.

4.142 In response to a similar question, the *United States* argues that because of the context of this dispute – involving the particular case of foreign confiscations, and the principle that Members are not required to give effect to foreign confiscations with respect to assets, including trademarks, in their territory – Section 211 is consistent with most-favoured-nation treatment obligations under either interpretation. Section 211 treats all nationals the same with respect to the ownership of trademarks associated with assets confiscated in Cuba, *and* the principle of non-recognition of foreign confiscations applies equally to all countries. The United States understands that the European Communities' claim that Section 211 violates the most-favoured-nation treatment obligation relates only to the first situation described in the Panel's question, i.e., that Section 211 violates TRIPS because, *with respect to the confiscations at issue in Section 211*, it gives advantages to one Member's nationals that are not granted to other Members' nationals. This is the argument to which the United States believes it has responded in stating that Section 211 provides identical treatment to all nationals. Because of this identical treatment, there is no MFN violation. Because the European Communities is only alleging an MFN violation based on the first situation described by the Panel, the United States argues that the Panel need not reach the question of whether TRIPS Article 4 applies in the second situation. The United States adds that it is also true, because of the special circumstance of foreign confiscations and their effect on assets within a Member's territory, that the principle reflected in Section 211 is a principle that applies in the United States regardless of the location of the confiscation.

3. Section 211(b) of the OAA

4.143 The *European Communities* argues that while the coverage of Section 211(b) appears to "parallel" the coverage of Section 211(a)(2), its precise scope is largely obscure. The absence of any legislative history in relation to

Section 211 adds to this obscurity. By way of speculation one might think that the drafters intended to cover rights flowing from treaties which are self-executory in the US legal system, i.e., where no act of Congress beyond ratification is needed. However, in the only case which has so far been decided by US Courts in relation to Section 211(b), the US District Court, with the subsequent approval of the Court of Appeals, has given Section 211(b) a wide scope[43].

4.144 From the foregoing, the European Communities concludes that the obligations flowing from the TRIPS Agreement - or put in the language of Section 211(b), the assertion of rights flowing from TRIPS - fall under Section 211(b).

4.145 The European Communities argues that it is noteworthy that the WTO Agreement (including the TRIPS Agreement) is not self-executing in the US legal order. This means that an individual cannot rely on TRIPS in a US Court but can only rely on the terms of the US implementing legislation.

4.146 The European Communities states that, given that Section 211(b) denies to "a designated national or its successor-in-interest" access to US courts for the recognition, enforcement or other validation for a trademark, trade name or commercial name, the same arguments as it used under Section 211(a)(2) apply – *mutatis mutandis* – to Section 211(b) as well.

4.147 The European Communities claims that, by denying any judicial enforceability of the targeted rights, Section 211(b) is at variance with Article 16.1 of the TRIPS Agreement for the reasons pointed out in its arguments made in respect of Section 211(a)(2). It also claims that Section 211(b) is at variance with the US obligations flowing from the first sentence of Article 42 of the TRIPS Agreement as it explained in respect of Article 211(a)(2).

4.148 Furthermore, the European Communities claims that Section 211(b) violates the US obligations under Article 2.1 of the TRIPS Agreement together with Articles 6*bis* (1) and 8 of the Paris Convention (1967) as set out under its arguments concerning Section 211(a)(2). Section 211(b) also violates the national treatment obligations of the United States as contained in Article 3.1 of the TRIPS Agreement and Article 2.1 of the TRIPS Agreement together with Article 2(1) of the Paris Convention (1967) for the reasons the European Communities points out in its arguments concerning Section 211(a)(2). Finally, the European Communities claims that Section 211(b) is incompatible with the United States'

---

[43] The European Communities quoted from the decision of the District Court: "Section 211 explicitly states that no court shall recognize 'treaty' rights of designated nationals. The further reference in that Section to § 44(b) of the Lanham Act should not be read to distinguish certain treaties from others. Both the text of § 44(b) and its legislative history indicate that the purpose of this Section was to execute all US treaty obligations respecting trademarks and trade names. *See* 15 U.S.C. § 1125 ('(t)he intent of this chapter is to ... provide rights and remedies stipulated by treaties and conventions respecting trade-marks, trade names, and unfair competition entered into between the United States and foreign nations'); S. Rep. No. 1333, 79th Cong., 2d Sess. 5 (1946) (stating that purpose of Lanham Act was 'to carry out by statute our international commitments to the end that American traders in foreign countries may receive the protection of their marks to which they are entitled')." *See* Havana Club Holding, S.A. v. Galleon, S.A., 62 F. Supp. 2d 1085, 1092-1093, (S.D.N.Y. 1999), confirmed 203 F. 3d 116 (2d Cir.2000), certiorari denied 121 S.Ct. 277 (2000).

obligations under Article 4 of the TRIPS Agreement for the reasons it mentioned in its arguments concerning Section 211(a)(2).[44]

4.149 The *United States* presented its arguments concerning both Section 211(a)(2) and Section 211(b) at the same time in its written submissions and oral statements. Its arguments concerning both provisions are contained above in those sections of this part of the report that summarize the parties' arguments in relation to Section 211(a)(2). In addition, the United States made the following remarks that concern specifically Section 211(b) in relation to the national treatment obligation.

4.150 The United States argues that US nationals may fall under Section 211(b) as successors to foreign trademark registrants. Section 211(b) specifically applies, by its own terms, to *all* successors in interest – whether US or not. Therefore, Section 211(b) does not violate national treatment obligations. In response to a question from the Panel, the United States emphasizes that Section 211(b) applies equally, without exception, to *any* national who asserts ownership rights derived from the subject confiscations, and so does not violate the national treatment obligation. Section 211(b) is addressed to designated nationals or their successors in interest (of whatever nationality) that base their US trademark registration application on a "home country" foreign registration. Such a trademark application benefits from certain advantages that are not available to those who do not file based on a home country registration. For instance, applications based on a home country registration do not require proof of actual use. "Designated nationals" may take advantage of the "home country" registration process, whereas US nationals may not. Therefore, to the extent that Section 211(b) might prevent a designated national from asserting purported ownership rights in a trademark that was registered based on a home country registration, the statute simply puts the designated national on an equal footing with US nationals, who have no access to that form of registration. As regards "successors in interest", all such successors are in the same position, regardless of nationality. If a US national could become a successor in interest - an assumption which according to the United States is doubtful[45] - he or she would be treated no better than successors in interest who are not US nationals. These factual situations show that, under Section 211(b), US nationals are treated no better than, and sometimes worse than, designated nationals.

D. Horizontal Issues

1. Principle of Non-Recognition of Foreign Confiscations

4.151 Before responding to the specific claims made by the European Communities in its first written submission, the *United States*, in its first written submis-

---

[44] In its first written submission and oral statement, the European Communities said that its arguments presented in relation to Section 211(a)(2) applied *mutatis mutandis* to Section 211(b). In its second written submission and oral statement, it discussed Section 211(a)(2) and Section 211(b) at the same time and reiterated its main arguments presented earlier in relation to Section 211(a)(2).

[45] *See* the US arguments cited in paragraph 4.121.

sion, takes up an issue to which it refers as the principle of non-recognition of foreign confiscations. It argues that it is an established rule of customary international law that a State may not expropriate private assets of nationals of other States in its territory unless the expropriation is (1) for a public purpose, (2) on a non-discriminatory basis and in accordance with due process of law, and (3) subject to prompt, adequate and effective compensation. In numerous judicial decisions spanning the past century, courts throughout the world have found similarly under their laws that foreign confiscatory decrees should be denied recognition in the forum States because they are repugnant to the nation's basic principles with respect to private property rights.[46] Those courts have found in the constitution and laws of the forum State emphatic pronouncements protecting property rights from uncompensated expropriation, and have had no difficulty concluding that those legal prescriptions are among the most fundamental principles of their systems. The courts have overwhelmingly held, accordingly, that it would be a flagrant violation of these principles if a foreign confiscation were given effect in the territory of the forum State.

4.152 According to the United States, this is as true in Europe as it is in the United States. One illustration of the European jurisprudence given by the United States is the multi-country litigation that arose out of the confiscation of the Koh-I-Noor trademark by the Communist revolutionary Government in Czechoslovakia.[47] Consistent with this practice in Europe, courts in the United States have steadfastly held that foreign confiscations will not be given effect within its jurisdiction. In case after case, courts in the United States have ruled that a foreign confiscation "is 'shocking to our sense of justice', and we need not enforce it here".

4.153 The United States argues that the unifying theme of the court decisions by European and US as well as other courts it has cited is that a foreign confiscation is contrary to the basic principles of the forum and will not be given effect in it. This principle – the *principle of non-recognition of foreign confiscations* – has been applied in a variety of settings. Not surprisingly, the most frequent case brought before the national courts is that of a foreign confiscation giving rise to a claim of title to property located in the forum. When the forum courts are called upon to adjudicate such a dispute, they routinely refuse to recognize the purported extraterritorial effects of the confiscation. Courts have also refused to recognize claims of title, based on a foreign confiscation, to property located in a third country at the time of the confiscation. In particular, courts have refused to

---

[46]   The United States cites numerous cases relating to extraterritorial confiscations with particular reference to trademarks. *See* Exhibit US-2, which refers to cases decided by courts of Argentina, Austria, Belgium, Brazil, France, Germany, Israel, Italy, the Netherlands, Norway, Spain, Sweden, Switzerland, the United Kingdom and the United States.

[47]   The United States submits that Koh-I-Noor L. & C. Hardtmuth was a Czechoslovak firm that owned registered trademarks throughout Europe and the United States. Following the Second World War, the company was expropriated without compensation by the Czechoslovak government. The government conveyed the assets of the company, including its trademarks, to a state-owned company, which then tried to assert rights to the trademark in various countries. The original owners of the confiscated company re-established their business in France and laid claim to those same trademarks. Courts across Europe refused to give extraterritorial effect to the confiscation.

give effect to the purported extraterritorial reach of a foreign confiscatory decree to trademarks registered in Berne.

4.154 The United States submits that Section 211 was enacted to reaffirm this principle with respect to trademarks, trade names and commercial names used in connection with businesses confiscated by Cuba, and to reaffirm and clarify the rights of the legitimate owners of such marks and names. Section 211(a)(1) provides that, absent consent of the original owner, a general licence from OFAC is unavailable for the registration or renewal of any trademark that is the same as or substantially similar to one used in connection with a business confiscated by Cuba.[48]

4.155 The United States submits that, as a complement to Section 211(a)(1), Section 211(a)(2) prevents the confiscating government and its successors in interest from asserting rights of ownership in trademarks used in connection with

---

[48] In response to a question from the Panel, the United States explains that, with respect to the substantive law concerning the ownership and protection of trademarks, Section 211 is a statutory articulation of a principle that is reflected in numerous US judicial decisions. It is not unusual in a common-law system for the legislature to elect to codify certain principles that have evolved in common law, for the sake of clarity and predictability.

The United States adds that procedurally, prior to Section 211(a)(1), a confiscating Cuban entity or its successors could register a trademark pursuant to an OFAC general licence (although the trademark could not be used in association with Cuban products because of the embargo). That registration, like all trademark registrations, was subject to challenge on the grounds that the trademark registrant was not the owner of the trademark. Such a challenge might be launched, for instance, by the original owner whose assets and trademark were confiscated in Cuba. A challenge could arise in a cancellation proceeding before the USPTO or in the context of litigation before a federal district court. After Section 211, if a confiscating entity or its successor registers a trademark used in connection with confiscated assets under cover of an OFAC general licence, that registration would be subject to challenge on the same grounds as before - that the registrant is not the proper owner of the mark.

The United States submits that Section 211 does clarify, moreover, that Cuban confiscating entities do not have any special favorable status in registering trademarks associated with assets they have confiscated. US courts do not give effect to foreign confiscations with respect to US assets, such as trademarks. However, OFAC had issued a general licence for the registration of trademarks in which Cuba or Cuban national have an interest – which would include confiscated marks. This created the possibility of confusion as to whether the United States was – exceptionally – allowing Cuban confiscating entities to claim trademark rights in the United States associated with the assets they had confiscated. This confusion was heightened by the fact that the USPTO, although tasked in part with assuring that registrants are the owners of the trademarks they claim, is not an agency generally called upon to consider questions arising from foreign confiscations. Added to this was the fact that, because Cuban trademarks cannot be used in the United States, there was no opportunity for the original owners to bring suit for infringement with respect to the confiscated trademarks.

The United States adds that Section 211 eliminates any possible confusion over any "special" status conferred on Cuban confiscating entities with respect to confiscated trademarks by providing that the OFAC general licence is not available for the registration of such trademarks. Thus it is made abundantly clear that the original owner of the trademark can challenge the ownership rights of the confiscating entity.

The United States argues that, for these reasons, Section 211 did not meaningfully change the legal situation with respect to those trademarks covered by its provisions compared to the situation under the pre existing law as concerns either the procedures relating to the acquisition and maintenance of rights relating to such marks (including procedural steps necessary to register or renew the registration of such marks); or the substantive law concerning the ownership and protection of such marks.

confiscated assets in US courts. Section 211(b) is a provision parallel to Section 211(a)(2). Whereas Section 211(a)(2) protects the rights of legitimate owners vis-à-vis designated nationals or their successors who would attempt to claim confiscation-derived trademark rights under common law or a registration, Section 211(b) extends this prohibition to designated nationals or their successors that base their US trademark registration on foreign registrations, through domestic laws intended to implement treaties. Section 211(b) prohibits the enforcement in the United States of rights based on foreign registrations in the case of a trademark, trade name, or commercial name confiscated by Cuba, except with the consent of the original owner.[49]

4.156 The *European Communities* contends that Section 211 has nothing to do with the well established US law and practice in relation to the domestic effects of foreign expropriations. Section 211 concerns exclusively the treatment of US trademarks and trade names against which the Cuban expropriations can have had no effects, and therefore the customary international law principles on expropriations raised by the United States to defend Section 211 are simply not relevant for the purposes of resolving this dispute.[50]

4.157 The European Communities asserts that, under public international law, the main principle to be recalled with regard to "ownership" is that, as a conse-

---

[49] In response to a question from the Panel, the United States explains that Section 211, in its entirety, reflects that ownership is a threshold issue and a basis for legal challenge in cases in which a party asserts rights in a trademark, trade name or commercial name. The overall purpose and effect of Section 211 is to emphasize that one may not claim rights of ownership derived from a confiscation. That purpose was accomplished by addressing or eliminating the procedural devices by which such a right of ownership could be asserted. This includes addressing the transactions or payments necessary to register a trademark, under Section 211(a)(1), or the ability to enforce a trademark in the US courts, under Sections 211(a)(2) and (b). Such thinking and drafting in procedural terms is not uncommon in the US legal system, which largely derives from case law rather than from declaratory provisions such as those characteristic of civil-law codes.

As a general matter, codification of legal principles is common in the US legal system. For example, it was not until 1996 that the concept of dilution was incorporated, at the federal level, into the Trademark Act. Prior to that time, while all fifty states had dilution statutes, plaintiffs and defendants alike were required to "prove" the concept and its applicability. Codification eliminated this time-consuming, economically wasteful step, making more efficient use of both judicial and consumer resources. Thus, the US system acknowledges the economic benefits that accrue when a time-honoured principle is committed to statutory form. Since codification is usually completed in response to a real or perceived need, not all principles of common law have been codified, nor does the codification necessarily address an issue as broadly as the common law principle. (For example, federal trademark law is not codified. The Trademark Act is only one legal vehicle relevant to federal trademark law.)

The United States adds that another consideration in the case of Section 211 is that, as a practical matter, not all courts see a variety of issues. In 1983, the Court of Appeals for the Federal Circuit was created specifically to address – among other specialty legal issues such as federal labor-relations cases – appeals in intellectual property cases, particularly patent cases. Thus, legislators have found it necessary and desirable to ensure that specialty areas of the law receive fair and knowledgeable treatment. Section 211 follows in this tradition, to ensure that courts that do not ordinarily hear confiscation cases are attuned to the intellectual property issues that may be raised by such cases.

[50] In response to a question from the Panel, the European Communities clarifies that it does not contend that Section 211 prejudicially affects the exercise of TRIPS protected legal rights created in its member States. It contends that Section 211 prejudicially affects the exercise of TRIPS protected legal rights created in the United States.

---

quence of the principle of sovereign equality of States, every State has the right to regulate the ownership of property in its own territory. This right includes the right to regulate how to acquire, enjoy, enforce and transfer property. It also includes the right to establish under which conditions the State may compulsorily take private property, in other words, nationalize, confiscate or expropriate it. A corollary of this principle is that a State is not required to accept another State's expropriation of property on the first State's territory.

4.158 In light of this principle, the European Communities states that it has never challenged that the United States is entitled not to recognize Cuban expropriations as changing the ownership of US trademarks and trade names.

4.159 However, the European Communities argues that, in light of the principle of sovereign equality of States, the United States is not entitled to refuse to recognize a change in ownership in an expropriating State of property that is incontestably under the jurisdiction of the expropriating State (business assets in Cuba) and to draw certain consequences therefrom.

4.160 In response to a question from the Panel, the European Communities states that the TRIPS Agreement *does not* require a WTO Member to recognize a confiscation of intellectual property in another country as regards the legal effect of that confiscation on the ownership of intellectual property protected in its own territory, in a third country, or even in the country where the confiscation took place.

4.161 In response to other questions from the Panel, the European Communities notes that, if a case with a factual situation similar to that of the Koh-I-Noor case, to which the United States had referred, would now arise in some EC member States' courts, the TRIPS Agreement would not require the courts to come to different conclusions. However, under the TRIPS Agreement a WTO Member remains also free to recognize ownership rights in the hands of the confiscation beneficiary.

4.162 In response to a further question, the European Communities clarified that in its view the TRIPS Agreement would not mandate different outcomes as regards the decisions, cited by the United States, where courts had refused to recognize claims of title, based on a foreign confiscation, to property located in a third country.

4.163 As regards protection of well-known marks under Article 6*bis* of the Paris Convention (1967) as incorporated into the TRIPS Agreement, the European Communities argues, in response to a question from the Panel, that in case an enterprise in country A which owned the well-known trademark in country B, is expropriated in country A, country B – on the basis of TRIPS – is free to recognize the original owner or the post-expropriation owner as the owner of the well-known trademark in its territory.

4.164 As regards Article 6*quinquies* of the Paris Convention (1967) as incorporated into the TRIPS Agreement, the European Communities argues, in response to another question, that it can see no provision in that Article which would forbid a Member, where an application covered by the provisions of Article 6*quinquies* is filed, to accept a certificate that was issued before the confiscation, because a WTO Member can renounce on the production of a certificate altogether.

4.165 Responding to the same question, the European Communities takes the view that under Article 6*quinquies* the country where registration is sought, is obliged to recognize the post-expropriation situation in the expropriating country and give full effects to an application based on this new situation. It adds that, in its view, the country where registration is sought has under this provision no right to question the existence of a trademark in the hands of an owner as defined by the laws of the country of origin.

4.166 The European Communities also explains, in response to a question from the Panel, that in its view Article 6*quinquies* D of the Paris Convention does not create a link between trademark ownership in the country of origin and the country where the benefit of Article 6*quinquies* is claimed. This provision only requires that *the trademark exists* in the country of origin, it does *not require* that *the applicant* is identical with the owner of the trademark in the country of origin.

4.167 Commenting on Section 211, the European Communities submits that confiscations of assets have frequently happened throughout the 20th century. It says that if it is true that the purpose of Section 211 is to deny recognition to these confiscations in the United States, it comes as a surprise to the European Communities that the United States has waited until 1998 to adopt for the first time legislation to pursue this objective. Similarly, the European Communities is surprised that it has taken the United States almost four decades to address problems caused by the situation flowing from confiscations in Cuba that mainly occurred around 1960. It also appears curious to the European Communities that numerous countries have operated uncompensated confiscations both before and after the Cuban revolution, but in relation to these uncompensated confiscations by other countries no provisions like Section 211 exist or have ever existed under US law.

4.168 The European Communities also argues that no other country in the world has a provision like Section 211 on its statute books, or at least no such statutory or regulatory provision has ever been communicated to the TRIPS Council under Article 63 of the TRIPS Agreement.

4.169 The European Communities also claims to be surprised to realize that Section 211 only applies to trademarks and trade and commercial names, but not to other intellectual property rights, given that, according to the United States, it is an application of the general principle of US law to deny effects to foreign uncompensated confiscations. Furthermore, no other intangible rights (such as, for example, receivables or bank accounts) or tangible assets are affected by Section 211 and no other equivalent provision under US law covering such assets would appear to exist or have ever existed.

4.170 In the view of the European Communities, the language of Section 211 is sufficiently straightforward to reasonably allow an appreciation of its scope and operation. In line with established rules on the issue of burden of proof, as expressed by the Appellate Body in *India – Patent Protection*[51], the burden to prove that Section 211 may mean something else than its plain text is squarely on the United States.

4.171 The European Communities claims that the United States in several instances deliberately mixes up the question of ownership of trademarks/trade names in Cuba and issues of ownership to trademarks/trade names in the United States. It argues that a good example of this kind of confusion can be found in the reply to question 21 from the Panel[52] where the United States states that "added to this was the fact that, because Cuban trademarks cannot be used in the United States, there was no opportunity for the original owners to bring suit for infringement with respect to the confiscated mark". Given the principle of territoriality of trademarks,[53] a Cuban trademark can under no circumstance be used against an infringement in the United States.

4.172 The European Communities notes the US assertion in that reply that "[f]or these reasons Section 211 did not meaningfully change the legal situation with respect to those trademarks covered by its provisions compared to the situation under the pre-existing law". In this respect, the European Communities refers to certain parts of its introductory remarks[54], and to the Havana Club trademark which, before Section 211 entered into force, was duly registered and renewed by the USPTO. The European Communities claims that these acts can no more be performed since Section 211 entered into force.

4.173 European Communities argues that the US jurisprudence cited by the United States carefully limits its considerations to the precise assets which were confiscated or were at least the target of the attempted confiscation. On the contrary, Section 211 extends its scope well beyond confiscated assets.

4.174 As to the targeted US trademarks and trade names under Section 211, the European Communities argues that any US trademark or trade name is a potential target, if the sign or combination of signs of which it is composed is the same or substantially similar to a trademark or trade name used in connection with a business or assets that were confiscated in Cuba. It is important to appreciate that this identity or similarity relates to the perception of the signs of which the trademark/trade name is composed. There is no need that the Cuban business effectively owned such a US trademark/trade name. According to the European Communities, the United States has confirmed that Section 211 applies in a situation in which no identical or similar trademark existed in the United States (in the hands of the expropriated business or in the hands of another person) at the time of the Cuban expropriations.[55] The European Communities argues that the US trademark/trade name does not have to have any factual or legal link with

---

[51] AB-1997-5, WT/DS50/AB/R, DSR 1998:I, 9, paragraph 74.
[52] The US response to question 21 is cited in footnote 48 above.
[53] In this regard, the European Communities refers to Article 6(3) of the Paris Convention.
[54] Cited in paragraphs 4.5-4.8 above.
[55] The European Communities refers to the US response to question 1(b). The United States explained that "[w]hether such a mark would come within the scope of Section 211 would depend on the facts. It may or may not be important to a court's determination of ownership of the mark that the mark existed in the United States at the time of confiscation".

a trademark/trade name which existed in the United States at the moment of the Cuban confiscation.

4.175 The European Communities submits that the trademark asset consists in exclusive rights relating to a sign in conjunction with a certain class of products. Section 211 does not only affect a US trademark in relation to the products which were covered by the trademark used in relation to the confiscated enterprise, but covers trademarks for any class of products. Also, Section 211 does not limit its scope to the same trademarks which were the object of the confiscation, but extends its scope to trademarks which are substantially similar to the ones used by the confiscated enterprise. The European Communities claims that it is obvious that a substantially similar trademark by its very definition has never been confiscated or attempted to be confiscated.

4.176 The European Communities further argues that trademarks can be abandoned by the respective owners through non-use and an intent to abandon. In this situation, the trademark falls into the public domain and anybody can apply for its registration and acquire ownership to it. Such abandoned trademarks are clearly covered by Section 211, without them being legally linked to previously confiscated trademarks.

4.177 The European Communities asserts these examples clearly demonstrate how Section 211 applies to US trademarks which had neither a factual nor a legal link with a Cuban enterprise using such a trademark. By its very broad wording, Section 211 applies to a US trademark which was never the property of the confiscated enterprise, or linked to it in any way. It is sufficient under Section 211 that the US trademark is the same or substantially similar to a trademark used in connection with a business that was confiscated. Section 211 does not require that the trademarks/trade names used with the confiscated Cuban enterprise existed in the United States, they can have existed anywhere in the world.[56]

4.178 As to the operation of Sections 211(a)(2) and (b), the European Communities argues that the ownership of a common-law trademark has to be strictly separated from the ownership of a registered federal trademark, and that the United States has been seeking throughout the proceedings before the Panel to mix up these two matters. To this end it reviews some basic features of the US system of trademark protection. According to the European Communities, a dis-

---

[56] In the view of the European Communities, the different decisions by US courts concerning disputes in relation to the US trademark and trade name "Havana Club" give a good practical illustration of how Section 211 works and why Section 211 is fundamentally different from the US jurisprudence on the effects of foreign confiscations. In one judgement, the US Federal District Court for the Southern District of New York recognized expressly that a Cuban enterprise (Cubaexport) is the owner of the US registered mark Havana Club. See Havana Club Holding, S.A. v. Galleon, S.A., 974.F.Suppl. 302 S.D.N.Y. 1997. The European Communities points out that in relation to this trademark a Cuban enterprise or its successor-in-interest are the rightfully registered owners of the trademark not only in the United States but in well over 100 countries and territories. The same court in a subsequent judgement in the same matter describes the object and purpose of Section 211 by saying at page 41 that "[t]his statute limits the registration and renewal of, and the assertion of trademark and trade name rights [...]". By applying Section 211(b) the Court refused the plaintiff's claim of trade name infringement, because it did not have the consent of the original owner of the trademark. See Havana Club Holding, S.A. v. Galleon, S.A., 62.F.Suppl. 2d 1085 S.D.N.Y. 1999.

tinction has to be made between so-called common law trademarks and registered trademarks. The common law of protection against unfair competition provides for an action to protect unregistered trademarks, service marks, trade names, designs and trade dress through actual use in commerce as long as they meet certain fundamental requirements for protection which may vary from State to State. Such common-law trademarks are typically territorially limited to the federal State or region where they are used. Registered federal trademarks under the Lanham Act are a completely different creature. A registered federal trademark may or may not be based on a pre-existing common law trademark. It is perfectly possible to obtain a registered trademark without having had any common-law trademark previously.

4.179 According to the European Communities, a US federal registered trademark is created by the act of registration. Before registration, a registered trademark does not exist and consequently there exists no owner of such right. Before such a registration is granted, the USPTO has to verify that the applicant meets all requirements for trademark registration. One of the elements to be verified is the use or intention to use the signs or combination of signs in commerce for the products concerned. This latter criterion and some other criteria can also be invoked by third parties. Once granted, a federal registered trademark becomes "incontestable" after five consecutive years of use and can no more be challenged by any contender who asserts prior rights. A similar effect occurs already after 5 years of registration.

4.180 The European Communities claims that this mechanism is one of the very reasons for the introduction of Section 211. The "Havana Club" trademark was duly registered in the USPTO in 1976 and had become by 1998, when Section 211 was adopted, incontestable. It is insofar also instructive that the USPTO has refused in 1994 and 1995 requests for the registration of a "Havana Club" trademark made by members of the Arechabala family, the former owners of the expropriated Cuban business which used the "Havana Club" trademark.[57]

4.181 As to the question of whether a US national can be the owner of a trade name or trademark targeted by Section 211, the European Communities argues that, given the fact that the trademarks and trade names targeted by Section 211 do not have to be legally traceable to a Cuban owner, the question if OFAC can and has already granted transfer licences is finally irrelevant, even though the text of the CACR is utterly clear that OFAC has the authority to grant such licences. As regards decisions of transfer, OFAC is only concerned with transactions in property in which Cuba or a Cuban national has an interest. It is not at all concerned with transactions in property owned by other persons.

4.182 The European Communities submits that the United States has repeatedly tried to excuse the TRIPS inconsistencies of Section 211 by referring to the uncertainty of how US courts might interpret this provision. It should be sufficient to recall that US courts are constitutionally required to fully respect federal stat-

---

[57] The European Communities adds that this is confirmed by the information available from the website of the USPTO in relation to the "Havana Club" trademark which shows that this registration has been subject to several cancellation attempts, all of them having been unsuccessful.

utes. In this context it is also noteworthy that the WTO Agreement (including the TRIPS Agreement) is not self-executing in the US legal order. This means that an individual cannot rely on TRIPS in a US court but can only rely on the terms of the US implementing legislation. Furthermore, it is well-established US jurisprudence that subsequent federal statutes have priority over previous international treaties concluded by the United States, thus preventing a US court from interpreting US domestic law in a treaty conform manner in case of conflict. This principle has been applied by a US court in a case referred to earlier[58] where the Court found that: "[...] Congress made clear its intention to repeal rights in marks and trade names derived from treaties, where those marks and trade names satisfy the requirements set forth in Section 211."

4.183 The European Communities argues that, as far as the USPTO is concerned, the clear wording of Section 211(a)(1), as implemented through Section 515.527(2) of the CACR, does not authorize to make payments to the USPTO necessary to file applications with the USPTO with respect to the registration and renewal of trademarks covered by Section 211. USPTO does not have any discretion to act otherwise.

4.184 The European Communities argues that the United States has put forward as its main defence the existence of a longstanding US policy against the recognition of foreign expropriations. The European Communities says that Section 211, which is allegedly a particular incarnation of this "longstanding policy", is in the view of the United States therefore exempted from TRIPS scrutiny. The European Communities argues that there exists nowhere in TRIPS a blanket exception that measures taken by a WTO Member would be exempted from TRIPS scrutiny, if the underlying policy considerations for these measures involve issues of foreign confiscations. The European Communities states that the United States has never pinpointed any such TRIPS provisions. According to the European Communities, the acceptance of any such blanket exception, be it for considerations of expropriations or for other reasons (e.g., to further public health or to foster the domestic industrialization), would render the TRIPS Agreement perfectly meaningless. Therefore, all measures taken by a WTO Member in relation to intellectual property rights covered by TRIPS have to meet the minimum standards of protection provided for by TRIPS. The European Communities argues that there can be no doubt – which according to it is not disputed by the United States – that the intellectual property rights covered by Section 211 are subject to TRIPS disciplines.

4.185 Commenting on the decisions by US courts to which the United States has referred in order to illustrate the US policy to disregard the effects of uncompensated confiscations by other countries in relation to non-nationals of such countries, the European Communities submits that the clear leitmotiv followed by the courts in these decisions consists in allocating ownership to the US rights as between different contenders. The European Communities argues that Section 211 pursues an approach which is diametrically opposed to the policy re-

---

[58] The European Communities refers to Havana Club Holding, S.A. v. Galleon, S.A., 62F., Supp. 2d 1085 S.D.N.Y. 1999.

flected in the jurisprudence referred to by the United States. Section 211 has to be systematically seen in the context of the system of US measures vis-à-vis Cuba, of which the Cuban Assets Control Regulation, to which Section 211 refers in several instances, is the pivotal piece of legislation. The purpose and object of these measures, as the name of the regulation already suggests, is not to allocate certain assets as between Cuba or Cuban nationals and others, but to control and curtail the exercise of legally undisputed ownership rights held by Cuba or Cuban nationals in relation to assets situated in the United States. The European Communities claims that the recognition of ownership of Cuba or Cuban nationals under US law in these assets is beyond doubt and a very precondition to the existence of the CACR.

4.186 The European Communities argues that all three operative parts of Section 211 start out from the basic assumption that the trademarks and trade or commercial names are lawfully owned by Cuba, a Cuban national or their successors-in-interest. Only if these designated nationals or successors-in-interest are considered as the lawful owners of the assets concerned, can they reasonably engage in a transaction in relation to these assets. This argument also applies to Sections 211(a)(2) and (b) because it does not make any sense to forbid US courts to recognize, enforce or otherwise validate the assertion of rights if there are no rights vested in the claimants in the first place.

4.187 The European Communities argues that another marked difference between Section 211 and the US jurisprudence in relation to foreign confiscations consists of the fact that this jurisprudence allocates the assets between two or more contenders. The European Communities claims that Section 211 operates whether or not there exists a contender. But even in cases where there exists a contender Section 211 will under no circumstances operate to allocate ownership rights. In other words, on the basis of Section 211(a)(2) and (b), the "original owner" will under no circumstances become the owner of the trademarks/trade/commercial names concerned. Thus the "original owner" will not be able himself to ask for injunctive relief or damages if somebody uses the disputed trademark or trade name without his consent. Sections 211(a)(2) and (b) will only grant the "original owner" a negative right to prevent somebody else from enforcing certain rights.

4.188 The European Communities argues that the owner of the confiscated business himself is given under Section 211 no cause of action or defence at all. He is not even a party - neither necessary nor permissible - to litigation involving the application of Section 211. Any infringer of a registered trademark can invoke Sections 211(a)(2) and (b) in an infringement procedure brought by the owner of the registered trademark. The infringer does not need to have the consent or authorization by the owner of the confiscated business to invoke this defence. The confiscated business may have ceased to exist altogether or the owner may have died without successors or simply disappeared.

4.189 The European Communities claims that the punitive character of the operation of Section 211 is clearly demonstrated. This provision is exclusively concerned with the discriminatory curtailment of trademarks and trade names in the hands of certain right holders, without giving any corresponding right to the owner of the business allegedly aggrieved by the foreign confiscation.

4.190 The European Communities argues that these operational features distinguish Section 211 in a fundamental way from the US jurisprudence on foreign expropriations which is concerned with the allocation of ownership as between several contenders. As the United States has rightly pointed out, US law and practice does indeed generally recognize the assets concerned in the hands of the pre-confiscation owner rather than in the hands of the beneficiary of the confiscation. To the contrary, Section 211 is only concerned with curtailing the use of an asset by its legal owner, without giving any corresponding benefit to the "original" owner.

4.191 The European Communities argues that the jurisprudence cited by the United States of both US and foreign courts that denies effects to foreign expropriations vis-à-vis domestic assets has nothing to do with Section 211. If, indeed, a US trademark or trade name was the object of a Cuban expropriation, this expropriation would – in light of the jurisprudence referred to by the United States – in all likelihood not be recognized and the pre-confiscation owner would continue to be the owner of the US rights. In this situation, Section 211 clearly has no role to play. The operation of Section 211 is diametrically opposed to the one described in this expropriation jurisprudence. It creates, in fact, detrimental effects for US assets based on events, which have taken place in Cuba in relation to assets outside the US. This could be described as a reversal of the principal of territoriality.

4.192 The European Communities further argues that the expropriation jurisprudence focuses on the asset and allocates the asset to persons independently of their respective nationality. To the contrary, Section 211 curtails trademarks and trade names only in the hands of certain nationals but not in the hands of others.

4.193 The European Communities submits that all this demonstrates beyond any reasonable doubt that Section 211 has nothing to do with the denial of recognition of domestic effects flowing from foreign expropriations, i.e., with the application of the principle of territoriality. Section 211 is exclusively concerned with the curtailment of the enjoyment of US trademarks and trade names in the hands of "undesirable" owners. Section 211 in reality has created yet another set of punitive measures targeted at Cuba and Cuban nationals and their successors-in-interest.

4.194 The European Communities recalls the US argument that no actual cases have occurred in which Section 211 has been applied and claims that, therefore, Section 211 cannot be considered contrary to any TRIPS obligation at this point in time. The European Communities submits that there exists a final judgement by the US Federal Court of Appeals for the Second Circuit in the Havana Club case in which Section 211(b) was applied. The European Communities adds that Section 211 contains clear and unequivocal instructions to the US executive and judicial branch of government without granting any degree of discretion. It argues that it is a well-established principle of WTO jurisprudence that national laws and regulations can be subject to scrutiny without having been effectively applied in individual cases and without the need for the complaining Member to have been directly affected by their operation.[59]

4.195 The Panel requested the *United States* to clarify which trademarks and other signs were covered by Section 211. In response, the United States submits, *inter alia*, that, in general terms, Section 211 addresses the issue of trademarks, trade names, and commercial names associated with business assets confiscated without compensation under circumstances where the "original owner" of the confiscated business has not provided a consent in respect of actions taken in relation to them. Therefore, a finder of fact such as a US court would have to determine whether each of the elements of Section 211 was met.

4.196 As regards the term "such a confiscated mark" used in Section 211(a)(2), the United States submits that the term serves two purposes. First, it is a short-hand way of referring to a trademark described in Section 211(a)(1), that is, "a mark, trade name or commercial name that is the same as or substantially similar to a mark, trade name or commercial name that was used in connection with a business or assets that were confiscated unless the original owner [...] has expressly consented". Second, the language "such confiscated mark" reflects that there is, under Section 211, a connection or link between the trademark whose enforcement is sought and the confiscation. Trademarks do not exist in a vacuum, but are linked to an underlying business asset. In situations covered by Section 211, that underlying business asset has been confiscated, the confiscating entity (or its successor in interest) is asserting ownership of the associated trademark by virtue of the confiscation of the asset, *and* there is a prior owner of the trademark used in connection with that asset. In this sense, it is the mark itself that has been confiscated. According to the United States, it appears that the Cuban confiscations did extend to the trademarks used in connection with the confiscated businesses, along with all the other assets of those businesses.

4.197 In response to a question whether Section 211 would apply to a trademark whose original owner has legally abandoned the trademark in the United States, the United States submits that this is a question that is left to the decision-maker. The United States argues that the core issue under Section 211 is trademark ownership. Therefore, a court could well decide that, under particular circumstances where a trademark has been legally abandoned, there is no original owner whose consent is required under Section 211.[60]

---

[59] The European Communities refers to the Appellate Body finding in the case of *India – Patents*, in which the existence of a violation of Article 70.9 of the TRIPS Agreement was confirmed without a single request for administrative protection having been made vis-à-vis the Indian authorities. Panel Report, *India - Patent Protection for Pharmaceutical and Agricultural Chemical Products – Complaint by the United States*, WT/DS50/R, adopted 16 January 1998, as modified by the Appellate Body Report, WT/DS50/AB/R, DSR 1998:I, 41. The European Communities also notes that the United States recently requested the establishment of a panel against Brazil, claiming violations in the area of patent protection. According to information available to the European Communities, not a single compulsory licence has been applied for or granted on the basis of the Brazilian provision in dispute to date.

[60] The United States submits that Section 211 does not specifically address the issue of abandonment. In general, any facts concerning the ownership of trademarks, including "abandonment" as defined by the Trademark Act at 15 U.S.C. 1127, could be raised and considered in any dispute over

4.198 According to the United States, the European Communities professes to embrace the recognized principle that Members do not have to give effect to foreign confiscatory decrees with respect to assets in their territory, but argues that its position in this dispute is unrelated to that principle. The United States argues that the principle *depends*, however, on Members being free under the TRIPS Agreement to determine the conditions under which a person can claim ownership in a trademark. If a Member is not free under the TRIPS Agreement to determine these substantive rules of ownership, as the European Communities contends, then a Member is not free to decide that it will not recognize the ownership of confiscating entities in trademarks; the European Communities cannot have it both ways. [61]

4.199 In the view of the United States, the European Communities takes a very expansive view of the requirements of Article 6*quinquies* of the Paris Convention. The United States argues that, where confiscated trademarks registered in Cuba are concerned, the European Communities is, in fact, demanding that the

---

ownership. "Abandonment" has two components, both of which must be proved. First, the use of the mark must have been voluntarily discontinued. Second, the discontinuation must be with the intent not to resume use. The United States says that two observations are relevant to whether the issue of abandonment has any practical significance in this dispute.

First, the United States submits that when the claimant to the mark has actual knowledge that the original Cuban owner's cessation of use was the result of a forcible takeover of his business, it would appear that the discontinuation of use was not voluntary, and was not accompanied by an intent not to resume use. Therefore, no issue of abandonment would be raised. In any event, the Lanham Act has codified the long-standing equitable "excusable nonuse" doctrine (i.e., the doctrine that nonuse attributable to special circumstances which excuse that nonuse does not give rise to an inference of an intent to abandon) with respect to the maintenance of a federal trademark registration under Sections 8 and 9 of the Trademark Act. An assertion of excusable non-use, if successful, would prevent registered marks from being considered abandoned; that same doctrine applies with equal force to common law trademark ownership rights in the United States. Consequently, a court could determine that the nonuse of a trademark in the United States because its original Cuban owner had his production facility in Cuba forcibly expropriated is excusable nonuse and does not result in an abandonment of that expropriation victim's US trademark rights.

Second, the United States submits that there is no TRIPS requirement that Members adopt a policy of abandonment. While Article 19.1 of the TRIPS Agreement forbids cancellation of a trademark based on non-use before the lapse of an uninterrupted period of at least three years of non-use, it does not require cancellation of a mark based on non-use. In fact, in some WTO Members, use is not a requirement for maintenance of a trademark registration. Thus, the mere fact of non-use is not synonymous with abandonment, either under the TRIPS Agreement or under US law.

[61] The United States further argues that first, the European Communities purports to embrace the principle that a Member does not have to give effect to foreign confiscations with respect to assets in that Member's territory. But then the European Communities presents, for purposes of *this* dispute, an interpretation of TRIPS and the Paris Convention that would nullify this very principle. The United States submits that if TRIPS and the Paris Convention require Members to register and protect all trademarks regardless of the registrant's ownership of the trademark, as the European Communities argues, then Members are powerless to deny ownership of trademarks in their territory to confiscating entities. According to the United States, this means that TRIPS and the Paris Convention require Members to give effect in their territory to foreign confiscations. The United States argues that, however, there is nothing in TRIPS that produces this result. Nothing in TRIPS requires the United States to declare that confiscating entities are the rightful owners of US trademarks and trade names associated with the confiscated assets. While TRIPS imposes numerous substantive and procedural obligations on Members with respect to trademarks, the standards for and means of determining trademark ownership are not among those obligations. According to the United States, this point is confirmed by the materials provided by WIPO.

United States give effect to confiscations with respect to assets within the United States. This is precisely what the many cases cited by the United States have refused to do, and what Section 211 addresses. The European Communities cannot avoid this contradiction between its position on Article 6*quinquies* (as well as on TRIPS Articles 15.1 and 16.1) and the principle of non-recognition of foreign confiscations, which the European Communities expressly accepts.

4.200   The United States claims that the European Communities, in its responses to questions from the Panel,[62] tries to navigate a course through the circumstances in which TRIPS *does* require a Member to confer trademark ownership on the entity that confiscated it, and those in which it does not. The United States argues that the European Communities does this with a view to preserve both its present position in this dispute that TRIPS dictates trademark ownership rules, on the one hand, and the principle that Members have the right not to recognize the ownership rights of confiscating entities, on the other. The United States argues that this is a distinction that cannot be maintained; either TRIPS does or it does not contain rules that require the United States to recognize a confiscating entity's ownership in a US trademark. According to the United States, the TRIPS Agreement does not contain such requirement; to say that there is such a TRIPS requirement, but that it is subject to exceptions, is not only to invent an "ownership" provision where there is none, but to craft detailed exemptions to that invented provision to accommodate the recognized principle of non-recognition.

4.201   The United States submits that the European Communities attempts to confuse the issue by arguing that Section 211 impermissibly extends the reach of the accepted principle of non-recognition of foreign confiscations. The United States recalls that the European Communities', in response to questions from the Panel[63], argues that the United States, through Section 211, denies the ability of a sovereign, such as Cuba, to make ownership decisions within its own territory. According to the United States, the European Communities would have the Panel believe that Section 211 is the United States' attempt to control creation and assignment of trademark, trade name and/or commercial name rights in other countries. The US submits that, in fact, Section 211 merely denies the extraterritorial effect of an uncompensated confiscation. Section 211 in no way addresses the validity, in a third country, of a particular trademark, trade name or business name. It simply points out that, despite validity in any other country, an assertion of rights in a trademark, trade name or business name associated with a business that was confiscated without compensation is not a valid assertion of rights in the United States – unless such assertion is made by the owner.[64]

---

[62]   The United States refers in particular to questions 42 and 43. The European Communities' response to question 43 is summarized in paragraph 4.160 above.

[63]   The United States refers to the European Communities' response to questions 40-42.

[64]   The United States argues that the inconsistencies in the European Communities' position are further highlighted by several of its responses to Panel questions. The United States recalls that the European Communities responded to Panel question number 46 that, after the nationalization of Compania Ron Bacardi in Cuba, the "trademark owners" (i.e., the original owners of the company, who had left Cuba to set up business in New York) asked the Danish authorities to change the Danish trademark registration to reflect the ownership of the new company in New York. The United States

4.202 The United States argues that the European Communities itself appears unsure about its argument that its interpretation of TRIPS has no relevance to the principle of non-recognition of foreign confiscations. The United States refers to a question the Panel posed to the European Communities on whether the Koh-I-Noor cases cited by the United States would have come out differently under the European Communities' interpretation of TRIPS, to which the European Communities replied, without elaboration, that it is "unlikely" that TRIPS would require a different outcome.[65] The United States claims that, in fact, however, the European Communities' argument in this proceeding - that the United States must register and enforce trademarks that are confiscated and duly registered in the country of origin - would compel a finding that the Czechoslovakian confiscating entity had an enforceable right to the Koh-I-Noor trademark outside of Czechoslovakia wherever it was registered by virtue of Article 6*quinquies* of the Paris Convention. This is a very different result from the original round of cases - and one that would find the EC member States powerless to prevent the assertion of ownership by that confiscating entity. The United States claims that it would appear that many of the cases it discussed in its first submission concerning the principle of non-recognition of foreign confiscations, in addition to the Koh-I-Noor cases, would have come out differently if the European Communities' interpretation of the Paris Convention had been adopted and applied.

4.203 The United States argues that the European Communities' assertion that the principle against the recognition of foreign confiscations is irrelevant to the present dispute is simply wrong.[66] The United States submits that "[t]he principle

---

wonders how did the Danish authorities justify simply changing the ownership of the Danish trademark from the confiscated Cuban company to a new New York company, if, as the European Communities maintains, Article 6*quinquies* requires that all duly registered foreign trademarks be registered and protected — without regard to any decision as to who the true owner of the trademark is. For the United States, the answer is that the Danish authorities were not compelled by anything in the Paris Convention to continue to recognize the trademark ownership of the confiscated Cuban registrant. The United States argues that it appears that the Danish authorities made some considered determination about who the true owner of the trademark was. This is precisely the determination that the European Communities now claims that Members are powerless to make. Under the European Communities' interpretation, it appears that Paris Convention Article 6*quinquies* would have prevented the Danish authorities from concluding that ownership of the trademark should be transferred. Likewise, if the TRIPS Agreement were applied to this situation in the manner urged by the European Communities, it appears that Articles 15.1 and 16.1 would have required the Danish authorities to maintain and enforce the trademark on behalf of the registrant - that is, the confiscated Cuban company. The United States adds that a similar question is presented with respect to the Bacardi trademarks in the United Kingdom.

The *European Communities* responds to the US arguments concerning the Danish Bacardi trademark by stating that it is exclusively the US legislation which is before this Panel. It adds that, however, it can see no element which would systematically distinguish this case from the Zeiss situation [another case referred to by the parties].

[65] The United States refers to the response to question 45. Subsequently, the European Communities clarified its position in response to question 72 by stating that the TRIPS Agreement would not mandate a different solution in the Koh-I-Noor chain of cases today.

[66] The United States draws attention in this regard to a "Declaration of Dissent" signed by a number of members of the European Parliament and submitted to the President of the European Commission to protest the European Communities' challenge to Section 211. The European Communities provided a copy of the reply by the President of the European Commission to the authors of the declara-

of non-recognition exists because Members exercise their right to determine who is and who is not the owner of assets on their territory, including trademarks. This is a right that the European Communities asserts was taken away by TRIPS. That the principle of non-recognition of foreign confiscations exists alongside of TRIPS and the Paris Convention means that the European Communities' interpretation of TRIPS is incorrect. This principle is, therefore, of utmost relevance in this dispute."

4.204 The United States submits that, contrary to the European Communities' statement which characterizes the United States as mixing up questions of ownership of trademarks in the United States and ownership of trademarks in Cuba, the United States position is clear: confiscating entities abroad may be able to assert ownership of assets in their own territory, but they cannot, by virtue of that confiscation, lay claim to assets in the United States.

4.205 The United States submits that the European Communities' logic, by contrast, appears to be as follows: (1) Every State has the right to regulate the ownership of property in its own territory. (2) Therefore, Cuba had a right to confiscate assets, including registered trademarks, in Cuba. (3) The United States is not obligated to accept an attempt by Cuba to confiscate property in the United States, but (4) the United States is obligated to recognize the change of title of property in Cuba "and to draw certain consequences therefrom". These "consequences" apparently include an obligation to recognize the ownership of confiscating entities with respect to trademarks in the United States. The United States claims that something is wrong with the European Communities' analysis: their conclusion flatly contradicts their opening assumption. The United States does not dispute in this proceeding the right of countries to regulate the ownership of assets in their own territories, although in fact those rights are subject to limitations. The United States does dispute, however, that this results in the United States not being able to regulate the ownership of trademarks in its territory under TRIPS.

4.206 The United States argues that the European Communities' sole claim in this dispute is that Section 211, on its face, violates the TRIPS Agreement – that is, that Section 211 requires that actions be taken that are inconsistent with the United States' TRIPS obligations. It does not allege, as it cannot, that Section 211 has caused any action to be taken that is inconsistent with TRIPS, and no such claims are within the Panel's terms of reference. The United States submits that, despite its claims that "the effects of Section 211 are likely to prejudice a great number of commercial relationships by EC enterprises not only with Cuban entities but other partners that fall within the scope of Section 211", the European Communities is unable to point to a single instance in which there has been any such prejudice, let alone whether any such prejudice would violate a TRIPS-protected right.

4.207 In support of this claim, the United States argues that over two years after enactment, and despite the thousands of trademarks the European Communities

---

tion. In addition, both parties provided information concerning the validity of one of the signatures in the declaration.

claims are potentially in "jeopardy", the European Communities cannot point to a single action taken in violation of TRIPS under Section 211. The European Communities speculates that Section 211 might prejudice the "legitimate economic expectations of EC economic operators" but has not shown that it has or that it will. It appears to the United States that even the European Communities concedes that the United States would be entitled under TRIPS not to give effect to a confiscatory decree with respect to trademarks located in the United States. The United States assumes that even the European Communities would admit that EC economic operators purchasing purported rights from the confiscating entity in such US trademarks have no legitimate economic expectation with respect to those US trademarks, or at least no legitimate expectations under the TRIPS Agreement. Whether other such economic operators would come within the scope of Section 211 is an issue that would have to be decided upon by the courts based on the facts of the case.

4.208 The United States further argues that the European Communities' concern with Section 211 is presumably not that it prevents the confiscating entity from asserting ownership in such a circumstance, which even the European Communities regards as legitimate, but that it supposedly goes far beyond such "legitimate" actions, into areas that the European Communities regards as illegitimate. The United States claims that this is where the European Communities' argument breaks down. Although the European Communities has speculated in a general way about how Section 211 might interfere with unspecified legitimate rights, it has not shown that Section 211 *mandates* that actions be taken that it considers contrary to TRIPS. This is the showing that the European Communities must make under the TRIPS Agreement to show that Section 211 is, on its face, inconsistent with TRIPS. The United States submits that the European Communities has failed to make any such showing.

4.209 The United States recalls that the European Communities suggests, for instance, that Section 211 is objectionable because, unlike in the jurisprudence on the non-recognition principle, its scope extends "well beyond confiscated assets" and would apply to trademarks that are used in connection with a different class of products than those subject to the confiscation. The United States responds that, in fact, however, Section 211 is directed at trademarks "used in connection with" the confiscated assets. It is thus simply not possible to conclude from Section 211 that trademarks having no relation to the products subject to the confiscation would be within the scope of Section 211. It adds that trade names are associated with the business itself, and not with any class of products.

4.210 The United States refers to the statement by the European Communities that Section 211 is objectionable because it is not aimed only at the same trademarks used in connection with confiscated assets, but also at trademarks "substantially similar" to the trademarks used in connection with confiscated assets. The United States responds that the point of trademark protection is to prevent consumer confusion as to the source of goods; a trademark that is "substantially similar" to another is as capable of creating confusion as a trademark that is "identical". For this reason one trademark can infringe another trademark if they are "substantially similar". It is in the context of trademark law that Section 211 focuses on identical or "substantially similar" trademarks. To speculate that a court or other decision-maker would use this provision to extend the scope of Section 211 to include completely separate and distinct trademarks from those used in connection with the confiscated assets is sheer fantasy.

4.211 According to the United States, the European Communities is distinguishing "TRIPS-inconsistent" Section 211 from the "TRIPS-consistent" principle of non-recognition of foreign expropriations, on the grounds that the latter is a principle of "allocation" of ownership between two contending parties, whereas the former - Section 211 - simply blocks the ownership of confiscating entities, without allocating it to anyone else. However, any dispute that may arise under Section 211 will also likely involve two parties who claim ownership of the trademark and will also therefore appear to "allocate" ownership – just as in the jurisprudence. Further, however, TRIPS says nothing about "allocation" of ownership; it does not say that Members' rules of trademark ownership must allocate the ownership of all trademarks to one party or another. It is simply silent on the issue of ownership. A Member's law might state that ownership of a trademark must be "allocated" to someone; but nothing in TRIPS would require this. As to the relevance of "abandonment", this is a legal determination that depends on the facts and on the intentions of the owner. TRIPS does not require that Members have a policy of "abandonment" at all; therefore, the impact of "abandonment" on Section 211 decisions has no relevance to an analysis of Section 211's TRIPS-consistency.[67] The United States argues further that the principle related to the extraterritorial application of foreign confiscatory decrees is articulated in the jurisprudence not as an "allocation" of rights to the original owner, but in terms of not recognizing the rights of the confiscating entities. The statements of principle expressed in the judicial decisions (e.g., foreign confiscations are "contrary to our public policy and shocking to our sense of justice and equity" and will not be given effect in the United States) do not reflect a mere neutral "allocation" of ownership rights.

4.212 The United States notes that the European Communities claims that under Section 211 "the 'original owner' will under no circumstances become the owner of the trademark/trade/commercial names concerned [...] Section 211(a)(2) and (b) will only grant the 'original owner' a negative right to prevent somebody else from enforcing certain rights." The United States argues that, assuming this distinction is relevant it is hard to see how Section 211 compels a US court *not* to find that the original owner is the owner of the trademark or trade name. Indeed, it would appear, to the contrary, that in any court proceeding under Section 211, a court will be called upon to determine who is and who is not the owner of the trademark or trade name, and that dispute may well involve the original owner and the confiscating entity. As to the observation that Section 211 "only" grants the original owner a negative right to prevent someone else from using the mark, the United States notes that this is precisely the right conferred on the owner of a registered trademark by Article 16.1 of TRIPS.

---

[67] *See* also footnote 61 above.

4.213 The United States argues that Section 211 reflects the principle that US courts will not give effect to foreign confiscations with respect to assets in the United States, and will not recognize the ownership of confiscating entities in trademarks used in connection with assets they have confiscated (absent the permission of the original owners). Whether the court will recognize the ownership of one entity or another in a particular case will depend on the particular facts presented to it. All of the factual variations proposed by the Panel in its questions to the United States would raise different issues that would be taken into consideration by the court in determining the ownership of the trademark or trade name concerned. The United States does not believe that it is possible to credibly assert that, presented with a particular set of facts, a court or other decision-maker will believe itself compelled by Section 211 to make a particular decision that is contrary to TRIPS. Certainly, the European Communities has not presented any evidence that this is so.

4.214 The United States submits that the European Communities has no basis to argue that the object of Section 211 is to "curtail the exercise of *legally undisputed ownership rights* held by Cuba or Cuban nationals in relation to assets situated in the US". According to the United States, the European Communities argues that ownership of the asset (i.e., the trademark or trade name) is assumed by US law, and that what Section 211 does is prevent the legitimate owner from enforcing his rights. The United States contends that, in light of the detailed description of US and European jurisprudence on the subject of recognition of foreign confiscations, it is incorrect that it is "legally undisputed" that confiscating entities have ownership rights in the United States with respect to trademarks used in connection with confiscated assets. It is *precisely* this ownership that *is* disputed under US law, both in the jurisprudence and in Section 211.

4.215 According to the United States, Section 211 requires a decision-maker to consider, based on the particular facts at issue, numerous "ownership" issues. Among others, it appears that the decision-maker must determine that a business or assets existed and that it was owned by someone; that the business or asset was taken away from that owner without the payment of just and adequate compensation; that there were trademarks, trade names or commercial names used in connection with that business or assets (under US law, "use" in connection with a business or assets may create ownership rights in the trademark, trade name or commercial name); that there is an "original owner" of the trademark trade name or commercial name; that the trademark, trade name or commercial name disputed under Section 211 is identical to, or substantially similar to the trademark, trade name or commercial name used in connection with the confiscated assets (which addresses in part who the owner of that trademark, trade name or commercial name is); and whether the original owner of the trademark, trade name, or commercial name has consented to its registration and/or use by someone else.

4.216 The United States submits that all of these questions raise "ownership" issues: they address the issue of who is, and who is not, the owner of the trademark, trade name or commercial name in the United States. Each of these questions must be resolved by the decision-maker on the basis of the particular facts before him or her, in order to decide whether Section 211 applies. If the answers to these questions establish that the confiscating entity is not the true owner of the trademark, trade name or commercial name (and does not have the consent of the original owner), then Section 211 directs the court not to "recognize, enforce or otherwise validate" any assertion of rights by that person. The outcome of the court's determination under Section 211 – that the assertion of rights by the confiscating entity not be recognized, enforced, or otherwise validated – cannot be read, as the European Communities apparently does, as a decision not to recognize, enforce or otherwise validate *legitimate* ownership rights. To the contrary, this outcome is the necessary result of the conclusion that the person asserting the rights has *no* such ownership rights.

4.217 The United States submits that there is nothing in Section 211 that mandates any particular result that is contrary to TRIPS. Its application under any particular set of facts can vary and will depend on numerous decisions made by the decision-maker relating to who is the true owner of the trademark, trade name or commercial name at issue. Further, these decisions are subject to administrative and judicial review. Consequently, it cannot be said that Section 211 is contrary to any provision of TRIPS.

4.218 The United States claims that the European Communities mischaracterizes Section 211 by suggesting that it targets trademarks and trade names that have nothing to do with the confiscated assets. In the view of the United States, this is apparently with a view to distancing the European Communities from the (well-founded) criticism that its position would create a requirement under TRIPS to recognize the effects of foreign confiscations. The European Communities' complaint appears to be that Section 211 targets trademarks that *look like* trademarks used in connection with confiscated assets, even though the trademarks might not have any legal or factual link to the confiscated assets or to trademarks associated with those assets. But the very fact that Section 211 is focusing on purported trademark rights asserted by entities that confiscated certain assets and the original owners of trademarks used in connection with those confiscated assets means that there is a link between the trademarks targeted by Section 211 and the confiscated assets.

4.219 According to the United States, the European Communities makes several assertions on the scope of Section 211. First, the European Communities maintains that Section 211 requires no factual or legal link between the trademark for which enforcement is being sought and a trademark or trade name that existed in the United States at the time of confiscation. For the United States it is not clear why it matters from a TRIPS point of view whether a trademark existed in the United States at the time of the confiscation. Whether it did or did not exist at the time of the confiscation is irrelevant to whether the United States has the right to determine whether the confiscating entity owns or does not own the trademark. Further, however, Section 211 only refers to the "original owner" of the trademark used in connection with the confiscated asset. Section 211 does not specify the location of the "use", but use of a trademark - even outside of the United States - can give rise to ownership of that trademark in the United States under

US law.[68] Therefore, a court might or might not find that the original owner owned a trademark in the United States at the time of the confiscation, and the court might or might not find that this is relevant. It is simply unclear how a court would resolve this ownership issue. The United States notes that the one case which the European Communities has repeatedly brought up as an illustration of how Section 211 might work — Havana Club — involved a trademark that *did* exist in the United States at the time of the confiscation.

4.220 According to the United States, the second assertion that the European Communities makes is that Section 211 targets trademarks that might cover products completely different from those subject to the confiscation. The United States submits that the European Communities does not say how this relates to any TRIPS obligation. The United States further responds that Section 211 requires that the trademark have been used in connection with the asset or business that was confiscated, and it focuses on protecting the interests of the "original owner" of the trademark used in connection with that asset or business. And, of course, trade names relate to the business itself, not to particular goods. The United States notes that, in the sole example that the European Communities cites - Havana Club - the US trademark at issue appears to have been used in connection with the exact product - rum - that was the subject of the confiscation.

4.221 The United States continues that the third assertion made by the European Communities is that Section 211 may be applied to prevent the assertion of ownership by confiscating entities in cases where the original owner has legally abandoned the US trademark. The United States responds that again it is not clear what significance this assertion has in terms of consistency with TRIPS. TRIPS does not require an abandonment policy at all, so the fact that it might not be applicable in certain circumstances would not violate TRIPS. The United States notes that the European Communities cites once again the judicial decision in the Havana Club case, and submits that the court in that case declined to find that, simply because the original owner had ceased to use that trade name, the original owner had lost his right to prevent the use of his trade name by someone else. The court also noted, by way of explanation of its decision, that "[i]t is not likely that Congress wished to disadvantage a company that understandably ceased to use its trade name after the confiscation of its business". In other words, the court specifically recognized that, in the context of the forced confiscation of the Havana Club distillery, it may be appropriate to conclude that the original owners did not voluntarily cease use of the trade name with the intent not to resume use.

4.222 According to the United States, the European Communities furthermore distinguishes Section 211 from the jurisprudence on non-recognition of foreign confiscations on the grounds that Section 211 targets trademarks that have never been confiscated and that "have existed in the hands of owners unrelated to the expropriated Cuban business or have only been created in the United States after

---

[68] *See* the United States' responses to questions from the Panel concerning the determination of the owner of a trademark under US law summarized in paragraphs 4.240-4.242 below.

the Cuban revolution." The United States responds that this is not accurate. If the trademarks are in the hands of "owners" unrelated to the confiscated business, Section 211 would not apply, because Section 211 only deals with the trademark ownership of those who derive their ownership from the confiscated business. If the claimant has no relationship whatsoever to the confiscated business, it is hard to see how Section 211 could be applied to that claimant. Further, if the trademarks were only created after the Cuban revolution, a court could well find that there is no "original owner" of the trademark other than the confiscating entity itself, and, therefore, no room for the application of Section 211. The distinctions drawn by the European Communities are simply not there, and even if they were, they do not make out a case that Section 211 is inconsistent with TRIPS.

4.223 The United States summarizes that the scope of Section 211 is not what the European Communities speculates. Further, even if the European Communities' description of the scope were accurate, the European Communities has failed to show that Section 211 is inconsistent with TRIPS.

4.224 According to the United States, the European Communities also purports to describe the "operation" of Section 211. It engages in the same amount of speculation that it did in describing Section 211's scope, and fails completely either to show that Section 211 requires the actions that it claims are required, or to demonstrate that those actions, even if they were required, are inconsistent with the United States' TRIPS obligations.

4.225 The United States submits that the European Communities first states that federally registered trademarks become "incontestable" after 5 years, and implies that the purpose and effect of Section 211 was to make Cubaexport's Havana Club "incontestable registration" contestable. The United States responds that this is incorrect. First of all, "incontestable" does not mean "unchallengeable": federal trademark registrations, no matter how old, are subject to challenge on bases that go to the ownership of the trademark. While emphasizing that the specific situation of "Havana Club" is not within the Panel's terms of reference, the United States notes that no one has made the statutory filing required for "incontestability", so "incontestability" is simply not an issue with respect to that trademark.

4.226 According to the United States, the European Communities complains that Section 211 does not give any rights to the original owner of the confiscated business - the European Communities appears even to allege that the original owner *cannot* be a party in an action in which Section 211 is involved - but only curtails the rights of certain right-holders; the European Communities says this demonstrates the "punitive" nature of Section 211. The United States responds that this is an odd assertion, because there appears to be little question but that Section 211, where it applies, would give the original owner of a trademark used in connection with confiscated assets - or his or her successor - the right to exclude the confiscating entity or its successor from using the mark or from asserting ownership in the mark. This is a significant right for the original owner. It may be true that a third party who is sued for infringement by the confiscating entity in the United States might be able to defend himself by saying that the confiscating entity cannot assert rights in a trademark that he does not own. But this is not unusual, and this is not "punitive". The defendant in a trademark action can always defend himself by saying that the plaintiff does not own the trademark that is allegedly infringed. If the plaintiff does not own the trademark, he cannot maintain a suit for infringement, even against a third party. In the US view, Section 211 does not propose anything unusual in this respect.

4.227 The United States submits that Section 211 does not mandate the kinds of decisions that the European Communities speculates might result from Section 211. According to the United States, the exact operation of Section 211 will depend on the facts before the decision-maker, but the core issue to be addressed is the identity of the owner of the trademark at issue. Further, even if the European Communities' speculations were accurate, they do not amount to a violation of TRIPS.

4.228 The United States concludes that it agrees with the European Communities that, if the principle of non-recognition of foreign confiscations is represented by one circle, and TRIPS by another, these circles do not intersect. That is because the issue of whether a confiscating entity can claim ownership of trademarks in the United States is not addressed by TRIPS: the rules for determining the owner of a trademark are left to national legislation. In the view of the United States, the problem with the European Communities' position is that if TRIPS *does* require Members to recognize all registrants as owners, as the European Communities argues, then Members are powerless to deny ownership of trademarks in their territory to confiscating entities. The United States contends that this is tantamount to a requirement that Members give effect to foreign confiscations with respect to trademarks in their territory. It is not enough to say, as the European Communities has, that there is a principle of non-recognition that relates to expropriations and is unaffected by TRIPS obligations. If Members are not compelled to give effect to foreign confiscations with respect to trademarks in their territory – and the European Communities agrees that Members are not – then the Panel must find that TRIPS itself does not compel Members to give such effect. The European Communities' interpretation of TRIPS does not permit such a finding. The correct interpretation of TRIPS requires it.

2.   Ownership of Trademarks

4.229 In their submission, the parties presented arguments on the issue of the determination of the owner of a trademark. As these arguments relate to all specific inconsistencies with the TRIPS Agreement alleged by the European Communities, they are summarized below in a thematic manner.

4.230 The *European Communities* argues that while it is true that WTO Members enjoy some leeway in relation to ownership, the TRIPS Agreement gives clear guidance for who has to be considered as the owner of an intellectual property right. The starting point is Article 1.3 of the TRIPS Agreement which refers to "[…] those natural and legal persons that would meet the criteria for eligibility for protection […]". This provision has to be read together with the relevant provisions on eligibility for protection in Part II of the Agreement for the intellectual property right concerned. For trademarks the relevant provision is Article 15 of the Agreement.

4.231 The European Communities submits that, furthermore, in each Section of Part II of the TRIPS Agreement the characteristics of the right holders are described. For example, in the copyright Section of TRIPS it is the author of the work[69] who is the owner of the rights granted in this Section and there does not exist ten thousand options of how to designate the author. An additional argument to support the view that TRIPS does define the owner of an intellectual property right can be drawn from Article 14*bis*(2) of the Berne Convention in which an exceptional grant of discretion is given to Members for the allocation of ownership to copyright in cinematographic works.

4.232 In response to a question from the Panel on whether the TRIPS Agreement defines who is the owner of a trademark, the European Communities submits that while TRIPS or the Paris Convention do not expressly define the owner of a trademark, it would appear that direct or indirect references to ownership in TRIPS as well as the Paris Convention give guidance to Members in order to establish ownership. Article 15.1 of the TRIPS Agreement establishes a link between the trademark and goods or services emanating from an undertaking. This would suggest that only an undertaking can be the owner of a trademark to distinguish its goods or services. This would appear to be confirmed by Article 16.1 of the Agreement which equates the owner of the trademark with the undertaking whose goods or services are distinguished by the trademark. Also Article 19.1 of the Agreement seems to equate the owner of the trademark to the undertaking using the trademark for its goods or services. Therefore, it would appear that the principal assumption contained both in TRIPS and the Paris Convention is that the owner of the trademark is the undertaking which uses the trademark to distinguish its goods or services.[70]

4.233 The European Communities further argues that WTO Members being completely free to allocate ownership of a trademark would lead to absurd results and would make Articles 16-21 of the TRIPS Agreement worthless.

4.234 In response to a question from the Panel on whether there could be any situations where the holder of a trademark registration would not be the same as the owner of that trademark, the European Communities submits that there can only be one owner (leaving the issue of co-ownership aside) of a trademark for a given class of products or services in a given territory. The signs or combination of signs in relation to a class of products or services only become a trademark upon registration. Prior to registration there exists no trademark. Therefore, there can be no conflict between a registration owner and another owner of the same

---

[69] The European Communities refers to Article 5 of the Berne Convention.

[70] The United States contends that an individual, e.g., an artist can own a trademark he has created and license its use (*see* paragraph 4.245 below). The European Communities responds that there exists no contradiction between its assertion that trademarks and trade names can only be owned by an "undertaking" and the US reference to "artists", because artists can of course be undertakings, which carry out an economic activity, and such an undertaking can be a natural or legal person alike.

trademark. Trademark registrations can be attacked by third parties – for example on grounds of priority – typically within a given timeframe. Such an attack – if successful – will defeat the trademark, it will not create another trademark for anybody else. This can only be achieved by subsequent – successful - registration. There exist situations where the trademark register (like for example a land register) is inaccurate and has to be rectified. In case the owner of a trademark dies or has transferred the trademark, the register has to be rectified and the heir or transferee be inscribed as owner.

4.235 In response to another question, the European Communities submits that, in relation to patents, Article 27.1 of the TRIPS Agreement has some common features with Article 15.1 of the Agreement. Here as well an invention is in itself no property right. Only the patent which is registered on the basis of an invention, which meets the requirements set out in Article 27.1, constitutes the property right. All patent systems in the world (with the exception of one) operate on the basis of the so-called first-to-file system. This means that the first registrant meeting the requirements set out in Article 27.1 is the owner of the patent. Nobody else can be the owner of this patent. This argumentation also applies – *mutatis mutandis* – to Article 25 of the Agreement for industrial designs, which in many countries are protected as design patents.

4.236 The *United States* submits that the Paris Convention, Article 1(1), established a "Union for the protection of industrial property". Article 1(2) states that "[t]he protection of industrial property has as its object", among other subjects, trademarks. Although the term "trademark" is not defined in the Paris Convention, one commentator on the Paris Convention noted in 1969 that "a *trademark* is usually defined as a sign serving to distinguish the goods of one enterprise from those of other enterprises. The proprietor of a trademark generally has the exclusive right to use the trademark, or variations of it, for the same or similar *goods*."[71] Further, possibly because the principle was so universally understood as necessary to the functioning of an industrial property system as to go without saying, the Paris Convention nowhere defines or describes who is the proprietor, or owner, of the trademark.

4.237 The United States elaborates that the decision on the identity of a trademark owner – who it is that may exclude others from using the mark – is, therefore, left to the domestic law of the Members of the Union. As one respected commentator has stated with respect to the Paris Convention, "[t]he question *whether* a person is the *proprietor* of the mark in a country of the Union will have to be decided according to the domestic legislation of that country".[72] The way in which the ownership of a trademark is determined under the US law is described in paragraph 4.242 below. The United States notes that in other Members, domestic law provisions on ownership of trademarks are different. There is nothing in the Paris Convention that dictates the content of domestic law on the subject of ownership. Although the substantive rules on ownership are left to the

---

[71] The United States refers to Bodenhausen, page 22. Emphasis by the author.

[72] Bodenhausen, at 125 (providing clarification as to who might be considered the proprietor of a mark for purposes of interpreting Article 6*septies* of the Paris Convention). (Emphasis by the author.)

domestic laws of the Members, a basic rule of the Convention under Article 2(1) is that, whatever the laws are, they must not grant fewer advantages to nationals of other Members than they grant a Member's own nationals.

4.238 The United States further explains that the TRIPS Agreement elaborates on certain provisions of the Paris Convention with respect to trademarks by, for instance, defining eligible subject matter for trademarks (Article 15.1), specifying the minimum exclusive rights which must accrue to owners of registered trademarks (Article 16.1), and making certain enforcement procedures available to right holders (e.g., Article 42). In these ways, it goes beyond the Paris Convention framework. But, as in the case of the Paris Convention, the TRIPS Agreement does not contain any provision that specifies how trademark ownership is to be determined; it leaves that determination to the national law of each Member, subject to the requirements of national treatment (Article 3) and most-favoured-nation treatment (Article 4), among other TRIPS disciplines.

4.239 In the US view, the Paris Convention and TRIPS rights with respect to trademarks accrue only to the *owner* of the intellectual property right, but the Paris Convention and the TRIPS Agreement do not provide substantive rules for determining who the owner of the trademark is.[73] The United States emphasizes, in particular, that there is nothing in the TRIPS Agreement that takes away the sovereign right of a Member to decide that a person who traces his or her purported ownership of a trademark to a confiscation is *not* the owner of that trademark in the jurisdiction of that Member.

4.240 As regards the determination of the ownership of a trademark under US law, the United States submits that, while "ownership" is generally established through use, there is a complex set of considerations that comes into play when decisions have to be made as to who owns a trademark, for instance, as between two users of the trademark, as between a distributor and a manufacturer, and as between related parties, each of whom claims ownership of the mark. Under US law, the owner of a mark is generally the party who controls the nature and quality of the goods sold or services rendered under the mark. Thus, the specific facts concerning the use of the mark are determinative of the issue of ownership in the United States.[74] This is true regardless of who has registered the trademark: if the person registering a trademark in the United States is not the true owner of the trademark under US law, the registration may be cancelled.

---

[73] The United States adds that it is for this reason that all responsible Members of the Paris Convention and TRIPS Agreement, including the European Communities, provide for the opportunity to challenge assertions of ownership and to cancel trademark registrations upon determination that the party asserting ownership rights is not, in fact, the true owner of the mark.

[74] United States adds that its domestic law reflects in numerous respects the importance of determining the identity of the owner of the trademark. The only proper party to apply for registration of a mark is the person who owns the mark. 15 U.S.C. 1051. Further, the applicant must be the owner of the mark for which registration is requested. If the applicant does not own the mark on the application filing date, the application is void.

An application filed by a party other than the owner of a mark is invalid, and this defect cannot be cured by amendment or assignment because the applicant did not have the right to apply on the assigned filing date. The statutory basis for this refusal is §1 of the Trademark Act, 15 U.S.C. §1051, and, where related-company issues are relevant, §§5 and 45, 15 U.S.C. §§1055 and 1127.

4.241 As regards the determination of "the original owner" referred to in Section 211, the United States submits that, in the context of a US court proceeding under Sections 211(a)(2) or (b), courts would use common law principles, based on the particular facts of the proceeding, to determine who the "original owner" is. Consistent with the principle of territoriality of trademarks, the "original owner" of the trademark, trade name, or commercial name would likely be determined under the law of the United States.[75] This principle would not be applied differently in the case of well-known trademarks: the owner of the trademark would be determined under the laws of the United States. The issue of who is a "successor-in-interest" would be determined under the contract and corporation law applicable on the facts of each case. Such determination would normally involve application of the personal law applicable to the original owner and its successors, unless such laws were found to violate the public order of the forum, in which case they would not be applied.[76]

4.242 In response to a question on the significance of a registration, the United States explains that, in the United States, registration is not conclusive of the ownership of a mark, and trademark rights acquired in the United States at common law exist independently of federal registration. Registration of a mark under the Trademark Act, 15 U.S.C. § 1051, *et seq.* confers *prima facie* presumptions of the registrant's ownership of the registered mark and of the registrant's exclusive right to use that mark in commerce. This is true in both administrative proceedings and in US courts. For instance, a registrant's claim to ownership of a mark can be defeated by a prior and continuous common-law usage of that mark or of a confusingly similar mark.

4.243 The United States claims that the European Communities has failed to present any legal support for its conclusion that TRIPS dictates how the owner of a trademark, trade name or commercial name is determined, and that it prevents Members from making their own determinations as to ownership. It further claims that, in trying to support its case, moreover, the European Communities fails to reconcile its position with the accepted principle against the extraterritorial recognition of foreign confiscations, contradicts its own arguments and the practices of its member States, and offers contorted interpretations of the TRIPS Agreement that are incorrect.

---

[75] In response to a question concerning Section 211(a)(1), the United States explains that Section 211(a)(1) focuses on trademarks that have an "original owner" and that have been "used" in connection with the confiscated assets or business. Such use – even outside the United States – can create ownership rights in the United States.

[76] In response to a question on by whom the determination of "the original owner" is made under Section 211(a)(1), the United States explains that, with the caveat that Section 211(a)(1) has not been applied, it is reasonable to assume that the determination of the original owner could be made by the USPTO, in the context of an opposition or cancellation proceeding, if the claimant sought to register a trademark in reliance on the general licence conferred by 31 CFR 515.527. This determination might also be made by OFAC, if (a) the claimant sought an OFAC ruling that he met the conditions for the general licence or (b) OFAC is called upon to consider whether a "general licence" registrant met the conditions for a general licence under Section 515.527, or whether that registrant should have requested a specific licence.

4.244 The United States argues that in neither its first submission nor its response to direct questions from the Panel has the European Communities been able to point to any provision of TRIPS that defines who is the owner of a trademark, or that prevents a Member from deciding that a confiscating entity is not entitled to own the trademarks used in connection with confiscated assets. The best the European Communities can offer is that "direct or indirect references to ownership in TRIPS as well as the Paris Convention give guidance to Members in order to establish ownership".[77] The United States claims that the conclusions that the European Communities draws from this apparently vague "guidance" are wrong. But the question is not whether references to ownership in the TRIPS Agreement "give guidance". The question is whether the TRIPS Agreement prevents any Member from refusing to give effect to a foreign confiscatory decree by deciding that it will not recognize the ownership of confiscating entities or their successors in such trademarks in the United States. The answer to this is "no": TRIPS does not require the United States to recognize such ownership with respect to US trademarks.

4.245 The United States submits that the European Communities' assertion that only an "undertaking" can be the owner of a trademark, because Article 15.1 establishes a link between the trademark and the goods or services emanating from an undertaking is untrue. An individual can own a trademark - e.g., a celebrity can own the trademark to his name, an artist can own the trademark to work he has created (e.g., Superman, or Spiderman) - and license the use of that trademark to a company that uses it in trade. This situation is specifically anticipated in Article 19.2.[78]

4.246 The United States argues that the European Communities' conclusion that signs only become a trademark upon registration and that prior to registration there exists no trademark is, while critical to the European Communities' interpretation, wrong. The United States argues that it is critical to the European Communities' interpretation because it is on this basis that the European Communities asserts that the trademark registrant and the trademark owner are, by definition, the same entity under the TRIPS Agreement, and that, therefore, TRIPS addresses the rules of trademark ownership whenever it addresses registration, as in TRIPS Article 16.1 and 15.1 It is on this basis that the European Communities concludes, "[t]herefore there can be no conflict between a registration owner and another owner of the same trademark".

4.247 The United States submits that this assertion is wrong because TRIPS was deliberately crafted to take into account both the civil law "registration" and the common-law "use" trademark systems. In the US common law system, trademarks are generally created by the use of the trademark in commerce to distin-

---

[77] Further, the United States disagrees with the European Communities that TRIPS Article 15.1 requires that all signs "capable" of being a trademark be registered as trademarks, regardless of whether the registrant is the true owner. Indeed, Article 15.1 does not contain an affirmative obligation to register all such trademarks, *even if* protection is sought by the true owner. Examples abound. For example, an applicant might properly be refused registration where the proposed mark is purely ornamental or functional, without source identifying capacity.

[78] *See* the EC response to the US arguments in footnote 70 above.

guish goods, not by the registration itself. Federal registration creates a presumption of trademark ownership, but that presumption is subject to challenge based on, among other things, who used the trademark first. TRIPS Article 16.1, which describes the rights conferred on the owner of a registered trademark, specifically states that these rights shall not "affect the possibility of Members making rights available on the basis of use". It is simply incorrect to assert, therefore, that under TRIPS, trademarks do not exist until they are registered. In the US system, they can and do exist, and they can and do have owners, without being registered. Nothing in TRIPS overturned this basic premise of US trademark law.

4.248   The United States adds that if, as the European Communities asserts, there can be no conflict between a registrant of a mark and another entity who claims ownership of the mark (because, by definition, these have to be the same entity), it is not clear on what basis the European Communities can protect "well-known" marks, as required by the Paris Convention.

4.249   Further, the United States claims that the European Communities' position seems internally inconsistent, because in response to a question from the Panel, the European Communities took the view that TRIPS does not address the relationship between principals and agents, and that this is a matter left for domestic rules.[79] The United States argues that rules that determine who - as between a principal and an agent - can be the owner of a trademark, are one aspect of the trademark ownership rules left to national law. For the United States it is not clear on what basis the European Communities claims that *this* aspect of ownership is left to national law, whereas *other* aspects of ownership are not.

4.250   The United States argues that the issue of trademark ownership, and whether TRIPS specifies the identity of the owner, is obviously important. It is because TRIPS does not specify the identity of the trademark owner that Members retain the right to adopt and enforce national rules of trademark ownership. This includes the right not to recognize the ownership of confiscating entities in trademarks used in connection with confiscated assets. From the US perspective, the EC view to the contrary appears to be based principally on an assumption that all signatories to the TRIPS Agreement have a trademark system in which registration itself creates both trademark rights and ownership rights, and that, in fact, TRIPS requires such a system. The United States submits that it does not

---

[79]   This question read: If an agent in country X seeks to register a trademark belonging to his or her principal in country Y without the principal's consent, does Article 15.1 require the trademark authority in country X to register the trademark? The European Communities responded that the relationship between principal and agent is not addressed in TRIPS. This relationship and its effects on third parties, including the question of validity of acts undertaken by the agent without the authorisation of the principal are governed by the domestic rules of the WTO Member concerned. In the hypothesis that these rules consider that the acts undertaken by the agent have to be attributed to the principal, an application for a trademark which meets the criteria set out in Article 15.1 of the TRIPS Agreement has to be registered, as long as no exception provision such as Article 6*quinquies* B of the Paris Convention applies. The situation contemplated by Article 6*septies* of the Paris Convention, which creates a number of special rights in the hands of a principal, starts out from the assumption that the trademark office has indeed granted the trademark or at least accepted the filing by an undisclosed agent acting without authority from the principal.

have such a system, and that TRIPS does not require such a system.[80] TRIPS leaves decisions of ownership to the Members, and, consistent with this freedom, the United States has many rules pertaining to who can be a trademark owner (including with respect to related parties and agents). TRIPS certainly permits other Members, including EC member States, to choose to equate registration with ownership,[81] but it in no way requires it.

4.251 The United States recalls in this context that EC member States such as Denmark and the United Kingdom have apparently considered it their right under the Paris Convention to transfer ownership of a trademark registration from a confiscating entity to the prior owners.[82] It claims, consequently, that whether registration is completely determinative of trademark ownership, even in the European Communities, appears questionable.

4.252 The United States asserts that, in sum, the European Communities' position that TRIPS does in fact determine who the owner of a trademark is, and that it prevents Members from determining ownership with respect to confiscated trademarks, has no support in the TRIPS Agreement and is inconsistent with both the European Communities' own arguments and the practices of its member States.

4.253 The United States argues that although TRIPS does not itself dictate who is an owner of a trademark under national law - leaving that issue instead to national rules - it does contain numerous disciplines and safeguards that prevent Members from abusing this freedom to benefit their own nationals or to unfairly curtail the trademark rights of others. The role of protections offered by the national treatment and most-favoured-nation provisions, among others, are significant. Given the broad variety of national rules among Members concerning the conditions for filing trademark registrations and rules of trademark ownership, a key safeguard against abuse — created by both TRIPS and the Paris Convention - is that whatever rules are in place, they cannot treat non-nationals worse than nationals, and they cannot treat the nationals of some nations worse than the nationals of others. These principles act as a powerful discipline on Members, in those areas, such as trademark ownership, that are left to national laws. Generally speaking, therefore, if those laws or rules are acceptable as imposed on the nationals of the Member, they may be imposed on the nationals of other Members. In the absence of specific rules defining who the trademark owner is, the national treatment and most-favoured-nation provisions, among other provisions, guard against abuse.[83]

---

[80] The United States notes that, for example, TRIPS Article 16.1 specifically states that the rights of owners of registered trademarks "shall not affect the possibility of Members making rights available on the basis of use".

[81] The United States adds this is true so long as such equation does not prejudice any existing prior rights and as long as the Members provide TRIPS-level protection for well-known marks.

[82] *See* footnote 64 above.

[83] The United States further argues that well-established jurisprudence under the GATT and WTO concerning the application of national treatment and most-favoured-nation provisions in the area of goods indicates the breadth of the protections offered by these provisions. While this jurisprudence has involved MFN and national treatment of goods under Articles I and III of GATT 1994, and not

4.254 The United States argues that it is not unusual that TRIPS would leave such a matter as trademark ownership to national legislation. Another obvious example under TRIPS and the Paris Convention relates to patents. Although TRIPS Article 27 describes patentable subject matter, it does not mandate whether the owner of a patent is the person who first made the invention, or the person who first filed a patent application claiming the invention. Under US law, when two people claim the same invention, the person who can prove that he or she made the invention first will be awarded ownership of the patent, assuming that the invention is patentable. By contrast, in most other WTO Members, ownership of a patent belongs to the first person to file a successful patent application. This key difference in determining the ownership of patent rights as between competing claimants is not resolved by the TRIPS Agreement or the Paris Convention; both are silent. The United States gives another example from the area of copyright.[84]

4.255 According to the United States, it is curious that the European Communities uses this difference to suggest that the patent provisions of TRIPS on protectable subject matter *do* dictate this aspect of patent ownership. After noting that one country (i.e., the United States) has a "first to invent system", the European Communities notes that other countries have a "first to file" system, and that "this means that the first registrant meeting the requirements set out in Article 27.1 TRIPS is the owner of the patent. Nobody else can be the owner of this patent." While this may be true of "first to file" systems, it is not true of "first to invent" systems, and nothing in Article 27.1 requires that a Member's laws incorporate a "first to file" system. The European Communities seems to believe that the TRIPS Agreement, which was specifically negotiated to accommodate both the US and the EC systems, in fact mandates the EC approach.

4.256 The United States claims that the fact that these differences among Members exist with respect to patents and copyrights has not detracted from the disciplines of the TRIPS Agreement with respect to these intellectual property rights. Similarly, in the trademark area, the lack of TRIPS rules concerning whether confiscating entities must be recognized as owners of trademarks in a Member's territory does not take away from the other TRIPS disciplines.

4.257 The United States reiterates that in its view the European Communities is seeking to re-interpret TRIPS and the Paris Convention so that these agreements accommodate only the civil law system of trademark law, and prohibit the US common law system. This is at the bottom of the European Communities' argu-

---

treatment of nationals under TRIPS, this jurisprudence is instructive in showing that national treatment and most-favoured-nation principles discipline Members' measures in areas where the WTO Agreements do not otherwise provide substantive rules. In addition to the most-favoured-nation and national treatment provisions, other TRIPS provisions also offer protections against abuse.

[84] According to the United States, it is well accepted that the Berne Convention and the TRIPS Agreement are silent regarding the definition of an "author" and, consequently, regarding the definition of an owner of a copyright. As explained in the WIPO Guide to the Berne Convention, the Berne Convention "does not specifically define the word 'author' because on this point too, national laws diverge widely, some recognizing only natural persons as authors, while others treat certain legal entities as copyright owners, some imposing conditions for the recognition of authorship which others do not accept". WIPO Guide to the Berne Convention, paragraph 1.16 (1978).

ment that, under TRIPS, trademarks only come into existence when they are registered, and that whoever registers the trademark "owns" the trademark. The United States contends that these assertions are not consistent with text of the TRIPS Agreement, and are entirely contrary to the US trademark system, in which trademarks are generally created by use and in which registration is *not* conclusive of ownership. TRIPS and the Paris Convention were specifically drafted to take into account both the civil law and the common law trademark systems, and cannot now be read to mandate the civil law system.

3. Burden of Proof

4.258 The *European Communities* argues that in line with established rules on the issue of burden of proof, as expressed by the Appellate Body in *India – Patent Protection*, the burden to prove that Section 211 may mean something else than its plain text is on the United States.

4.259 Before responding to the specific claims made by the European Communities in its first written submission, the *United States*, in its first written submission, questions whether the European Communities as the complaining party has submitted arguments and evidence sufficient to raise a presumption that the US measures are inconsistent with its obligations under TRIPS Agreement. The United States recalls that the Appellate Body stated in *United States—Measures Affecting Imports of Woven Wool Shirts and Blouses from India* that the burden of proof rests upon the party, whether complaining or defending, who asserts the affirmative of a particular claim or defence. If that party adduces evidence sufficient to raise a presumption that what is claimed is true, the burden then shifts to the other party, who will fail unless it adduces sufficient evidence to rebut the presumption.[85] Under this rule, as recently applied to the TRIPS Agreement in *Canada – Patent Term*,[86] the European Communities has the initial burden of establishing a *prima facie* case of inconsistency with a particular provision of the TRIPS Agreement by adducing sufficient evidence to raise a presumption that its claims are true. Only upon establishing a *prima facie* case of inconsistency would any burden shift to the United States to refute the claim of inconsistency.

4.260 The United States argues that, in this dispute, the European Communities has not sustained its burden of establishing a *prima facie* case that Section 211 is inconsistent with any provision of the TRIPS Agreement. It has not presented sufficient evidence of any inconsistency to create a presumption that its claims are true. There is little specificity or substance to the European Communities' argument and what little there is – while insufficient to create a presumption of inconsistency – is easily refuted.

4.261 The United States further argues that the European Communities' claims with respect to Sections 211(a)(1) and (b) completely ignore well-established doctrines with respect to the ownership of trademarks and well-established poli-

---

[85] WT/DS33/AB/R, adopted 23 May 1997, p. 14, DSR 1997:I, 323, at 335.
[86] *Canada – Term of Patent Protection*, WT/DS170/R, upheld by Appellate Body, adopted, 12 October 2000, DSR 2000:XI, 5121, paras. 6.8-6.11.

cies against extraterritorial recognition of foreign confiscations. In addition, in maintaining that Section 211(b) is inconsistent with a number of TRIPS Articles, the European Communities states that "the precise scope" of Section 211(b) is "largely obscure". It then offers an interpretation "[b]y way of speculation" and some dictum from a court case. Since it is the European Communities' burden to *demonstrate* that Section 211(b) is inconsistent with TRIPS, the European Communities' admission that it does not know exactly what Section 211(b) covers is evidence that the European Communities has not sustained its burden in this dispute.

4.262 Referring to the first written submission by the European Communities, the United States claims that the European Communities has done little more than quote or restate various provisions of US law, quote or restate various TRIPS provisions, and ask the United States to prove that Section 211 is consistent with TRIPS. This reverses the proper allocation of burdens.

V.   ARGUMENTS OF THE THIRD PARTIES

Nicaragua[87]

5.1   Concerning the right of private ownership, *Nicaragua* states that the right to ownership is the most complete right that a person may have over property. It is the real right par excellence; it is absolute, in that its holders are fully entitled to enjoy and dispose of what belongs to them with no limitations other than those accepted by them or imposed by the law in the public interest or in defence of another person's rights. Ownership, while comprising an element of appropriation and personal use, also comprises a social element in that it contributes to ensuring the life and welfare of the community.

5.2   Article 44 of the Constitution of Nicaragua stipulates as follows: "The right of private ownership of movable and immovable property and of the instruments and means of production is guaranteed. By virtue of the social function of property, for reasons of public utility or social interest, the right is subject to the limits and obligations imposed by the law. Immovable property (...) may be the subject of expropriation in accordance with the law following the cash payment of fair compensation (...). The confiscation of property is prohibited (...)."

5.3   Nicaragua argues that within the territory of a State, the exercise of territorial powers by another State is prohibited except with the consent of the former, i.e., unless there is an international agreement or convention regulating the exercise of such powers. On the basis of this principle and of the above-cited constitutional article, the Government of Nicaragua does not recognize rights based on acts of confiscation ordered by other States. Indeed such acts are incon-

---

[87]   In a letter, dated 5 January 2001, *Canada* stated that in its view, the dispute raises important issues, including the scope of national and most-favoured-nation treatment under the TRIPS Agreement. However, in view of the issues that have been defined by the submissions already made, it informed the Panel that it would not be filing a written submission in the proceedings. It added that it remained highly interested in the issues that may be addressed in the course of the Panel's deliberations. *Japan* did not make a submission.

sistent with its basic constitutional principles governing the right of private ownership.

5.4   Intellectual property constitutes a special case, and is therefore regulated individually on the grounds that it involves a right by which property is submitted to the absolute and exclusive will and action of the holder.

5.5   Thus, intellectual property rights are protected by the provisions of international agreements such as the Paris Convention (1967), the Berne Convention (1971), the Rome Convention (1961), the Washington Treaty, and the TRIPS Agreement. But in addition to being protected under those agreements, they have been recognized in the principal declarations on human rights:

(a)   Through the recognition of the right of ownership in general; and

(b)   implicitly, through the recognition of the right to participate in the cultural life of a country.

5.6   According to Article 17 of the Universal Declaration of Human Rights, "Everyone has the right to own property alone as well as in association with others. No one shall be arbitrarily deprived of his property". A similar provision appears, *inter alia*, in the American Declaration of the Rights and Duties of Man and the International Covenant on Economic, Social and Cultural Rights of the United Nations.

5.7   According to Article 14 of the Convention Relating to the Status of Refugees, in respect of the protection of industrial property, such as inventions, designs or models, trademarks, trade names, and of rights in literary, artistic and scientific works, a refugee shall be accorded in the country in which he has his habitual residence the same protection as is accorded to nationals of that country. In the territory of any other Contracting States, he shall be accorded the same protection as is accorded in that territory to nationals of the country in which he has his habitual residence." This reaffirms the obligation of every State to afford protection to the legitimate holder of intellectual property rights, even when such rights have been damaged through actions in time of war.

5.8   Concerning the TRIPS Agreement and the Paris Convention (1967), Nicaragua states that in the international society of today, States are the subject of international law par excellence. States are legal persons acting through their executive, legislative or judicial bodies, which, in their turn, are subject to the domestic laws of the State. In this sense, domestic law facilitates compliance with international law, which is not only applicable externally, i.e., at the level of inter-State relations, but must also be observed within the State, i.e., in relations between the State and individuals under its jurisdiction.

5.9   Both the TRIPS Agreement and the Paris Convention are agreements which establish minimum standards for the protection of intellectual property rights, and the members of those Agreements are free to grant more extensive protection to intellectual property through their domestic laws.

5.10   Nicaragua considers that neither the TRIPS Agreement nor the Paris Convention stipulates the way in which Members of the WTO or of the Union, under the Paris Convention, must determine the criteria to be observed with respect to the acquisition of intellectual property rights.

5.11   In this respect, Article 1.1 of the TRIPS Agreement states that Members may, but shall not be obliged to, implement in their law more extensive protection than is required by the TRIPS Agreement, provided that such protection does not contravene the provisions of the Agreement. Similarly, the Agreement excludes from its scope the notions of creation, exhaustion or amendment of intellectual property rights.

5.12   Article 2 of the Paris Convention (1967) clearly lays down the principle of compliance with domestic legislation and territoriality of industrial property. Nicaragua considers that every State has the sovereign right to determine how intellectual property rights are acquired under its domestic law.

5.13   Nicaragua is of the view that ownership of or acquired rights to intellectual property in a third country cannot be based on an act of confiscation in another country under international law. As this issue is not clearly regulated in the TRIPS Agreement or in the Paris Convention, each State is entitled to act in accordance with its domestic legislation.

VI.   FACTUAL INFORMATION PROVIDED BY THE INTERNATIONAL BUREAU OF WIPO

6.1   On 1 February 2001, the *Panel* sent a letter to the International Bureau of the WIPO, which is responsible for the administration of the Paris Convention (1967). In that letter, the Panel noted that the parties to the dispute refer to the provisions of the Stockholm Act of 1967 of the Paris Convention, the substantive provisions of which have been incorporated into the TRIPS Agreement by its Article 2.1. These provisions include, in particular, Articles 2(1), 6, 6*bis*, 6*quinquies*, and 8 of the Paris Convention. Given that the International Bureau of WIPO is responsible for the administration of that Convention, the Panel requested any factual information available to the International Bureau on the provisions of the Paris Convention (1967) relevant to the dispute, in particular the negotiating history and subsequent developments concerning those provisions referred to by the Parties to the dispute. As regards Article 6*quinquies*, the Panel requested any factual information on its intended scope.

6.2   The Panel noted that the Parties had also raised the question of whether and, if so, in what way the provisions of the Paris Convention (1967) regulate how the owner of a trademark has to be determined under domestic law of Paris Union members. The Panel expressed its interest in any factual information on the way this issue might have been addressed in the negotiating history of the Convention or in subsequent developments.

6.3   The *International Bureau of WIPO* provided such information in a letter dated 2 March 2001. Annexes to the letter contain excerpts from the records of the conferences for the conclusion and revision of the Paris Convention. The following contains a summary of a "Note on certain questions regarding the Paris

Convention raised by the World Trade Organization" that was attached to the letter.[88]

Article 2(1) of the Paris Convention (1967)

1. *International Conference for the Protection of Industrial Property (Paris, November 1880)*

6.4   In his welcoming remarks, the French Minister for Agriculture and Commerce (Mr. Tirard) stated that the Conference could not achieve a complete international treaty of industrial property, in view of the difficulties of States with an immediate unification of all national laws. The conference should rather strive to find the means for constituting a union which, without encroaching on the domestic legislation of the contracting states, would assure national treatment and lay down a number of uniform general principles.

6.5   In the negotiation regarding Article 2, the French delegate (Mr. Jagerschmidt), who had prepared the preliminary draft, pointed out that, in order to be acceptable, the convention would have to respect the internal legislation of all contracting States to the extent possible, and to restrict it to an obligation to extend national treatment to foreigners. Such an approach would also be acceptable to countries which, like the Netherlands and Switzerland, did not protect patents under their national law, because they would not be obliged to treat foreigners better than their own citizens. In the course of the discussion, the national treatment principle was clarified by the deletion of the word "réciproquement" from the original draft.

6.6   The discussions focused, in particular, on two questions: whether Contracting States were free to extend national treatment to nationals of countries which were not party to the Union, which led to the inclusion of Article 3 in the text of the Convention; and whether the national treatment obligation extended to procedural formalities, which led to the adoption of paragraph 3 of the Final Protocol.

6.7   The Final Protocol also included, in paragraph 4, a reservation by the delegation of the United States of America, which was, however, deleted when the United States did not sign the Convention at the conference in 1883.

2. *Brussels Conference, First session (December 1897)*

6.8   The United States of America had proposed a restriction of the principle of national treatment as regards fees and the issue of patentability. This proposal was, however, not adopted by the conference.

---

[88]   References to the attachments to the Note have been omitted from the summary.

3. *Washington Conference (May 15 - June 2, 1911)*

6.9   The International Bureau and the Delegation of France had proposed a number of amendments to Article 2. Following the discussion in the sub-committee, these amendments were generally adopted by the Conference.

4. *The Hague Conference (November 1925)*

6.10   The International Bureau and the Delegations of France, Morocco and the United States of America had proposed a number of amendments to Article 2. The proposals made by the International Bureau and France were adopted by the Conference. According to the proposal of the United States of America, every country would have had the right to impose upon nationals of the other countries the fulfilment of some or all of the conditions imposed on its nationals by those countries. This proposal found no support and was withdrawn.

6.11   The provision was not discussed at the subsequent Conferences of 1934 (London), 1958 (Lisbon), 1967 (Stockholm), and at the Revision Conference of 1980-1981.

*Article 6, 6*bis*, and 6*quinquies *of the Paris Convention (1967)*

6.12   The origin of Article 6/6*quinquies* of the Paris Convention (1967) can be found in the agreement reached by the delegates discussing the principle of national treatment for nationals of countries of the Union (Article 2). In the absence of harmonization of trademark law and with regard to the wide divergences then existing between the different national systems, the determination of signs eligible for registration constituted for the delegates to the International Conference for the Protection of Industrial Property a major question.

1. *International Conference for the Protection of Industrial Property (Paris, November 1880)*

6.13   The origin of the provisions on trademarks of the Paris Convention can be found in Article 5 of the preliminary draft convention prepared by the French Government (Mr. Jagerschmidt) for the International Conference on the protection of industrial property (November 1880). The authentic French version of this Article reads as follows:

> "La propriété des dessins ou modèles industriels et des marques de fabrique ou de commerce sera considérée, dans tous les États de l'Union, comme légitimement acquise à ceux qui font usage, conformément à la législation du pays d'origine, desdits dessins et modèles et marques de fabrique ou de commerce."

6.14   According to its drafter, this Article intended to solve the problems arising from the differences relating to trademark application formalities in the different States. Its aim was to state a principle, then existing in certain states through bilateral agreements, "aux termes duquel les marques d'un pays sont admises telles quelles dans l'autre, pourvu que le déposant fournisse la preuve qu'elles ont été régulièrement déposées dans le premier pays".

6.15   This Article, discussed and revised several times, was adopted, in second reading, in the authentic French version as follows:

"Toute marque de fabrique ou de commerce régulièrement déposée dans le pays d'origine sera admise au dépôt et protégée telle quelle dans tous les autres pays de l'Union.

Sera considéré comme pays d'origine le pays où le déposant a son principal établissement.

Si ce principal établissement n'est point situé dans un des pays de l'Union, sera considéré comme pays d'origine celui auquel appartient le déposant. Le dépôt pourra être refusé, si l'objet pour lequel il est demandé est considéré comme contraire à la morale ou à l'ordre public."

2.   International Conference for the Protection of Industrial Property (March 1883)

6.16   During the first meeting of the conference on March 6, 1883, the need to clarify the scope of this Article (renumbered as Article 6) was raised by the delegate of Spain and the observation made by the delegation of Belgium. However, since it was not possible at this stage of the Conference to amend the draft convention, it was decided to insert in the Final Protocol of the Conference a paragraph clarifying the meaning of the first sentence of Article 6. This paragraph was discussed and unanimously adopted in the second plenary meeting (Second meeting) of the Conference on March 12, 1883.

6.17   Article 6 adopted in Paris on March 20, 1883, reads as follows (WIPO translation):

"Article 6: [1] Every trademark duly filed in the country of origin shall be accepted for filing and protected in its original form in the other countries of the Union. [2] The country in which the applicant has his principal establishment shall be considered as the country of origin. [3] If the principal establishment is not situated in one of the countries of the Union, the country to which the applicant belongs shall be considered as the country of origin. [4] The filing may be refused if the object for which it is requested is considered as contrary to morality or public order."

6.18   Paragraph 4 of the Final Protocol (dated of March 20, 1883) reads as follows (WIPO translation):

"4. [1] Paragraph [1] of Article 6 should be understood in the sense that no trade mark may be excluded from protection in one of the States of the Union for the sole reason that it does not comply, with regard to the signs of which it is composed, with the conditions of the laws of that State, provided it complies on this point with the laws of the country of origin and that it has been properly filed there. Subject to this exception, which only concerns the form of the mark, and subject to the provisions of the other Articles of the Convention, each State shall apply its domestic law. [2] In order to avoid improper interpretation, it is understood that the use of public armorial bearings and decorations may be considered as contrary to public order, in the sense of the last paragraph of Article 6."

3. Brussels Conference, First Session (December 1897)

6.19   Due to the unclear scope of Article 6, it was proposed at the first session of the Brussels Conference to merge Article 6 and Paragraph N° 4 of the Final Protocol. These proposals were extensively discussed in the Sub-Committee on Trademarks. However, since it was impossible to reach an agreement on a revised Article 6, no decision was taken and the provisions relating to this Article and the N° 4 of the Final Protocol were considered unchanged for the time being.

4. Brussels Conference, Second Session (December 11-14, 1900)

6.20   In a Note addressed by the Government of Belgium to the States attending the 1897 conference, it was recalled that the UK delegation had accepted, at the First Session of the Conference, to maintain Article 6 and paragraph N° 4 of the Final Protocol as they were, provided that all Member States remained free to keep their national legislation with regards to trademarks. Considering the general agreement of the Members States in favor of the maintenance of Article 6 in its form, it was decided to keep this Article unchanged.

5. Washington Conference (May 15 - June 2, 1911)

6.21   The question relating to a new drafting of Article 6 which would include paragraph N°4 of the Final Protocol as well as the need to clarify the notion of "public order" in Article 6 led to a new proposal on this Article, prepared by the International Bureau and submitted at the Washington Conference. In the preliminary draft convention, Article 6 was renumbered as draft Article 9. A number of proposals were made by several delegations. On the basis of these proposals, discussions in the Sub-Committee on Trademarks on a renumbered Article 6 (formerly draft Article 9) were held on seven different points and it was decided that paragraph N° 4 of the Final Protocol should be deleted. The only amendment affecting the first paragraph of Article 6 concerns the change of the words "registered" ("*enregistré*") instead of "filed" ("*déposé*"). Discussion on the French and German proposals, which aimed at specifying, by a limitative enumeration, the cases under which it would be permitted to a State to refuse a mark already filed in another State of the Union (trademarks infringing rights of third parties; lack of distinctive character) led to some amendments in this respect, as did discussions on the Swiss proposal, which tended to prohibit the use of state emblems, armorial bearings, flags as trademarks.

6.22 It was also decided to clarify Article 6 in an Ad Article 6 to the Final Protocol of June 2, 1911, which reads in English (WIPO translation):

(1) It is understood that the provision contained in the first paragraph of Article 6 does not exclude the right to require from the applicant a certificate of proper registration in the country of origin, issued by the competent authority.

(2) It is understood that the use of public emblems, signs or decorations which has not been authorized by the competent authorities, or the use of official signs and hallmarks indicating control and warranty adopted by a country of the Union, may be considered as contrary to public order in the sense of No. 3 of Article 6.

(3) However, marks which contain the reproduction of public emblems, decorations or signs with the authorization of the competent authorities shall not be considered contrary to public order.

(4) It is understood that a mark may not be considered as contrary to public order for the sole reason that it does not conform to a provision of the law relating to marks, except where such provision itself relates to public order.

(5) The present Final Protocol, which shall be ratified at the same time as the Act concluded this day, shall be considered as an integral part of that Act and shall have the same force, validity and duration.

6. *The Hague Conference (November 1925)*

6.23 The Act of The Hague, adopted by the Conference on November 6, 1925, included the following changes:

- The first and second paragraphs of Article 6 remain unchanged. However, in the third sub-paragraph of paragraph 2 of Article 6, paragraph 4 of the ad Article 6 of the Final Protocol of Washington was inserted. Paragraphs 2 and 3 of the Final Protocol relating to State emblems have been merged in a new Article 6*ter*.

- The third paragraph had been amended with regards to the notion of "country of origin".

- In the fourth paragraph, the proposal from the German delegation relating to the principle of independence of trademarks had not been accepted but the proposal from United Kingdom had been included.

6.24 Following a proposal from Belgium, a new paragraph 5 had been added according to which "the benefit of priority shall be accorded to applications for the registration of marks filed within the period fixed by Article 4, even when registration in the country of origin does not occur until after the expiration of such period".

6.25   A sixth paragraph was also added, combining the first paragraph of *Ad Article 6* of the Final Protocol of Washington and a proposal from the delegation of the United Kingdom.

6.26   A new Article 6*bis* introduced a special provision on the protection of well-known marks.

7.   *London Conference (May-June 1934)*

6.27   The London Act of the Convention, adopted at a Diplomatic Conference on June 2, 1934, introduced important amendments to Article 6 of the Paris Convention, including its reorganization and renumbering in paragraphs from A to F (instead of 1 to 6). Some amendments were also made to Article 6*bis*.

6.28   Changes affecting paragraph 6A (previously 6(1)) read: "Every trademark duly registered in the country of origin shall be accepted for filing and protected in its original form in the other countries of the Union, *subject to the reservations indicated below. These countries may, before proceeding to final registration,* require *the production of* a certificate of registration in the country of origin, issued by the competent authority. No authentication shall be required for this certificate."

6.29   Other amendments concerned paragraph 6B (previously 6(2)) to which the following sentence was added in its sub-paragraph 3: "...marks which are contrary to morality or public order, *in particular those of such a nature as to deceive the public.*" In addition the following new sub-paragraph was added: "*(2) Trademarks shall not be refused in the other countries of the Union for the sole reason that they differ from the marks protected in the country of origin only by elements that do not alter the distinctive character and do not affect the identity of the marks in the form in which these have been registered in the said country of origin.*"

6.30   Finally, a new paragraph D was introduced with the following wording: "*When a trademark has been duly registered in the country of origin and then in one or more of the other countries of the Union, each of these national marks shall be considered, from the date of its registration, as independent of the mark in the country of origin, provided it conforms to the domestic legislation of the country of importation.*"

6.31   With regards to Article 6*bis*, the following amendments were introduced in its paragraph (1): "The countries *of the Union* undertake, either administratively if their legislation so permits, or at the request of an interested party, to refuse or to cancel the registration of a trademark which *constitutes* a reproduction, imitation *or translation*, liable to *create* confusion, of a mark considered by the competent authority of the country of registration to be well known in that country as being already the mark *of a person entitled to the benefits of the present Convention* and used for *identical* or similar goods. *These provisions shall also apply when the essential part of the mark constitutes a reproduction of any such well-known mark or an imitation liable to create confusion therewith.*"

8. Lisbon Conference (October 6-31, 1958)

6.32   The Lisbon Act of the Convention, adopted at a Diplomatic Conference on October 31, 1958, introduced major amendments to Article 6 of the Paris Convention. It was decided to separate its provisions into two different Articles, which remain unchanged today: a revised Article 6 to deal with the principle of independence of trademarks, and a new Article 6*quinquies* for which new paragraphs were constituted from texts that were in the former Article 6. In this respect, the Proposal by the International Bureau with Explanatory Memorandum discussed in the Third Committee as well as the Analytical Report from the International Bureau provides a thorough analysis of the different steps of the discussions since the origin of the clause "telle quelle" in 1883.

Article 8 of the Paris Convention (1967)

1.   International Conference for the Protection of Industrial Property (Paris, 1880)

6.33   The chairman of the conference explained that the provision was deemed necessary in view of French court decisions according to which a trade name, which was part of a trademark, was lost together with the trademark when the public became possessed of its other elements.

6.34   The discussion addressed, inter alia, the question whether contracting states should extend protection to nationals of countries that were not party to the convention.

6.35   The obligation to protect trade names was therefore contained in Article 8 of the original text of 20 March 1883 which, in the authentic French version, read as follows:

> **Article 8**. Le nom commercial sera protégé dans tous les pays de l'Union sans obligation de dépôt, qu'il fasse ou non partie d'une marque de fabrique ou de commerce.

6.36   The provision reads as follows in English (WIPO translation):

> **Article 8**. A trade name shall be protected in all the countries of the Union without the obligation of filing ("*dépôt*"), whether or not it forms part of a trade mark.

2.   Conference of 1911 at Washington

6.37   The International Bureau had proposed the inclusion of an additional paragraph (2) specifying the content of the protection required to be extended to trade names. However, following a decision of the competent sub-committee, the Conference maintained the original language.

3.   The Hague Conference (1925)

6.38   The inclusion of a reference to registration had been proposed in the drafting committee, and was adopted by the general committee as well as the plenary. The provision read as follows: "A trade name shall be protected in all the countries of the Union without the obligation of filing ("*dépôt*") *or registra-tion* ("*enregistrement*"), whether or not it forms part of a trade mark."

4. London Conference (1934)

6.39   The Delegation of the United States of America had suggested to define the notion of trade name, and to enlarge its scope of protection. The Conference, however, found that the proposal needed further study, and decided to include the issue among the "*Résolutions et voeux*" of the Conference.

6.40   The provision was not discussed at the subsequent Conferences of 1958 at Lisbon, of 1967 at Stockholm, and at the Revision Conference of 1980-1981.

Determination of trademark ownership

6.41   Even though some provisions of the Paris Convention refer to the concept of trademark ownership (Article 5C(2) and (3), and Article 6*septies*: "proprie-tor", Article 6*ter*(1)(c): "owner", Article 6*bis*(1) "being already the mark of a person entitled to the benefits of this Convention"), no provision addresses the question how the owner of a trademark has to be determined under the domestic law of States party to the Paris Convention.

6.42   The general approach of the Paris Convention with regard to trademarks is illustrated by Paragraph (4) of the Final Protocol to the Original text of March 20, 1883 which, in the authentic French version, reads as follows:

"... Sauf cette exception, qui ne concerne que la forme de la mar-que, et sous réserve des dispositions des autres Articles de la Con-vention, la législation intérieure de chacun des Etats recevra son application."

1. International Conference for the Protection of Industrial Property (Paris, 1880)

6.43   The question of trademark ownership was not directly addressed at that conference. It was, however, of some relevance in the context of the discussion of other issues:

6.44   In the context of the provision concerning the right of priority, the Bel-gian delegate Demeur proposed to grant that right to the "author" of a patent, industrial design or trademark. This was opposed by the Swedish delegation who held that the provision should only address the priority of filing, while the ques-tion of ownership should be regulated by the legislation of Contracting Parties and determined by their courts. As a consequence, the wording "Any person who has duly filed an application..." was adopted.

6.45   The provision regulating the protection of marks registered in one country of the Union in the other countries of the Union, had, in the original draft, used the word "property". Delegates agreed, however, that the provision did not ad-dress the question of trademark ownership, and decided not to use the word "property" in the text of the provision, which then became Article 6, and which is now contained in Article 6*quinquies*.

6.46   Also discussed was the question whether the provision required that the registration was valid in the sense that it had given rise to a right of ownership in the country of origin. The conference, however, adopted the view expressed by the delegate of Sweden, Lagerheim, that a "regular" filing was sufficient and that the question of validity was left to the national courts.

2.   The Hague Conference (1925)

6.47   Article 6*bis* was adopted at this conference. The negotiating history, however, does not contain a discussion of the question of ownership. The proposal of the International Bureau merely refers to the difficulties of finding a text that could be applied both in countries where trademark rights were acquired according to priority of use as well as in countries where the priority of registration was decisive.

3.   Lisbon Conference (1958)

6.48   At this conference, Article 6*bis* was modified to oblige Contracting Parties to allow for prohibitions of unauthorized use of well-known marks. The proposal of the International Bureau points out that in 29 of the - then - 44 Contracting States of the Paris Convention trademark rights were based on priority of use and that an effective protection of well-known marks in such countries required the possibility of prohibiting the use of such marks.

6.49   Article 6*septies* was also adopted at this conference. The negotiating history, however, does not contain a discussion of the question of ownership. The Delegation of Japan had originally objected to the provision on the grounds that under its law everyone could apply for the registration of a trademark, but withdrew this objection in the course of the discussions.

VII.   INTERIM REVIEW

7.1   On 18 June 2001, the European Communities and the United States requested the Panel to review, in accordance with Article 15.2 of the DSU, certain aspects of the interim report that had been transmitted to the parties on 11 June 2001. The European Communities and the United States did not request an interim review meeting. Pursuant to paragraph 19 of the Working Procedures for the Panel dated 9 November 2000, the United States and the European Communities each commented on the other party's requests in communications dated 20 and 21 June 2001, respectively.

7.2   The European Communities requests that we delete paragraph 8.101 for the sake of clarity and consistency with paragraphs 8.100 and 8.102. The European Communities is of the view that the situation contemplated in paragraph 8.101 is of a purely hypothetical nature while the situation described in paragraphs 8.100 and 8.102 refers to an existing situation under Section 211(a)(2).

The United States disagrees with the European Communities that paragraph 8.101 is purely hypothetical and argues that it provides helpful explanatory guidance to aid the United States in determining how to respond to our finding that Section 211(a)(2) is inconsistent with Article 42 of the TRIPS Agreement. We stated in paragraph 8.98 that the term "right holder" "refers not only to an owner of an intellectual property right but also to others who may have legal standing in the jurisdiction in question to assert rights, such as a holder of a registration who may be considered the presumptive owner of a registered trademark." We went on to state in the following paragraph that "this presumptive owner must have access to civil judicial procedures that are effective in terms of bringing about the enforcement of its rights until the moment that there is a determination by the court that it is, in fact, the owner of the trademark that it has registered or that there is some other disqualifying ground which is compatible with international obligations." Our statement contained in paragraph 8.101 that a registrant who has been determined by the court not to be the owner of the trademark may not have any right to enforce under Article 42 of the TRIPS Agreement is a logical extension of the aforementioned paragraphs. Therefore, we decline to make the change requested by the European Communities.

7.3   The United States requests that we reconsider our conclusion that Section 211(a)(2) is inconsistent with Article 42 of the TRIPS Agreement. The United States argues that nothing in Section 211(a)(2) precludes any person from asserting ownership rights in a trade name or trademark—including a trademark registrant—from having access to civil judicial procedures that would bring about the enforcement of the rights being asserted until the moment that there is a determination by the court that such a person is, in fact, not the true owner of the trademark. The United States contends that a trademark registrant would have a full opportunity to avail himself or herself of a presumption of trademark ownership under general trademark law to substantiate his or her claim to ownership, to contest any opposing claim—including any claim based on Section 211(a)(2)—and to present relevant evidence. According to the United States, if, after a full hearing of relevant evidence, the court determines that the registrant is not the rightful owner of the trademark under US law, then the suit would be dismissed. The United States contends that the outcome is not "preempted *a priori* by legislation." The European Communities notes that the United States is reiterating its views already presented to the Panel. We note that the arguments advanced by the United States are similar to the ones it made in its written submission and oral statement.[89] In making our finding, we considered these arguments carefully and then concluded that Section 211(a)(2) is inconsistent with Article 42 because it limits, under certain circumstances, right holders' effective access to and, hence, the availability of civil judicial procedures. We remain of the view that our analysis and conclusion are correct and therefore decline to make the change requested by the United States.

---

[89]   *See* US First Submission, para. 88; and US First Oral Statement, para. 40.

7.4   The United States requests that we exercise judicial economy with respect to the issue of whether the scope of the TRIPS Agreement includes trade names. The United States notes that Parts II, III and IV of the TRIPS Agreement do not mention trade names but argues that it is not clear that this means that obligations under Article 8 of the Paris Convention (1967) are not incorporated into the TRIPS Agreement. The United States argues that the words of the text should be given their full meaning. In referring to the negotiating history, the United States argues that the language "[i]n respect of" may have nothing to do with limiting the incorporation of the Paris Convention (1967) obligations. In the view of the United States, the negotiating history supports the conclusion that the Article 2.1 language was intended to resolve the debate among negotiators as to whether undisclosed information/trade secrets would be considered to be intellectual property and was not intended to limit the commitment to comply with the Paris Convention (1967). The United States also argues that other parts of the TRIPS Agreement cast doubt on our approach to the issue of the scope of the TRIPS Agreement. Specifically, the United States argues that Article 39 contains obligations related to ensuring effective protection against unfair competition under Article 10*bis* of the Paris Convention (1967). The United States notes that unfair competition, like trade names, is not specifically identified as one of the seven categories of intellectual property in Part II of the TRIPS Agreement and that under our approach, unfair competition would be outside the scope of the TRIPS Agreement. The United States argues that our approach would require the words "in respect of" to have different meanings for different types of rights. The United States finally argues that it is unclear how our approach to the scope of the TRIPS Agreement would be applied with respect to the provisions of the Berne and Rome Conventions that are relevant to the TRIPS Agreement. The European Communities states that it cannot agree with the United States' request because the United States mentions the principle of judicial economy for the first time in the proceeding and points out that it requested a finding of TRIPS inconsistency of Sections 211(a)(2) and 211(b) in relation to trade names.

7.5   We are cognizant of WTO jurisprudence on judicial economy. However, we note that the complaining party, the European Communities, specifically claimed in its request for the establishment of a panel that Sections 211(a)(2) and 211(b) are inconsistent with Article 2.1 of the TRIPS Agreement in conjunction with Article 8 of the Paris Convention (1967).[90] The European Communities specifically requested the Panel to find that Sections 211(a)(2) and 211(b) are inconsistent with Article 2.1 of the TRIPS Agreement in conjunction with Article 8 of the Paris Convention (1967).[91] We note that our task, as set out in Article 11 of the DSU, is to make an objective assessment of the

---

[90]   *See* WT/DS176/2. Thus, the issue related to trade names under Article 2.1 of the TRIPS Agreement in conjunction with Article 8 of the Paris Convention (1967) clearly comes within our terms of reference.

[91]   *See* paragraphs 3.1 and 3.3, *supra.*

matter before us and "make such findings as will assist the DSB in making the recommendations or in giving the rulings provided for in the covered agreements." Moreover, we note that the aim of the dispute settlement mechanism as set out in Article 3.7 of the DSU is to "secure a positive solution to a dispute" and that the recommendations and rulings of the DSB are to be "aimed at achieving a satisfactory settlement of the matter" as set out in Article 3.4 of the DSU. In our view, determining whether Sections 211(a)(2) and 211(b) are consistent with Article 2.1 of the TRIPS Agreement in conjunction with Article 8 of the Paris Convention (1967) entails considering whether the scope of the TRIPS Agreement includes trade names.[92] Therefore, we decline to make the change requested by the United States.

7.6   The United States pointed out few clerical errors and we took account of them and consequently made certain changes in certain headings in section IV.C.2, and paragraphs 8.86, 8.124, 8.126 and 8.133.

VIII. FINDINGS

A.   Measures at Issue

8.1   The measure in dispute, Section 211 of the Omnibus Appropriations Act of 1998 (the "OAA") which the US Congress passed on 21 October 1998, and the provisions referred to therein are reproduced in this part of the report:

> SEC. 211.   (a)(1) Notwithstanding any other provision of law, no transaction or payment shall be authorized or approved pursuant to section 515.527 of title 31, Code of Federal Regulations, as in effect on September 9, 1998, with respect to a mark, trade name, or commercial name that is the same as or substantially similar to a mark, trade name, or commercial name that was used in connection with a business or assets that were confiscated unless the original owner of the mark, trade name, or commercial name, or the bona fide successor-in-interest has expressly consented.
>
> (2)   No U.S. Court shall recognize, enforce or otherwise validate any assertion of rights by a designated national based on common law rights or registration obtained under such section 515.527 of such a confiscated mark, trade name, or commercial name.
>
> (b)   No U.S. court shall recognize, enforce or otherwise validate any assertion of treaty rights by a designated national or its successor-in-interest under Section 44(b) or (e) of the Trademark Act of 1946 (15 U.S.C. 1126 (b) or (e)) for a mark, trade name, or commercial name that is the same as or substantially similar to a mark, trade name, or commercial name that was used in connection with a business or assets that were confiscated unless the original owner

---

[92]   *See* paragraph 8.41.

of such mark, trade name, or commercial name, or the bona fide successor-in-interest has expressly consented.

(c)   The Secretary of the Treasury shall promulgate such rules and regulations as are necessary to carry out the provisions of this section.

(d)   In this section:

(1)   The term "designated national" has the meaning given such term in section 515.305 of title 31, Code of Federal Regulations, as in effect on September 9, 1998, and includes a national of any foreign country who is a successor-in-interest to a designated national.

(2)   The term "confiscated" has the meaning given such term in section 515.336 of title 31, Code of Federal Regulations, as in effect on September 9, 1998.

8.2   Section 515.305 of title 31 Code of Federal Regulations ("CFR"), which defines "designated national", states:

For the purposes of this part, the term *designated national* shall mean Cuba and any national thereof including any person who is a specially designated national.

8.3   Section 515.306 of 31 CFR, which defines "specially designated national", states:

(a)   The term specially designated national shall mean:

(1)   Any person who is determined by the Secretary of Treasury to be a specially designated national,

(2)   Any person who on or since the "effective date" has acted for or on behalf of the Government or authorities exercising control over a designated foreign country, or

(3)   Any partnership, association, corporation or other organization which on or since the "effective date" has been owned or controlled directly or indirectly by the Government or authorities exercising control over a designated foreign country or by any specially designated national.

8.4   Section 515.336 of title 31 of the CFR defines the term "confiscated" and states:

As used in Section 515.208, the term *confiscated* refers to:

(a)   The nationalization, expropriation, or other seizure by the Cuban Government of ownership or control of property, on or after January 1, 1959:

(1)   Without the property having been returned or adequate and effective compensation provided; or

      (2)   Without the claim to the property having been settled pursuant to an international claims settlement agreement or other mutually accepted settlement procedure; and

    (b)   The repudiation by the Cuban Government of, the default by the Cuban Government on, or the failure of the Cuban Government to pay, on or after January 1, 1959:

      (1)   A debt of any enterprise which has been nationalized, expropriated, or otherwise taken by the Cuban Government;

      (2)   A debt which is a charge on property nationalized, expropriated, or otherwise taken by the Cuban Government; or

      (3)   A debt which was incurred by the Cuban Government in satisfaction or settlement of a confiscated property claim.

8.5   Section 211(a)(1) was implemented in the Cuban Assets Control Regulations, Section 515.527(a) of 31 CFR of which provides:

    (a)(1)   Transactions related to the registration and renewal in the United States Patent and Trademark Office or the United States Copyright Office of patents, trademarks, and copyrights in which the Government of Cuba or a Cuban national has interest are authorized.

    (2)   No transaction or payment is authorized or approved pursuant to paragraph (a)(1) of this section with respect to a mark, trade name, or commercial name that is the same as or substantially similar to a mark, trade name, or commercial name that was used in connection with a business or assets that were confiscated, as that term is defined in section 515.336, unless the original owner of the mark, trade name, or commercial name, or the bona fide successor-in-interest has expressly consented.

B.   *Findings and Recommendations Requested by the Parties*

8.6   Findings and recommendations requested by the parties are reproduced in this part of the report.

8.7   The European Communities alleges that:

    (a)   Section 211(a)(1) of the OAA is inconsistent with Article 2.1 of the TRIPS Agreement in conjunction with Article 6*quinquies* A(1) of the Paris Convention (1967) and Article 15.1 of the TRIPS Agreement;

    (b)   Section 211(a)(2) of the OAA is inconsistent with Article 2.1 of the TRIPS Agreement in conjunction with Articles

2(1), 6*bis* (1) and 8 of the Paris Convention (1967), and Articles 3.1, 4, 16.1 and 42 of the TRIPS Agreement; and

(c)   Section 211(b) of the OAA is inconsistent with Article 2.1 of the TRIPS Agreement in conjunction with Articles 2(1), 6*bis* (1) and 8 of the Paris Convention (1967), and Articles 3.1, 4, 16.1 and 42 of the TRIPS Agreement.

8.8   In the view of the European Communities, these measures cause prejudice to the legitimate rights of trademark owners and owners of trade/commercial names, thus nullifying and impairing the rights of the European Communities.

8.9   The European Communities requests the Panel to find that the United States has violated its obligations under Articles 3.1, 4, 15.1, 16.1 and 42 of the TRIPS Agreement as well as Article 2.1 of the TRIPS Agreement in conjunction with Articles 2(1), 6*bis* (1), 6*quinquies* A(1) and 8 of the Paris Convention (1967) and recommend that the United States bring its domestic legislation into conformity with its obligations under the TRIPS Agreement.

8.10   The United States requests the Panel to find that Section 211 of the OAA is not inconsistent with Articles 3.1, 4, 15.1, 16.1 or 42 of the TRIPS Agreement, or with Article 2.1 of the TRIPS Agreement in conjunction with Articles 2(1), 6*bis* (1), 6*quinquies* A(1) and 8 of the Paris Convention (1967) and reject the claims of the European Communities in their entirety.

C.   Preliminary Matters

1.   Factual Information from the International Bureau of WIPO

8.11   As mentioned previously, at the first substantive meeting, we informed the parties of our intention to seek information from the International Bureau of the World Intellectual Property Organization ("WIPO") pursuant to Article 13 of the DSU. The International Bureau of WIPO is responsible for the administration of the Paris Convention (1967) for the Protection of Industrial Property.

8.12   Article 13.1 of the DSU states that a panel has "the right to seek information and technical advice from any individual or body which it deems appropriate."[93] Article 13.2 further provides that panels may "seek information from any relevant source and may consult experts to obtain their opinion on certain aspects of the matter."

---

[93]   The first time a panel requested the International Bureau of WIPO to provide information in relation to an agreement administered by the International Bureau of WIPO was when the Panel in *United States—Section 110(5) of the US Copyright Act* ("*US—Section 110(5)*"), WT/DS160/R, adopted 27 July 2000, DSR 2000:VIII, 3769, requested information pertaining to the provisions of the Paris Act of 1971 of the Berne Convention (1971). In *India—Quantitative Restrictions on Imports of Agricultural, Textile and Industrial Products* ("*India—Quantitative Restrictions*"), WT/DS90/R, adopted 22 September 1999, DSR 1999:V, 1799, para. 5.12, the Panel stated that "Article 13.1 of the DSU entitles the Panel to consult with the IMF in order to obtain any relevant information relating to India's monetary reserves and balance-of-payments situation which would assist us in assessing the claims submitted to us."

8.13   Pursuant to this authority vested in panels under Article 13, we requested, in a letter dated 1 February 2001, the International Bureau of WIPO to provide us with factual information, in particular the negotiating history and subsequent developments, concerning the provisions of the Paris Convention (1967) relevant to the dispute, including Articles 2(1), 6, 6*bis*, 6*quinquies* and 8 of the Paris Convention (1967). With respect to Article 6*quinquies*, we requested any factual information on its intended scope. We also requested the International Bureau of WIPO to provide any factual information on whether the provisions of the Paris Convention (1967) regulate how the owner of a trademark is to be determined under domestic law of the Paris Union members. The International Bureau of WIPO responded to our request on 2 March 2001.

2.   Rules of Interpretation

8.14   Along with agreements governing trade in goods and services, protection of intellectual property rights as encapsulated in the TRIPS Agreement consti- tutes an integral part of the Marrakesh Agreement Establishing the World Trade Organization (the "WTO Agreement"). As such, the TRIPS Agreement is one of the "covered agreements" and is therefore subject to the DSU.[94] Article 3.2 of the DSU provides that panels are to clarify the provisions of "covered agreements" in accordance with customary rules of interpretation of public international law.

8.15   In *United States—Standards for Reformulated and Conventional Gaso- line*, the Appellate Body stated that the fundamental rule of treaty interpretation as set out in Articles 31 and 32 of the Vienna Convention on the Law of Treaties (the "Vienna Convention")[95] had "attained the status of a rule of customary or general international law".[96] Pursuant to Article 31(1) of the Vienna Convention, the duty of a treaty interpreter is to determine the meaning of a term in accor- dance with the ordinary meaning to be given to the term in its context and in light of the object and purpose of the treaty.

8.16   If, after applying the rules of interpretation set out in Article 31(1), the meaning of the treaty term remains ambiguous or obscure or leads to a result that is manifestly absurd or unreasonable, Article 32 allows the treaty interpreter to have a recourse to "supplementary means of interpretation, including the pre- paratory work on the treaty and the circumstances of its conclusion."[97] We will

---

[94]   Appellate Body Report, *India—Protection for Pharmaceutical and Agricultural Chemical Prod- ucts* ("*India—Patents*"), WT/DS50/AB/R, adopted 16 January 1998, DSR 1998:I, 9, para. 29.
[95]   Vienna Convention on the Law of Treaties, done at Vienna, 23 May 1969, 1155 U.N.T.S. 331; (1969) 8 International Legal Materials 679.
[96]   Appellate Body Report, *United States—Standards for Reformulated and Conventional Gasoline* ("*US—Gasoline*"), WT/DS2/AB/R, adopted 20 May 1996, p. 17, DSR 1996:I, 3, at 16. *See* also Ap- pellate Body Report, *Japan—Taxes on Alcoholic Beverages* ("*Japan—Alcoholic Beverages*"), WT/DS8/AB/R, WT/DS10/AB/R, WT/DS11/AB/R, adopted 1 November 1996, p. 11, DSR 1996:I, 97, at 105; Appellate Body Reports, *India—Patents*, WT/DS50/AB/R, DSR 1998:I, 9, para. 46; *European Communities—Customs Classification of Certain Computer Equipment* ("*EC-Computer Equipment*"), WT/DS62/AB/R, WT/DS67/AB/R, WT/DS68AB/R, adopted 22 June 1998, DSR 1998:V, 1851, para. 84; and *United States—Import Prohibition of Certain Shrimp and Shrimp Prod- ucts* ("*US—Shrimps*"), WT/DS58/AB/R, adopted 6 November 1998, DSR 1998:VII, 2755, para. 114.
[97]   Appellate Body Report, *EC—Computer Equipment*, DSR 1998:V, 1851, para. 86.

apply the principles enunciated by the Appellate Body in the *United States— Gasoline* to interpret the relevant provisions of the TRIPS Agreement throughout the report, including the provisions of the Paris Convention (1967) incorporated into the Agreement.

3.   Burden of Proof

8.17   The issue of burden of proof is an area in which WTO jurisprudence is well-established. The Appellate Body stated in *United States—Measures Affecting Imports of Woven Wool Shirts and Blouses* that:

> ...the burden of proof rests upon the party, whether complaining or defending, who asserts the affirmative of a particular claim or defence. If that party adduces evidence sufficient to raise a presumption that what is claimed is true, the burden then shifts to the other party, who will fail unless it adduces sufficient evidence to rebut the presumption.[98]

8.18   Once the Panel determines that the party asserting the affirmative of particular claim or defense has succeeded in raising a presumption that its claim is true, it is incumbent upon the Panel to assess the merits of all the arguments advanced by the parties and the admissibility, relevance and weight of all the factual evidence submitted with a view to establishing whether the party contesting a particular claim has successfully refuted the presumption raised. In the event that the arguments and the factual evidence adduced by the parties remain in equipoise, the Panel must, as a matter of law, find against the party who bears the burden of proof.

8.19   Thus, it is for the European Communities as the complaining party to submit arguments and evidence sufficient to raise a presumption that the US measures are inconsistent with its obligations under TRIPS Agreement. If the European Communities successfully raises such a presumption, the Panel's task becomes a matter of weighing the arguments and evidence available to it to determine whether, on balance, the Panel is convinced that the US measures are inconsistent with the provisions of the TRIPS Agreement. We will apply the principles enunciated by the Appellate Body in *United States—Shirts and Blouses* in examining the consistency of Section 211. We note that this dispute concerns a review of a regulatory text in light of the TRIPS Agreement and does not deal with any private litigation.

4.   Scope of the TRIPS Agreement

8.20   In this dispute, the European Communities requests the Panel to evaluate the consistency of Section 211 with various provisions of the TRIPS Agreement. We note that Section 211 contains a reference to "mark, trade name, or commer-

---

[98]   Appellate Body Report, *United States—Measures Affecting Imports of Woven Shirts and Blouses* (*"US—Shirts and Blouses"*), WT/DS33/AB/R, adopted 23 March 1997, p. 14, DSR 1997:I, 323, at 335.

cial name that is the same as or substantially similar to a mark, trade name, or commercial name that was used in connection with a business or assets that were confiscated" in various paragraphs. Accordingly, in examining whether Section 211 is consistent with the provisions of the TRIPS Agreement invoked by the European Communities, we are initially obliged to consider the extent to which those provisions apply to trademarks, trade names and commercial names referred to in Section 211.

8.21   Trade name is defined under the Lanham Act as "any name used by a person to identify his or her business or vocation". The United States pointed out that trade name and commercial name are synonymous under the Lanham Act. In light of this fact, a reference in this report to trade names will include commercial names.

8.22   We note that in its claims, the European Communities specifically invoked Article 2.1 of the TRIPS Agreement in conjunction with Article 8 of the Paris Convention (1967) in its request to find Sections 211(a)(2) and (b) inconsistent with Article 8 which provides that trade names are to be protected by the signatories of the Paris Convention (1967). In light of this, we consider it necessary to determine whether the scope of the TRIPS Agreement includes trade names. Were we to determine that trade names are not covered by the TRIPS Agreement, our analysis of the measure in relation to the legal basis cited by the European Communities will be limited to trademarks only.

(a)   Whether the Scope of the TRIPS Agreement Encompasses Trade Names

8.23   This Section examines whether the scope of TRIPS Agreement includes trade names. The initial focus of the analysis is the examination of the definition of the term "intellectual property" which is defined in Article 1.2 of the TRIPS Agreement as follows:

> For the purposes of this Agreement, the term "intellectual property" refers to all categories of intellectual property that are the subject of *Sections 1 through 7 of Part II.* (emphasis added)

8.24   Sections 1 through 7 of Part II of the TRIPS Agreement deal with the following categories of intellectual property: copyright and related rights; trademarks; geographical indications; industrial designs; patents; layout-designs (topographies) of integrated circuits; and protection of undisclosed information. The categories of related rights covered by Article 14 are protection of performers, producers of phonograms and broadcasting organizations.

8.25   Categories of protectable subject matters not dealt within Sections 1 to 7 of Part II of the TRIPS Agreement are not included in the definition of "intellectual property" in Article 1.2. That is, Sections 1 to 7 of Part II do not contain any reference to trade names as a category that comes within the definition of the term "intellectual property".

8.26   We interpret the terms "intellectual property" and "intellectual property rights" with reference to the definition of "intellectual property" in Article 1.2 of the TRIPS Agreement. The textual reading of Article 1.2 is that it establishes an inclusive definition and this is confirmed by the words "all categories"; the word "all" indicates that this is an exhaustive list. Thus, for example, the national and most-favoured-nation treatment obligations contained in Articles 3 and 4 of the TRIPS Agreement that refer to the "protection of intellectual property" would be interpreted to mean the categories covered by Article 1.2 of the TRIPS Agreement. We consider the correct interpretation to be that there are no obligations under those Articles in relation to categories of intellectual property not set forth in Article 1.2, e.g., trade names, consistent with Article 31 of the Vienna Convention.

8.27   Based on these reasons, we can provisionally conclude that trade names are not covered by the TRIPS Agreement.

8.28   In determining whether the scope of the TRIPS Agreement includes trade names, however, it must be noted that Article 2.1 of the TRIPS Agreement incorporates Article 8 of the Paris Convention (1967) into the TRIPS Agreement. Article 8 of the Paris Convention (1967) deals with the protection of trade names and states:

> A trade name shall be protected in all the countries of the Union without the obligation of filing or registration, whether or not it forms part of a trademark.

8.29   Article 2.1 of the TRIPS Agreement states:

> *In respect of* Parts II, III and IV of this Agreement, Members shall comply with Articles 1 through 12, and Article 19, of the Paris Convention (1967). (emphasis added)

8.30   The second subclause of Article 2.1 obliges Members to comply with the provisions of the Paris Convention (1967) which are identified in that provision.[99] However, the second subclause is conditioned by the first subclause: Members shall comply with the obligations "*[i]n respect of* Parts II, III and IV of this Agreement". As the ordinary meaning of the term "in respect of" is in "relation [to], connection [with], reference [to]"[100] and it refers to Parts II, III and IV explicitly, we consider that Members have to comply with Articles 1 through 12 and 19 of the Paris Convention (1967) "in respect" of what is covered by those parts of the TRIPS Agreement identified therein, namely copyright and related rights; trademarks; geographical indications; industrial designs; patents; layout-designs (topographies) of integrated circuits; and protection of undisclosed information.

8.31   Pursuant to Article 32 of the Vienna Convention, a treaty interpreter may have a recourse to supplementary means of interpretation, including negotiating history, in order to confirm the interpretation derived after applying Article 31 of the Vienna Convention. In this regard, we also consider the negotiating history of Articles 1.2 and 2.1 of the TRIPS Agreement. As will be shown below, the

---

[99]   Article 2.1 of the TRIPS Agreement refers to the substantive provisions of the Paris Convention (1967).

[100]   *The New Shorter Oxford English Dictionary*, (Clarendon Press, 1993), p. 2565.

historical record confirms our interpretation concerning the scope of the TRIPS Agreement.

8.32   The effective negotiation stage of the TRIPS Agreement began in Spring 1990 with the submission of five draft legal texts to the Uruguay Round Negotiating Group on TRIPS by the European Communities, the United States, Japan, 15 developing countries and Switzerland. Proposals made by the European Communities in document MTN.GNG/NG11/W/68 of 29 March 1990 and the United States in document MTN.GNG/NG11/W/70 of 11 May 1990 limit the scope of "intellectual property" to subject matters identified in Part II of the TRIPS Agreement. In introducing its proposal in document MTN.GNG/NG11/W/74, the Japanese delegation explained that it "provided for the protection of *seven types of rights*". The proposal by a group of 15 developing countries in document MTN.GNG/NG11/W/71 contained specific proposals on patents, marks, geographical indications, copyright and neighbouring rights, and integrated circuit layout-designs. Switzerland circulated a "draft amendment to the GATT" in document MTN.GNG/NG11/W/73 of 14 May 1990. It differed from the other proposals in that it had an open-ended coverage. Its Article 100 on "Scope and Coverage" stated as follows:

> This Part of the General Agreement applies in respect of all contracting parties which accept or accede to it (hereinafter the PARTIES) and to *all areas of intellectual property law, including* copyright and related rights, trademarks, geographical indications, including appellations of origin, industrial designs, patents, layout-designs (topographies) of integrated circuits, and proprietary information. (emphasis added)

8.33   This broader scope was questioned by other delegations when Switzerland introduced its submission. The following discussion was recorded in the minutes of the meeting of the Negotiating Group of 14-16 May 1990:

> Some participants said that the phrase "all areas of intellectual property law" could have a different meaning in different jurisdictions. They wondered whether all participants would have a common understanding of the outer limits of the agreement envisaged. The representative of Switzerland, in response, said that the phrase took into account that intellectual property was a field in evolution. His delegation believed that the general provisions of national treatment and MFN should apply to future IPRs. A participant expressed support for the approach taken in the provisions on national treatment and MFN, which allowed exemptions only when absolutely necessary and well justified.[101]

8.34   An Annex to the Chairman's Report to the Group of Negotiations on Goods on the Status of Work in the TRIPS Negotiation Group of 23 July 1990 (MTN.GNG/NG11/W/76) contained the first Chairman's text of a draft agree-

---

[101]   *See* document MTN.GNG/NG11/21, para. 38, 22 June 1990.

ment. In essence, the structure of that text corresponds to that of the final text of the TRIPS Agreement. In this report, the Chairman explained the following:

> The two basic approaches to the negotiations on TRIPS are identified in the text by the letters A and B. These approaches differ not only in substance but also in structure. In broad terms approach A envisages a single TRIPS agreement, encompassing all the areas of negotiation and *dealing with all seven categories of intellectual property* on which proposals have been made; this agreement would be implemented as an integral part of the General Agreement. Approach B provides for two parts, one on trade in counterfeit and pirated goods (reflected in Part IX of the attached text) and the other on standards and principles concerning the availability, scope and use of intellectual property rights (reflected in Parts I-VIII). Under this approach, the latter part would *cover the same categories of intellectual property as approach A, with the exception of the protection of trade secrets*, which its proponents do not accept as a category of intellectual property; this part would be implemented in the "relevant international organization, account being taken of the multidisciplinary and overall aspects of the issues involved". (emphasis added)

8.35   Paragraph 1 of Part II contained the following provision on the "Scope and Coverage":

> For the purposes of this agreement, the term "intellectual property" refers to all categories of intellectual property that are the subject of Sections ... to ... of Part III. This definition is without prejudice to whether the protection given to that subject matter takes the form of an intellectual property right.

8.36   Part III of the text provided standards in the following areas: copyright and related rights, trademarks, geographical indications including appellations of origin, industrial designs, patents, layout-designs of integrated circuits and protection of undisclosed information.

8.37   Eventually, a "Draft Final Act Embodying the Results of the Uruguay Round Multilateral Negotiations" (document MTN.TNC/W/35/Rev.1 of 3 December 1990) was submitted to the Brussels ministerial conference (the Brussels draft). Article 1.2 of the draft agreement provided that

> For the purposes of this Agreement, the term "intellectual property" refers to all categories of intellectual property that are the subject of Sections ... to ... of Part II.

8.38   The definition of "intellectual property" in the Chairman's draft text of July 1990 and the Brussels draft are essentially similar. Subsequently, the text remained the same in the Draft Final Act Embodying the Results of the Uruguay Round of Multilateral Trade Negotiations of 20 December 1991 (MTN.TNC/W/FA, the so-called Dunkel draft) and, apart from referring to "Members" instead of "PARTIES", in the final text of the TRIPS Agreement.

8.39   As regards the provision now contained in Article 2.1 of the Agreement, a difference between the Chairman's text of July 1990 and the Brussels draft was the addition of the words "in respect of Parts II, III and IV of this Agreement". Text to this effect first appeared in an informal draft of 20 November 1990. The records do not contain information on the purpose of the addition but the language of this provision, contained in Part I of the Agreement, suggests that Members are to comply with the Paris Convention (1967) provisions to the extent that they relate to Part II—i.e., the relevant categories of intellectual property rights regulated in the agreement—Part III (enforcement) and Part IV (acquisition).

8.40   The negotiating history confirms the view that trade names are not covered by the TRIPS Agreement.

8.41   In view of the above, we conclude that the categories of intellectual property covered by the TRIPS Agreement are those referred to in Article 1.2. Article 8 of the Paris Convention (1967) is relevant as part of the TRIPS Agreement to the extent that it may affect the protection of the categories of intellectual property covered by the Agreement. As trade names are not a category of intellectual property covered by the TRIPS Agreement, Members do not have obligations under the TRIPS Agreement to provide protection to trade names.[102] Therefore, we will limit our findings to an examination of the consistency of the provisions of Section 211 that relate to trademarks with the provision of the TRIPS Agreement.

D.   Consistency of Section 211(a)(1) with Article 15.1 of the TRIPS Agreement

1.   Whether Section 211(a)(1) is Consistent with Article 15.1 of the TRIPS Agreement

8.42   The European Communities claims that Section 211(a)(1) disallows any transaction related to the registration and renewal of trademarks with the USPTO in which Cuba or a Cuban national has an interest. Specifically, the European Communities argues that Section 211(a)(1) operates to prevent an act (i.e., the payment of the required fees) that must be performed by the right holder in order to register a mark or to ensure the renewal of a trademark that was duly registered in the United States. According to the European Communities, Article 15.1 of the TRIPS Agreement stipulates an obligation on Members to register trademarks that meet the requirements set out in the provision, subject to the exceptions set out in Article 6*quinquies* B of the Paris Convention (1967). The European Communities argues that because trademarks targeted by Section 211(a)(1) satisfy the criteria set forth in Article 15.1 of the TRIPS Agreement and therefore

---

[102]   Article 2.2 of the TRIPS Agreement makes it clear that WTO Members who are also members of the Paris Convention continue to have obligations to each other in relation to trade names under that Convention. In addition, Article 15.2 of the TRIPS Agreement lays down that when a Member denies registration of a trademark on other grounds than those contained in Article 15.1, it shall not derogate from the provisions of the Paris Convention (1967).

constitute a "sign, or combination of signs" that are eligible for registration as trademarks, Section 211(a)(1) is inconsistent with Article 15.1.

8.43   The European Communities is of the view that registration under Article 15.2 can only be refused in the exceptional cases expressly mentioned in the TRIPS Agreement and Paris Convention (1967). The European Communities argues that in the absence of a specific optional or mandatory exception, a request for registration has to be granted under Article 15.1 of the TRIPS Agreement.

8.44   The United States argues that Article 15.1 simply describes what subject matter is protectable as a trademark and that the limitation imposed on the ability of a Member to deny registration of a trademark under Article 15.1 relates only to the question of whether such signs are capable of distinguishing good(s). The United States therefore claims that because Section 211(a)(1) has nothing to do with whether certain signs are capable of constituting trademarks and has only to do with who may assert the rights in such a trademark, Section 211(a)(1) is not inconsistent with Article 15.1 of the TRIPS Agreement.

8.45   The United States argues in addition that even if Article 15.1 were to be construed to impose on a Member an affirmative obligation to register those trademarks that it considers "eligible for registration", such an obligation is limited by Article 15.2 of the TRIPS Agreement. The United States asserts that Article 15.2 does not require that the grounds for the denial be expressly contemplated in the Paris Convention (1967); it is enough that the denial itself be consistent with the Paris Convention (1967), i.e., that it is not inconsistent with the Member's obligation under that Convention. Therefore, the United States argues, denying a trademark registration on the ground that the person applying for registration is not the true owner of the trademark is not inconsistent with Article 15.1 and does not derogate from any provision of the Paris Convention (1967) under Article 15.2 of the TRIPS Agreement.

8.46   The European Communities disagrees with the US view that Article 15.2 of the TRIPS Agreement allows a Member to deny registration of a trademark so long as the ground for denial is not inconsistent with the provisions of the Paris Convention (1967).

8.47   Article 15.1 of the TRIPS Agreement states:

Section 2: Trademarks

Protectable Subject Matter

Any sign, or any combination of signs, capable of distinguishing the goods or services of one undertaking from those of other undertakings, shall be capable of constituting a trademark. Such signs, in particular words including personal names, letters, numerals, figurative elements and combinations of colours as well as any combination of such signs, shall be eligible for registration as trademarks. Where signs are not inherently capable of distinguishing the relevant goods or services, Members may make registrability depend on distinctiveness acquired through use. Members may require, as a condition of registration, that signs be visually perceptible.

8.48   Article 15.2 of the TRIPS Agreement states:

Paragraph 1 shall not be understood to prevent a Member from denying registration of a trademark on other grounds, provided that they do not derogate from the provisions of the Paris Convention (1967).

8.49   Article 15.1 sets out which signs or combinations of signs—including in particular personal names, letters, numerals, figurative elements and combinations of colours—shall be eligible for registration as trademarks.[103] The subheading of Article 15 is "Protectable Subject Matter" and paragraph 1 suggests that the "subject matter", the ordinary meaning of which is "the topic dealt with or the subject represented in a debate, exposition, or work of art",[104] is signs or any combination of signs. Based on the ordinary meaning of the term "subject matter" and in light of the second sentence which reads "[s]uch signs...shall be eligible for registration as trademarks", the "subject matter" in relation to trademarks is signs. If these signs are "capable of distinguishing the goods or services of one undertaking from other undertakings," they become eligible for trademark registration, provided that registration is not denied on "other grounds" as set out in Article 15.2 of the TRIPS Agreement. An obligation to make certain signs eligible for protection without it being understood that such signs are to be protectable would be meaningless and inconsistent with the objectives of the TRIPS Agreement as set out in the preamble and Article 7 of the TRIPS Agreement. Such interpretation is borne out contextually by Article 15.2 of the TRIPS Agreement which provides that "paragraph 1 shall not be understood to prevent a Member from denying registration on other grounds".

8.50   Article 15.1 of the TRIPS Agreement specifies the form of signs that are eligible for registration as trademarks whereas Article 15.2 does not prevent Members from denying registration of trademarks on "other grounds". In light of the explicit reference to paragraph 1, we consider that Article 15.2 has to be read in tandem with Article 15.1 to ascertain its meaning.

8.51   Article 15.2 states that Members are not prevented from denying registration of trademarks on "other grounds" so long as such grounds do not "derogate" from the provisions of the Paris Convention (1967). Thus, if a measure comes within the scope of "other grounds", a Member may deny trademark registration to signs that meet the requirements of Article 15.1. It is in this context that we assess the consistency of Section 211(a)(1) with Article 15.1 of the TRIPS Agreement.

---

[103]   Article 15 is contained in Part II of the TRIPS Agreement entitled "Standards Concerning the Availability, Scope and Use of Intellectual Property Rights" which contains seven sections that describe categories of subject matter, specify requirements that must be fulfilled before the subject matter is conferred the protection in the form of a particular intellectual property right and then specifies those rights and their duration.

[104]   *The New Oxford Dictionary of English,* (Oxford University Press, 1998), p. 1849.

8.52   In interpreting Article 15.2, we are guided by the customary rules of interpretation of public international law as set out in Article 31(1) of the Vienna Convention which provides that the treaty interpreter is to determine the meaning of a term in good faith in accordance with the ordinary meaning to be given to the term in their context and in light of object and purpose of the treaty. We also note that Article 32 of the Vienna Convention allows the treaty interpreter to have recourse to supplementary means of interpretation, including the negotiating history of the TRIPS Agreement provisions in dispute, to confirm the meaning resulting from the application of Article 31 of the Vienna Convention.

8.53   We first turn to the term "other grounds" and note that the ordinary meaning of the word "other" is defined as "different or distinct from that *already mentioned*"[105] and "ground" is defined as "a foundation or basis; points relied on".[106] Based on the ordinary meaning, we are of the view that the term "other grounds" can mean grounds "different or distinct from that already mentioned" in Article 15.1 of the TRIPS Agreement. The term "other grounds" is followed by the second part of the sentence of Article 15.2 which reads "provided that *they* do not derogate from the provisions of the Paris Convention (1967)." As the word "they" refers to "other grounds", we consider that Members can deny trademark registration on "other grounds" provided that they do not "derogate", the ordinary meaning of which is "take away (something from a thing) so as to lessen or *impair* it...To detract from",[107] from the provisions of the Paris Convention (1967). Based on the ordinary meaning of the term "derogate", Article 15.2 does not prevent a Member from denying trademark registration so long as the grounds for such denial are not inconsistent with its obligations under the Paris Convention (1967).

8.54   The European Communities argued that trademark registration under Article 15.2 of the TRIPS Agreement can only be refused pursuant to specific provisions set out in the TRIPS Agreement and Paris Convention (1967) and that such provisions are Articles 22.3, 23.2 and 24.5 of the TRIPS Agreement and Articles 6(2), 6*ter* and 6*quinquies* B of the Paris Convention (1967). We do not agree that "other grounds" for denial of registration are limited to those set out in Articles 22.3, 23.2 and 24.5 of the TRIPS Agreement and Articles 6(2), 6*ter* and 6*quinquies* B of the Paris Convention (1967). As we are examining "other grounds" that do not "derogate from the provisions of the Paris Convention (1967)", the EC's reference to the provisions of the TRIPS Agreement is inappropriate. The provisions cited by the European Communities are, on the one hand, provisions that contain reasons for denying trademark registration and, on the other hand, provisions that set out reasons which Members cannot invoke to deny trademark registration and therefore must be granted registration. As we are focusing on "other grounds" that do not "derogate" from, or impair, the provisions of the Paris Convention (1967), only the latter category of reasons are relevant. By asserting that only those provisions for denying trademark registration

---

[105]   *Black's Law Dictionary*, (West Publishing Co., Fifth Edition), p. 992.
[106]   *Ibid.*, p. 633.
[107]   *The New Shorter Oxford English Dictionary, supra*, p. 652.

to which it referred encompass the universe of "other grounds", the European Communities requires us to read the final words of Article 15.2 as if it stated "provided that they do not derogate from the provisions concerning the denial of registration of the Paris Convention (1967)." Such interpretation would oblige us to read into Article 15.2 words that are not there, something that panels are enjoined from doing.

8.55   Having determined that "other grounds" for denying trademark registration may be grounds that are not specifically identified in the TRIPS Agreement, including those provisions of the Paris Convention (1967) that are incorporated therein, we are required to address *whether* denying trademark registration on the basis that the applicant is not the proper owner under US law of "a mark...that is the same as or substantially similar to a mark...that was used in connection with a business or assets that were confiscated"[108] (hereinafter "trademarks used in connection with confiscated assets") comes within the scope of the term "other grounds" as set out in Article 15.2 of the TRIPS Agreement. The United States does not dispute the fact that signs covered by Section 211(a)(1) may be eligible for registration under Article 15.1 of the TRIPS Agreement but argues that Article 15.1 does not prevent it from denying trademark registration to an eligible sign on the ground that the applicant is not the owner of the trademark used in connection with confiscated assets.

8.56   In examining this issue, we consider that Article 6(1) of the Paris Convention (1967) serves as a useful context. Article 6(1) of the Paris Convention (1967) states that "[t]he conditions for the filing and registration of trademarks shall be determined in each country of the Union by its domestic legislation." The language contained in Article 6(1) of the Paris Convention (1967) lends credence to the view that Members have the right, subject to the national and most-favoured-nation treatment and other safeguards contained in the TRIPS Agreement, to require, as a condition for filing and registration, that the applicant be the owner of the trademark, unless there are specific provisions in the Paris Convention (1967) that are an exception to Article 6(1) and that regulate trademark registration so extensively as to restrict the ability of a Member to deny trademark registration for reasons related to ownership. That is, subject to the proviso in the previous sentence, the TRIPS Agreement and the provisions of the Paris Convention (1967) incorporated into the TRIPS Agreement do not prohibit Members from denying the registration of a trademark on the ground that the applicant is not the owner of the trademark as defined in their respective domestic legal system. Thus, we consider that "other grounds" for denying trademark

---

[108]   The United States argued that the customary international law on expropriations is clear in that a state may not expropriate private assets of nationals of other states in its territory unless the expropriation is (1) for public purpose, (2) on a non-discriminatory basis and in accordance with due process of law and (3) subject to prompt, adequate and effective compensation. We note that public international law on what constitutes a lawful taking of private party by a state is not fully settled and subject to an ongoing discussion. However, we recognize that there are bilateral treaties that specify, as a matter of private international law, what constitutes a lawful taking. For the purposes of this dispute, we do not need to determine what constitutes a lawful taking or whether the business or assets, including trademarks covered by Article 211, were lawfully expropriated by Cuba.

registration under Article 15.2 may encompass a measure that denies trademark registration on the basis that the applicant is not the owner of the trademark.

8.57   We are very cognizant of the potential abuse that might arise in connection with any national legislation that seeks to arbitrarily regulate the ownership of intellectual property. The TRIPS Agreement, however, is not without safeguards against potential abuse. Article 1.1 of the TRIPS Agreement states that "Members shall give effect to the provisions of this Agreement." We construe this sentence to mean that Members are to give effect to rights and obligations contained in the TRIPS Agreement and that Members are not to enact measures that would negate such rights and obligations. In addition, Articles 3 and 4 of the Agreement require a Member to accord national and most-favoured-nation treatment to the nationals of other Members. Moreover, Article 7 of the TRIPS Agreement states that one of the objectives is that "[t]he protection and enforcement of intellectual property rights should contribute...to a balance of rights and obligations." We consider this expression to be a form of the good faith principle. The Appellate Body in *United States—Shrimps* stated that this principle "controls the exercise of rights by states. One application of this principle, the application widely known as the doctrine of *abus de droit*, prohibits the abusive exercise of a state's rights and enjoins that whenever the assertion of a right 'impinges on the field covered by [a] treaty obligation, it must be exercised bona fide, that is to say reasonably.' An abusive exercise by a Member of its own treaty right thus results in a breach of the treaty rights of the other members and, as well, a violation of the treaty obligation of the Member so acting."[109] Members must therefore implement the provisions of the TRIPS Agreement in a manner consistent with the good faith principle enshrined in Article 7 of the TRIPS Agreement.

8.58   Based on the reasons aforementioned, if Section 211(a)(1) is domestic legislation that denies trademark registration on the basis that the applicant is not the proper owner under US law, it comes within the purview of "other grounds" as set out in Article 15.2 and, hence, is consistent with Article 15.1 of the TRIPS Agreement.

8.59   The European Communities argued that Section 211 curtails the use of an asset by its legal owner and that any transaction such as simple licensing agreement to a joint venture operation between a designated national and an EC economic operator can be jeopardized by the curtailment flowing from Section 211. While it is true that Section 211(a)(1) has the practical effect of denying trademark registration or renewal of trademarks,[110] an examination of the language of

---

[109]   Appellate Body Report, *United States—Shrimps*, DSR 1998:VII, 2755, para. 158.

[110]   We note that Section 211(a)(1) does not explicitly state that registration or renewal of underlying marks shall be denied. Section 211(a)(1) prohibits any "transaction or payment" related to the registration and renewal of underlying marks and names unless the original owner of the mark consents. The term "transaction" is defined in Section 515.309 of 31 CFR as "any payment or transfer to such designated foreign country or national thereof" and "transfer" in turn is defined in Section 515.310 of 31 CFR as "any actual or purported act or transaction...the purpose, intent, or effect of which is to create...transfer, or alter...any right, remedy, power, privilege, or interest with respect to any property". The term "property" is defined in Section 515.311 of 31 CFR to include trademarks. Thus, the

Section 211(a)(1) indicates that it is a measure that deals with ownership of trademarks used in connection with confiscated assets. Section 211(a)(1) states:

> Notwithstanding any other provision of law, no transaction or payment shall be authorized or approved pursuant to section 515.527 of title 31, Code of Federal Regulations, as in effect on September 9, 1998, with respect to a mark, trade name, or commercial name that is the same as or substantially similar to a mark, trade name, or commercial name that was used in connection with a business or assets that were confiscated unless the original owner of the mark, trade name, or commercial name, or the bona fide successor-in-interest has expressly consented.

8.60   The language of Section 211(a)(1) addresses the rights of a person registering a trademark to assert an ownership interest in the trademark concerned. Section 211(a)(1), together with OFAC regulations, creates an additional procedural step that relates to the registration of a trademark or the renewal of a trademark registration in the United States, namely the requirement that an applicant obtain a licence—a general or a specific licence—in order to be able to pay the registration or renewal fee. In the absence of such a licence, the applicant is not able to pay the required fee and this, in turn, results in the rejection of the application. As a part of this procedure, the US authorities examine, in the case where the trademark in question is one that was used in connection with confiscated assets, whether the applicant is the proper owner of that trademark in accordance with US law or has the consent of the original owner or the latter's successor-in-interest. If a trademark was used in connection with confiscated assets, the failure to obtain the required consent or to meet the condition of being the proper owner as defined under US law has the practical effect of denying trademark registration. However, if the applicant is the original owner under US law or has the consent of such original owner or its bona fide successor-in-interest, the licence will be granted and, hence, the trademark will be registered or the registration will be renewed. For these reasons, we consider that Section 211(a)(1) is domestic legislation, as envisaged in Article 6(1) of the Paris Convention (1967), that requires the applicant to be the owner of a trademark or have its consent or be a successor-in-interest as a condition for filing and registration and therefore comes within the purview of "other grounds" as set out in Article 15.2. Hence, we conclude that Section 211(a)(1) is consistent with Article 15.1, subject to review below of additional arguments advanced by the European Communities in respect of Article 15.1.

---

denial of registration or renewal is the effect of not authorizing or approving "any transaction or payment" which prevents a designated national from paying the necessary filing fee for the registration or renewal of a trademark with the USPTO.

2. Consideration of Other Arguments of the European Communities

(a) EC's Argument that Section 211(a)(1) Denies Registration to Signs of Trademarks that Meet the Requirements of Article 15.1

8.61   The European Communities argues that the scope of Section 211 includes those trademarks that did not exist in the United States at the time of the confiscation and were acquired thereafter in the United States. The European Communities asserts that Section 211 applies to US trademarks that have neither a factual nor legal relationship with the confiscated Cuban business or assets. The European Communities claims that Section 211 is inconsistent with Article 15.1 because the signs constituting trademarks used in connection with confiscated assets that meet the criteria set out in Article 15.1 can come within the purview of Section 211(a)(1) and therefore be denied registration as trademarks.[111]

8.62   To deal with the EC's argument, we are obliged to examine first how the United States determines trademark ownership under its laws. We then consider whether Section 211(a)(1) is consistent with Article 15.1 of the TRIPS Agreement. Such consideration also raises the issue of the extent to which ownership is regulated in the TRIPS Agreement.

8.63   According to the United States, trademark ownership is generally established through use and thus the owner of a trademark is generally the party who controls the nature and quality of the goods sold or services rendered under the trademark.[112] The United States indicated that the original owner under Section 211 would be determined pursuant to the relevant US laws and that use even outside of the United States may be relevant in this regard.[113] The United States argued that the TRIPS Agreement, including the provisions of the Paris Convention (1967) incorporated into the TRIPS Agreement, does not provide substantive rules for determining the ownership of a trademark. The European Communities, while stating that the TRIPS Agreement does not expressly define the

---

[111]   *See* EC's First Submission, para. 42 and EC's Second Oral Statement, para. 38.

[112]   The *Trademark Manual of Examining Procedure*, Section 1201.01 states:

Section 1(a) of the Trademark Act, 15 U.S.C. Section 1051(a), states, "The owner of a trademark used in commerce may apply to register his or her trademark under this act...." An application for trademark registration under Section 1(A) or Section 44 of the Act must include "a statement to the effect that the person making the verification believes himself, or the firm, corporation, or association in whose behalf he makes the verification, to be the owner of the mark sought to be registered...." 15 U.S.C. Section 1051(a)(1)(A). Similarly, an application under Section 1(b) must include a statement to the effect that the person making the verification believes the applicant to be entitled to use of the mark in commerce. 15 U.S.C. sec. 1051(b)(1)(A). ...The owner of a mark is the party who controls the nature and quality of the goods sold or services rendered under the mark. Thus, the specific facts concerning the use of the mark are determinative of the issue of ownership.

[113]   The United States submitted that "Section 211(a)(1) focuses on trademarks that have an 'original owner' and that have been 'used' in connection with confiscated assets or business. Such use—even outside the United States—can create ownership rights (*i.e.*, 'protection') in the United States." *See* US Response 67(b).

owner of a trademark,[114] advanced the view that the TRIPS Agreement provides clear guidance to determine ownership of trademarks and that Article 15.1, by establishing a link between the trademark and goods or services emanating from an undertaking, suggests that only an undertaking can be the owner of a trademark which distinguishes its goods or services.

8.64   We note that trademark ownership is generally determined by use under US law. According to the United States, use of trademark outside the United States can establish ownership in the United States. We also note that under Section 211, the relevant US authorities will examine whether the applicant has the consent of the original owner of the trademark in the event that the trademark in question is one that was used in connection with confiscated assets. We consider that the newly introduced procedure under Section 211 whereby the US authorities determine whether the applicant is the original owner of the trademark or has the consent of the original owner in respect of trademarks used in connection with confiscated assets is consistent with the US approach that determines ownership based on use because a party who used a trademark in Cuba can acquire ownership in the United States on the basis of that use.[115] Article 16.1 of the TRIPS Agreement, the pertinent part of which states that "[t]he rights described above shall not...affect the possibility of Members making rights available on the basis of use", supports the view that a Member can determine the owner of a trademark based on use.[116] Accordingly, because the use of a trademark within or outside the United States can establish ownership, we do not consider that the scope of Section 211 is overly broad either in temporal or geographical terms.

8.65   In respect of the EC's argument that signs constituting trademarks used in connection with confiscated assets that meet the criteria set out in Article 15.1 can come within the purview of Section 211(a)(1) and therefore be denied regis-

---

[114] *See* EC's Response 50. The WIPO Note adds that "[e]ven though some provisions of the Paris Convention refer to the concept of trademark ownership (Article 5C(2) and (3), and Article 6*septies*: 'proprietor', Article 6*ter* (1)(c): 'owner', Article 6*bis* (1) 'being already the mark of a person entitled to the benefits of this Convention'), no provision addresses the question how the owner of a trademark has to be determined under the domestic law of States party to the Paris Convention."

[115] *See* footnote 113, *supra.*

[116] The European Communities argued that prior to registration, there exists no trademark and that the holder of the registration of a trademark is by definition the owner of that trademark. The United States, on the other hand, argued that the TRIPS Agreement was drafted to take into account both the civil law "registration" and the common law "use" systems and that the TRIPS Agreement does not require a trademark system in which registration itself creates both trademark rights and ownership rights. The United States submitted that, under US law, registration is not conclusive of the ownership of a trademark and common law trademarks exist independently of federal registration. The United States argued that registration of a trademark under the Trademark Act confers *prima facie* presumptions of the registrant's ownership of the registered trademark and of the registrant's exclusive right to use that trademark in commerce. We are of the view that the TRIPS Agreement does not contain any provision that would require Members to equate the holder of a trademark registration with the owner of that trademark. We note that Article 16 of the TRIPS Agreement provides that rights conferred under that Article are not to affect the possibility of Members making rights available on the basis of use. To the extent that rights are granted and ownership determined on the basis of use, a trademark can exist before the registration. Safeguarding the interests of an owner of a trademark acquired through use against a subsequent applicant of a trademark registration is not inconsistent with the TRIPS Agreement.

tration as trademarks, we note that Section 211(a)(1) does not deny trademark registration to those signs that constitute trademarks as such; it denies trademark registration to those who are not deemed to be the proper owner under US law. Thus, the effect of Section 211(a)(1) is that the original owner, the successor-in-interest or a person who has the original owner's or the successor-in-interest's consent can register the signs constituting trademarks that were used in connection with confiscated assets which meet the requirements of Article 15.1 because they are considered the proper owner under Section 211(a)(1). It is also for this reason that we do not share the EC's view that Articles 16 to 21 of the TRIPS Agreement would be reduced to inutility; the original owner, the successor-in-interest or a person who has the original owner's or the successor-in-interest's consent would obtain rights and benefits stemming from these provisions. Therefore, Section 211(a)(1) is not inconsistent with Article 15.1 on the basis that Section 211(a)(1) denies trademark registration to those signs constituting trademarks that were used in connection with confiscated assets which meet the requirements of Article 15.1.

> (b)   EC's Argument that Section 211(a)(1) Applies to Other Classes of Products; Extends its Scope to Include Similar Trademarks; and Applies to Abandoned Trademarks

8.66   The European Communities made three arguments related to the scope of Section 211.[117] First, the European Communities argued that Section 211 applies to classes of products other than those covered by the trademarks that were used in connection with confiscated assets. Second, the European Communities submitted that Section 211 extends its scope to include substantially similar trademarks, which according to the European Communities, by definition have not been confiscated. Third, the European Communities claimed that the reach of Section 211 extends to those trademarks used in connection with confiscated assets acquired by a person other than the original owner or its successor-in-interest after such original owner or its successor-in-interest has abandoned the trademark in the United States. In this regard, the European Communities claimed that if a trademark has been abandoned, anyone can apply for its registration and acquire ownership.

8.67   In relation to the EC's argument that Section 211(a)(1) would apply to classes of products other than those covered by the trademarks that were used in connection with confiscated assets, we see no basis to interpret Section 211(a)(1) so that it would apply to classes of products other than those covered by "a mark that was used in connection with a business or assets that were confiscated". The language of Section 211(a)(1) links a trademark to confiscated assets and does not refer to types of products or assets other than confiscated assets. We note that trademarks give rights in respect of the same or similar goods and in light of this principle, we are of the view that Section 211(a)(1) would not be construed so as

---

[117]   The European Communities stated that Section 211 extends "well beyond confiscated assets." *See* EC's First Oral Statement, paras. 48 to 52.

to apply to classes of products unrelated to those covered by the trademarks used in connection with confiscated assets. Accordingly, for the reasons set out above, we reject the EC's argument that Section 211(a)(1) would apply to classes of products other than those covered by the trademarks that were used in connection with confiscated assets.

8.68   Turning to the EC's argument that Section 211(a)(1) applies to similar trademarks, we note that Section 211(a)(1) states that no transaction or payment shall be authorized with respect to a trademark that is "substantially similar" to a trademark that was used in connection with confiscated assets. Although the regime of ownership is not to be equated with the regime of protection (which has important implications for this case),[118] it is recalled that the primary function of a trademark is to distinguish trademarked goods or services of an enterprise from others in order to help consumers identify a product. If the owner of a trademark who produces certain goods is unable to exercise exclusive rights to protect itself against infringing competitors who might take advantage of the reputation of the trademark by selling identical or similar products in the marketplace using that trademark, the trademark could not serve its function. The protection afforded to the owner must include not only identical trademarks but also similar trademarks. Otherwise, third parties would be able to take advantage of the reputation of a trademark by using a similar sign so as to confuse consumers in the marketplace and thereby undermine the function of trademarks. In recognition of the important function of trademarks, Article 16.1 of the TRIPS Agreement states that "[t]he owner of a registered trademark shall have the exclusive right to prevent all third parties...from using...*similar signs* for goods or services *which are...similar* to those in respect of which the trademark is registered where such use would result in a likelihood of confusion." In light of the function of trademarks and because the protection afforded to the owner of a trademark includes preventing third parties from using "similar" trademarks, we reject the EC's argument that the United States is in violation of its obligations under the TRIPS Agreement because the scope of Section 211(a)(1) is overly broad in that it includes similar trademarks.

8.69   With respect to the argument related to abandoned trademarks, we understand the European Communities to argue that the signs of abandoned trademarks used in connection with confiscated assets meet the requirement under Article 15.1 and are therefore eligible for registration as trademarks, provided that they are not denied registration on "other grounds" under Article 15.2. In response to a question we posed, the United States argued that in particular circumstances where a trademark has been legally abandoned, there is no original owner whose consent is required under Section 211. We note that abandonment of a trademark is determined by the national laws of each Member. In case of an abandonment, the owner relinquishes title to the ownership of the trademark concerned. Based on this principle, if the original owner abandons a trademark, i.e., relinquishes the title to the ownership of a trademark, such original owner no longer has rights that are to be protected. In light of the US response, we under-

---

[118]   For a discussion on the regime of ownership, *see* para. 8.108, *infra.*

stand that Section 211(a)(1) would not be applicable in such circumstances. On this basis, we reject the EC's argument concerning abandoned trademarks.

3.   Overall Conclusion with Respect to Article 15.1

8.70   Based on our consideration of the issues above, we confirm our finding in paragraph 8.60 and reject the further arguments advanced by the European Communities. We find that Section 211(a)(1) is not inconsistent with Article 15.1 of the TRIPS Agreement because the term "other grounds" as used in Article 15.2 of the TRIPS Agreement may include a measure that denies trademark registration on the basis that the applicant is not the owner under national, in this case, US law and Section 211(a)(1) is a measure that deals with the ownership of trademarks used in connection with confiscated assets.

E.   Consistency of Section 211(a)(1) with Article 2.1 of the TRIPS Agreement in Conjunction with Article 6quinquies (a)(1) of the Paris Convention (1967)

1.   Whether Section 211(a)(1) is Consistent with Article 2.1 of the TRIPS Agreement in Conjunction with Article 6quinquies A(1) of the Paris Convention (1967)

8.71   The European Communities claims that Section 211(a)(1) is inconsistent with Article 6*quinquies* A(1) of the Paris Convention (1967) as incorporated into the TRIPS Agreement because it prevents the owner of a trademark registered in another WTO Member from acquiring or maintaining a trademark registration in the United States by foreclosing the possibility of paying the required fees necessary for the registration and renewal. The European Communities argues that all trademarks duly registered in the country of origin are covered by Article 6*quinquies* A(1). In the view of the European Communities, the scope of Article 6*quinquies* A(1) is not limited to the form of a trademark. Consequently, it argues that the Member in which a registration is sought does not have the right to question the existence of a trademark in the hands of an owner as defined by the laws of the country of origin. Furthermore, the European Communities argues that, in any event, the scope of Article 6*quinquies* A(1) is irrelevant for the resolution of the dispute because Section 211(a)(1) denies registration to those trademarks that meet the particular conditions of the US legislation as to the form.

8.72   The United States argues that nothing in Article 6*quinquies* A(1) of the Paris Convention (1967) requires it to accept the registration or renewal of trademarks if the person registering or renewing is not the true owner of the trademark under US law. The United States argues that Article 6*quinquies* A(1) of the Paris Convention (1967) does not require it to recognize and enforce trademarks used in connection with assets that have been confiscated—i.e., expropriated without compensation—from their rightful owners. The United States contends that the Paris Convention (1967) and the TRIPS Agreement do not contain any provision that specifies how trademark ownership is determined but leaves such determination to the national laws of each Member, subject to the requirements of national and most-favoured-nation treatment.

8.73   According to the United States, Article 6*quinquies* A(1) is directed at the form of the trademark: in cases where a trademark would normally be ineligible for registration because of its form—for instance because it contains foreign language terms or proper names—Members are required to accept and protect such trademarks "as is" or "in their original form" if they are duly registered in their country of origin. The United States argues that this provision was necessary because of differences in domestic legislation with regard to the form of the trademark. It is the view of the United States that Article 6*quinquies* A(1) does not eliminate Members' ability to determine that, with respect to issues other than form, a trademark will not be registered or protected. The United States contends that Article 6*quinquies* A(1) does not prevent a Member from denying registration of a trademark duly registered abroad, where the registrant is not the true owner of the mark and Section 211(a)(1), therefore, is not inconsistent with Article 6*quinquies* A(1).

8.74   We first examine the EC's claim that Section 211(a)(1) is inconsistent with Article 6*quinquies* A(1) of the Paris Convention (1967) on the basis that Article 6*quinquies* A(1) requires that all trademarks duly registered in the country of origin are to be accepted for filing and protected "as is" in other Members. We note that through their incorporation, the substantive rules of the Paris Convention (1967), including the provisions of Article 6*quinquies*, have become part of the TRIPS Agreement and as provisions of that Agreement have to be read as applying to all Members. Article 6*quinquies* A(1) of the Paris Convention (1967) states:

> Every trademark duly registered in the country of origin shall be accepted for filing and protected as is in the other countries of the Union, subject to the reservations indicated in this Article. Such countries may, before proceeding to final registration, require the production of a certificate of registration in the country of origin, issued by the competent authority. No authentication shall be required for this certificate.[119]

8.75   There are essentially two conditions that must be fulfilled before "every trademark" is to be accepted for filing and protected "as is" by other Members. The first condition is that the trademark has to be "duly registered" and the sec-

---

[119]   Article 6*quinquies* A(1) reads in French:

> Toute marque de fabrique ou de commerce régulièrement enregistrée dans le pays d'origine sera admise au dépôt et protégée telle quelle dans les autres pays de l'Union, sous les réserves indiquées au présent article. Ces pays pourront, avant de procéder à l'enregistrement définitif, exiger la production d'un certificat d'enregistrement au pays d'origine, délivré par l'autorité compétente. Aucune légalisation ne sera requise pour ce certificat.

We note that under Article 29(1)(c) of the Paris Convention (1967), the French text shall prevail in case of differences of opinion of the various texts. As regards the Marrakesh Agreement Establishing the World Trade Organization, including the TRIPS Agreement annexed to it, English, French and Spanish texts are equally authentic.

ond condition is that the trademark has to be duly registered "in the country of origin". Thus, the benefits under Article 6*quinquies* A(1) can be claimed only if there is a registration in the country of origin. This requirement is reinforced by Article 6*quinquies* D which states that "[n]o person may benefit from the provisions of this article if the mark for which he claims protection is not registered in the country of origin." Upon meeting these conditions, "every trademark" is to be accepted for filing and protected "as is" ("telle quelle" in French) by other Members, subject to the grounds for denying registration as trademarks as set out in Article 6*quinquies* B.

8.76   The ordinary meaning of the term "as is" is defined as "in the existing state, things being what they are".[120] The French term "telle quelle" is defined as "à l'état naturel, *sans arrangement*; *sans modification*. Comme il est, avec ses inconvénients et ses avantages, ses qualités et ses défauts." [121]

8.77   We note that the term "as is" refers to the word "trademark" and that this is apparent in the French text which, according to Article 29(1)(c) of the Paris Convention (1967), is the text which shall prevail in cases of differences of opinion on the interpretation of the various texts. The term "telle quelle" in the feminine form refers to "marque de fabrique ou de commerce" which is also feminine. This textual element already indicates that the form of a trademark should be accepted "as is" by the authorities of "the other countries of the Union", especially since the term "telle quelle" in French refers primarily to the form of an object. That the correct interpretation covers only the form of the trademark which must be accepted in the country in which it is filed for registration and protection is further confirmed when one considers the context of this provision. We are of the view that in this respect Article 6*quinquies* C(2), Article 6(1) and (3), and Article 2 deserve particular scrutiny.

8.78   Article 6*quinquies* C(2) states that no trademark shall be refused in other countries of the Union only because it differs from the mark protected in the country of origin in respect of elements inter alia that "do not alter its distinctive character and do not affect its identity *in the form in which it has been registered* in the ... country of origin". (emphasis added) There is a clear and direct link between paragraph C(2) and paragraph A(1) of Article 6*quinquies*. They both speak of the same situation, namely the filing for registration and protection in one country of the Union of a trademark registered in another country of the Union. It is clear that what is important under paragraphs C(2) and A(1) of Article 6*quinquies* is the form in which the trademark has been registered.

8.79   Article 6, paragraphs 1 and 3 state two principles, namely (1) that the domestic legislation of each country of the Union shall determine the conditions for filing and registration of trademarks, and (2) that filing, registration or renewal of the trademark in the country of origin is not required for acceptance in other countries; in other words "the independence" or "territorial limitation" of trademarks according to their country of registration. These principles set out in Article 6 of the Paris Convention (1967) would be reduced in their effectiveness be-

---

[120]   *The New Shorter Oxford Dictionary, supra*, p. 123.
[121]   *Le Robert Dictionnaire de la Langue Française*, (Dictionnaires Le Robert, 1985), p. 199.

yond the bounds of the reasonable if Article 6*quinquies* A(1) were to be interpreted to mean that every trademark registered in one country of the Union would have to be accepted "as is" in all its aspects and in its totality in every other country of the Union. In such case, little would remain of the freedom of each country to lay down the rules for filing and registration because nearly every foreign trademark would have to be accepted for registration in all its aspects. Equally, the "territoriality" or "independence" of trademarks would be severely curtailed if every trademark registered in one country would have to be accepted in another in all its aspects. Article 6*quinquies* clearly constitutes an exception to or limitation on Article 6. So long as that exception or limitation is restricted to problems arising from the form of the trademark registered in one country and offered for registration in another country (and which otherwise might be refused there for reasons of pure form), both provisions can each be given their effectiveness.[122]

8.80   Article 2 of the Paris Convention (1967) lays down the national treatment principle. This is one of the foundations of the Convention. Article 6*quinquies* goes beyond national treatment in that it prescribes that the authorities accept for filing and protection trademarks which according to rules applicable in their own country they might be entitled to refuse. In that regard, Article 6*quinquies* has, in our view, correctly been described as a "national treatment plus" provision. If this provision were to be interpreted as covering every trademark in all its aspects, the national treatment plus provision would acquire such importance as to make the fundamental rule of Article 2 virtually meaningless. This cannot have been the intention of the drafters. Again, both provisions can each deploy their full utility only if it is accepted that national treatment remains one of the main principles of the Convention, which is superseded only in a limited number of cases, namely only when the form of the trademark concerned needlessly stands in the way of a certain uniformity of trademarks in different countries of the Union for the same right holder.

8.81   On the basis of the textual and contextual arguments discussed above, we arrive at the conclusion that the broad interpretation given by the European Communities must be rejected. As will be seen below, the historical record confirms our narrower interpretation.

---

[122] The principle of effective interpretation or "l'effet utile" or in Latin *ut res magis valeat quam pereat* reflects the general rule of interpretation which requires that a treaty be interpreted to give meaning and effect to all the terms of the treaty. For instance, one provision should not be given an interpretation that will result in nullifying the effect of another provision of the same treaty. For a discussion of this principle, *see Yearbook of the International Law Commission*, 1966, Vol. II A/CN.4/SER.A/1966/Add.1 p. 219 and following. *See* also *e.g., Corfu Channel* Case (1949) *I.C.J. Reports*, p. 24 (International Court of Justice); Territorial Dispute Case (Libyan Arab Jamahiriya v. Chad) (1994) *I.C.J. Reports*, p. 23 (International Court of Justice); and *Oppenheim's International Law* (9th ed., Jennings and Watts eds., 1992), Vol. 1, 1280-1281. *See* Appellate Body in *US—Gasoline*, p. 12 ("An interpreter is not free to adopt a reading that would result in reducing whole clauses or paragraphs of a treaty to redundancy or inutility"); *Japan—Alcoholic Beverages*, p. 12; and Panel Report, *Korea—Definitive Safeguard Measure on Imports of Certain Dairy Products* ("*Korea— Dairy*"), WT/DS98/R, DSR 2000:I, 49, para. 7.37.

8.82   The documents concerning the Lisbon Conference of 1958 provided by WIPO in response to our request make it unequivocally clear that from the very beginning of the Paris Convention's history, the predecessor provisions to Article 6*quinquies* had been largely drafted in the same wording but had been since considered somewhat opaque. As a matter of fact, it was necessary, in order to arrive at the final adoption of the predecessor provisions, to adopt an agreed interpretation of that provision in the form of paragraph 4 of the final Protocol of 1883.[123] This agreed interpretation is very clear in stating that the predecessor provision of Article 6*quinquies* is an exception to the rule that the legislation of the Members of the Union remains applicable and is restricted only to the form of the trademark. Later on, this agreed interpretation was set aside at the Washington Conference of 1911 and this may have reduced its value as a possible interpretative tool under Article 31(3)(a) of the Vienna Convention.[124] Nevertheless, it remains part of the historical record and its interpretation is moreover confirmed by what transpired at the Lisbon Conference of 1958, at which the present text of Article 6*quinquies* was finalized. At the Lisbon Conference, the issue of the interpretation of Article 6*quinquies* A(1) was discussed in the clearest manner imaginable in response to a proposal from the United Kingdom and the then Federation of Rhodesia and Nyasaland which aimed to reduce this provision to a mere national treatment provision. On this occasion the President described how the two proponents wanted to eliminate what he described as "le principe de la marque 'telle quelle'." He described how this principle foresaw that any mark duly registered in a country would be accepted for registration in another country "sans adjonction" and added "toutefois, ce principe concerne uniquement la forme de la marque et non son contenu".[125] Nowhere in the record of the Lisbon Conference is there any indication at all that any delegation took issue with this view of the provision at issue. Therefore, when the delegations later voted in favour of maintaining the principle of the "marque telle quelle", they did this with the full knowledge of the interpretation given by the President of the Conference.[126] We, therefore, conclude that the historical record bears out our interpretation based on textual and contextual elements.

---

[123]   The text of paragraph 4 adopted at the 1883 Conference of Paris reads as follows: 4. Le paragraphe 1er de l'article 6 doit être entendu en ce sens qu'aucune marque de fabrique ou de commerce ne pourra être exclue de la protection dans l'un des États de l'Union par le fait seul qu'elle ne satisferait pas, au point de vue des signes qui la composent, *aux conditions de la législation de cet État*, pourvu qu'elle satisfasse, sur ce point, à la législation du pays d'origine et qu'elle ait été, dans ce dernier pays, l'objet d'un dépôt régulier. Sauf cette exception, *qui ne concerne que la forme de la marque*, et sous réserve des dispositions des autres articles de la Convention, la législation intérieure de chacun des États recevra son application. (…) (emphasis added). *See* Annex II to the letter from WIPO, pp. 24-27, p. 32.

[124]   According to the Paris Centenary 1983, "it is generally believed that such omission did not alter the intended sense of 'telle quelle' as it was made explicit in 1883." Paris Centenary 1983, WIPO Publication No. 875. Annex X to the WIPO letter. Bodenhasuen expressed a similar view: "it is not possible to conclude from this discussion that agreement was reached regarding a different scope of application of the provision." *See* Bodenhausen, *Paris Convention for the Protection of Industrial Property*, (United International Bureaux for the Protection of Intellectual Property, 1968), p. 110.

[125]   Annex VII to the WIPO letter, p. 600.

[126]   Annex VII to the WIPO letter, p. 751

8.83   The ordinary meaning of the term "as is" and read in its context and as confirmed by the negotiating history indicates that Article 6*quinquies* A(1) addresses the form of the trademark; that is, those trademarks duly registered in one country, even when they do not comply with the provisions of domestic law of a Member concerning the permissible form of trademarks, have nevertheless to be accepted for filing and protection in another country. Therefore, we do not agree with the EC's assertion[127] that the Member in which registration is sought does not have any right to question the existence of a trademark in the hands of an owner as defined by the laws of the country of origin. However, as we noted above in our examination of Section 211(a)(1) in relation to Article 15.1 of the TRIPS Agreement, Section 211(a)(1) is a measure that regulates ownership and does not deal with the form of the signs of which the trademark is composed. For these reasons, Section 211(a)(1) is not inconsistent with Article 6*quinquies* A(1) of the Paris Convention (1967).

> 2.   *Consideration of Other Arguments of the European Communities*
>
> (a)   EC's Argument that Section 211(a)(1) Denies Registration "as is" to Signs of Trademarks that Meet the Conditions as to the Form Required under Article 6*quinquies* A(1)

8.84   The European Communities argued that the scope of Section 211 includes trademarks that did not exist in the United States at the time of the confiscation but were acquired thereafter in the United States. The European Communities also argued that Section 211(a)(1) is inconsistent with Article 6*quinquies* A(1) because, even if Article 6*quinquies* A(1) were limited to the form of the sign, Section 211(a)(1) denies acceptance for filing and protection on an "as is" basis to those trademarks that do not comply with the provisions of the domestic law of a Member with respect to the permissible form.

8.85   In dealing with the EC's argument that the scope of Section 211 includes trademarks that did not exist in the United States at the time of the Cuban confiscation, we stated previously that trademark ownership is generally determined on the basis of use under US law and that the relevant US authorities will examine whether the applicant is the proper owner of the trademark in the event that the trademark is one that was used in connection with confiscated assets. We concluded that determining the owner of a trademark based on use is not inconsistent with the TRIPS Agreement and that the scope of Section 211 is not overly broad either in temporal or geographical terms.[128]

---

[127]   *See* EC's Second Oral Statement, para. 41. We note that this position appears to be inconsistent with the EC's assertion that the TRIPS Agreement does not require a WTO Member to recognize a confiscation of intellectual property in another country as regards the legal effect of that confiscation on the ownership of intellectual property protected in the country where the confiscation took place. *See* EC's Response 43.

[128]   *See* our discussion in paras. 8.59 and 8.60, *supra.*

8.86   In respect of the EC's argument that Section 211(a)(1) denies acceptance for filing and protection on an "as is" basis even to those trademarks that meet the particular conditions of the US legislation as to the form, we determined previously that Section 211(a)(1) does not deny protection of trademarks as such and that the effect of Section 211(a)(1) is that the original owner, the successor-in-interest or a person who has the original owner's consent can register the trademarks that were used in connection with confiscated assets. The effect of Section 211(a)(1) is that the original owner, the successor-in-interest or a person who has the original owner's or successor-in-interest's consent are not prevented from having their trademarks accepted for filing and protection on an "as is" basis under Article 6*quinquies* A(1). We note that Section 211(a)(1) denies acceptance for filing and protection on an "as is" basis to those who are not the original owner or do not have its consent or the consent of the successor-in-interest but does not deny acceptance for filing and protection of trademarks that meet the particular conditions of the US law as to the form. Therefore, Section 211(a)(1) is not inconsistent with Article 6*quinquies* A(1) on the basis that it denies acceptance for filing and protection on an "as is" basis to those trademarks that meet the particular conditions of the US law as to the form.

> (b)   EC's Argument that Section 211(a)(1) Applies to Other Classes of Products; Extends its Scope to Include Similar Trademarks; and Applies to Abandoned Trademarks

8.87   The European Communities argued that Section 211(a)(1) applies to classes of products other than those covered by the trademark that was used in connection with confiscated assets; extends its scope to include substantially similar trademarks; and applies to trademarks abandoned by the original owner or its successor-in-interest.

8.88   These arguments put forward by the European Communities are the same as the ones advanced in relation to Article 15.1 and therefore raise the same issues. Accordingly, we refer to the reasons stated in paragraphs 8.67, 8.68 and 8.69 and confirm that the conclusions stated therein apply equally in relation to Article 6*quinquies* A(1).

> 3.   *Overall Conclusion with Respect to Article 6quinquies A(1)*

8.89   We conclude that Article 6*quinquies* A(1) addresses the form of the trademark and therefore find that Section 211(a)(1) is not inconsistent with Article 6*quinquies* A(1) of the Paris Convention (1967) as incorporated into the TRIPS Agreement by means of a reference in its Article 2.1.

F. Consistency of Section 211(a)(2) with Articles 42 and 16.1 of the TRIPS Agreement

1. General Remarks

8.90   The European Communities claims that Section 211(a)(2) prevents the owner of a registered US trademark from using a US court to enforce its rights, and that the measure denies standing to certain owners of US rights to initiate or maintain proceedings in a US court to enforce the rights conferred on these parties through the Lanham Act. The European Communities argues specifically in relation to Article 42 of the TRIPS Agreement that, by expressly denying the availability of US courts to enforce the rights targeted by its provisions, Section 211(a)(2) constitutes a violation of the US obligations under the first sentence of Article 42 of the TRIPS Agreement. As regards Article 16 of the Agreement, it argues that, given that trademarks as all other intellectual property rights are primarily enforced in the United States, like in most WTO Members, in the civil judicial system, the denial of access to the US court system for certain trademark owners is tantamount to depriving the right holders of their exclusive rights altogether.

8.91   We note that the EC's arguments relating to Articles 16.1 and 42 of the TRIPS Agreement are closely related. Given that in both cases the claim is based on alleged denial of enforcement possibilities—the European Communities argues in relation to Article 16 that the denial of access to civil procedures is tantamount to depriving the right holders of the rights to which they should be entitled under that Article—we find it appropriate first to examine the alleged breach of the enforcement provisions of the TRIPS Agreement contained in Article 42. We will then turn to the EC's arguments that concern Article 16.1. In doing so, we are nonetheless cognizant that both Articles have their separate significance; Article 42 defining the procedural rights accruing to right holders and Article 16 defining the exclusive rights deriving from ownership.

2. Whether Section 211(a)(2) is Consistent with Article 42 of the TRIPS Agreement

8.92   The European Communities alleges that Section 211(a)(2) is inconsistent with Article 42 of the TRIPS Agreement. It argues that by expressly denying the availability of US courts to enforce the rights targeted by Section 211(a)(2), the measure constitutes a violation of the United States' obligations under the first sentence of Article 42 of the TRIPS Agreement. The European Communities contends that Article 42 together with Articles 44-46 and 50 of the Agreement requires WTO Members to provide remedies expressly stipulated therein.

8.93   The United States argues that Article 42 applies only to intellectual property rights "covered by this Agreement" and that it does not require Members to provide right holders with procedures to enforce rights that do not exist. According to the United States, if a purported intellectual property right is not "covered by this Agreement", a Member is under no obligation to enforce it through its civil judicial system. The United States claims that Section 211(a)(2) constitutes substantive rules governing ownership of trademark rights and it does not affect the availability of judicial procedures to any party asserting a right to a trademark. The United States contends that nothing in Section 211(a)(2) precludes the person asserting ownership rights in the trademark from having a full opportunity to substantiate his claim to ownership and to present all relevant evidence.

8.94   Article 42 of the TRIPS Agreement states:[129]

Fair and Equitable Procedures

Members shall make available to the right holders (footnote 11) civil judicial procedures concerning the enforcement of any intellectual property right covered by this Agreement. Defendants shall have the right to written notice which is timely and contains sufficient detail, including the basis of the claims. Parties shall be allowed to be represented by independent legal counsel, and procedures shall not impose overly burdensome requirements concerning mandatory personal appearances. All parties to such procedures shall be duly entitled to substantiate their claims and to present all relevant evidence. The procedure shall provide a means to identify and protect confidential information, unless this would be contrary to existing constitutional requirements.

_____

Footnote 11: For the purpose of this Part, the term "right holder" includes federations and associations having legal standing to assert such rights.

8.95   In considering the EC's claims, our starting-point is the ordinary meaning to be given to the terms of the treaty in their context and in the light of its object and purpose. The first sentence of Article 42 requires Members to make available civil judicial procedures to right holders. The ordinary meaning of the term "available" is "having sufficient force or efficacy; effectual; valid".[130] The ordinary meaning of the term "available" would suggest that right holders are entitled under Article 42 to have access to judicial procedures which are effective in terms of bringing about the enforcement of their rights covered by the Agreement when this is warranted.[131]

_____

[129] Article 42 is contained in Section 2 of Part III of the TRIPS Agreement. That Section is entitled "Civil and Administrative Procedures and Remedies". Article 49 of that Section on "Administrative Procedures" provides that "[t]o the extent that any civil remedy can be ordered as a result of administrative procedures on the merits of a case, such procedures shall conform to principles equivalent in substance to those set forth in this Section".
[130] *Black's Law Dictionary, supra*, p. 123.
[131] Although the rule of exhaustion of local remedies is not applicable in this case, as the interpretation and application of a treaty between states is what is primarily at issue rather than the infringement of rights of individuals, it bears pointing out that in cases involving this rule it has been universally recognized that the remedies available under national law must be "effective" in nature, i.e., they must open the possibility of a genuine remedy for the (private) complainant. *See* Jennings ad Watts, eds., *Oppenheim's International Law*, 9th ed., Vol I, pp. 522-566; and Ian Brownlie, *Principles of Public International Law*, 5th ed., p. 500-501.

8.96   While the European Communities has focused its arguments on the first sentence of Article 42, it alleges that Section 211(a)(2) is inconsistent with the whole Article 42. We note that under the fourth sentence of Article 42 "[a]ll parties to such procedures shall be duly entitled to substantiate their claims and to present all relevant evidence". The ordinary meaning of the term "substantiate" is to "demonstrate or verify by evidence".[132] This fourth sentence elaborates on one aspect of the effectiveness of judicial procedures, namely that the parties must have an effective opportunity to fully present their case before the court reaches its conclusions.

8.97   In interpreting Article 42, we look next at its context. The Article appears in Section 2 of Part III of the TRIPS Agreement, which deals with the enforcement of intellectual property rights. The inclusion of this Part on enforcement in the TRIPS Agreement was one of the major accomplishments of the Uruguay Round negotiations as it expanded the scope of enforcement aspect of intellectual property rights. Prior to the TRIPS Agreement, provisions related to enforcement were limited to general obligations to provide legal remedies and seizure of infringing goods. Article 41 of Section 1 of Part III lays down the general obligations applicable to all enforcement measures. It provides, *inter alia*, that "Members shall ensure that enforcement procedures as specified in this Part are available under their law so as to permit effective action against any act of infringement of intellectual property rights covered by this Agreement" (paragraph 1) and that "[p]rocedures concerning the enforcement of intellectual property rights shall be fair and equitable" (paragraph 2). Article 42—together with the other provisions of Section 2 of Part III—elaborates upon the general obligations contained in Section 1 of the same Part in respect of civil and administrative procedures and remedies. As concerns the requirement of effectiveness, the object and purpose of the enforcement provisions of Part III is expressed in the Preamble to the Agreement, which recognizes the need of "the provision of effective and appropriate means for the enforcement of trade-related intellectual property rights".

8.98   As regards the term "right holders" in the first sentence of Article 42, the accompanying footnote 11 states that "the term 'right holder' includes federations and associations having legal standing to assert such rights". The footnote refers to the legal capacity of right holders to assert rights. It denotes that the term "right holders" as used in Article 42 (in contrast to the term "owner of a registered trademark" used in Article 16.1) refers not only to an owner of an intellectual property right but also to others who may have legal standing in the jurisdiction in question to assert rights, such as a holder of a registration who may be considered the presumptive owner of a registered trademark.

8.99   As we have already noted, in the United States, the registration of a trademark confers a *prima facie* presumption of the registrant's ownership of the registered trademark. This means that, in the United States, the holder of a registration is deemed to be the owner unless otherwise proven. A person who enjoys the presumption of being the owner of a trademark under US law must be enti-

---

[132]   *The New Shorter Oxford English Dictionary, supra*, p. 3124.

tled to a level of protection of its rights that meets the US obligations under the TRIPS Agreement, including Article 42. Consequently, in our interpretation, this presumptive owner must have access to civil judicial procedures that are effective in terms of bringing about the enforcement of its rights until the moment that there is a determination by the court that it is, in fact, not the owner of the trademark that it has registered or that there is some other disqualifying ground which is compatible with international obligations.

8.100 We note the US argument that Section 211(a)(2) does not affect the availability of judicial procedures to any party to assert a right to a trademark. However, given the clear wording of Section 211(a)(2) which provides that "[n]o U.S. court shall recognize, enforce or otherwise validate any assertion of rights" in certain circumstances, we fail to see how a right holder would be able effectively to assert its rights under these circumstances.[133] While Section 211(a)(2) would not appear to prevent a right holder from initiating civil judicial procedures, its wording indicates that the right holder is not entitled to effective procedures as the court is *ab initio* not permitted to recognize its assertion of rights if the conditions of Section 211(a)(2) are met. In other words, the right holder is effectively prevented from having a chance to substantiate its claim, a chance to which a right holder is clearly entitled under Article 42, because effective civil judicial procedures mean procedures with the possibility of an outcome which is not preempted *a priori* by legislation.

8.101 We note that it would be another matter were a court to decide, after making available effective civil judicial procedures to the holder of a trademark registration, that the registrant is not the true owner of the trademark in question. In such a situation, there may no longer be rights to be enforced under Part III of the Agreement, including its Article 42.

8.102 However, given that Section 211(a)(2) limits, under certain circumstances, right holders' effective access to and, hence, the availability of civil judicial procedures, we find that Section 211(a)(2) is inconsistent with Article 42 of the TRIPS Agreement.

3. Whether Section 211(a)(2) is Consistent with Article 16.1 of the TRIPS Agreement

8.103 The European Communities argues that the denial of access to US courts for certain trademark owners is tantamount to depriving those right holders of their exclusive rights under Article 16.1. It subsequently argues that the denial of judicial remedies for certain trademark owners constitutes a serious curtailment of their exclusive rights. According to the European Communities, there is no other legal or practical way in the United States, other than through recourse to US courts, to prevent third parties who do not have the owner's consent from using identical or similar signs.

---

[133] Applying Section 211(b) to a trade name issue, a District Court ruled that "§ 211 prevents HCI [the plaintiff] from asserting its claims for trade name infringement". *See Havana Club Holdings, S.A. v. Galleon S.A.*, 62F., Supp.2d 1085 (S.D.N.Y. 1999).

8.104 The United States argues that, under Article 16.1, the "owner" of the trademark is not necessarily the same as the person who has registered the trademark. The United States argues that, while a US federal trademark registration carries with it the legal presumptions of ownership, validity and priority, all of these presumptions are subject to challenge. If a person other than the registrant can show a superior claim to the trademark based, for example, on prior use, that person can be adjudged the true "owner" of the trademark. The United States submits that Article 16.1 specifically anticipates that the owner of a trademark—the person in a position to assert exclusive rights under domestic law—may be someone other than the person who has registered the trademark. The United States supports its position by noting that the last sentence of Article 16.1 states that the rights guaranteed by Article 16.1 do not "affect the possibility of Members making rights available on the basis of use", and that this sentence also provides more generally that the Article 16.1 rights "shall not prejudice any existing prior rights". It argues that the determination of existing prior rights, like the determination that trademarks are acquired through use, is a question of national law not dealt with in the TRIPS Agreement. The United States argues that it is not denying exclusive rights to the owner of the registered trademark, which is the obligation set forth in Article 16.1 The United States, therefore, concludes that Section 211(a)(2) is not inconsistent with Article 16.1 of the TRIPS Agreement.

8.105 The United States submits that, even if Section 211(a)(2) was deemed inconsistent with Article 16.1, it would still be consistent with the TRIPS Agreement because it applies only to a very narrow and specified class of potential right holders, i.e., those whose trademarks are the same as or substantially similar to trademarks that were used in connection with a business or assets that were confiscated. Therefore, according to the United States, it is "limited" and would meet the requirements of Article 17. The European Communities contends that Section 211(a)(2) does not come within the "limited" exception of Article 17 because the owner of the registered trademark is completely deprived of his exclusive rights granted under Article 16.1 and such deprivation cannot be considered a "limited" exception under Article 17.

8.106 Article 16.1 states:

Rights Conferred

The owner of a registered trademark shall have the exclusive right to prevent all third parties not having the owner's consent from using in the course of trade identical or similar signs for goods or services which are identical or similar to those in respect of which the trademark is registered where such use would result in a likelihood of confusion. In case of the use of an identical sign for identical goods or services, a likelihood of confusion shall be presumed. The rights described above shall not prejudice any existing prior rights, nor shall they affect the possibility of Members making rights available on the basis of use.

8.107 The first sentence of Article 16.1 requires Members to confer an exclusive right to "[t]he owner of a registered trademark" so as to prevent third parties from using identical or similar signs in the course of trade for goods or services where such use would result in a likelihood of confusion. The last sentence indicates that these rights shall not prejudice any existing prior rights, and that Members are not prevented from making available rights on the basis of use. It is apparent that the last sentence, *inter alia*, accommodates those jurisdictions where trademarks may be acquired through use, e.g., common law trademarks in the United States. Thus, Article 16.1 recognizes that exclusive rights can be conferred on the owner of a trademark who may have established ownership either through registration or use.

8.108 We are concerned here, however, with the exclusive rights accruing to the owner of a registered trademark under Article 16.1.[134] Neither Article 16.1 nor other provisions contained in the TRIPS Agreement define how the owner of a trademark is determined.[135] Article 16.1 mentions neither "the registered owner of a trademark" nor "the owner of the registration" but refers to "the owner of a registered trademark", from which we draw the conclusion that the wording of Article 16.1 contemplates different forms of entitlements existing under the laws of Members. Although the European Communities argued that the TRIPS Agreement contains some guidance about who should be considered the owner, it acknowledged that the TRIPS Agreement, including the provisions of the Paris Convention (1967) incorporated into it, does not contain a definition of the owner of a trademark.[136] The ordinary meaning of the word "owner" is "[t]he person who is vested the ownership, dominion, or title of property, proprietor. He who has dominion of a thing, real or personal, corporeal or incorporeal, which has a right to enjoy and do with as he pleases."[137] The ordinary meaning does not provide further clarity on *how* the owner of a trademark is to be determined. To determine who the owner of a registered trademark is, it is necessary to have a recourse to the national law of the Members. We conclude that Article 16.1 lays down certain exclusive rights flowing from the ownership of a registered trademark which must be respected by all Members and accorded by them to the "owner" of that trademark; but the TRIPS Agreement does not contain a

---

[134] We are not concerned here with an "assertion of rights by a designated national based on common law rights" referred to in Section 211(a)(2) because the first sentence of Article 16 does not deal with such rights. Rather, our focus is on the non-recognition, enforcement or validation of assertion of rights, including the exclusive rights set out in Article 16.1, of designated nationals who have obtained, pursuant to a general OFAC licence, registration of trademarks used in connection with confiscated assets.

[135] Cf. our discussion in paras. 8.56 and 8.57.

[136] *See* the EC's Response 50.

[137] *Black's Law Dictionary, supra,* p. 996. In comparison, we note that the French text of Article 16.1 of the Agreement uses the term "le titulaire d'une marque de fabrique ou de commerce enregistrée" and the Spanish text the term "el titular de una marca de fábrica o de comercio registrada". The dictionary meaning given to the term "le titulaire" is "qui posséde juridiquement" (*Le Petit Robert,* Dictionnaire de la langue française (2000), p. 2529). The dictionary meaning given to the term "el titular" is "quien goza legítimamente de un derecho declarado o reconocido a su favor" (*Diccionario de Ciencias Jurídicas, Politicas y Sociales* (1984), p. 749).

regime of ownership of trademarks that is valid for and applicable to all Members.

8.109 We noted earlier that in the United States the ownership of a trademark is generally established through use and concluded that the TRIPS Agreement does not prevent a Member from determining the title to ownership of a trademark based on use. In the United States, the registration of a trademark confers a *prima facie* presumption of the registrant's ownership of the registered trademark and of the registrant's exclusive right to use that trademark in commerce; but these presumptions are subject to challenge and possible reversal, e.g., in case a person other than the registrant shows a superior claim.

8.110 It is incumbent on us to verify whether Section 211(a)(2) denies the owner of a registered trademark the exclusive rights set out in Article 16.1. In the United States, the holder of a federal trademark registration is presumed to be the owner of the registered trademark. It follows from the provisions of Article 16 that such presumptive owner must be entitled to the exclusive rights referred to in that Article. However, the presumptive ownership is subject to challenge in a proceeding before the Trademark Trial and Appeal Board or before a federal court. Until the moment that the presumption regarding the validity of the registration is successfully challenged through court or administrative proceedings, the presumptive owner must be entitled to protection pursuant to Article 16.

8.111 We note that the EC's claim in relation to Article 16.1 focuses on the alleged denial of access to US courts which, in its view, is tantamount to depriving right holders of their rights as set out in Article 16.1. We concluded earlier that Article 42 requires the United States to make available to the holder of a trademark registration effective civil judicial procedures, i.e., with the possibility of an outcome which is not pre-empted *a priori* by legislation, to assert its rights to the registered trademark. Under the exceptional circumstances dealt with under Section 211(a)(2), there may be a successful challenge concerning the *prima facie* ownership rights in relation to the registration, obtained by a designated national pursuant to a general OFAC licence without the consent of the original owner, of a trademark used in connection with confiscated assets. In circumstances where the presumptive ownership would be successfully challenged within effective civil judicial procedures, the provisions of Section 211(a)(2) would not stand in the way of the person whom the court would deem to be the proper owner of the trademark under US law from asserting its rights. In this way, Section 211(a)(2) allows for the person whom the court considers to be the proper owner of the registered trademark under US law to be granted exclusive rights. The European Communities has not provided any evidence to us that would enable us to conclude that US courts would interpret Section 211(a)(2) in a manner that would deprive a person, who has been determined by the court to be the owner of a registered trademark, of its exclusive rights.

8.112 For the reasons set out above, we find that the European Communities has not proved that Section 211(a)(2) is inconsistent with Article 16.1 of the TRIPS Agreement.

G. Consistency of Section 211(a)(2) with Article 2.1 of the TRIPS Agreement in Conjunction with Article 6bis (1) of the Paris Convention (1967)

1. Whether Section 211(a)(2) is Consistent with Article 2.1 of the TRIPS Agreement in Conjunction with Article 6bis (1) of the Paris Convention (1967)

8.113 The European Communities claims that Section 211(a)(2) denies protection to certain trademarks indiscriminately whether or not they are well-known and that it is, therefore, inconsistent with Article 6*bis* (1) of the Paris Convention (1967) as incorporated into the TRIPS Agreement by its Article 2.1. In particular, it argues that Cuba, a Cuban national or its foreign successor-in-interest will not be able to apply for refusal or cancellation of a requested registration nor will they be in a position to seek to prohibit the use of such a trademark. It further argues that, given its broad language, Section 211(a)(2) applies to all kinds of trademarks, registered trademarks, common-law trademarks and well-known trademarks.

8.114 The United States contends that Section 211(a)(2) is not inconsistent with Article 6*bis* (1) of the Paris Convention (1967) because it provides that Members shall undertake to refuse or cancel a registration, or prohibit the use of a trademark, when the competent authorities of that Member consider that the trademark is well-known in that Member's territory "as being already the mark of" another person claiming protection under that Article. According to the United States, Section 211(a)(2) would only come into play when US courts determine that the US trademark is not "the mark of" the confiscating entity or its successors in interest. The United States argues that Article 6*bis* specifically reserves to "the competent authority" of the Member the determination of whether a trademark is well-known as being already the mark of a particular person. The United States argues that if, under US law, the confiscating entity does not have any rights of ownership in the trademark, the trademark cannot, as a matter of law, be "well-known as being already the mark of" the confiscating entity.

8.115 Paragraph 1 of Article 6*bis* of the Paris Convention (1967), as incorporated into the TRIPS Agreement, reads as follows:

> The countries of the Union undertake, ex officio if their legislation so permits, or at the request of an interested party, to refuse or to cancel the registration, and to prohibit the use, of a trademark which constitutes a reproduction, an imitation, or a translation, liable to create confusion, of a mark considered by the competent authority of the country of registration or use to be well known in that country as being already the mark of a person entitled to the benefits of this Convention and used for identical or similar goods. These provisions shall also apply when the essential part of the mark constitutes a reproduction of any such well-known mark or an imitation liable to create confusion therewith.

8.116 We note that Article 6*bis* of the Paris Convention (1967) requires Members to refuse or cancel registrations in certain situations. However, Section 211(a)(2) does not deal with the refusal or the cancellation of registrations. The European Communities did not explain whether and to what extent Section 211(a)(2) overlaps or conflicts with Article 6*bis* in this regard. Hence, we do not consider that the European Communities presented evidence and legal arguments that are sufficient to demonstrate that Section 211(a)(2) is inconsistent with US obligations under Article 6*bis* of the Paris Convention (1967). Therefore, the Panel is not able to reach a conclusion that the Section 211(a)(2) would be inconsistent with Article 6*bis* in this regard.

8.117 Article 6*bis* also requires Members to prohibit the use of a well-known trademark in certain situations. In response to a question, the European Communities gave the following example of a situation under which Section 211(a)(2) could violate the US obligations under Article 6*bis* (1): if the "Havana Club" trademark were not registered in the United States, but the United States were to recognize it as a well-known mark in the sense of Article 6*bis*, the operation of Section 211(a)(2) would not allow the person entitled to the protection of this well-known trademark to prevent somebody else from using this trademark in the United States.

8.118 We note that the European Communities argued that the TRIPS Agreement does not require a WTO Member to recognize a confiscation of intellectual property in another country as regards the legal effect of that confiscation even in the country where the confiscation took place.[138] Consistent with this view, it further argued that under Article 6*bis* of the Paris Convention (1967) as incorporated into the TRIPS Agreement, a WTO Member is free to recognize the original owner or the post-expropriation owner of a confiscated trademark as the owner of the well-known trademark in its territory.[139] The European Communities appears to be in agreement with the United States in this respect.

8.119 We also note that the European Communities has not brought evidence to allow us to compare the "rights … based on common law rights or registration obtained under such Section 515.527" referred to in Section 211(a)(2) with the obligations contained under Article 6*bis*. For example, the European Communities did not provide any information on how US courts would apply common law rights in this regard; in the absence of any such evidence, we cannot presume that US courts would apply common law rights inconsistently with the US obligations under the TRIPS Agreement. However, to the extent Section 211(a)(2) would affect the exercise of the rights that should be provided to a right owner under Article 6*bis*, the European Communities did not claim that Section 211(a)(2) would prevent US courts from recognizing such rights in the hands of the original owner of the trademark used in connection with confiscated assets, its successor-in-interest or a person who has the consent of the original owner or its successor-in-interest. In considering the example cited by the European Communities above, Section 211(a)(2) would not prevent the original

---

[138] *See* EC's Response 43.
[139] *See* EC's Response 57.

owner of a well-known trademark, its successor-in-interest or a person who has the consent of the original owner or its successor-in-interest from exercising its rights in the circumstances described in that example.

8.120   We agree with the parties that a WTO Member is not required to give the benefit of Article 6*bis* to the confiscating entity or its successor-in-interest; the competent authority of a WTO Member may consider the well-known trademark as being the mark of the person who owned the trademark prior to the confiscation. We note that Section 211(a)(2) relates to a situation where rights are being asserted by the confiscating entity or its successor-in-interest without the consent of the original owner. It does not concern a situation where the original owner itself, the successor-in-interest or another person who has the consent of the original owner or the successor-in-interest would assert these rights. Hence, to the extent that the coverage of Section 211(a)(2) might extend to the protection that should be made available under Article 6*bis*, nothing in Section 211(a)(2) would prevent US courts from providing that protection to the person who is considered the proper owner of a confiscated well-known trademark under US law, i.e., the original owner, its successor-in-interest or the person who has the consent of the original owner or the successor-in-interest.

8.121   Accordingly, based on the reasons set out above, we find that Section 211(a)(2) is not inconsistent with Article 6*bis* of the Paris Convention (1967) as incorporated into the TRIPS Agreement.

>
> *H.*   *Consistency of Section 211(a)(2) with Article 2.1 of the TRIPS Agreement in Conjunction with Article 8 of the Paris Convention (1967)*
>
> *1.*   *Whether Section 211(a)(2) is Consistent with Article 2.1 of the TRIPS Agreement in Conjunction with Article 8 of the Paris Convention (1967)*

8.122   In light of our finding in paragraph 8.41 that the categories of intellectual property covered by the TRIPS Agreement are those referred to in Article 1.2 of the TRIPs Agreement and that Members do not have obligations under the TRIPS Agreement to provide protection to trade names, we find that Section 211(a)(2) is not inconsistent with Article 2.1 of the TRIPS Agreement in conjunction with Article 8 of the Paris Convention (1967).

> I.   Consistency of Section 211(a)(2) with Article 3.1 of the TRIPS Agreement and 2.1 of the TRIPS Agreement in Conjunction with Article 2(1) of the Paris Convention (1967)
>
>> 1.   Whether Section 211(a)(2) is consistent with Article 3.1 of the TRIPS Agreement and Article 2.1 of the TRIPS Agreement in conjunction with Article 2(1) of the Paris Convention (1967)

8.123   The European Communities argues that Section 211(a)(2) is inconsistent with Article 3.1 of the TRIPS Agreement at two levels. According to the European Communities, Section 211(a)(2) is inconsistent with Article 3.1 because the provision applies in respect of "designated nationals" which are basically comprised of Cuba and Cuban nationals. The European Communities also argues that at the level of successors-in-interest, the statutory language refers only to nationals of a foreign country without referring to US nationals.

8.124   The United States argues that under Section 211(a)(2) US courts are not to recognize, enforce or validate any assertion of rights in a confiscated trademark by a designated national or a national of any foreign country who is a successor-in-interest to the designated national. The United States notes that the statutory language does not include US nationals when describing successor-in-interest but argues that US nationals cannot even become a successor-in-interest to a designated national without first obtaining a specific licence from OFAC and points out that OFAC has never issued such a specific licence. The United States argues that any transaction by which a US national might become a successor-in-interest to a Cuban confiscating entity is prohibited under 31 CFR 515.201. The United States adds that a measure is inconsistent on its face only if it mandates WTO-inconsistent actions.

8.125   The national treatment principle has historically been an important part of the international agreements on intellectual property rights. The national treatment principle has been a requirement since the inception of the Paris and Bern Conventions in the late nineteenth century and the principle is encapsulated in Article 3.1 of the TRIPS Agreement. Article 3.1 in pertinent part states:

> Each Member shall accord to the nationals of other Members treatment no less favourable than it accords to its own nationals with regard to the protection (footnote 3) of intellectual property....

Footnote 3: For the purpose of Articles 3 and 4, "protection" shall include matters affecting the availability, acquisition, scope, maintenance and enforcement of intellectual property rights as well as those matters affecting the use of intellectual property rights specifically addressed in this Agreement.

8.126 The national treatment provision as embodied in Article 2(1) of the Paris Convention (1967) contains a statement similar to Article 3.1 of the TRIPS Agreement:[140]

> Nationals of any country of the Union shall, as regards the protection of industrial property, enjoy in all the other countries of the Union the advantages that their respective laws now grant, or may hereafter grant, to nationals; all without prejudice to the rights specially provided for by this Convention. Consequently, they shall have the same protection as the latter, and the same legal remedy against any infringement of their rights, provided that the conditions and formalities imposed upon nationals are complied with.

8.127 Violation of Article 3.1 of the TRIPS Agreement occurs when a complaining party demonstrates (1) the existence of a measure in a Member that affects the "availability, acquisition, scope, maintenance and enforcement of intellectual property rights as well as those matters affecting the use of intellectual property rights specifically addressed" in the TRIPS Agreement and (2) that such measure provides less favourable treatment to the nationals of other Members in connection with protection of intellectual property rights.

8.128 The first issue to be examined is whether Section 211(a)(2) affects the "availability, acquisition, scope, maintenance and enforcement of intellectual property rights as well as those matters affecting the use of intellectual property rights specifically addressed" in the TRIPS Agreement. We note that both parties do not dispute that Section 211(a)(2) affects protection of intellectual property rights as defined in footnote 3 of the TRIPS Agreement. We therefore examine whether Section 211(a)(2) accords protection of intellectual property rights that is less favourable to the nationals of other Members than that it accords to US nationals.

8.129 The language of Article 3.1 of the TRIPS Agreement is similar to that contained in III:4 of the GATT 1994.[141] A major difference between the national treatment principle as set forth in Article 3.1 of the TRIPS Agreement and Article III:4 of the GATT 1994 is that the national treatment attaches to the intellectual property right holder under Article 3.1 whereas it attaches to the goods un-

---

[140] Both Article 3.1 of the TRIPS Agreement and 2(1) of the Paris Convention (1967) deal with "protection" of intellectual property. Article 3.1 refers to "treatment no less favourable" while Article 2(1) refers to "the same protection...and same legal remedy". We do not purport to determine whether the expression "treatment no less favourable" means "the same protection...and same legal remedy". However, given the common objective of according non-discriminatory treatment to foreign nationals in respect of protection of intellectual property, a finding of inconsistency under Article 3.1 could also lead to the same finding under Article 2.1 of the TRIPS Agreement in conjunction with Article 2(1) of the Paris Convention (1967).

[141] Article III:4 of the GATT 1994 states:
> The products of the territory of any contracting party imported into the territory of any other contracting party shall be accorded treatment no less favourable than that accorded to like products of national origin in respect of all laws, regulations and requirements affecting their internal sale, offering for sale, purchase, transportation, distribution or use.

der Article III:4. In construing Article 3.1 of the TRIPS Agreement, Article III:4 can serve as a useful context.

8.130 The term "treatment no less favourable" was expressly interpreted by the Panel in *United States—Section 337of the Tariff Act of 1930* as requiring Members to provide equality of competitive conditions for imported products in relation to domestic products. The Panel in *United States—Section 337* stated:

> ...the "no less favourable" treatment requirement set out in Article III:4, is unqualified. These words are to be found throughout the General Agreement and later agreements negotiated in the GATT framework as an expression of the underlying principle of equality of treatment of imported products as compared to the treatment given either to other foreign products, under the most favoured nation standard, or to domestic products, under the national treatment standard of Article III. The words "treatment no less favourable" in paragraph 4 call for effective equality of opportunities for imported products in respect of the application of laws, regulations and requirements affecting the internal sale, offering for sale, purchase, transportation, distribution or use of products. This clearly sets a minimum permissible standard as a basis.[142]

8.131 Similarly, the Panel in *Canada—Import, Distribution and Sale of Certain Alcoholic Drinks by Provincial Marketing Agencies* examined a Canadian measure in relation to Article III:4 of the GATT 1947 and stated that "by allowing the access of domestic beer to points of sale not available to imported beer, Canada accorded domestic beer competitive opportunities denied to imported beer".[143] The relevant standard of examination to determine whether the nationals of other Members are treated "less favourably" than the nationals of the concerned Member under Article 3.1 of the TRIPS Agreement is whether the measure provides effective equality of opportunities as between these two groups in respect of protection of intellectual property rights.

8.132 The European Communities claimed that Section 211(a)(2) is inconsistent with the national treatment principle at the level of designated nationals and successors-in-interest. The European Communities argued that, by curtailing the protection of trademarks held by "designated nationals" while granting US nationals the full enjoyment of their rights, Section 211(a)(2) discriminates against the "designated nationals" in breach of the national treatment principle. In respect of successors-in-interest, the European Communities argued that Section 211(a)(2) denies protection to foreign successors-in-interest while US suc-

---

[142] Panel Report, *United States—Section 337 of the Tariff Act of 1930* ("*US—Section 337*"), BISD 36S/345, adopted 7 November 1989, para. 5.11.
[143] Panel Report, *Canada—Import, Distribution and Sale of Certain Alcoholic Drinks by Provincial Marketing Agencies* ("*Canada—Marketing Agencies*"), BISD 39S, adopted 18 February 1992, para. 5.6.

cessors-in-interest can enjoy their rights to trademarks used in connection with confiscated assets.[144]

8.133 Section 211(a)(2) provides that no US courts are to recognize, enforce or validate any rights by a "designated national" based on registration of trademarks obtained through a licence from OFAC. We note that the term "designated national" is defined in Section 211(d)(1) to include (1) Cuba, (2) any Cuban national, (3) "a specially designated national" or (4) "a national of any foreign country who is a successor-in-interest to a designated national." We consider that the term "designated national" must be read as a whole and cannot be segregated into two tiers. We note that "designated national" is defined to include "[a] national of *any foreign country* who is a successor-in-interest to a designated national" and does not include US nationals. Thus, it is plausible that while a foreign national who is a successor-in-interest to a designated national may not have its rights to the underlying mark recognized, enforced or validated, a US national who is a successor-in-interest to a designated national can have US courts recognize, enforce or validate rights in respect of the underlying mark that was registered pursuant to a specific licence granted by OFAC. Such differential treatment in respect of intellectual property right protection could be considered to provide a less favourable treatment to nationals of other Members as it denies effective equality of opportunities to non-US nationals in the United States.

8.134 However, the United States argued that Section 211(a)(2) is not inconsistent with Article 3.1 on the basis that US nationals, although not specifically set out in the measure, cannot become successors-in-interest to designated nationals because Section 515.201 of 31 CFR prohibits US nationals from becoming successors-in-interest without obtaining a specific licence from OFAC. The United States submitted that OFAC has never issued a specific licence to a US national for the purpose of becoming a successor-in-interest to trademarks that were used in connection with confiscated assets. The United States asserted that a law is only WTO-inconsistent on its face if it mandates WTO-inconsistent actions and that if the law allows the national authority to act in manner consistent with the WTO Agreement, panels should not assume that a Member will use its discretion in a manner contrary to its international obligations.

8.135 Although the term "designated national" is defined to include a national of any foreign country who is a successor-in-interest, we note that Section 515.201 of 31 CFR imposes a general prohibition on US nationals from becoming successors-in-interest unless OFAC grants a specific licence. The question that needs to be addressed in determining the consistency of Section 211(a)(2) with the national treatment principle is whether OFAC accords a

---

[144] The United States, on the other hand, argued that "[o]ne cannot assess consistency with national treatment and MFN by focusing on only one part of the law. The law has to be considered as a whole. If a provision of U.S. law stated that a certain treatment would be provided to (1) domestic products and (2) imported products, it would be nonsensical to analyze a 'first tier' (domestic products) in isolation, and conclude that the law violates national treatment. Similarly, in Section 211, there are not separate 'tiers'; the law, read as a whole, does not violate the national treatment or most favoured nation provisions of TRIPS." *See* US Rebuttal Submission, para. 48.

more favourable treatment to US nationals in considering whether to grant licences to US nationals to become successors-in-interest.

8.136 The Appellate Body noted in *United States—Antidumping Act of 1916* that the concept of mandatory and discretionary legislation was developed by various GATT panels to determine when legislation as such, rather than the specific application of that legislation, was inconsistent with a Contracting Party's GATT 1947 obligations.[145] In *United States—Measures Affecting the Importation, Internal Sale and Use of Tobacco*, the Panel was required to examine Section 1106(c) of the 1993 Budget Act.[146] The Panel in *United States—Tobacco* stated:

> In view of the fact that USDA had as yet not amended its inspection fee structure in line with the statutory amendment of Section 1106(c), the main question that arose for the Panel's analysis was whether this Section of the 1993 Budget Act mandated action inconsistent with Article VIII or whether it merely gave the U.S. Government the discretion to act inconsistently with Article VIII. Panels had consistently ruled that legislation which mandated action inconsistent with the General Agreement could be challenged as such, whereas legislation which merely gave the discretion to the executive authority of a contracting party to act inconsistently with the General Agreement could not be challenged as such; only the actual application of such legislation inconsistent with the General Agreement could be subject to challenge.[147]

8.137 The Appellate Body referred to the above paragraph and stated that "the relevant discretion, for purposes of distinguishing between mandatory and discretionary legislation, is a discretion vested in the *executive branch* of government."[148] OFAC is part of the executive branch which has the discretion to grant specific licences to US nationals to become a successor-in-interest to a "designated national".

8.138 The United States asserted that OFAC has never granted a specific licence to US nationals so as to allow any US nationals to become a successor-in-interest to a "designated national" and the European Communities did not demonstrate that OFAC acted in a manner inconsistent with the national treatment principle as encapsulated in Article 3 of the TRIPS Agreement and Article 2.1 of the TRIPS Agreement in conjunction with Article 2(1) of the Paris Convention (1967).

---

[145] Appellate Body Report, *United States—Antidumping Act of 1916* ("*US—1916 Act*"), WT/DS136/AB/R, WT/DS162/AB/R, adopted 26 September 2000, DSR 2000:X, 4793, para. 88.

[146] Section 1106(c) of the 1993 Budget Act required that fees for inspecting imported tobacco "be comparable to the fees and charges fixed and collected for services provided in connection with tobacco produced in the United States". *United States—Measures Affecting the Importation, Internal Sale and Use of Tobacco* ("*US—Tobacco*"), BISD 41S, Volume I, adopted 4 October 1994, para. 114.

[147] Panel Report, *US—Tobacco*, para. 118.

[148] Appellate Body Report, *United States—1916 Act*, DSR 2000:X, 4793, para. 89.

8.139 In respect of original owners, Section 211(a)(2) does not accord a treatment less favourable to foreign original owners than it accords to original owners who are US nationals with respect to protection of intellectual property rights.

8.140 Because US nationals are unable to obtain licences so as to become a successor-in-interest and OFAC has not granted any such licence for such purpose and in light of our conclusion that Section 211(a)(2) does not accord a treatment less favourable to foreign original owners than it accords to original owners who are US nationals, we find that Section 211(a)(2) is not inconsistent with Article 3.1 of the TRIPS Agreement and Article 2.1 of the TRIPS Agreement in conjunction with Article 2(1) of the Paris Convention (1967).

J.   Consistency of Section 211(a)(2) with Article 4 of the TRIPS Agreement

1.   Whether Section 211(a)(2) is Consistent with Article 4 of the TRIPS Agreement

8.141 The European Communities argues that the dichotomy created by Section 211(a)(2) distinguishes between Cuba or Cuban nationals and others, the latter being US nationals or nationals of any other country. The European Communities contends that therefore this provision not only discriminates between Cuban nationals and US nationals (violation of national treatment obligation) but also creates a *de jure* discrimination between Cuba/Cuban nationals and other non–US nationals by denying protection of intellectual property rights held by Cuban nationals while granting such protection to nationals of other countries. The European Communities therefore argues that Article 211(a)(2) is inconsistent with the US obligations under Article 4 of the TRIPS Agreement.

8.142 The United States argues that Section 211(a)(2) does not limit its scope to Cuba and Cuban nationals because US courts will not enforce or recognize any assertion of rights to underlying marks and underlying names by any successors-in-interest—whether Cuban or not—to any Cuban entitities claiming rights based on confiscated assets. The United States alleges that it does not matter that the rights associated with the confiscated assets are transferred by the confiscating entity to a Cuban, European or US national because US courts will not recognize those assertions of rights as regards trademarks in the United States. The United States argues that Section 211(a)(2) does not grant an "advantage, favour, privilege or immunity" to the nationals of, for instance, France that it does not grant to the nationals of Cuba in respect of protection of intellectual property rights.

8.143 In response to the question as to whether Article 4 of the TRIPS Agreement allows a Member to have a certain policy applicable to confiscations of trademarks in one Member on the condition that all WTO Member nationals are treated similarly or whether Article 4 requires that a similar policy be applied to confiscations of trademarks in all other Members, the European Communities states that the most-favoured-nation treatment flowing from Article 4 attaches to persons and not to situations. The European Communities argues, therefore, that Article 4 requires that all nationals of other Members be treated similarly in respect of a certain event. In response to the same question, the United States submitted that because the European Communities is alleging a violation of the most-favoured-nation principle based on the first situation described by the Panel, there is no need to examine the question of whether Article 4 applies to the second situation.

8.144 Article 4 of the TRIPS Agreement states:

Most-Favoured-Nation Treatment

With regard to the protection of intellectual property, any advantage, favour, privilege or immunity granted by a Member to the nationals of any other country shall be accorded immediately and unconditionally to the nationals of all other Members.

Footnote 3: For the purpose of Articles 3 and 4, "protection" shall include matters affecting the availability, acquisition, scope, maintenance and enforcement of intellectual property rights as well as those matters affecting the use of intellectual property rights specifically addressed in this Agreement.

8.145 For the purposes of determining whether Section 211(a)(2) is consistent with Article 4 of the TRIPS Agreement, we need to determine whether, with regard to protection of intellectual property, "any advantage, favour, privilege or immunity" that is accorded to the nationals of one Member is not being accorded to the nationals of other Members. That is, we will consider whether Section 211(a)(2) accords any advantage, favour, privilege or immunity that is accorded to certain foreign nationals while such advantage, favour, privilege or immunity is being denied to Cuban nationals. In this regard, our analysis will focus on whether Section 211(a)(2) accords advantage, favour, privilege or immunity to nationals other than Cubans that it does not so accord to Cubans, be they the owner before the confiscation on the one hand, or the confiscating entity or its successor-in-interest after the confiscation on the other hand. As the parties requested that we make a determination of the consistency of Section 211(a)(2) in relation to the Cuban confiscation, our examination and finding will be limited to the Cuban confiscation. Our analysis is thus without prejudice to the findings that we would have made had a broader claim relating to Article 4 been made. We note that neither party disputes that Section 211(a)(2) affects "protection" of intellectual property rights as defined in footnote 3 of the TRIPS Agreement.

8.146 We recall that the term "designated national" means Cuba, a Cuban national, a specially designated national or a national of any foreign country who is a successor-in-interest to a designated national. Pursuant to Section 211(a)(2), US courts will not recognize, enforce or validate any assertion of rights by a Cuban national or any other foreign national in respect of trademarks used in connection with confiscated trademarks. Section 211(a)(2) does not discriminate between Cuban nationals and other foreign nationals in respect of trademarks used in connection with confiscated assets that were acquired by the confiscating entity or its successor-in-interest after the confiscation. If the confiscating entity or its successors-in-interest, irrespective of whether they are Cuban or other foreign nationals, do not have the consent of the original owner, they cannot assert any rights based on common law rights or registration to the trademarks that were used in connection with confiscated assets.

8.147 In respect of original owners, there is nothing in the language of Section 211(a)(2) that limits the class of original owners based on nationality. All original owners, irrespective of whether they are Cuban or other foreign nationals, whose trademarks were used in connection with confiscated assets, are covered.

8.148 Based on the foregoing reasons, we conclude that Section 211(a)(2) does not deny Cuban nationals any advantage, favour, privilege or immunity that it accords to other foreign nationals. We therefore find that Section 211(a)(2) is not inconsistent with Article 4 of the TRIPS Agreement.

K. Consistency of Section 211(b) with Article 16.1 of the TRIPS Agreement

1. Whether Section 211(b) is Consistent with Article 16.1 of the TRIPS Agreement

8.149 The European Communities notes that the coverage of Section 211(b) appears to "parallel" the coverage of Section 211(a)(2) but the "precise scope is obscure." The European Communities submits that it can be speculated that the drafters intended to cover rights flowing from self-executing treaties but also takes the view that the TRIPS Agreement is not self-executing. The European Communities refers to a US district court case that construed the scope of Section 211(b) broadly. The European Communities argues, therefore, that obligations stemming from the TRIPS Agreement come within the ambit of Section 211(b). The European Communities claims that the arguments made in relation to Section 211(a)(2) apply *mutatis mutandis* to Section 211(b) and submits that Section 211(b) is inconsistent with Article 16.1

8.150 The United States argues that Section 211(b) is similar to Section 211(a)(2) in that it applies to a person who claims a right to a trademark in the United States by virtue of foreign registration. The United States argues that, under Section 211(b), a confiscating entity or its successor-in-interest cannot claim ownership rights to that trademark in the United States by virtue of foreign registration. The United States uses the same arguments its advanced in respect of Article 211(a)(2) to claim that Section 211(b) is not inconsistent with Article 16.1.

8.151 Section 211(b) states:

> No U.S. court shall recognize, enforce or otherwise validate any assertion of *treaty rights* by a designated national or its successor-in-interest *under Section 44(b) or (e) of the Trademark Act of 1946* (15 U.S.C. 1126 (b) or (e)) for a mark, trade name, or commercial name that is the same as or substantially similar to a mark, trade name, or commercial name that was used in connection with a

business or assets that were confiscated unless the original owner of such mark, trade name, or commercial name, or the bona fide successor-in-interest has expressly consented. (emphasis added)

8.152 The statutory language of Section 211(b) states that "treaty rights…under Section 44(b) and (e) of the Trademark Act of 1946" asserted by a designated national or its successor-in-interest are not to be recognized, enforced or validated. Sections 44(b) and (e) of the Trademark Act of 1946 state:

(b)   Any person whose country of origin is a party to any convention or treaty relating to trademarks, trade or commercial names, or the repression of unfair competition, to which the United States is also a party, or extends reciprocal rights to nationals of the United States by law, shall be entitled to the benefits of this section under the conditions expressed herein to the extent necessary to give effect to any provision of such convention, treaty or reciprocal law, in addition to the rights to which any owner of a mark is otherwise entitled by this Act.

(e)   A mark duly registered in the country of origin of the foreign applicant may be registered on the principal register if eligible, otherwise on the supplemental register herein provided. Such applicant shall submit, within such time period as may be prescribed by the Director, a certification or a certified copy of the registration in the country of origin of the applicant. The application must state the applicant's bona fide intention to use the mark in commerce, but use in commerce shall not be required prior to registration.

8.153 We note that the EC's argument that Section 211(b) is inconsistent with Article 16.1 is rather tentative. The European Communities stated that the coverage of Section 211(b) "appears to 'parallel'" the coverage of Section 211(a)(2) but then stated that "its precise scope is largely obscure."[149] The European Communities then went on to argue "[b]y way of speculation" that "one might think that the drafters intended to cover rights flowing from treaties which are self-executory [sic] in the US legal system". Referring to a US district court case that deals with Section 211(b), the European Communities concluded that obligations flowing from the TRIPS Agreement come within the scope of Section 211(b), noting that the issue of whether the TRIPS Agreement is self-executing "can be left open [although] the language of Section 102(a) of H.R. S 5110…would appear to militate against such self-executory [sic] character." While we appreciate the EC's assertion that the statutory language of Section 211(b) is allegedly obscure, under the well-established WTO jurisprudence pertaining to burden of proof, it is the European Communities, as the complaining party, that must submit arguments and evidence sufficient to raise a presumption that the United States acts inconsistently with its obligations under Article

---

[149] EC's First Submission, para. 67.

16.1 of the TRIPS Agreement. The Appellate Body in *United States—Shirts and Blouses* stated:

> [I]t is a generally-accepted canon of evidence in civil law, common law and, in fact, most jurisdictions, that the burden of proof rests upon the party, whether complaining or defending, who asserts the affirmative of a particular claim or defence. If that party adduces evidence sufficient to raise a presumption that what is claimed is true, the burden then shifts to the other party, who will fail unless it adduces sufficient evidence to rebut the presumption.[150]

8.154 In respect of applying the principle enunciated in *United States—Shirts and Blouses*, the Appellate Body stated:

> In accordance with our ruling *United States—Shirts and Blouses,* the Panel should have begun analysis of each legal provision by examining whether the United States and Canada had presented *evidence and legal arguments sufficient to demonstrate that the EC measures were inconsistent with the obligations assumed by the European Communities* under each Article of the *SPS Agreement* addressed by the Panel....[151] (emphasis added)

8.155 Thus, our task is first to determine whether the European Communities, as the complaining party, presented evidence and legal arguments *sufficient* to demonstrate that Section 211(b) is inconsistent with the US obligations under the TRIPS Agreement. The European Communities argued that, based on a paragraph contained in an opinion of a US district court case,[152] obligations flowing from the TRIPS Agreement fall under Section 211(b). The European Communities then argued that the arguments used under Section 211(a)(2) apply *mutatis mutandis* to Section 211(b) and referred to the arguments contained in paragraph 50 of its first written submission.[153] This paragraph referred to by the European Communities quotes Article 16.1 of the TRIPS Agreement and states the following:

---

[150] Appellate Body Report, *United States—Shirts and Blouses*, p. 14, DSR 1997:I, 323, at 335.
[151] Appellate Body Report, *European Communities—Mesures Concerning Meat and Meat Products (Hormones)* (*"EC—Hormones"*), WT/DS26AB/R, WT/DS48/AB/R, DSR 1998:I, 135, para. 109.
[152] The district court in *Havana Club Holding, S.A. v. Galleon, S.A..*, 62 F. Supp. 2d 1085, 1092-1093, (S.D.N.Y. 1999) stated:
> Section 211 explicitly states that no court shall recognize "treaty" rights of designated nationals. The further reference in that Section to § 44 (b) of the Lanham Act should not be read to distinguish certain treaties from others. Both the text of § 44(b) and its legislative history indicate that the purpose of this Section was to execute all U.S. treaty obligations respecting trademarks and trade names. See 15 U.S.C. § 1125 ("(t)he intent of this chapter is to ... provide rights and remedies stipulated by treaties and conventions respecting trade-marks, trade names, and unfair competition entered into between the United States and foreign nations"); S. Rep. No. 1333, 79th Cong., 2d Sess. 5 (1946) (stating that purpose of Lanham Act was "to carry out by statute our international commitments to the end that American traders in foreign countries may receive the protection of their marks to which they are entitled"). See Exhibit EC-18.
[153] *See* EC's First Submission, para. 69.

Given that trademarks as all other intellectual property rights, are primarily enforced in the US, like in most WTO members, in the civil judicial system, the denial of access to the US Court system for certain trademark owners is tantamount to depriving the rightholders of their exclusive rights altogether. There exists no other legal or practical way to prevent third parties not having the owner's consent from using in the course of trade identical or similar signs in the US than the possibility to have recourse to the US judicial system.

8.156 The United States in turn argued that the European Communities failed to sustain its burden of establishing a *prima facie* case that Section 211 is inconsistent with any provisions of the TRIPS Agreement. In connection with Section 211(b), it is worth noting that the United States argued in its first written submission:

In this dispute, the EC has not sustained its burden of establishing a *prima facie* case that Section 211 is inconsistent with any provision of the TRIPs Agreement....In addition, in maintaining that Section 211(b) is inconsistent with a number of TRIPs articles, the EC states that "the precise scope" of Section 211(b) is "largely obscure." It then offers an interpretation "[b]y way of speculation" and some dictum from a court case. Since it is the EC's burden to *demonstrate* that Section 211(b) is inconsistent with TRIPs, the EC's admission that it does not know exactly what Section 211(b) covers is evidence that the EC has not sustained its burden in this dispute.[154]

8.157 The European Communities does not further explain in its subsequent submission or oral statements precisely how Section 211(b) is inconsistent with US obligations under the TRIPS Agreement.[155] In particular, the European Communities did not produce any analysis of Sections 44(b), other than citing the paragraph from the US district court case mentioned above,[156] and 44(e) of the Trademark Act of 1946 to which Section 211(b) explicitly refers and for which there presumably exists ample record. There is no explanation as to the meaning of various terms contained in Sections 44(b) and (e) of the Trademark Act of 1946 or how they operate or apply in relation to Section 211(b). The European Communities does not, for example, explain what the term "benefits of this Section" as used in Section 44(b) means and how a person is entitled to such benefits "to the extent necessary to give effect to any provision of such convention, treaty". With respect to Section 44(e), it would appear to transform the pro-

---

[154] *See* US First Submission, paras. 22 and 23.
[155] *See* EC's First Oral Statement, para. 25 which refers to EC's First Submission, para. 67. The European Communities does state, in relation to Article 17 of the TRIPS Agreement, that "the outright denial of judicial enforceability goes beyond 'a small diminution of the rights in question', thus excluding the limited nature of the exception." *See* EC's First Oral Statement, para. 71; EC's Second Submission, para. 61; and EC's Second Oral Statement, para. 42.
[156] *Havana Club Holding, S.A. v. Galleon, S.A.*, 62 F. Supp. 2d 1085, 1092/1093, (S.D.N.Y. 1999). *See* Exhibit EC-8.

vision of Article 6*quinquies* A(1) of the Paris Convention (1967) into US national law. However, it is not clear how Section 211(b) speaks of "treaty rights" because Section 44(e) does not refer to any treaty in contrast to Section 44(b). We note, in any event, that the European Communities did not make any argument in respect of Section 44(e).

8.158   Based on our review of the evidence and legal arguments provided by the European Communities, we do not consider that they are sufficient to demonstrate that Section 211(b) is inconsistent with US obligations under the TRIPS Agreement, including Article 16.1. There needs to be more analysis supported by evidence and legal arguments to show that Section 211(b) is inconsistent with Article 16.1 of the TRIPS Agreement. Were we to examine Section 211(b) based on the limited evidence and legal arguments presented to us, we would find ourselves speculating about the meaning of various terms contained in Sections 44(b) and (e) of the Trademark Act of 1946 and how they operate, a task we are reluctant to undertake. We are also of the view that speculating as to the meaning of the terms contained in Sections 44(b) and (e) of the Trademark Act of 1946 and their application would raise a due process concern because the United States, after having claimed that the European Communities failed to sufficiently demonstrate that Section 211(b) is inconsistent with the US obligations under the TRIPS Agreement, would be denied the opportunity to present arguments in support of its position in relation to Section 211(b), including Sections 44(b) and (e) of the Trademark Act of 1946.

8.159   For these reasons, we conclude that the European Communities, as the complaining party, has not presented evidence and legal arguments sufficient to demonstrate the violation it alleges. Therefore, it has not been proved that Section 211(b) is inconsistent with Article 16.1 of the TRIPS Agreement.

2.   *Whether Section 211(b) is Consistent with Article 42 of the TRIPS Agreement*

8.160   The European Communities argues that for the reasons contained in paragraph 51 of its first written submission, Section 211(b) is inconsistent with Article 42 of the TRIPS Agreement. That paragraph states that "[b]y expressly denying the availability of US courts to enforce the rights targeted by Section 211(a)(2)", it constitutes a violation of the US obligations under Article 42 of the TRIPS Agreement.

8.161   The United States argues that Section 211(b) constitutes substantive rules governing the ownership of trademark rights, not jurisdictional or standing rules regarding access to the court system. The United States argues that nothing in Section 211(b) precludes the person asserting ownership rights in the trademark from having a full opportunity to substantiate his claim to ownership and to present all relevant evidence.

8.162   We note that it is plausible that similar concerns mentioned in respect of Section 211(a)(2) might arise in connection with Section 211(b). However, as we noted above, the European Communities did not explain the meaning of various terms contained in Sections 44(b) and (e) even though Article 211(b) explicitly refers to "treaty rights...under sections 44(b) or (e)". Therefore, for the reasons set out in paragraphs 8.157 and 8.158, it has not been proved that Section 211(b) is inconsistent with Article 42 of the TRIPS Agreement.

> *3.   Whether Section 211(b) is Consistent with Article 2.1 of the TRIPS Agreement in Conjunction with Article 6bis (1) of the Paris Convention (1967)*

8.163 The European Communities uses the same arguments set out in paragraph 8.113 above to argue that Section 211(b) is inconsistent with Article 2.1 of the TRIPS Agreement in conjunction with Article 6*bis* (1) of the Paris Convention (1967). The United States makes arguments set out in paragraph 8.114 to argue that Section 211(b) is not inconsistent with Article 2.1 of the TRIPS Agreement in conjunction with Article 6*bis* (1) of the Paris Convention (1967).

8.164 For the reasons set out in paragraphs 8.157 and 8.158, it has not been proved that Section 211(b) is inconsistent with Article 2.1 of the TRIPS Agreement in conjunction with Article 6*bis* of the Paris Convention (1967).

> *4.   Whether Section 211(b) is Consistent with Article 2.1 of the TRIPS Agreement in Conjunction with Article 8 of the Paris Convention (1967)*

8.165 In light of our finding in paragraph 8.41 that the categories of intellectual property covered by the TRIPS Agreement are those referred to in Article 1.2 of the TRIPS Agreement and that Members do not have obligations under the TRIPS Agreement to provide protection to trade names, we find that Section 211(a)(2) is not inconsistent with Article 2.1 of the TRIPS Agreement in conjunction with Article 8 of the Paris Convention (1967).

> *5.   Whether Section 211(b) is Consistent with Article 3.1 of the TRIPS Agreement and Article 2.1 of the TRIPS Agreement in Conjunction with Article 2(1) of the Paris Convention (1967)*

8.166 The European Communities argues that, under Article 3.1 of the TRIPS Agreement, a Member cannot treat a national of another Member less favourably than it treats its own nationals in relation to intellectual property rights.[157] The European Communities argues that Section 211(b) is inconsistent with the national treatment principle contained in Articles 3.1 and 2.1 of the TRIPS Agreement in conjunction with Article 2(1) of the Paris Convention (1967) because "designated national" is defined as Cuba, Cuban nationals and specially designated nationals who are denied protection of their intellectual property rights in the United States while US nationals enjoy such protection.[158] The European

---

[157] *See* EC's First Submission, para. 57.
[158] *See* EC's First Submission, para. 58; EC's Second Submission, para. 64; and EC's Second Oral Statement, para. 44.

Communities claims that at the level of successors-in-interest, the language specifically singles out foreign successors-in-interest for the curtailment of their rights while successors-in-interest who are US nationals are not subject to such curtailment.[159]

8.167   The European Communities notes that the text of Article 3.1 of the TRIPS Agreement and Article 2(1) of the Paris Convention (1967) are not identical but argues that the underlying objective of both provisions are the same, i.e., to prohibit treatment that differs as a consequence of the nationality of the right holders.[160] The European Communities argues that the *de jure* discrimination created by Section 211(b) between Cuban right holders on the one hand and US right holders on the other constitutes a violation of Article 2(1) of the Paris Convention (1967) as well as Article 3.1 of the TRIPS Agreement.[161]

8.168   The United States argues that Section 211(b) applies, by its own terms, to designated nationals and to any successor-in-interest, whether Cuban or not. According to the United States, Section 211(b) applies to any person, whether Cuban or not and whether US or not, who claims a registration under US law by virtue of foreign registration of a trademark used in connection with confiscated assets.

8.169   The examination of the consistency of Section 211(b) with Article 3 of the TRIPS Agreement and Article 2.1 of the TRIPS Agreement in conjunction with Article 2(1) of the Paris Convention (1967) is identical to our examination of Section 211(a)(2). That is, we need to consider whether Section 211(b) affects protection of intellectual property rights as defined in footnote 3 of the TRIPS Agreement and whether Section 211(b) provides less favourable treatment to nationals of other Members in connection with such protection of intellectual property rights.

8.170   As stated previously, neither party disputes that Section 211(b) affects protection of intellectual property rights. Our task, therefore, is to examine whether Section 211(b) accords protection of intellectual property rights that is less favourable to the nationals of other Members than that it accords to US nationals.

8.171   Section 211(b) states that US courts shall not recognize, enforce or validate any assertion of treaty rights by a "designated national or *its successor-in-interest*". The difference between Section 211(a)(2) and Section 211(b) is that the latter contains the additional term "its successor-in-interest" whereas the former just refers to "a designated national". Moreover, the term "its successor-in-interest" as set out in Section 211(b) is not limited to foreign nationals which means that it includes US nationals. This would mean that any transfer of trademarks used in connection with confiscated assets to any national, including US nationals, would be subject to Section 211(b). For these reasons, Section 211(b)

---

[159]   *See* EC's First Submission, para. 58; EC's First Oral Statement, para. 78; EC's Second Submission, para. 64; and EC's Second Oral Statement, para. 44.
[160]   *See* EC's First Submission, para. 60.
[161]   *See* EC's First Submission, paras. 61 and 71.

does not accord a treatment less favourable to nationals of other Members than it accords to US nationals.

8.172 Similarly, in respect of original owners, Section 211(b) does not accord a treatment less favourable to foreign original owners than it accords to original owners who are US nationals.

8.173 Based on the reasons stated above, we conclude that Section 211(b) is not inconsistent with Article 3.1 of the TRIPS Agreement and Article 2.1 of the TRIPS Agreement in conjunction with Article 2 of the Paris Convention (1967).

6.   *Whether Section 211(b) is Consistent with Article 4 of the TRIPS Agreement*

8.174 The European Communities argued that Section 211(a)(2) is inconsistent with the most-favoured-nation treatment obligations contained in Article 4 of the TRIPS Agreement. The European Communities contends that Section 211(b) not only discriminates between Cuban nationals and US nationals but also creates a *de jure* discrimination between Cuba/Cuban nationals and other non-US nationals by denying protection of intellectual property rights held by Cuban nationals while granting such protection to nationals of other countries.[162]

8.175 The United States argues that Section 211(b) does not grant an "advantage, favour, privilege, or immunity" to non-Cuban nationals that they do not grant to Cuban nationals. The United States contends that neither one nor the other can enforce a trademark based on a foreign confiscation. The United States further argues that US courts will not enforce or recognize an asserted rights to trademarks used in connection with confiscated assets by any successor-in-interest, whether Cuban or not.

8.176 As we are faced with the same issue that was examined in connection with Section 211(a)(2), we refer to our reasons set out in paragraphs 8.145 to 8.147 and find that Section 211(b) is not inconsistent with Article 4 of the TRIPS Agreement.

IX.   CONCLUSIONS AND RECOMMENDATIONS

9.1   In light of the findings above, we conclude that:

(a)   Section 211(a)(1) is not inconsistent with Article 15.1 of the TRIPS Agreement;

(b)   Section 211(a)(1) is not inconsistent with Article 2.1 of the TRIPS Agreement in conjunction with Article 6*quinquies* A(1) of the Paris Convention (1967);

(c)   it has not been proved that Section 211(a)(2) is inconsistent with Article 16.1 of the TRIPS Agreement;

---

[162]   *See* EC's First Submission, paras. 62, 64 and 71; and EC's First Oral Statement, para. 79.

(d)   Section 211(a)(2) is inconsistent with Article 42 of the TRIPS Agreement;

(e)   Section 211(a)(2) is not inconsistent with Article 2.1 of the TRIPS Agreement in conjunction with Article 6*bis* of the Paris Convention (1967);

(f)   Section 211(a)(2) is not inconsistent with Article 2.1 of the TRIPS Agreement in conjunction with Article 8 of the Paris Convention (1967);

(g)   Section 211(a)(2) is not inconsistent with Article 3.1 of the TRIPS Agreement and Article 2.1 of the TRIPS Agreement in conjunction with Article 2(1) of the Paris Convention (1967);

(h)   Section 211(a)(2) is not inconsistent with Article 4 of the TRIPS Agreement;

(i)   it has not been proved that Section 211(b) is inconsistent with Article 16.1 of the TRIPS Agreement;

(j)   it has not been proved that Section 211(b) is inconsistent with Article 42 of the TRIPS Agreement;

(k)   it has not been proved that Section 211(b) is inconsistent with Article 2.1 of the TRIPS Agreement in conjunction with Article 6*bis* of the Paris Convention (1967);

(l)   Section 211(b) is not inconsistent with Article 2.1 of the TRIPS Agreement in conjunction with Article 8 of the Paris Convention (1967);

(m)   Section 211(b) is not inconsistent with Article 3.1 of the TRIPS Agreement and Article 2.1 of the TRIPS Agreement in conjunction with Article 2(1) of the Paris Convention (1967); and

(n)   Section 211(b) is not inconsistent with Article 4 of the TRIPS Agreement.

9.2   In light of the above and in accordance with Article 3.8 of the DSU, we further conclude that there is nullification or impairment of the benefits accruing to the European Communities under the TRIPS Agreement.

9.3   We recommend that the Dispute Settlement Body request the United States to bring its measures into conformity with its obligations under the TRIPS Agreement.

ANNEX I

(WT/DS176/2 of 7 July 2000)

UNITED STATES – SECTION 211 OMNIBUS APPROPRIATIONS ACT OF 1998

Request for the Establishment of a Panel by the European Communities and their member States

The following communication, dated 30 June 2000, from the Permanent Delegation of the European Commission to the Chairman of the Dispute Settlement Body, is circulated in accordance with Article 6.2 of the DSU.

On behalf of the European Communities and their member States, we hereby submit the following request for consideration at the next meeting of the Dispute Settlement Body. Section 211 United States Omnibus Appropriations Act of 1998 was signed into law on 21 October 1998 (Pub. Law. 105-277(1998); hereafter "Section 211"). The main substantive provisions of Section 211 are contained in its paragraphs (a)(1), (a)(2) and (b). Section 211, paragraph (a)(1), was implemented in the Cuban Assets Control Regulations (31 CFR 515) effective as of 10 May 1999 (64 FR 25808).

1. *Section 211, paragraph (a)(1) United States Omnibus Appropriations Act of 1998*

Section 211, paragraph (a)(1), concerns transactions or payments pursuant to section 515.527 of title 31 of the U.S. Code of Federal Regulations, i.e. the registration or renewal in the United States Patent and Trademark Office of a trademark, trade-name or commercial name. Section 211, paragraph (a)(1), limits the right to register or renew in the United States Patent and Trademark Office a trademark, trade-name or commercial name that is the same as or substantially similar to a trademark, trade-name or commercial name that was used in connection with a business or assets that were confiscated as defined in section 515.336 of title 31 of the U.S. Code of Federal Regulations (see Section 211, paragraph (d)(2)) in so far as the registration or renewal requires the express consent of the original owner or his bona fide successor-in-interest of the trademark, trade-name or commercial name.

The European Communities and their member States consider that Section 211, paragraph (a)(1) is in contradiction with several provisions of the WTO Agreement on Trade-Related Aspects of Intellectual Property Rights (hereafter "TRIPs Agreement"), and notably its Article 2, paragraph 1, in conjunction with Article 6 *quinquies*, paragraph A(1) of the

Paris Convention for the Protection of Industrial Property (1967), and Article 15, paragraph 1.

2.   *Section 211, paragraph (a)(2) United States Omnibus Appropriations Act of 1998*

Section 211, paragraph (a)(2), concerns the assertion before U.S. courts of rights based on common law rights or on a registration obtained under section 515.527 of title 31 of the U.S. Code of Federal Regulations of such a confiscated trademark, trade-name or commercial name. It follows that Section 211, paragraph (a)(2), refers to trademarks, trade-names or commercial names as defined in Section 211, paragraph (a)(1), i.e. that are the same as or substantially similar to trademarks, trade-names or commercial names that were used in connection with a business or assets that were confiscated. Under Section 211, paragraph (a)(2), U.S. courts shall not recognize, enforce or otherwise validate the assertion of such rights by a designated national. Designated nationals are defined in section 515.305 of title 31 of the U.S. Code of Federal Regulations and include nationals of any foreign country who are successors-in-interest to a designated national (see Section 211, paragraph (d)(1)).

The European Communities and their member States are of the view that Section 211, paragraph (a)(2) violates several provisions of the TRIPs Agreement, and notably its Article 2, paragraph 1, in conjunction with Articles 6 *bis*, paragraph (1), and 8 of the Paris Convention for the Protection of Industrial Property (1967), and Article 16, paragraph 1, which oblige WTO Members to provide protection for trademarks, trade-names or commercial names. In addition, this provision violates the enforcement provisions under the TRIPs Agreement, and notably its Article 42. Furthermore, Section 211, paragraph (a)(2) is in breach of Article 3, paragraph 1, and Article 2, paragraph 1, of the TRIPs Agreement, in conjunction with Article 2, paragraph (1), of the Paris Convention for the Protection of Industrial Property (1967), which provide that each WTO Member shall accord to the nationals of other WTO Members treatment no less favourable than it accords to its own nationals. Lastly, Section 211, paragraph (a)(2) violates Article 4 of the TRIPs Agreement which provides that any advantage granted by a WTO Member to the nationals of any other country shall be accorded immediately and unconditionally to the nationals of all other WTO Members.

3.   *Section 211, paragraph (b) United States Omnibus Appropriations Act of 1998*

Section 211, paragraph (b), concerns the assertion before U.S. courts of treaty rights under sections 44(b) or (e) of the Trademark Act of 1946 (15 U.S.C. 1126(b) or (e)) for trademarks, trade-names or commercial names that are the same as or substantially similar to trademarks, trade-names or commercial names that were used in connection with a business or assets that were confiscated. Under Section 211, paragraph (b), U.S. courts shall not recognize, enforce or otherwise validate the assertion of such rights by a designated national. Furthermore, under Section 211, paragraph (b), U.S. courts shall not recognize, enforce or otherwise validate the assertion of such rights unless the original owner or his bona fide successor-in-interest of the trademark, trade-name or commercial name has expressly consented.

The European Communities and their member States consider that Section 211, paragraph (b), is in contradiction with Article 2, paragraph 1, of the TRIPs Agreement in conjunction with Articles 2, paragraph 1, 6 *bis*, paragraph (1), and 8 of the Paris Convention for the Protection of Industrial Property (1967), and Articles 3, paragraph 1, 4, 16, paragraph 1, and 42 of the TRIPs Agreement.

In a communication dated 7 July 1999 (WT/DS176/1-IP/D/20), the European Communities and their member States requested consultations with the United States of America pursuant to Article 4 of the Understanding on Rules and Procedures Governing the Settlement of Disputes contained in Annex 2 of the WTO Agreement (hereafter "the DSU") and Article 64.1 of the TRIPs Agreement. Such consultations, which were held on 13 September and 13 December 1999, have led to a better understanding of the respective positions, but not to a satisfactory resolution of the dispute.

Accordingly, the European Communities and their member States request the establishment of a panel pursuant to Article 6 of the DSU and Article 64.1 of the TRIPs Agreement to examine the matter in the light of the relevant provisions of the TRIPs Agreement and to find that the United States of America fails to conform to the obligations contained in the provisions of the TRIPs Agreement here above mentioned and thereby nullifies or impairs the benefits accruing directly or indirectly to the European Communities and their member States under the TRIPs Agreement.

The European Communities and their member States request that the panel be established with the standard terms of reference as provided for in Article 7 of the DSU.

ANNEX II

(WT/DS176/3 of 27 October 2000)

UNITED STATES – SECTION 211 OMNIBUS APPROPRIATIONS ACT OF 1998

*Constitution of the Panel Established at the Request of
the European Communities and their member States*

Note by the Secretariat

1.　At its meeting on 26 September 2000, the DSB established a panel pursuant to the request of the European Communities and their member States (WT/DS176/2), in accordance with Article 6 of the DSU.

2.　At that meeting, the parties to the dispute agreed that the Panel should have standard terms of reference. The terms of reference are the following:

"To examine, in the light of the relevant provisions of the covered agreements cited by the European Communities and their member States in document WT/DS176/2, the matter referred to the DSB by the European Communities and their member States in that document and to make such findings as will assist the DSB in making the recommendations or in giving the rulings provided for in those agreements."

3.　On 17 October 2000, the European Communities and their member States requested the Director-General to determine the composition of the Panel, pursuant to paragraph 7 of Article 8 of the DSU. Paragraph 7 of Article 8 provides:

"If there is no agreement on the panelists within 20 days after the date of the establishment of a panel, at the request of either party, the Director-General, in consultation with the Chairman of the DSB and the Chairman of the relevant Council or Committee, shall determine the composition of the panel by appointing the panelists whom the Director-General considers most appropriate in accordance with any relevant special or additional rules or procedures of the covered agreement or covered agreements which are at issue in the dispute, after consulting with the parties to the dispute. The Chairman of the DSB shall inform the Members of the composition of the panel thus formed no later than 10 days after the date the Chairman receives such a request."

4.   On 26 October 2000, the Director-General accordingly composed the Panel as follows:

Chairman: Mr. Wade Armstrong

Members: Mr. François Dessemontet

Mr. Armand de Mestral

5.   Canada, Japan and Nicaragua reserved their rights as third parties to the dispute.

Cumulative Index of Published Disputes